§ ANTIQUES AS AN INVESTMENT

Antiques as an Investment

Richard H. Rush

Drawings by Julia Rush

BONANZA BOOKS · NEW YORK

0-517-N08397

Antiques As An Investment, by Richard H. Rush

© MCMLXVIII by Richard H. Rush

This edition published by Bonanza Books
a division of Crown Publishers, Inc.,
by arrangement with Prentice-Hall, Inc.

b c d e f g h

Library of Congress Catalog Card Number: 68–10170
Manufactured in the United States of America

CONTENTS

§ *This book is dedicated to those who love to collect and to live with fine antiques—and to those who are opening the door to the adventure of collecting antiques—and to my daughter, Sallie, who still has ahead of her the joys, discoveries and adventures in this world so full of beautiful and interesting things*

Pavillon de Musique d'epoque Louis XVI. Courtesy Connaissance Des Arts.
(Photo by Jacqueline Guillot)

Introduction

THE UNITED STATES AND, IN FACT, the entire Western world are entering a period of antique boom. Prices of antiques have been rising rapidly in the past several years, and if the factors that are responsible continue in force, the price rise cannot help but accelerate within the next few years. There is now developing a notable shortage not only of good antiques but of *any* antiques. Certainly this situation has prevailed in the past, in periods like the middle 1920's. However, that antique boom subsided in the 1930's, and antiques then became more plentiful. But they are again becoming scarce, and the supply of the much wanted eighteenth-century types is ever diminishing. High prices may lure some antiques out of private homes, and the death of antique owners will bring some onto the market. But the fact remains that the supply is diminishing and the demand increasing to such an extent that if the economic prosperity of the Western world continues, the boom must accelerate.

At the present time we are moving at a tremendous rate of speed into a new "Age of Elegance." Antiques are the very epitome of this Age, and they go along with large, luxurious homes, with yachts and with Rolls-Royces. As long as this movement continues, antiques will be in progressively greater demand.

When one sees French antiques on display at the Parke-Bernet Galleries in New York, he can hardly help but come to the conclusion, "These are the finest and the ultimate in antiques." But although this attitude may be correct today, it certainly was not correct in the late 1930's, just prior to the war. At that time French antiques were a drug on the market. And we can be fairly certain that at some time in the future French antiques will not be the ultimate. Antique styles are a matter of fashion. For that matter, the collecting of antiques is a fashion. Whereas today the emphasis is more and more on antiques, we can be certain that there will be a time in the future when the ownership of antiques will be relatively unimportant, just as such ownership has been unimportant during certain periods in the past—the 1930's for instance. The emphasis on certain antique styles, and the emphasis on antiques in general, are subject to changes in taste and fashion.

Antiques cost increasingly more money, and to a great extent these monetary values are based on intangibles. One can look at a Louis XV commode and place

1

a certain value on it simply by studying the prices realized in the antique market. But if he learns that there is a name stamped on the commode, let us say the name Bernard van Riesen Burgh II (stamped BVRB), the value of the piece is at least doubled in his mind—and in the market. This is an intangible value simply based on the identification of the maker.

But what if the piece is not a BVRB and not made in the period of Louis XV? Instead, it is an excellent, recent reproduction. Whereas the genuine Louis XV commode might have been worth $30,000, and the BVRB stamp might have made it worth $60,000, the fact that it is a recent reproduction reduces its value to under $3,000.

If the Louis XV commode is not a recent reproduction (the last fifty years, let us say) but was made just a little later than the reign of Louis XV—perhaps in the reign of the next king, Louis XVI (still comfortably within the "Golden Eighteenth Century")—the commode, although "antique," is not what it purports to be. Its value is thus highly problematical. It could be worth up to $10,000, but in the international antique market its value is uncertain.

Possibilities such as these must always be explored by all intelligent antique buyers, both individual collectors and dealers.

There are several purposes in writing this book. The first is simply a desire to rationalize price movements by different styles of antique furniture over the years in order to show (1) the effects of prosperity on antique sales, (2) changes in taste, (3) alternating periods of preference for antiques and for "modern."

The book also has as a fundamental purpose the instruction of potential antique buyers on approximate amounts to pay for particular pieces of antique furniture. It is thus a kind of "how-to-do" book.

In the late spring of 1966, the author visited two regional antique shows in the New York City area. One dealer at each of these shows offered for sale *half* of a chest-on-chest. Each was offered as a complete piece of antique furniture. The sellers did not bother to point out that the buyer would have half of an antique— something of problematical value that would be most difficult to dispose of at anything like the asking price except to an uninformed buyer.

At another antique show a highboy was offered for sale with the feet cut off and then reglued in place. This mutilation, even though the original feet were stuck back on, reduced the value of the antique by possibly as much as one-half. Again, it is problematical whether anyone with knowledge of antiques would want to buy the piece should the person stuck with it ever want to resell it.

In a small New York auction a pair of "Louis XV" chairs was recently offered for sale. A large cardboard sign on the seat of one of them proclaimed the name of the maker. The only trouble was that the chairs were recent fakes. The "wormholes" were drilled perfectly straight—in one end and out the other—so that it appeared the primary objective of the worm was to get in and out of the wood in the shortest possible elapsed time! In the case of one "wormhole" the drill had slipped, leaving marks on the surface nearly an inch long. Yet these fakes were sold as genuine antiques of the period.

If this book can help the inexperienced antique buyer to determine what is genuine and what is fake, and can indicate a reasonable price range for each antique, it will have served a major purpose.

The recognition of quality is not always instinctive. To a large extent it must be learned, and if the many descriptions and illustrations in this book provide even a small start for the prospective antique buyer in recognizing what is fine and beautiful it will have accomplished a great deal.

Enough statistical material on comparative price rises by types of antiques is included in this study to allow the reader to draw some tentative conclusions on which antiques are the best investment. The types rising the fastest are certainly candidates for investment, while "slow starters" may offer even greater potentialities. Antiques in general cost a good deal of money, and any prudent antique buyer wants to know that for a relatively large outlay of cash he is securing the same approximate value in antiques. He also wants to be reassured to some extent that if he ever has to resell he will either make money or, at the least, lose as little as possible.

The auction houses, as a general rule, provide the best hunting ground for the inexperienced antique buyer. (But it must be noted that the auction houses' descriptions and attributions are by no means infallible.) At the same time, various conditions at auctions may result in artificially low prices to the auction *seller* of antiques. This situation points to another purpose of the book—information to the prospective antique seller on what to expect for what he wants to sell.

The largest market for all auction houses is probably the dealer market. The dealer purchases for resale. But a survey made of antique dealers throughout the country indicates that the auction houses are not reaching many dealers who could well buy at auction. Thus this book may benefit the auction houses to some small extent.

Antiques and antique prices are important to study for another reason: The majority of the products of the furniture industry at all times are directly related to antiques, and this statement holds true of products turned out in 1900 as well as those of today. There are relatively few new forms in the furniture industry, and most of the total product can be related upon brief examination to well-known types of antiques—Italian Renaissance, Venetian of the eighteenth century, Chippendale, etc.

Antique vogues have had another effect on the furniture industry: The manufacture of reproductions. Reproductions are more or less faithful copies of historical styles of furniture. All through recent history, reproductions of two types have been made: (1) faithful copies bought by those who cannot afford the originals of the period or for some other reason do not want originals, and (2) modern, well-designed pieces based on historical styles. Sometimes reproductions form a large percentage of total furniture output and sometimes a small percentage, depending on whether antiques are in vogue at the time.

The field of antiques is bewildering to many prospective buyers because of the technical factors which determine prices. In addition, many prospective antique buyers simply do not know what the market has to offer. They often have a vague yearning for antiques, but just which kind they do not know. They do not know what Jacobean antiques are. Nor do they quite understand the meaning of Regency. This book traces prices for 23 distinct types of antiques. It should thus educate the antique buyer in how to recognize these 23 types and see which best suit his needs and pocketbook. The various types of antiques are set in a historical background as a matter of general interest and as an aid in remembering them.

The one clear fact that emerges from the research for this book is that there is a market price for almost all antique furniture. While it is true that the price is most certainly not as easy to determine as the price of a share of stock, nevertheless it can be determined within limits. For a piece of antique furniture, or a painting, or any item within the general overall category of art and antiques, *market value or fair value is the price that the usual kind of dealer who handles the particular item is likely to receive for it in the process of normal selling.* A *bureau plat* made by Bernard van Riesen Burgh II and sold by French and Company of New York in the normal course of business would be sold at what should be considered the fair market price. If, on the other hand, French and Company were anxious to cut its inventory, as when it moved to its new Madison Avenue quarters, the prices received could be expected to be very much under market—as they were in actuality.

On the other hand, if a Second Avenue New York shop should happen to run across the BVRB *bureau plat*, that shop could not be expected to secure the high price that French and Company could secure. If, in addition, the *bureau plat* cost the Second Avenue shop a good deal of money in relation to its capital (and it almost certainly would), that shop might sell the piece for a quick but small profit.

Recently the Parke-Bernet Galleries sold the Anton Meister Collection, including many enormous vases. The prices received seemed to be on the low side. It was noted that most pieces went to dealers, and many pieces to just a few dealers. These few dealers specialized in such items and could be expected to tap the market for them better than the Parke-Bernet Galleries could. Then too, for many items, if not most, an auction house is below retail stores in price. The late Leslie Hyam, president of Parke-Bernet Galleries, stated that auction prices were from 10 percent to 75 percent of retail prices. He was probably not far wrong, except that auction houses probably secure the highest prices obtainable for certain items such as Impressionist and Modern paintings.

What is an antique? More things are probably sold as antiques which are not antiques than the entire sales of genuine antiques. This does not mean that more fakes are sold than genuine pieces. Rather, it means that pieces are sold which are not old enough to be considered antique. Until 1966, the United States Customs Bureau classified a piece of furniture as antique if it was made prior to 1830. Now the Florida Implementation Legislation provides that anything over one hundred years old is considered an antique. Thus, until this change in the law, no Victorian furniture whatever was classified as antique. The importance of a piece of furniture coming within this antique classification is that it is permitted to come into the

United States duty free. The Customs Bureau thus has a gigantic job to do, and a job calculated to enrage a great number of Americans who buy nonantique furniture abroad under the impression that they are buying antiques.

Today, furniture made later than 1830 is not usually considered important by most of the antique industry. In fact, furniture made later than 1820 is not considered of very great importance. The great body of fine antiques was made prior to 1800.

The Office of Price Administration of World War II issued a regulation on November 11, 1944, which bears quoting: "Antiques for the purpose of this exemption are (1) old objects such as furniture, tableware, household articles, etc. (if an article is less than 75 years old it will ordinarily not be considered an antique within the meaning of this exemption) which (2) tend to increase rather than decrease in value because of age; which (3) are purchased primarily because of their authenticity, age, rarity, style, etc., rather than for utility; and which (4) are commonly known and dealt in as antiques by the trade." The cutoff year is of course very liberal. Otherwise the definition speaks for itself and has a great deal of merit. (Note the cutoff year does not correspond with the Customs cutoff year of 1830.)

The Morgan Act of 1906 (sponsored by J. Pierpont Morgan who wanted to import large quantities of antiques) did a great deal to develop antique buying in the United States. *The New York Times* of April 29, 1937, flatly states that this Act established the antique industry in this country. The Act allowed the duty-free entry of art and antiquities over one hundred years old (made prior to 1806).

In 1906 such imports amounted to $478,000. In the next year this total rose to $1,636,049. By 1910 it had risen to $2,500,000, and by 1919 the total was $21,619,543. In 1937 the United States Treasury Department noted that $640,633,302 in "aged pieces" had entered this country in 28 years. It also noted that 75 percent of the total import of so-called antiques since 1906 were fakes.

At this point I would like to mention that the primary data used in the preparation of this book are the sales catalogues of the following New York and London auctions—the Parke-Bernet Galleries, and prior to the organization of this firm, Anderson Galleries and the American Art Association (all located in New York City); and Sotheby's and Christie's in London. Usually only illustrated antiques were used in the price computations, since a visual study is required to determine the specific characteristics and quality of each antique, and to determine whether the catalogue description tallies with the appearance of the antique.

But it is certainly not enough to study antiques from photos and to record their prices. Much is unrealistic in such an analysis. Pictures can go only so far, and they are limited in helping to distinguish a genuine antique from a reproduction, or from a fake, or from a piece one hundred years old as compared with a genuine antique of the eighteenth century. Therefore this auction price recording and analysis was backed up by visits to auction houses over a period of years.

Many books and articles on auctions and their prices ignore the fact that there is more than one auction house in America and more than two in England. For the past five years the author has visited most of the New York City auction houses every time they have made an offering, and has studied the antiques prior to sale. In this way a considerably broader view and larger sample were obtained of what was offered in relation to what price was realized in the sale.

Probably almost as many antiques are offered in all the smaller New York City auctions combined as by the one house of Parke-Bernet. Certainly the total number of pieces of furniture (antiques and more recent furniture) offered by the smaller houses far exceeds the Parke-Bernet offerings. A certain type buyer predominates at these smaller auctions. Another type predominates at Parke-Bernet. But only by visiting a majority of the auctions can a total picture of antiques sold at auction in New York be obtained . . . and more antiques by far are sold in New York than in any other city in the United States.

The auction price analysis has been supplemented by visits to dealers not only in New York but in other cities. In each city where the author has lectured on art and antiques, an attempt was made to visit a representative group of antique dealers to determine what was being offered and at what prices.

Last year the author and his wife were certainly candidates for the distinction of being the largest private buyers of furniture in New York. They had the colossal job of furnishing not one, but two large houses, one with 16 rooms and the other with 15—31 rooms in all. By no means were all antiques purchased, although a good proportion were antiques. Many of the purchases fell into the Victorian category; and the combination of antiques, Victorian items and furniture not old enough to merit either distinction resulted in two homes which were certainly livable as well as enriched by some good antiques.

Actual purchase of antiques is perhaps the best way to learn about them. When one prepares to spend $1,000 for a pair of chairs, a good deal more is usually done than to exclaim, "How lovely they are! Here is your check for $1,000!" Unless he is a fool, the buyer tries to make sure that the chairs are in effect antiques, and not 50-year-old or 100-year-old chairs, or reproductions or clever fakes. He likes to know he has purchased $1,000 worth of chairs, not $200 worth. A study before as well as after purchase adds immeasurably to a person's discriminatory powers in antiques.

The author and his wife have visited the Biennial Art and Antiques Fair in Florence, Italy, ever since it was organized, and on each of their trips to Europe have visited several hundred antique dealers, examined their wares and obtained prices—in England, Holland, Germany, France and Italy.

The antiques market is a world market, and most antiques of the Western world sold at auction are sold in New York, London and Paris. There is some arbitrage among these three centers, although not as much as in paintings, where shipment is much easier as well as much cheaper in relation to the value of any particular item. There is some shipment of antiques not only between European countries but between the United States and many cities of Europe.

Are Antiques a Good Investment?

Are antiques increasing in price? This is the first subquestion to answer, and it started this entire study. The overall answer is yes, antiques are increasing in price. The next question concerns *which* antiques are increasing in price. The answer is that probably all antiques are increasing in price in the middle 1960's, the time this study was made.

Actually, however, there is hardly any such overall category as "antiques." The generic term "antiques" covers very different types of old furniture, and there is for example a vast difference between Renaissance Italian and Louis XVI. The difference is not only in period made and country of origin. It is not simply that the furniture of the Renaissance is large, extremely heavy and generally made of very dark wood, while that of Louis XVI is smaller by far, lighter in weight and usually lighter in color. The prices of these two types of antique furniture are very different, and the price histories vary even more. And while both types of antiques have experienced a price rise in recent years, that of Louis XVI has skyrocketed while Renaissance furniture can be characterized as a "late starter."

Some antiques are increasing in price rapidly; some at a very slow pace. What the growth relationship will be in the future is another matter, and a question on which this book tries to shed some light.

When we try to assess antiques as an investment we, of course, bring antiques into the investment arena. Here we must compare antiques with real estate and with stocks and bonds, as well as with other items which might be collected—glassware, porcelain, paintings, watches, coins, stamps and even buttons. It is not the purpose of this book to compare antiques with these other things, because few antique buyers will make a comprehensive study and arrive at the conclusion, "I'm buying antiques because they are a better investment than municipal bonds." This book is directed to answering the question, "What has happened to the price of antiques over the years, what is happening now, and what is likely to happen in the future? And to *which* antiques?" For the prospective buyer it tries to answer the question, "If I put a sum of money of investment size into antiques, what is likely to happen to my investment?"

This book also has a negative element. It tries to answer the question, "Will I lose less, or possibly make money, by buying antiques, since I know with very little analysis that if I buy new furniture it will decline in value as the years go by?"

One must probably come to the conclusion, if he is assessing antiques purely as an investment, that there are better types of investments which can be made. Some go up faster. Some give cash returns in the form of dividends or interest. Some can be sold for profit more quickly and at a more easily determined price. And, very importantly, other types of investments do not soon fill up the home and start pushing out into the warehouse, they do not require moving vans and packers to handle them, they do not entail storage charges each month, and they do not require attention from time to time if they are to be kept from collapsing.

By way of apology as a close to this Introduction, an apology when one is considering antiques solely from an investment point of view, it should be pointed out that the furniture of the eighteenth century, purely as *furniture*, has probably never been equaled in originality, quality of workmanship and sheer beauty, and to surround oneself with fine antiques produces a psychic income that few investments can come close to matching.

THE DRAWING ROOM, SUTTON PLACE.   This room combines the comfort of twentieth-century overstuffed chairs and sofas with the beauty and elegance of fine antiques and important Old Master paintings.   *Courtesy of Mr. J. Paul Getty.* *(Photo: Sargent/Gamma Ltd., Guildford, England)*

CHAPTER ONE

The "Age of Elegance"

T HE HOME OF THE SOCIALLY AND economically prominent of today is usually a home characterized by large size, traditional architecture, spacious rooms and fine interiors. The first two paragraphs of a recent *New York Times* article commenting on this trend bear quoting:

> Be they ever so homelike, there is nothing humble about apartments and houses that contain more than $1 million worth of art and furnishings. Manhattan is loaded with such living quarters.
>
> Since the war, affluent New Yorkers, some of whom have great taste, have indulged themselves in the kind of extravagances usually associated with the eighteen-nineties and the nineteen-twenties. They have hung their bedrooms with 18th-century French chandeliers, replaced their doorknobs with gold handles, installed crystal wall sconces in their closets, and run expensive carpets into the kitchen and up the bathroom walls.

Periodically in New York City, tours of outstanding homes and apartments are arranged. A fee is charged to visitors and the proceeds go to charity or some other worthy cause. One such tour in the Spring of 1967 was the Finch College Alumnae Club Tour. A catalogue was prepared covering each apartment. The important furnishings and paintings were listed in some detail. Without exception, the main feature of these apartments was antique furniture, most of which was of museum quality.

For an enormous segment of the public, the interior decorator sets the style. If the interior decorator says a particular item is the thing to buy for the home, that is it. If the interior decorator says another item should go because it is out-of-date, it frequently goes.

At the 1965 National Decorator and Design Show held in New York City, about three-quarters of the exhibits of the decorators contained either antiques or true reproductions of antiques. In some instances there was limited admission to a particular display, so that one had to inquire whether a particular piece of furniture was a genuine antique or a reproduction. It is interesting to note that when this question was asked of some of the decorators they were slightly outraged that anyone would suggest that they would display anything other than a genuine antique. The emphasis and the premium were placed on authentic pieces.

A photograph in a magazine most characteristic of this return to the "Age of Elegance" showed an antique frame that was made to hold an Old Master painting. The frame contained no painting, but was used instead to outline the interior of a room. The frame gave the impression of being a window through which one viewed what lay beyond. The room was spacious, to say the least. The ceiling was very high, and at the far end was a French eighteenth-century marble fireplace. The walls of the room were white and covered with gilded moldings. The furniture was almost all Louis XV and Louis XVI. There was no modern piece of furniture to be seen.

In August 1965 there was a newspaper account of a new bank that was about to open on Fifth Avenue in New York. Depositors—exactly eight hundred would be accepted—had to make formal application and undergo rigid scrutiny; accounts must contain a minimum of $25,000. The newspaper account also mentioned that members would "conduct their financial affairs in the surroundings of Louis XVI decor."

Such an establishment is a far cry from banks built on New York's Fifth Avenue five to ten years ago, banks that pride themselves on freedom from decoration, freedom from clutter, and complete orderliness so that passersby cannot help but be impressed with the utter simplicity and neatness as they look through an enormous plate glass window into the perpetually lighted interior.

"Elegance" is more and more the theme of home-furnishing manufacturers and stores. One manufacturer's ad shows a room filled with the furniture of the Louis'. It is captioned "Elegance is in the Air . . . When Pieces like these are in the Room."

One of the leading hardware stores in Norwalk, Connecticut, long known for its large stock of paints, tools and hardware, advertises the "Regency Bathroom."

This identification of a product with the "height of elegance" is used more and more. For three years one of the leading men's suit manufacturers has used castles as the background for his suits. The models stand outside these highly imposing structures, and some of the elegance and majesty of the castles is presumably transferred to the suits.

Sometimes "Age of Elegance" advertising seems to go a little far. One of these extreme ads shows a boy driving a motorcycle with a girl perched behind him on the tandem seat. This is usual enough. What is not usual is the object she is clutching in her hand—an antique picture frame!

Measures of the Return to the "Age of Elegance"

To a student of style history, it is obvious that interior design and decoration are turning to the antique at an almost incredible rate of speed. But to the person who is interested in style only as an incidental part of life, this may not be so immediately obvious. For the purpose of determining how rapidly the "Age of Elegance" is coming upon us, a review of magazines and newspapers was made to find out by years how many articles on antiques and antique interiors were carried, and how many advertisements appeared which used antiques and antique design as a major theme. We were interested in determining how rapidly the Age of Elegance was developing in *recent* years rather than over a period of decades.

As far as antiques are concerned, *The New York Times Magazine* is considered neutral. It presents what is, not what it would like to see happen style-wise.

We reviewed four issues of the December 1965 *New York Times Magazine*, along with the Sunday edition of the paper. *Twenty-seven* advertisements stressed antiques and antique interiors or themes; *five* stressed modern. We then took a count of the Sunday advertisements stressing antiques five years earlier—December 1960. There were then *eight* ads predominantly antique in character.

Next we moved back to December 1955 and reviewed the advertisements of *The New York Times Magazine* in that month. Not one ad emphasized antiques. The December 4, 1955, issue contained an article entitled "Just in from France." The article did not illustrate one antique or one reproduction of an antique, or any item of any kind directly dependent on antiques.

This analysis was done on advertisements no more than ten years old. As we moved towards the present, more and more advertisements emphasized the elegant and the old. In the December 4, 1960, issue of the magazine an ad reads: "Just this adherence to unique and tasteful creativity exploiting past and lasting glories, or present and future splendors makes —— one of the most important establishments of its kind in the world . . . truly one of America's oldest and largest furniture, decorating and carpet sources."

The ad straddled the old and the new, yet was worded so that the clear emphasis is on elegance.

Next we move forward five years to December 1965. The December 5 issue of the magazine contains an ad which reads, "A Rembrandt for $60" in huge letters. The ad then continues: "Who says masterpieces have to cost a King's ransom? Take our Rembrandt raincoat lining for example."

In the same issue of the magazine another ad reads, "Not every man who wears ———— clothes has a cooperage at his castle."

It was logical to make a similar analysis of the magazine *Interior Design* to determine trend in style in recent years. Again the December issues were studied and the antique advertisements tabulated.

As in the *New York Times* study, the increase in advertisements using strict antiques (or reproductions so close to antiques as to be faithful copies of them) is quite clear, with the greatest increase in the past five years.

The "Age of Elegance"

It is certainly appropriate that the style of the 1960's be titled the "Return to the Age of Elegance." In history there were several periods of elegance. One of the most notable, probably *the* most notable, was the era of Louis XV and Louis XVI. The elegance was so extreme, and the wealth of the possessors so great as compared with the great masses of Frenchmen, that one of the bloodiest revolutions

in all history resulted. It is ironical that this is the elegance—that of the Louis'—
that is the most wanted today, not only by Americans, but by most collectors of
the Western world.

But the era which is most commonly known as the "Age of Elegance" is the
era of the Prince Regent of England. The Regent occupied this status from 1811
to 1820 when his father, George III, the English monarch at the time of the
American Revolution, was mentally incompetent to rule. In 1820 the Prince
Regent ascended the throne as George IV. Practically, the Regency Period is
sometimes dated as early as 1795 when the Prince of Wales, later to become the
Prince Regent, married Caroline of Brunswick.

The Prince Regent led the country to new heights of elegance and high living.

The extreme plushness of this era is well expressed by L. G. G. Ramsey in his
Introduction to *The Connoisseur Period Guide—the Regency Period* (Reynal &
Company, New York: 1958) ". . . the height of magnificence in Regency exoticism
was reached in the Royal Pavilion at Brighton. . . ." The banqueting room is
illustrated on the cover of the book. There are 24 chairs at a table which is
covered by a tablecloth touching the floor. There are four immense *torchères* which
appear to be about 12 feet tall; the main chandelier appears to weigh at least a
ton, and the ceiling looks like it is about 30 feet high. The walls are covered with
oriental designs and carved woodwork and plasterwork. The rug would seem to be
about 60 feet long and perhaps 25 feet wide, a rug which could only be described
as a "palace size."

Clifford Musgrave sums up the characteristics of this "Age of Elegance" in
Architecture and Interior Design, "It is in such monumental interiors that the
decorative art of the Regency period attained its zenith of richness as its moment
of historical triumph".

While we have a long way to go in our interior design and furniture to merit
such descriptions, there is little question that we are moving in that direction.

The Trend Away from Elegance

From the point of view of interior decoration and furnishing, the most important
single event in the past half century was the Exposition Décoratif held in Paris in
1925. The impact of this display of interior design, decoration and furniture was
no less than monumental. Strange as it may seem from our present-day vantage
point, the theme of this Exposition was completely opposed to antiques and
historical design. Cubism, one of the most "modern" of designs, had been known
for a decade or more at the time of this Exposition and was being used in home
and commercial interiors, but the Exposition drew together the forces of Modernism.

There were various forces at work which made the ideas embodied in the
Exposition Décoratif take hold and become, for a time, the style setter. In the
1920's there was considerable emphasis on democracy and social revolution
throughout the Western world. Trivial as the change may seem, at this time
dining room and kitchen in many instances became one. It was in the 1920's that
the stage was set for the great social revolution which took place in the 1930's—in

the United States this involved the Roosevelt reforms and social assistance.

When one style of anything stays in for a time it tends to become tiresome. The upswept tail of the Cadillac, which set the style from 1948 on, disappeared by degrees after it had reached a peak in the "jet aircraft tails" of 1959.

In the same way the owners of homes with lavish interiors began to focus their attention not on the elegance but on the clutter. The number of people accumulating anything at all in the early 1930's was relatively small indeed, and the sheer necessity of getting or holding a job took the emphasis off building ornate interiors. In her excellent article in the February 4, 1965, issue of *Country Life* entitled "The Fashionable Interior, 1925–50," Madge Garland says of the new simplicity (or functionalism, as it was sometimes called):

> Cornices, dadoes, moulding and panelled doors were removed, and the horizontal lines that were the hallmark of the new style in all countries, and which had been made possible by new structural techniques, were echoed by such devices as removing the chimneypiece and running a straight shelf over a built-in electric fire to the return wall. Built-in units replaced heavy furniture. . . . Patterned carpets and wallpapers were, of course, taboo. . . . Although it was forthrightly stated that the unadorned was the natural expression of the Mechanical Age, few interiors were as austere as the purists would have them.

Style is a peculiar thing. It secures adherents with the same degree of fervor as revolutionaries. The adherents of functionalism were as dedicated as the Abstract Expressionist faddists of the late 1950's and early 1960's, and both seemed about as dedicated as the original Marxists and the German National Socialists. Under such circumstances it was a long and slow process to throw out the "New Modernism"; even by suggesting that there might be another style of interior design, decoration and furniture just as good, one might find himself scorned as a person with too little artistic and intellectual insight to attempt to comprehend the "deep social and intellectual significance of Modernism."

The Turning Point in the "Elegant Emphasis"

The "Return to the Age of Elegance" has taken place at a remarkable rate of speed. The year 1965 probably recorded the greatest change in emphasis, and it is being exceeded by the late Sixties. Let us go back to 1950 and note the interior vogue at that time in order to get some historical perspective.

In 1950 a book appeared on interior design and decoration which was most competent. One of the chapters in this book is entitled "Modern is Here to Stay." This chapter mentions that modern appeals to teenagers and to the younger married couples "because it fulfills the functional needs of their individual interests better than the traditional furniture."

The same book comments on antique furniture styles. In regard to French Louis XIV furniture it states: that the "fancy gilt ormolu" and "extreme ostentatiousness" are "highly indigestible."

It goes on to say that Renaissance furniture does not belong in an American house.

At the February 12, 1966, Parke-Bernet sale in New York, a Renaissance Italian *credenza* brought a price far higher than it would have brought a year before or even six months before. This furniture is again coming into vogue rapidly.

Let us quote from *Modern Furniture*, another competent book on home decoration also published in 1950. The first quotation is even more startling than the quotes from the book just cited:

> The French decorative styles have never achieved real popularity in this country, a fact easily understood when you realize that the French period styles reflect the life and taste of kings, and very extravagant kings at that. Only a magician could adapt the extravagances of French court styles to the modest proportions and simple background of the average American five-room house or apartment of today.

Modern Furniture has more to say about modern style, however:

> Already the spirit of the new furniture is evident. It is light in weight and often has a knock-down, you-can-take-it-with-you angle.

> Large flat unbroken surfaces.
> Unusual woods and light natural finishes.
> Flush edges.
> Plain surfaces or rather the absence of carvings.
> Horizontal movement.
> Simple, geometric shapes: cubes, squares, circles.
> Dynamic balance, or informal balance.
> Plywood in thin bent or molded forms.
> The absence of conspicuous drawer pulls and hardware.
> Unusual materials: foam rubber, plastics, glass, cork, light metals.
> More outdoor furniture.
> Plain fabrics and shaggy textures are probably the most characteristic features of modern fabrics. Rough textures have become so important that it would almost seem that the modern school had invented the word.

We can go down the list, almost to the item, and reverse each one if we want to arrive at the characteristics of what is most in vogue today. Large, flat, unbroken surfaces are not used. Carving is wanted; plywood was an interesting experiment, and is now used chiefly on "price furniture" because it is cheap and sturdy. The most wanted drawer pulls in the world are the elaborate French, and the finest of all French pieces have elaborate drawer pulls and bronze trim. Inconspicuous drawer pulls were often put on eighteenth-century American and English furniture, but most of these have now been removed as a matter of course, and replaced with old brass or faithful reproductions. Handwoven fabrics, tapestry coverings, silk and velvet are the accepted upholstering materials, and if these coverings are also "of the period" the antique is in the unique category.

Modern Furniture further states, "It is already clear that modern houses and modern furniture, with minor changes and refinements, will be the popular forms for the next 50 years."

The popular house of the late 1960's is the traditional house. These predominate in new construction, particularly in the east. The most sought-after furniture is antique furniture.

So-called modern furniture has its place in contemporary homes and apartments with limited space. Its trouble is that it becomes obsolete extremely quickly. What was modern in 1950 is outmoded today. The purchase of such "modern" furniture in 1950 by a newlywed couple would mean that, if they could afford to be up-to-date, they would have to refurnish completely by 1970—just when their children were of college age. If styles of modern furniture change in the future as rapidly as they have in the past, this couple would have to buy a new round of modern furniture in 1982. If they are fortunate and styles do not change too fast, they might keep that round of modern furniture for the rest of their lives and still not be too greatly out-of-date. But such furniture does become out-of-date in fifteen years, and one has only to visit secondary auctions where such furniture is sold to note the price depths to which it falls. At least one forecast can be made with absolute finality: If antique furniture should drop at all in value in the next fifteen years, it will not drop nearly as fast as the modern furniture of today.

One final semirelevant comment might be made on the modernity of antique furniture. In the mid-Sixties the most up-to-date character was James Bond, the famous "007." In his appearance in *Thunderball*, the first piece of furniture one becomes aware of is a Louis XVI commode which appears to be either a genuine antique or an exact reproduction. As the scene changes the next items of furniture noted are two French Empire chairs. Then the scene changes again and one sees what seem to be two eighteenth-century landscapes. Quite clearly the most "modern" things are antiques and Old Masters!

THE MAIN GALLERY OF THE AMERICAN WING. "The most spectacular museum event in the last twenty years was the opening of the American Wing by the Metropolitan Museum on November 11, 1924" (*Antiques* magazine, 1925). The Metropolitan Museum of Art.

CHAPTER TWO

The Fashion of Collecting Antiques—
A Historical Perspective

I T IS THE FASHION TODAY TO COLLECT antiques. So imbedded in our present-day thinking is the desirability of owning antiques that it is difficult to realize that it was not always the fashion. In the middle 1930's there was not this great demand for antiques. There were collectors who had come through the Depression, and who were buying throughout that period, who continued to buy after the Depression was over. But filling one's home with antiques or even spreading around a substantial number of antiques among more modern furniture was not "the thing." It was not what interior decorators emphasized, and it was not the predominant decor which appeared in the fashion and home furnishing magazines.

These are major criteria for determining whether there is a fashion for collecting antiques:

1. The decor of the homes of social leaders
2. The decor of the homes of *nouveaux riches*
3. Emphasis by interior decorators
4. Emphasis in fashion and home furnishing magazines

It should be stressed that collectors generally continue buying through feast and famine. If they are interested in Renaissance Italian furniture they continue buying it whether it is in or out of fashion. When they are in pinched economic times they may buy less, and if dividends and capital gains are good they buy more. But their buying neither determines nor greatly influences fashion unless these collectors are social leaders or for some other reason are emulated by others.

J. Paul Getty is such a collector. He was probably buying the most heavily when antiques in general were out of fashion, and he was buying French antiques of the eighteenth century when they were at one of their historical low points price-wise. Furthermore he did this buying at a time when he was decidedly not in the public eye and was anything but a style innovator. He was purely and simply a collector who loved French antiques, and who at the same time probably looked upon them as an excellent investment. They were so low in price that in view of their intrinsic quality they had nowhere to go but up.

17

Origin of Antique Collecting in America

Antique collecting in America was by no means dead until the 1920's, although it received its real impetus in that decade. In November 1916 the furnishings of the Davanzati Palace in Florence, Italy, were sold in New York in the famous Volpi sale. This sale grossed almost $1,000,000. The so-called Riccio oil burner realized $66,000, a sizable sum even today.

Antique collecting in America had some sort of beginning in the Philadelphia Exposition of 1876. American relics were displayed and created a certain stimulus to collecting. The primary interest seemed to be, however, the glorification of the past of the United States of America, and this motive persisted well into the 1920's. Today the motive is to collect beautiful and well-made antiques, but not solely or even primarily because they represent the heritage of this country.

By the 1880's collecting in America had increased enough for newspaper cartoons to appear showing "long-beards" rooting around in trash cans for antiques. This is often the first kind of recognition of a new movement. Anything new seems to elicit a good deal of antagonism until it is well established.

The Hudson-Fulton Celebration in 1907 was probably the most significant exhibition of American historical furniture to be held in this country. Until that time there was an extremely limited group of collectors interested in American antiques, and American as well as other antiques were of almost no public interest.

The next milestone in the development of antique collecting in America was the gift by Mrs. Russell Sage of over six hundred pieces of American furniture to the Metropolitan Museum of Art in New York.

In 1914 the Clarence J. Dearden Collection of American and English furniture was sold. This sale was considered more of a novelty than anything else, as were the items offered to the public.

In 1918 the idea of American antiques apparently took hold in the Metropolitan Museum of Art, for in that year the Museum bought the George S. Palmer Collection from New London, Connecticut.

An event took place in 1921 which, on its face, would not seem of great significance to the collecting of antiques. But it was actually a milestone, and probably as important as any other event in the history of American collecting. In that year *Antiques* magazine was founded (its first issue appeared in 1922). The inauguration of a new magazine is of course a reflection of interest, and of enough interest to make the project economically feasible. *Antiques* reflected the growing interest in antiques, but it was a pioneering effort which in itself pushed forward the collecting of antiques.

In the Twentieth Anniversary Issue of *Antiques* (January 1942) in an article entitled "Milestones," Charles Messer Stow calls the opening of the American wing by the Metropolitan Museum of Art on November 11, 1924, "The most spectacular museum event in the last twenty years." The public began to take great interest in American antiques as was evidenced by some 300,000 visitors in eleven months; and other museums followed suit by opening American wings or American period rooms.

In the following year, 1925, the Metropolitan bought the Louis Guerineau Myers Collection of Queen Anne furniture made in Philadelphia; and in 1926 J. Pierpont Morgan gave the Wallace Nutting Collection of very early American furniture to the Wadsworth Atheneum in Hartford, Connecticut.

In January 1925 American pewter was exhibited in the Twentieth Century Club in Boston. At the same time a show of antique furniture took place (The Park Square Show) which possibly did as much to promote the "Early American Style" in decor as any other single event.

Two events of significance further reflecting the growing interest in collecting and promoting antiques took place in 1927. The Museum of the City of New York was opened, and Colonial Williamsburg was opened in Virginia with its authentic building, furnishings and even curtains and upholstering materials made regardless of cost, so long as they were of the type used in the Colonial Period.

In 1929 one of the greatest exhibitions of antique furniture was held—the Girl Scouts Loan Exhibition of American furniture. The items were supplied from private collections, and the number on display was enormous. A large illustrated catalogue was prepared. One of these catalogues came up for sale in a lot of many books at the Plaza Art Galleries in 1964, but it was certainly not a featured publication. I did not bother to buy the lot just to get this one catalogue. When I told the librarian at the Parke-Bernet Galleries that I had seen this catalogue but did not buy it, she said: "Too bad. It alone is worth about $75 at auction!" So the Girl Scouts Loan Exhibition (for the benefit of the Girl Scouts of America) is still of considerable importance.

In the same year, 1929, the famous Reifsnyder sale took place in New York. This was one of the leading auctions of American furniture in history. The quality of items offered will almost certainly never be equaled in the future, simply because a collection of this importance does not exist today outside museums. This was a benchmark in the sale of American antiques.

The first major antique show in the United States was held in New York City at the Commodore Hotel in 1929. This was to be followed by many more Commodore Hotel shows. Boston and Philadelphia then followed suit with shows.

In 1930 Francis P. Garvan gave Yale University a huge collection of furniture, silver, paintings, glass and prints, and in 1932 he gave Yale an additional collection of sporting prints. In 1931 when things, including the stock market, were pushing toward an economic bottom, the Garvan Collection of American furniture brought $424,852. (Later we will indicate the course of antique prices in periods of economic decline.) But the important thing about the Garvan Collection is that it was composed of top-grade American antique furniture. Some of it had been purchased from the Reifsnyder Collection which was sold in 1929, and some had come from the comparable Flayderman Collection which was also sold earlier. Probably no sale of American antique furniture which may be held in the future can equal the Garvan Collection either.

In the year 1932, the very bottom of economic activity, the Myers sale of American furniture was held. Again, museum-quality American furniture came onto the market, pieces which are not likely to be equaled in any future sale.

Henry Ford in 1934 opened Greenfield Village in Dearborn, Michigan, with its excellent collection of American furniture.

In 1935 another major sale took place—the Francis Shaw sale of Salem, Massachusetts, furniture. Salem is one of the half dozen cities in the United States that produced the finest American furniture in the eighteenth century.

These then are the leading events in the development of antique collecting in America. They are also the leading events in the development of collecting *American* antiques. And those who write in America tend to emphasize American collectors and American antiques, as is only natural. In Italy we would think English antiques did not exist; in Paris English antiques are of secondary importance; in London the finest Italian antiques often do not bring prices comparable to their quality—certainly not comparable to what the same pieces would bring in Rome. So it is in America. We are most concerned about American collectors and American antiques.

Antique Furniture Collecting in England

One of the most notable sales was the Hamilton Palace sale in England which was held in 1882. In five days £397,562 worth of antiques and related items was sold. This represented almost $2,000,000, a large sum even today. Some of the individual items sold, as will be seen later, brought enormous sums.

It will appear, as we outline the history of collecting, that it is most difficult to determine when collecting began. Certainly the earlier we go in the history of collecting the more important the collecting of other things seems to be as compared with collecting antique furniture.

In the middle of the nineteenth century, however, a significant change in the collection of antique furniture took place. Antique collecting at this time went middle class. It was no longer the exclusive pastime of the wealthy. Writers like Lucy Orrinsmith and Lady Barker managed to secure some interest on the part of the middle class in collecting old Spanish cabinets, Chinese and Japanese screens, and classical furniture made in the late eighteenth and early nineteenth centuries. Having begun in Boston, the revival of old furniture had by 1856 become a "freak of fashion."

By 1884 there is reference to the "antique craze." This seemed to cause the journal *Cabinet Making and Upholstery* a great deal of concern: "There is little doubt but the manufacture of antiques has become a modern industry."

The first issue of *The Connoisseur*, September–December 1901, mentions the great increase in collectors and the increase in prices in the 1880's over the 1870's and 1860's caused by the increased desire for things old and beautiful and rare. According to the same issue of *Connoisseur*, prices for even ordinary English furniture were ". . . double and treble those of a few years ago."

There is also mention of Hepplewhite and Chippendale chairs being returned to the drawing room from the servants quarters after the owners had noticed the high prices such pieces were now commanding.

And *The Connoisseur*, May–August 1905, shows the great interest in antiques at that time. Such comments could almost have been written today:

The taste for antiques is largely on the increase. Formerly the exclusive possession of the connoisseur of ample means, it has, through the influence of public collectors and the literature devoted to them, now extended to a much wider field. No home, however unassuming, having any pretensions to refinement, is nowadays without some indication of its owner's love of beautiful old things in the shape of a cabinet of china, examples of old silver or old ivory, or a few pieces of eighteenth century furniture.

One of the results of the growth of this taste has been a great scouring of likely and unlikely places for specimens to supply the demand, for the requirements of museums and the zeal of rich collectors have locked up, so to speak, so many of the choicer works for the term of their natural lives, that diligent search has had to be made to find genuine pieces to satisfy the needs of that larger public which, while not aspiring to possess the unattainable great examples, is educated enough and critical enough not to be imposed upon by counterfeits.

. . . there are still opportunities for judicious investment in antique furniture. It needs no argument to show that genuine pieces must, as they become more difficult to obtain, appreciate in market value.

Collecting After the Fall of France

The Bastille was stormed by the French Republicans in 1789. The furniture guilds which produced the superb French furniture of the eighteenth century were dissolved in the following year, and in 1792 there began what was probably the greatest sale of paintings, art objects and antiques in history.

Later, on September 30, 1793, the sale of the furniture from Versailles Palace began. (Louis XVI had been guillotined by the time notice of the sale went out, and the queen, Marie Antoinette, was to follow him shortly.) Each day the sale started at 10 A.M. and continued until 8 P.M. There were 17,182 items in the catalogue, and they were sold without regard to order. The sale required one year. The various items were sold for a fraction of their present worth. The Republicans were so intent on getting rid of the monarchy that they exempted from taxes all pieces of furniture which bore the arms or monograms of the king and queen provided a foreigner bought these items and cleared them out of the country.

The great *ébéniste* Riesener saw an economic opportunity in this sale and bought back a number of the pieces of furniture he had made for the royal court, counting on the Terror to "blow over." But he was more wrong than he knew. Not only did the Terror fail to "blow over" until Napoleon Bonaparte came to the throne and reestablished the monarchy in 1804, but the style of furniture Riesener made— Louis XVI—did not return to popularity in Riesener's lifetime.

The chronicle of Christie's *Since the War, 1945–1958*, prepared by Denys Sutton, states that the English collectors were buying French furniture in the eighteenth century and continued to do so into the nineteenth century. French pieces were imported, for example, by Horace Walpole (1717–1797) who was known to have made purchases on his visits to Paris of furniture and *objets d'art*. The Prince Regent and George Watson Taylor, the West Indies magnate, both took full advantage of the dispersal of the French collections including the Royal collection, and Lord Yarmouth purchased furniture on the Regent's behalf in

London, and in Paris after the Napoleonic Wars. In 1802 Sir John Dean Paul went to Paris to visit the "curiosity shops" in order to purchase "furniture and works of art . . . pillaged during the Terror." The desire and taste for French furniture was definitely widespread in England and later in the nineteenth century such personages as the 4th Marquess of Hertford and the Rothschilds were avid buyers of major works by the French *maîtres ébénistes*. Denys Sutton further states that early in the 1850's Christie's supplied Lord Hertford with photographs of important French antiques that were to be auctioned. Interest in the eighteenth century was more prevalent at this time than is usually realized. In his "Dutch" style house, of 1862, one of Thackeray's treasured possessions was a Louis XV table which featured the French crown and royal cipher.

Earlier Collecting

From 1775 to the fall of the Bastille in 1789 the price of furniture rose, but this was essentially new furniture then turned out by the *maîtres ébénistes*, and it rose in response to the demands of the nobility and the wealthy mercantile class—like any other product would in the face of increasing demand. But with the onset of the Terror in 1789 and Napoleon's looting of the art treasures of Europe, collecting went into something of an eclipse and remained there for perhaps half a century.

There were no French and Companys, no Durand-Ruels, no Parke-Bernet Galleries and Sotheby's until well into the nineteenth century. Furniture dealing, even furniture dealing in the finest works of art, was in the hands of curiosity shops and what today would be considered secondhand dealers and junk shops.

But let us again try to locate the *beginning* of collecting. And to try to locate this particular era we must move far back in time.

Maurice Rheims in his *Strange Life of Objects* (New York: Atheneum Publishers, 1961) says: "But it was not until the second century B.C. that the Romans began to foreshadow the juvenile American passion for anything that belonged to the cultural past: they invented the modern idea of 'collecting.' "

During four centuries the Romans collected almost every masterpiece they could—often as the spoils of war. Greek art was particularly popular and avidly collected and displayed in the public squares.

Collecting became very fashionable in Rome. Romans, even as today, opened their homes on certain days to show their private collections and Caesar gave his treasures to the city as a sign of his affection for his people. In A.D. 71 great crowds in Rome came to see the tables of the Laws and the seven-branched candlestick captured from the Jews.

But even this period was not the one which saw the dawn of collecting. In the fifth century B.C. the Greeks made inventories of objects in their treasure houses and temples. It was apparently at this time that the wealthy upper class as individuals first adopted the fashion of adorning their homes with fine objects.

Frank Arnau in *3000 Years of Deception in Art and Antiques* (London: Jonathan Cape, 1961) states: "Around 180 B.C. Eumenes II built the famous

altar at Pergamum. He collected 'art treasures of some antiquity' and his brother Attalus II 'old paintings'—evidence that even in this period antiques were being hoarded and 'famous *old* murals, which were not purchasable, were copied.' "

Collecting died with the collapse of Rome in the early part of the Christian era, and it is of tremendous significance that it died because those who collected, the wealthy classes, collapsed. Both Greek and Roman art declined and remained dormant for five hundred years until Constantinople rose to preeminence and treasure houses were again in vogue. Charlemagne (742–814) ushered in a new era of collecting antiques.

Between the tenth and twelfth centuries collecting went out of fashion. Then the French House of Valois, which came into power in 1328 in the person of Philip VI, started collecting and placing a premium on antiques.

By 1492 one of the greatest private collections of art and antiques was assembled. Possibly it has not been equaled since. This was the Medici Collection. By the close of the fifteenth century this collection was not only so extensive but so fine as to be beyond belief.

We might continue with the rise and fall of collecting antiques up to the present time, but most of the collecting had to do with art and antiquities and not with furniture of ancient vintage. This brief summary of the high points of the history and origin of collecting indicates several facts:

1. The wealthy classes are for the most part the collectors.
2. They emulate the rulers and the nobles who were the first to make great collections of art and antiquities.
3. They collect when they have military security and a stable government.
4. Collecting antiques is an exponent of leisure.
5. Considerable wealth is required on the part of the upper classes before they satisfy basic wants and turn to collecting.
6. When governmental and social organization disintegrates, collecting goes under a cloud.

Thus in the heyday of the Greek Empire there was great emphasis on collecting. The same collecting took place in the heyday of the Roman Empire which succeeded the Greek. With the fall of the Roman Empire there was no collecting until the stable French House of Valois appeared. During the Renaissance, when the extremely wealthy ruling families such as the House of Medici appeared, collecting reached a new high. It reached another high under the stable French governments of Louis XIV, XV and XVI.

With the overthrow of the French royal house and nobility at the end of the eighteenth century and the establishment of Republicanism, collecting again came to an end. It had a brief revival with the establishment of Napoleon's First Empire. But with his downfall collecting went into the doldrums for half a century, to rise again in England and in other areas peopled by the wealthy classes created by the nineteenth-century Industrial Revolution.

The Renaissance Collection of Colonel Luigi Grassi, which was sold by The American Art Association, January 20–22, 1927. This was the style of furnishing so popular early in this century.

CHAPTER THREE

Changing Furniture Vogues

THE MOST SIGNIFICANT CHANGE IN furniture fashion to take place in recent decades is the tremendously increased preference for the eighteenth-century French style—the furniture of Louis XV and Louis XVI. The rapidity with which this change in fashion took place is illustrated by quotations from the Parke-Bernet Galleries' annual reports:

June 1951——"The traditional popularity of fine English and American 18th–early 19th century furniture was reaffirmed during the season. . . ."

No mention was made of French furniture, although some quotations on French furniture were given under the heading of HIGH PRICES—along with other kinds of furniture. The top price for a French piece was $5,000, while an American piece brought $16,000.

June 1952——"English and American 18th century furniture maintained its long time popularity. . . . However, a large part of the buying public sought French furniture."

In the 1952 annual report, at least mention was made of French furniture.

June 1956——"Outstanding among sales of American furniture and objects of art. . . . Connoisseurs of English antiques added numerous fine specimens to their collections this season. . . . The elegance of French and other Continental art, particularly of the 18th century, both in furniture and *objets d'art*, has long been popular among discriminating collectors."

Here the order of preference seems to be, according to the Galleries: (1) American, (2) English, and (3) French, with French popular with the "discriminating collectors," not with the general buying public.

June 1957——"French and English XVIII century furniture and objects of art formed two major categories of sales held during the season. Among outstanding prices realized for fine examples of French origin were. . . ."

For the first time French furniture was placed ahead of other kinds in the summary, and the price quotes for French came ahead of quotes on other kinds of furniture.

June 1958——"As to the distinguishing characteristics of the season, French XVIII century cabinetwork, European and Chinese porcelains, early silver, and Americana continued in high favor. . . . The continuing demand for the finest

25

French XVIII century cabinetwork and *objets d'art* was affirmed by the following outstanding prices. . . . Collectors of English antiques were offered many opportunities for important acquisitions this season. . . . Fine American furnishings from several important collections appeared during the season. . . ."

In this report French furniture was placed ahead of *all* other categories of objects sold through these auction galleries. Such furniture obviously stands at the top of the preference list, while the collectors of other types of furniture still have "something to buy." This switch in positions is clear if one refers back to the 1952 report.

June 1959——"In the field of furniture, it was again French examples of the XVIII century with American second, which led in appeal. . . . Connoisseurs of English antiques added numerous fine specimens to their collections this past season."

Here English furniture appears to be a kind of "afterthought."

June 1960——"In antique furniture, French XVIII century held its dominant place, with American second and English third."

June 1961——"As to trends in collecting, one season is too short a time to establish anything very positive in this connection, but it seems that French XVIII century furniture with modern paintings continue in widest popularity. . . ."

When one considers that a major gallery handles everything from Georgian silver to tapestries to porcelains, the extreme preference for French furniture seems clear.

July 1962——"In other categories we found that collectors' appetite for French XVIII century furniture showed no abatement."

The picture is painted here of a buying public waiting to "wolf down" French pieces as soon as they are placed on the display floor! The market most certainly seems no longer confined to the "discriminating collectors" referred to in the 1956 report.

June 1963——"Keenest bidding interest and largest attendance at exhibitions and sales were directed to modern paintings and French XVIII century furniture."

Here the implication is that in *numbers* of buyers alone the preference is for French furniture. It is most interesting to note that although "top prices" were quoted for a number of pieces of French furniture, not one price quote was given for a piece of English or American furniture!

June 1964——"Modern painting and French XVIII century furniture continued as the most favored by current collectors, with American furniture a close second. . . . Sales of furniture, porcelain, glass, silver and other decorations, rugs and objects of art totaled $6,989,052, with American examples frequently equaling the perennially popular French XVIII century pieces."

This report implies that collectors in general and as an extensive group prefer French furniture, but it is also clear that American furniture is the runner-up and is being emphasized again, and a new trend might seem to be appearing. This foreshadowing is correct. It was borne out by the Andrew Varick Stout sale of early 1966 in which several pieces of American furniture reached five figures, one

American chair bringing $24,000, another $27,000, a third $18,000 and a little table bringing $23,000.

Thus, to summarize, in the space of one decade French eighteenth-century furniture rose to absolute dominance in the preference of buyers in general, and while American was always in demand throughout the period, it was overshadowed for a time by French. Now, however, French seems to be taking on something of the importance of Rembrandt in the art field.

The human mind has a number of "built in biases," and one of the most noticeable is the bias that "what *is* will continue forever." When the stock market is rising, for instance, there is the generally prevalent feeling that it will continue to rise forever, and when particular stocks are in vogue there is the feeling among members of the investment community that they will be in demand indefinitely.

Now the fashion is French furniture, and it is most difficult to see any other price movement for this furniture but up.

The French Vogue

Let us trace the preference for French furniture. In order to determine trends, a number of magazines were reviewed from the early years of this century up to the present time. A few magazines and other periodicals were traced back much earlier, but we are concerned in this chapter with fairly recent vogues rather than ancient history. *Antiques* magazine was first published in 1922, and the great majority of all issues of that magazine were read in order to determine price trends and preferences.

No matter how far back in history we go, there was no French antique vogue in the sense that it exists today. One might draw a parallel between the French vogue and the Rolls-Royce vogue. In America there was never a Rolls-Royce vogue until the last few years. A decade ago the total of Rolls-Royce and Bentley cars sold per year in the United States was a few hundred. Now New York seems alive with Rolls-Royces. There is certainly a Rolls-Royce vogue in that there are disproportionately more Rolls-Royces on the street as compared with other makes of cars *when one looks at the recent past*. But the vogue is not of the ubiquity to force a person to stop buying Chevrolets and buy a Rolls-Royce (or even stop buying Cadillacs, for that matter).

When we talk about the French vogue we are talking about a preference that can be expressed, and is expressed, by relatively few furniture buyers. While we see the shift in preference to French furniture by reviewing the annual reports of the Parke-Bernet Galleries, this French demand is actually "on top" of the already existing demand for American and English furniture. While French furniture was selling for ever-increasing prices because it was so much in demand in recent years, American and English furniture was selling for increasing prices too. Demand for these two types was also increasing—but not quite so fast as demand for French.

It was made somewhat clear in the chapter on the "Age of Elegance" that the type furniture most synonymous with elegance at the present time is French furniture of Louis XV and Louis XVI design, and there is no other period in history in which such a tremendous appeal to appreciate French furniture was made to the general public through newspaper and magazine advertising.

As early in the history of *Antiques* magazine as February 1923 (less than a year after the first issue of this magazine appeared), there was a full-page advertisement for French furniture. It occupied the back inside cover. In this era there was at least some interest in French furniture. That French furniture was then in demand is attested to by the fact that in the same year *Antiques* reported that Sir Anthony Rothschild purchased a Louis XV table by Cosson for the huge sum of £4,935 ($22,553). The September 1923 issue reported that a sale of Louis XV and Louis XVI furniture brought £20,398.

There is little more mention of French furniture in this magazine devoted to antiques until January 1927. In that issue there was an advertisement for a Louis XVI screen and two *Directoire* chairs.

The overall attitude toward French antiques in the period of the 1920's is perhaps best illustrated by a quotation from an advertisement of one of the large antique furniture dealers. The ad was for a Louis XV armchair, a beautiful piece of furniture in gros point needlework. The ad reads, "It was from French master-works in furniture of the period of Louis XV that the English school of Chippendale received much of its inspiration." This is elegance by association. The piece of French furniture is related to the accepted elegant Chippendale. The issue of the magazine was July 1928. During the 1920's French furniture was conspicuous by its absence from *Antiques* magazine.

In May 1930 the Barnet Lewis sale in London was described in *Antiques*, and the conclusion was that French furniture was badly off in price. For two hundred lots only £18,758 was received—$91,164, or $455 per lot. A pair of Louis XVI settees and eight *fauteuils* brought 810 guineas (about $4,050). In 1898 this same suite had brought 3,100 guineas ($15,500). It had lost three-quarters of its value in the later year. A *Régence* commode and *cartonniere* that had brought £540 in 1898 brought only £90 in 1930—one sixth of its earlier price. Finally, an oval table that had possibly once belonged to Marie Antoinette brought 340 guineas in 1903 and only 140 in 1930.

While it may seem like probing too far into the ancient past to go back to 1898 in order to make a price comparison with 1930, the time span is the same as between 1934 and 1966. It is not so long as it might seem—and the price drop was enormous.

Actually the earlier French vogue, such as it was, continued after the turn of the twentieth century. *Connoisseur* magazine stated in the September–December 1901 issue: "While the prices of fine old French mounted furniture quite hold their own, there has been a more rapid appreciation lately of really high class English furniture of the 18th Century. Sheraton with original decoration has risen rapidly in the past two or three years as well as Chippendale."

French furniture was still bringing high prices two years later. The January–April 1903 issue of *The Connoisseur* remarked: "The furniture sold in January included few pieces of any importance and the prices were in no way remarkable. The only piece that fetched a really high figure was a Louis XVI parquetry commode which realized £2,415 at Christie's on the 23rd."

In the January–April 1920 issue, *The Connoisseur* stated, "French furniture in many cases surpassed the 1,000 guinea standard at Rutley, Lodge, Claggate (Messrs. Castiglione and Scott) whilst Messrs. Knight, Frank and Rutley have scored a trail of eminently successful auctions both at their Hanover Square Galleries and at numerous country seats. . . ."

1920, five years before the start of our systematic recording of antique prices, it was something of an achievement for French furniture to reach the 1,000-guinea mark ($3,660). Today a piece of French furniture which realized ten times this figure—$36,600—*might* get such notice.

In May 1930 a drop in French prices is cited in *The Connoisseur* while the appreciation in price of old English oak furniture is pointed out. There was a definite falling off in the popularity of French furniture as compared with some other types of antiques. Again, in the June issue of the same year, it is pointed out that English furniture is the furniture most in demand, not French.

At about this place in antique history the furniture of the Louis' was at something of a low point and certainly was not popular in America. This is recorded in "Art and Artful Art," as told to Edward Smith, in the June 1, 1929, *Saturday Evening Post*, "Out of these woods, plus marble, stone, onyx, gold, silver, baser metals, silks, satins, downs, damasks, velvets, brocades, tapestry, ivory, agate and what not else, the French furniture makers produced those marvelous and sometimes ludicrous works of theirs which appeal so powerfully to some tastes."

The April 1931 issue of *Antiques* remarks that French Provincial furniture was down in price.

By 1939, although there were many sales of French furniture, the September issue of *Antiques* cites a Louis XV acajou desk that brought $1,500. This was about the low point for French furniture in recent times.

Throughout the 1940's French furniture was in relative obscurity. The June 1943 issue of *Antiques* points out that French furniture was low in price. As far as advertisements of French furniture are concerned, they are conspicuous by their absence. In the June 1954 issue of the magazine, an eighteenth-century inlaid breakfront commode with a marble top, made in 1785, was advertised for $325.

The year 1953 might be characterized as the year of the emergence of French furniture. *Antiques* magazine in its October issue contained a full-page advertisement by French and Company which illustrated a Louis XV sofa. Charles Patterson of New York advertised two Louis XVI *fauteuils*. Isabella Barclay of New York advertised a pair of Louis XV *canapés*, and John Vesey of New York even advertised a nineteenth-century French birdcage.

The magazine in its December issue of the next year commented that French furniture was rising in price, and it is absolutely clear that of all antiques French dominated as far as popularity and general interest were concerned, although prices were still certainly under eighteenth-century American furniture prices.

The March 1960 issue contained more French pieces of furniture advertised for sale than probably any other issue of the magazine published up to that time. The January issue of the same year contained an article on the royal *ébéniste* David Roentgen, and the March issue contained another article on the same maker. The September issue commented on the height of French antique prices.

Side Effects of the Eighteenth Century French Boom

In almost all fields of antiquities there is a trend toward items of more recent date. From the French Impressionist and Post-Impressionist paintings, interest moved to the French Modern School (which actually began about 1905). From Italian Renaissance paintings interest moved to Italian Baroque, and as interest in Baroque increases and prices rise, as they have been doing recently to rather astronomical levels, interest moves to nineteenth-century Italian painting. In the same way, as eighteenth-century British art is cleared from the market—Gainsborough, Romney, Reynolds, Lawrence, Raeburn, Hoppner, etc.—nineteenth-century British art takes on interest in the market and prices rise.

Connaissance magazine for June 1961 comments that the prices at the Murat Sale increased the price of Empire furniture, and confirmed the rise in the price of nineteenth-century furniture.

But there is a backward movement of interest in the market too. *Connaissance* for April 1961 states that there is a rise in seventeenth-century furniture (e.g. a pair of Louis Treize armchairs—$2,350 . . .) and even in the earlier furniture of the fifteenth and sixteenth centuries, but in a far less spectacular fashion. The prices still indicate some reluctance on the part of collectors. The principal reasons for this are that they are cumbersome, have restricted usefulness, and do not mix easily with later furniture. They also present problems of authenticity. However, they go very well with contemporary decor.

Another quote (*Connaissance,* March 1961) indicates both the preeminence of Louis XV furniture and a rebirth of pre-eighteenth century (Louis XIII) furniture:

> The price of $8,060 for a Louis XV writing table and $7,830 for a side table in the Paris salerooms illustrates the continuing vogue for this type of furniture on the art market everywhere. Nevertheless French taste shows signs of being more eclectically inclined and oriented towards the works of other periods. The tremendous rise in the price of Eighteenth Century furniture has caused Louis XIII furniture to be commonly regarded as cheap (and justly so compared to Louis XV). But in fact there is a rise in this field also. For instance, a pair of Louis XIII armchairs fetched $2,880 on the Paris market and a *bergère* armchair of the same period $888 at Lausanne. Such prices obtained only for Louis XV until recently.

By 1964 there was an interest in furniture of periods very much later than that of Louis XV and XVI, and *Connaissance* for October 1964 comments, "There is an increasing interest in Charles X chairs."

Vogues Prior to the French Vogue

The purpose of the reviews of price history for the various types of furniture is to show preferences. Sometimes these preferences are so strong as to amount to a vogue. In this chapter, however, we are pointing out *dominating* vogues—vogues that are so strong as to influence antique buyers and nonantique buyers as well. When advertisements for women's hose and men's suits use French antiques as the dominant background, then it seems obvious that French is the dominating vogue.

To find a vogue as all-pervasive as French, we must go back to the 1920's. The January 1942 issue of *Antiques* magazine, the Twentieth Anniversary Issue, describes the spirit of collecting in this unforgettable era: "Every collector who was active in the lush, flush years prior to the debacle of 1929 looks back on that period with a certain nostalgia, and with, perhaps, a mingled amusement and amazement. There was an excitement about collecting in those days, an abandon in acquisition, a keenness of rivalry, a madness in prices that will probably never be equaled."

As far as America is concerned, the vogue was a "simple early American" furniture vogue that took hold in roughly the year 1925 and continued *into* the Depression. As late as February 1930, long after the stock market crash, *Antiques* magazine states, "The collecting public has gone mad!"

The emphasis in the era of the 1920's, especially after 1925, was on cottage furniture. The March 1927 issue of *Antiques* magazine states: "At Sotheby's the other day . . . a set of plain old Windsor side chairs was sold (eight, I think there were) that realized £58—a staggering sum for ordinary Windsor chairs over here. Such things show which way the wind blows; and it seems as if the vogue for simplicity were spreading to England."

The June 1926 issue of *Antiques* states, "The prices of simple cottage furniture are twice those of last November."

The March 14, 1925, issue of *The Saturday Evening Post* contains an article by M. L. Blumenthal entitled "Antiqueering." It states that ten or twenty years prior to this date old furniture brought little, but now antiques were a craze. The fashion, the article continues, is for early American, not English or continental furniture, with curly maple, pine, walnut and oak favored.

The Philadelphia Centennial of 1876, as mentioned in Chapter II, started the Americana vogue, but to only a very limited extent. In the 1890's the collecting of Americana took a fresh start. After the Free Silver scare had passed, prosperity returned, and large sums of money were made by an increasingly large group of people. Yachts and country estates were the things for the wealthy to have, and along with these luxuries went American antiques. But it was not until certain events took place in and around the 1920's that Americana of the more simple variety took firm hold on a major segment of the furniture-buying public. The Centennial stressed Americanism and patriotism. So did World War I, and this feeling appears to have been very much stronger at that time than it is today.

It is no wonder, then, that with the tremendous development of public interest in antiques a class of collectors of Americana should develop. The early interest in the cottage or primitive American furniture was in pine. Then the interest shifted to maple, and from there it went to the fine early eighteenth-century furniture of the William and Mary period.

The early American vogue was well recognized by the *Literary Digest* in an article which appeared in the April 11, 1925, issue entitled "The Day of the American Antique." The article states that fifteen years prior to this date there was no boom in American antiques. This view corresponds with that of the leading American dealer, Israel Sack, who in the January 1955 issue of *Antiques* magazine stated, "In 1904 when I started as a dealer in Boston, the few collectors of Americana were considered eccentric and American creations merely as crude country versions of English contemporary designs."

By the bottom of the Depression the early American simple furniture boom was about over, and Edwin Lefevre, writing in *The Saturday Evening Post* of October 29, 1932, in an article entitled, "Deflated Antiques" states, "The early American pine fad is dead." He goes on to state that while this furniture was crude and ugly, it was a part of America and American history. Mr. Lefevre continues: "I don't think anyone can deny that antiques have followed closely the course of the stock market, or did until the rally began in Wall Street. But antiques have not rallied."

Antiques were still booming to a certain extent well after the stock market crash. There is some evidence that antiques lag behind business conditions in general, both in the recession phase of the business cycle and in the recovery phase, and that they have a cycle which varies in length and amplitude from the general business cycle.

The simple American antique furniture boom did, however, die with the onset of the Depression, and no vogue came in to replace it. Fine eighteenth-century English and American furniture rose in popularity and continued to be the most sought-after furniture until French eighteenth-century antiques took over, but the English and American furniture never commanded the general public attention that American cottage furniture did in the 1920's or French furniture in the later 1950's and 1960's.

The Renaissance Furniture Boom

In 1914 the Clarence J. Dearden collection of antique American and English furniture was sold. The sale was something of a novelty. Collectors of such furniture were relatively few, although there had been some collectors of Americana as early as the turn of the century. Still, at this late date in antique collecting history there was not even a glimmering of an American antique vogue.

Since the early part of the Twentieth Century the wealthiest members of the American community had been buying Renaissance Italian furniture to fill their palatial homes and apartments. But these buyers were relatively few. However, in November 1916 the furnishings of the Davanzati Palace in Florence, Italy, were auctioned in New York. This sale was a milestone in collecting history. It realized very nearly $1,000,000 in all.

From this date, and particularly after the war ended in 1918, a Renaissance vogue took over in the United States. This was the era of building apartment houses and theaters. As well as can be remembered, the dominant furniture was Renaissance Italian for the lobbies. Even the names of a vast number of theaters reflected the Renaissance vogue—"Palace." Woodwork and plasterwork, including trim, were mostly in the early Italian style.

Related antiques also boomed in America as well as in England. The corresponding Anglo-Saxon furniture was Jacobean, also massive and dark. A. Stainforth states in "An Antique Dealer's Yesterdays" (*Antiques*, January 1942), "Between 1915 and 1925, the greatest demand was for the very early and primitive pieces. Carved chairs in the Jacobean style, court cupboards and Hadley chests of the Pilgrim century. . . ."

By the mid-1920's the early American vogue had taken over, but it had not by any means killed the popularity of the Renaissance and related styles. As late in the economic decline as the summer of 1930, one simple three-cornered chair in the Figdor Collection brought $23,000. But by 1947 Helen Comstock, writing in *Antiques* magazine, mentions that Italian Renaissance furniture has been gradually replaced by Americana collections.

Leslie A. Hyam, late President of the Parke-Bernet Galleries, says in his July 8, 1955, annual report, "Fashions come and go; the dark and cumbrous furniture of the Renaissance has disappeared from the American domestic scene."

Similarly, the June 1960 issue of *Fortune* magazine states, "Heavy, dark Spanish and Italian Renaissance . . . has never recovered from the 1929 crash." An article entitled "Hedge Against Inflation" in the November 19, 1962, issue of *Barrons* points out that whereas the huge Renaissance pieces brought thousands of dollars in the 1920's, these pieces now bring $100 or less.

The late Leon Medina had in his New York gallery dozens of these huge old pieces. To some extent he was probably living in the era of the 1920's and earlier, when such pieces were the height of expensive fashion. He used to point out pieces that originally sold for many thousands of dollars—he would gladly have sold them for $500 each or less.

But times change, and one day in the early 1960's I walked into his huge showrooms to find them almost denuded of these old pieces. Just one dealer from Europe, he told me, had come in and purchased all of the missing items. In fact, that dealer had offered to purchase every stick of this old furniture that he had in stock. But since Mr. Medina wanted to have some stock in order to remain in business, he refused to sell all of the items. Such a mass purchase is most unusual in any kind of business at any time.

Connaissance magazine in the May 1964 issue had this to say about the early style: "Furniture of the Middle Ages and the Renaissance is showing a certain hesitant return to fashion. Twelve years or so ago certain European collectors were showing an interest in it."

While the individual chapters in the book show changes in preference over the years, the three styles of antique furniture outlined in this chapter illustrate what might be called "all pervasive fashions," fashions that were so dominant and so impressed on the public mind that they constituted a major vogue. But perhaps it is well to end this chapter on fashion by quoting the antiques writer Thomas Hamilton Ormsbee, editor of the *American Collector*: "Nothing is more certain than change. Looking back a short twenty years (from 1942), one finds many of antiquities that are the most sought after today either neglected entirely or so far down in the lists of also-rans that only a few collectors saw any merit in them."

Special Antique Show display featuring Duncan Phyfe furniture. The sofa table by Duncan Phyfe is a rare piece and the market price is $7,500 today. The Phyfe work table was sold for about $1,500, the pair of Roman-style Phyfe chairs in the foreground for under $1,000 each, and the settee sold for about $4,700. The Federal mirrors (Albany, circa 1800) are worth $3,500-$4,500 each. The American Hepplewhite secretary sold for about $5,000 and the Rhode Island Hepplewhite, shield-back, side chairs sold for $1,200 each, $4,500 for the set of four. The Phyfe "S" scrolled armchairs sold for about $6,000 the pair. *(Photo: Courtesy of Ginsburg & Levy, Inc., New York)*

CHAPTER FOUR

The Market Price of Antiques

I N THE FALL OF 1959 MY WIFE AND I made a trip through Europe visiting about 700 art and antique dealers and 64 art museums. The primary purpose of our trip was to see the art of Europe and to buy Old Master paintings for our collection.

It became obvious about halfway through our trip that there was such a thing as the international "art market," and that there was an international market price. This means that the price of a painting by an artist whose works come up for sale reasonably periodically in the major art centers of the world—London, New York and Paris—tends to be about the same regardless of whether the painting is sold in London, New York or Paris. The value of this painting is what it will bring at retail in the normal course of business when offered by one of the larger art dealers. Naturally, the painting must be fully authenticated as to authorship.

International Antique Market and International Antique Price

Although my wife and I were avidly buying antiques as early as 1955, our primary interest was in the collection of paintings, and our 1959 trip was directed to the study and acquisition of paintings. On our many subsequent trips we also studied the antique market and purchased antiques for our home.

Investigations during our trips led us to the conclusion that the price of antiques (like paintings) traded on the international market *tends* to be about the same regardless of what dealer handles them, and regardless of whether he is renowned or not, large or small, located in an exclusive or less exclusive area.

In the United States we studied market prices intensively for a period of about seven years, mainly in the American art and antique center of New York, but also throughout the country as we went on our tours and lectured on art and antiques and their values.

This tendency to sell at the same price exists because (1) almost every dealer tends to buy at auction in the auction center nearest him. His buying price is thus comparable to that of other dealers in the same city who buy in the same auction or auctions. (2) All dealers see the prices brought at auction, and these auction prices guide each dealer in pricing his own merchandise. (3) Most dealers get the catalogues of the Parke-Bernet Galleries, Sotheby's and Christie's in London, or perhaps the catalogues of just one or two of these houses. The list of prices is sent later, and many dealers attach these price lists to each catalogue. This is an international guide to prices. In recent years there has appeared a summary price sheet on art and antiques which is published in New York, and many dealers (as well as buyers) get this price sheet. Many dealers also get the auction catalogues and price sheets of a number of the other world auction houses.

The National Bias and Its Effect

A piece of Venetian furniture, let us say a green Venetian poltrone (armchair), usually brings more in Italy than anywhere else in the world. The Italians prefer this furniture. Of course, the Italian inflation has sent people with money scurrying to invest in things which will not decline in value with rising prices. This fear, coupled with excess funds, has made the antique market boom in Italy perhaps more than in any other country.

This same poltrone will bring less money if offered by the Parke-Bernet Galleries in New York, and it seems to bring still less money when offered at auction in London. If there are twelve matching poltroni the set will bring upwards of $12,000 in Italy. The same set offered in New York is not likely to bring this sum, and in London it might bring only $6,000.

Theoretically, the large auction house gets the best price for antiques as well as art. But the smaller New York auctions seem to get as high a price for certain antiques as the major house, and these certain antiques are French of the period of the Louis'.

There is an established international price for most fine antiques. Once in a while a buyer can find a pair of outstanding Chippendale chairs of the period in New York. Almost every dealer, large and small, knows the value of such chairs. They are an extreme rarity on the international antique market and are much in demand. I have never seen any dealer or any auction house in the country offer a fine pair of Chippendale chairs that brought much under what they would have brought if offered by a major dealer in New York or London. Every dealer knows the market price of such a pair of chairs closely enough never to offer such a pair at much under the market.

Sources of Prices Over the Years

Dealers are loathe to open their books for price analysis. What they get for their furniture is their business, and it is too easy to trace the price of an antique from an auction to the ultimate customer. Dealers obviously do not like such a process, particularly if the results are put in print!

The next best thing is the international auction, and this is the main source of prices used in this book. The prices realized even by the largest auction houses—Parke-Bernet, Sotheby's and Christie's—tend to be below the market price; and it bears repeating that the market price is that price realized by a leading dealer offering fine antiques in the normal course of business.

The late Leslie Hyam of the Parke-Bernet Galleries stated that his house secured prices from 10 percent to 75 percent of retail. Of course, he could have added that for some unique items the fact that everyone knew of their availability at the auction and had to come there to compete with other buyers meant that a price at least as high as the dealer's price was achieved. The Fragonard that was sold from the Erickson Collection by the Parke-Bernet Galleries for $875,000 could probably not have realized as high a price if offered by any dealer in the world!

All the prices of the illustrated antiques offered by the Parke-Bernet Galleries from the year 1925 to the present were studied and recorded for this book. In almost no case was an unillustrated antique recorded or the price used in this study. We wanted to see what was offered for sale. Words mean something, but illustrations mean far more. If the description did not seem to fit the illustration, the price was not used. On the other hand, at certain times in the past particular items were not in great demand, and the gallery did not illustrate such items. Victorian furniture has usually not merited illustration, at least until recently. Since Victorian furniture has long been at the bottom of the price and preference list, it is not likely that the auction house will err in labeling something Victorian that is not.

The year 1925 was taken as the starting point for the study because it represents a base from which to measure the rise into the boom of 1929. From there the effect of the Great Depression on antique prices can be measured. Next, antique prices in the gradual return to normalcy of the late 1930's are recorded, including the price behavior in the short depression of 1938.

Then the prices going into the war, during the war and coming out of the war were recorded; and finally the postwar behavior of prices up to the present near-boom in antiques.

The American prices recorded were those of the Parke-Bernet Galleries, and before that gallery came into existence of the American-Anderson Galleries. Prior to that merger, prices of the American Art Association Galleries were used as well as those of Anderson Galleries. The study thus covers the leading American auction houses.

The same period was covered for the leading London houses—Sotheby's and Christie's. The years from 1925 to 1965 were studied and recorded.

Minor Auction Houses

At least as many items of antique furniture are offered for sale by the lesser New York auction houses as by the Parke-Bernet Galleries. We have regularly visited the majority of these auction houses in New York for a period of about seven years. They include the following: Plaza Art Galleries, Coleman Auction Galleries, Savoy Art and Auction Galleries, Fischer Auction Gallery, Astor Birnbaum Galleries and Manhattan Galleries.

(Of course, there are still other galleries that offer art and antiques at auction in New York. Most are in Manhattan. But other auctions in the other boroughs sometimes offer among lesser items a few excellent antiques and Old Master paintings.)

Although most of the above-listed galleries prepare auction catalogues, there are usually few or no illustrations. There are also no price lists printed up as there are in the case of the Parke-Bernet Galleries, Christie's and Sotheby's. A purely statistical study is thus impossible as far as these other auction houses are concerned. There is no way to chronicle these prices except to attend the displays and then sit in at the auctions themselves and record prices, or else secure the priced catalogues from someone who did attend the actual auctions.

Printed Sources of Market Information on Antiques

The antique market did not suddenly start in the year 1925, the base or starting year of this study. Collecting antiques began long before that. Thus, the most significant sales in the nineteenth century were reviewed for the purpose of price recording.

One of the most valuable sources of information on antiques, especially for the American buyer (and particularly for the buyer of American antiques), is *Antiques* magazine. Almost every issue of this magazine was read in some detail from its inception in the year 1922. At one time the magazine had an art market column, one particularly directed toward the London market for antiques. In almost every issue antiques were offered for sale by various firms, and occasionally prices were quoted.

The Connoisseur magazine was organized in 1901, and the majority of the issues of this magazine have also been reviewed. Here there have been scholarly articles on French furniture of the era of Louis XVI, on Sheraton, etc.; the earlier articles are particularly scholarly.

Another much used source has been *Connaissance* magazine. While the magazine is in French, for a time certain market comments were translated into English. This was an invaluable source of information on French furniture and its market peculiarities. It is also the best source of information on the Paris market—and this is a rather unique market. French furniture is best understood and appreciated in France, as is to be expected. There are most definite market biases in Paris, and these are explained in great detail in *Connaissance*. These biases will be discussed in the chapters on the furniture of the Louis'.

Another excellent source of information on the antique market has been *Country Life* magazine. This English magazine concentrates strictly on the London market. It almost never is concerned with American antiques because so few are offered for sale in London. It is most concerned with the finer English antiques, but also with fine French pieces, many of which have been sold in London at extremely high prices in recent years. This magazine comments on quality and discusses present prices as compared with historical prices. The information obtained from it has been of great assistance in getting a feel of the London market as well as in securing detailed descriptions of particular pieces.

The excellent facilities of the Bridgeport, Connecticut, Public Library were used for the review of *The New York Times* from the turn of the century to the present time. The purpose of such review was to note what sales were considered important, what pieces brought high prices, what types of antiques were in demand at different times, and during what periods antique collecting was pursued and during what periods antique collecting was considered unimportant. This *New York Times* review was important in that advertisements were studied which dealt with antiques and with decorating.

Major magazines were also reviewed for articles dealing with antiques from the turn of the century up to the present time. The most valuable group of articles was found in *The Saturday Evening Post* in the middle 1920's. Article after article appeared in this era in the *Post*, many of which were extremely scholarly. It is obvious that antiques were a primary concern of a very large group of people at the time.

Many reference sources were used to locate articles or antiques. The further back one goes in these summaries of source materials, the fewer are the articles on the subject of antiques. We thus see the increasing importance of antiques as time goes on. The process was by no means one of constant build-up, however.

Weaknesses in Using Auction Prices to Trace Historical Market Movements

1. The auction market is generally below the retail market, especially for the type of antiques sold by the larger and more important dealers.

2. Generally, only the illustrated antiques were made use of in determining the course of the auction market. But many many other items were sold in every auction that were not illustrated. Of course, in the last seven years in New York almost every auction, large and small, was visited by the author in advance of the sale so that pieces offered could be inspected. This is a good sample of antiques offered in these later years. Interviews with collectors, dealers and auction officials were used to supplement our sample and confirm our opinions.

The fact remains, however, that the best items were generally the illustrated ones. They were illustrated because the auction house wanted prospective buyers to realize what fine things were going and thereby be induced to attend the auction sale.

3. The auction market is only a part of the antique market, and a large amount of goods goes from sellers or their estates direct to dealers for resale. The rarity of good French antiques in the smaller auction houses in New York suggests that in many cases the auction houses purchase certain items as well as entire estates and offer them for resale at auction. Some take the best French antiques and offer them to the leading dealers in French antiques since the auction houses can expect to get the highest prices from these specialty dealers.

It must also be remembered that a good many of the items offered at auction do not come from individuals who are moving away or from the estates of the rich. They come from dealers who think they may do well by auctioning them. And the auction house itself, sometimes facing a paucity of good antiques, will ask dealers to put in items. One dealer whom I have known for years always put in one excellent Dutch picture as a favor to his friend the auctioneer. This painting was so high in quality that it alone drew in several buyers. But the dealer always had a high reserve on the picture and it never sold. It was always there to do service again in another auction. The same for an eighteenth-century English chest-on-chest. I have seen this chest reappear at the same auction house for almost a year. The last time I saw it was the day I wrote this page.

4. These "come ons," plus items with reserves so high that they will never sell, to some extent vitiate auction prices as a measure of the market. I bid on an item that the auctioneer started at $10. I bid it up patiently by $5 jumps until I got to $110. At that point I got tired and it went, or *maybe* it went, for $115. The alacrity with which I was raised each time, without any hesitation on the part of the only other bidder, suggests that the owner was there protecting his item—he would have protected it much more. Where the auction house itself owns an item, and the smaller houses often do, the house often bids against the customer. Such an auction is of course no auction at all, and the house might just as well place price tags on the items and forget about the machinations of the auction procedure. Not all the smaller houses do this, however.

5. In many furniture auctions of smaller size, a ring of dealers is formed. One dealer is designated to do the bidding, and the rest sit back and offer no competition. If the spokesman gets the item, a second auction, or knock-out, is held and attended only by the dealers in the ring. It is held right after the main auction, and may even be held in the street. The one who bids the most gets the item, and the difference between what the ring paid for the item at the real auction and this second, higher price is divided among the members of the ring, depending on how long each one stayed in the bidding. (Those remaining the longest get most of the excess of the second price over the first, or real, auction price.) Now the *true* price is this knockout price. This price most nearly approximates the market price. The first price is only a monopoly price which is artificially low because competition among a group of buyers is eliminated through mutual agreement.

The existence of such a ring is not subject to debate, although dealers vigorously deny its existence. It is a fact. And despite the fact that such rings are against the law in England, they exist there just as they do here.

One major world auction house has a good customer. He buys Impressionist and French modern paintings in the high price category. This collector has a relative who is an artist, and the collector is interested in promoting her work. He thus has induced the major auction house to sell her paintings. They otherwise would not be likely to handle the work of this artist as the artist is not well-known enough to command an interest at auctions. Each time the paintings by his relative are offered at auction, this collector goes to the auction and bids on them. He always gets the paintings.

Prices established by such methods are not market prices at all and are useless for recording purposes. Only the underbids, if these were real, could be used as any measure of the market price.

6. One cannot be sure of exactly what he is looking at in the catalogue illustrations. The quality of Old Master paintings is often judged from a black-and-white photo. This is standard procedure all over the world for judging the quality of paintings.

But it is vastly more difficult to judge by photo the authenticity as well as the quality of an antique. Thus in some cases we have to rely heavily on the authentications prepared by the auction houses. These are generally good *for all houses*, both large and small. They are probably at least 80 percent accurate, and many of the descriptions err on the *conservative* side.

An eighteenth-century painting does not look like a nineteenth-century one even in a black-and-white photo. But it is tremendously difficult, if not impossible, to distinguish by looking at a photo between a genuine eighteenth-century antique and one made in the nineteenth century *in the manner of* the eighteenth-century piece. It is difficult enough if one spends some time actually examining the piece itself, opening the drawers, looking at the bottom, and tearing the upholstery off, as buyers do at many auctions.

The selling price of a piece is a measure of its authenticity. This is, of course, circular reasoning, and we are saying that because a piece brought a high price it must be genuine and fine. And usually those who pay high prices—dealers and the ultimate customer—do not part with money easily, thus providing a certain proof of authenticity.

There is little deliberate misrepresentation in the major as well as the minor auction houses in New York and probably in London. However, the auctioneer who has an item for sale which no one in his right mind could conceivably want, may say, "Now here is a thing of beauty, a real treasure that the most discriminating collector will be proud to own." But he usually does not say, "This is Louis XV of the period."

7. When the price of American Telephone and Telegraph is quoted at $60 per share at one time and $68 at another time, we know that the market has risen from $60 to $68. We are talking about exactly the same thing—one share of American Tel and Tel common. But when we say the price of Louis XV furniture rose 50 percent in the year, we are on much less certain ground. No two items of furniture are exactly alike, and thus no two prices are exactly comparable. In a few rare instances, which we will cite later, the same piece may go through auction twice and thus the prices are directly comparable, but such instances are few and far between.

8. Foreign exchange rates offer a major problem. We have converted

foreign currencies to dollars for comparability. In 1949 the pound sterling was the equivalent of $3.68. Then it went to $2.80.* If we were tracing antique prices in England and converting them to dollars, then obviously this mechanical procedure of devaluation of the pound sterling would have indicated that the antique market declined in price. It did for Americans, but this is not the type of decline we are interested in. (Many British products came within the reach of American pocketbooks, but it cannot be said that the *prices* declined from 1949 to 1950.) We must adjust either mathematically or by estimate where devaluations take place. Some adjustment is also required where the official government exchange rate varies from the free rate which, although often a black market rate, is in effect the real rate. As late as 1963 people came up to me in the street in Naples and offered me the currencies of major European countries at discounts if I would give them American dollars.

9. No adjustment has been made for the changing purchasing power of money. The procedure which would have to be developed where a number of foreign currencies are concerned is very complicated. Deflationary techniques are to a great extent opinion, and there is a question as to the value of such techniques to the student of the antique market.

10. There is difficulty in using three markets for recording prices (New York, London and Paris). Each market has its own bias. English antiques of the eighteenth century are almost unknown in the Paris market. But strangely enough, the average French antique of the eighteenth century tends to bring a little more in the United States than it does in Paris. Consequently, when we record the prices of French antiques sold in New York and in Paris, with conversion to dollars of the franc prices, these two sets of prices vary because of market bias and are thus not always strictly comparable. This market bias is even more true of antiques than of paintings since a painting can easily be packed and shipped to a market in which it can secure a higher price.

Price History by Types of Antiques

One could refer to a "School" of Antiques—Chippendale or William and Mary —as he would refer to a School of Painting—the Impressionists or seventeenth-century Dutch. But antiques are not generally referred to as belonging to a particular "School." We will simply call them *types* or categories of antiques.

The types of antiques we have traced in this book are those which are *traded in substantial dollar volume on the international antique market*. Chippendale furniture is in this category. So is French Empire furniture, or just Empire as it is generally called. Some excellent furniture was produced in Holland in the eighteenth

*Until November 1967 when it went to $2.40.

century. It is sold on today's market in Holland in very large volume. It is also sold on the international market—but not in sufficient quantity to make a price history valuable or even possible.

Some of the types of antiques we have traced present problems in that at some time in the span of years we have chosen to trace price history, the type antique was of relatively little importance. For this reason it did not merit detailed catalogue explanations and minute descriptions of the decoration, the shape of the legs, the type feet, etc. In fact, some Jacobean furniture in England was sometimes referred to as "antique furniture" without any reference to seventeenth century or to Jacobean. It was given no positively identifying description. The same was true in the early years of price recording for such presently outstanding types of antiques as Chippendale and Queen Anne.

By the international market we mean London, New York and Paris. We have relied most heavily on the prices secured at Sotheby's, Christie's and the Parke-Bernet Galleries. The Paris auctions sell the most French furniture, as might be expected. And they trade relatively little English and American furniture—again, as would be expected. We have used Paris prices only in the past dozen years, and we have used them to a considerable extent to show market bias. If one wants a good set of French furniture of good average quality, it should probably be bought in Paris. There it can be obtained much more easily than anywhere else. In the United States such average pieces would often bring much higher prices, and, I believe, even in the secondary auctions here.

Then too, this book is written in English. It is therefore directed at English-speaking people, and the "English-speaking" markets are New York and London. They are the natural markets for English-speaking people.

Types of Antiques Reviewed

Below are listed the types or categories of antiques for which we have recorded prices from 1925 (in some cases earlier) to the present. Some earlier prices for important sales were recorded, and in a few cases the earliest obtainable prices were searched for in order to determine approximately when antiques began to have value *as antiques* and not simply as useful pieces of furniture.

FRENCH ANTIQUES
Louis XIV
Régence
Louis XV
Transition
Louis XVI
French Provincial
Directoire
Empire

ITALIAN ANTIQUES
> Renaissance
> Venetian and other eighteenth-century painted Italian

ENGLISH ANTIQUES
> Jacobean
> William and Mary
> Queen Anne
> Chippendale
> Hepplewhite
> Adam
> Sheraton
> Regency
> Victorian

AMERICAN ANTIQUES
> William and Mary
> Queen Anne
> Chippendale
> Hepplewhite
> Sheraton
> Duncan Phyfe
> Victorian
> American Country

The following types of antiques were not reviewed in detail either because (1) they were not on the market in sufficient volume to warrant a price study, or (2) they were strictly nineteenth-century furniture and thus not antiques, or (3) they are foreign to Western international antique markets even though they may be prominent in other parts of the world:

FRENCH ANTIQUES
> Gothic (1100–1500)
> Renaissance (1500–1625)
> Louis XIII (1625–1643)
> Consulate (1799–1804)
> Restoration—Louis XVIII (1814–1824)
> Charles X (1824–1830)
> Louis Philippe (1830–1848)

ITALIAN ANTIQUES
> Eighteenth-century natural wood furniture

ENGLISH ANTIQUES
> Gothic (1100–1500)
> Early Tudor (1509–1558)

AMERICAN ANTIQUES
> Pilgrim Century—seventeenth century
> Empire

DUTCH ANTIQUES OF THE EIGHTEENTH CENTURY
SPANISH RENAISSANCE ANTIQUES
GERMAN AND AUSTRIAN ANTIQUES
IRISH AND SCOTCH ANTIQUES (for the most part)
ANTIQUES OF OTHER COUNTRIES BASED ON DESIGNS OF THE LOUIS'
CHINESE FURNITURE

Masterpieces and Average Pieces

Although it is possible to classify antiques of a particular type, such as American Chippendale, into an infinite variety of classes from the best to the poorest, it is also possible to establish the empirical categories of "masterpieces" and "average antiques." The block-front slant-top Chippendale desk appearing on the cover of Wallace Nutting's *Furniture Treasury* is a masterpiece in every sense of the word, while there are many Chippendale slant tops to be found in dealers' shops and in many auctions that can simply be considered good average pieces. The block front illustrated should presently be worth about $35,000 or possibly more, while the average piece going through a minor auction might be bought for as low as $500.

The block front is bought either by the most discriminating collector or by a museum. Such items are rare indeed, and when they do get into the hands of dealers or come up at auction there are many, many collectors waiting for them. They usually do not last long in the dealer's stock, and they always bring high prices.

The high grade and the average markets do not necessarily move together. If we compare the 1963–1964 season with the 1964–1965 season, we find that the market price of these two categories of antiques varied significantly. The top category rose, but average antiques rose much more. The latter was caused by more mass buying for decorative purposes and not so much by the buying of discriminating and wealthy collectors.

It is not easy to make this dichotomy, and to a certain degree it is an artificial one. It is arbitrary but it exists, and where it can be made for the purpose of price tracing it will be made.

LOUIS XIV DINING ROOM. *Courtesy Chicago Art Institute and Mrs. James Ward Thorne.*

CHAPTER FIVE

Louis XIV
1643–1715

THE FURNITURE OF LOUIS XIV IS A PRELUDE to the furniture that exerted the greatest stylistic influence on European furniture design of any furniture ever made. So dominant was the style of Louis XV and of Louis XVI that we refer to these two styles as the "furniture of the Louis'."

Louis XIV furniture is very much like the furniture of the same period in the other countries of Europe and like the Jacobean style in England. With Jacobean (1603–1649) we include Cromwellian (1649–1660) and English Restoration (1660–1689). In actuality, the long reign of Louis XIV (1643–1715) included the two later English styles of William and Mary (1689–1702) and Queen Anne (1702–1714). The similarity between the Louis XIV furniture and that of England prior to the two styles of William and Mary and Queen Anne is most striking. Under Louis XIV the chief elements of the Louis XV style were conceived.

Elevation of the Role of Furniture Under Louis XIV

The events leading up to the organizations and mechanism by which the superb French furniture of the eighteenth century was produced in large measure explain why the furniture achieved such importance.

Under Louis XIII (1601–1643) his chief advisor, Cardinal Mazarin, built what was considered the finest palace in all Europe. The cardinal, and not the king, owned the finest palace at this time.

Louis XIII was followed by Louis XIV, who reigned from 1643 to 1715— 72 years. The entire reign of Louis XIV is characterized by a series of military victories that established France as the dominant military power in Europe. Along with military success goes self-glorification and the peace of mind required to emphasize material things. The "things" soon turned out to be splendors which went along with the epithet of Louis XIV—"the Sun King."

Louis XIV began building the Palace of Versailles in 1661. Just prior to this time Louis' minister of finance, Nicholas Fouquet, who apparently had aspirations plus a love of splendor similar to Cardinal Mazarin's, entertained the entire French court at his magnificent Château de Vaux-le-Vicomte. So extravagant was this affair that an investigation of his finances followed; it was discovered that he had built and furnished his château with state plus royal funds, whereupon he was condemned to prison in 1659.

Fouquet had had an entire tapestry plant established at Maincy which supplied the artisans who worked on his château. Louis XIV moved this plant to Gobelins on the outskirts of Paris and there established the *Manufacture Royal des Meubles de la Couronne*. This move was highly important, for now the king took over the tapestry plant and raised its status to a crown organization.

In the beginning the plant was largely staffed by foreigners. (Earlier, Cardinal Mazarin had imported skilled craftsmen from Italy and the Low Countries.) The regulations of the Gobelins plant favored training the children of the plant's staff, so that in time the trained workmen became almost entirely French. This policy obviously helped to develop French industry.

The head of the plant was Charles LeBrun. LeBrun was later appointed First Painter to the King. He was an indefatigable worker and supervised everything from tapestry to furniture—in detail. A man of great prestige who reported directly to the king, he was extremely important in developing French furniture into its eighteenth-century eminence.

Two years after this move from Vaux to Gobelins, Louis XIV started work on Versailles Palace. In 1682, over twenty years later, he moved his entire court to Versailles. Until this time there was no single central location of the court of France. The emphasis of Louis XIV was on one magnificent group of buildings to house him and his court, and this was to be a reflection and a symbol of his greatness. The stage was thus set for the magnificent furniture that was to follow. It was only natural that the nobles should follow their leader and try both to emulate him and to outdo each other in magnificence of home and interior decoration. But the nobles were not the only patrons of the furniture industry in the early eighteenth century. The wealthy commercial classes were, too. Without this additional demand the industry could not have grown to the size and eminence it ultimately attained.

Characteristics of the Furniture of Louis XIV

In the early part of the reign of Louis XIV, the furniture was not much different from the furniture of the same period in other parts of Europe—or in England. Only late in his reign did the characteristic elements of the furniture of the Louis' develop, and even then the style was not fully developed.

These were the primary characteristics of the Louis XIV furniture for most of the reign of that monarch:

1. Rectangular structure and straight lines.
2. Large size and heavy. The pieces could not be moved about easily. They generally stayed where they were placed, particularly in the palaces and châteaux. The pieces were solidly constructed so they had considerable durability.

3. Predominantly dark wood, especially in the early years of Louis XIV. Oak and walnut were used and some fruitwood such as lime and pear. Later, lighter woods were introduced.

4. The use of underbracing in almost all pieces. The furniture in general was far more durable than that of Louis XV or Louis XVI.

5. Tapestries and velours with large and elaborate designs.

6. Carving as the chief means of ornamentation. It was often very elaborate.

These are the elements typical of Louis XIV furniture, the characteristics which one thinks of first as epitomizing the style. But under Louis XIV the basic elements of the furniture of Louis XV had their beginnings. We thus in effect have two Louis XIV styles: the old, heavy, rectangular style so like the contemporary styles of other European countries, and the new style which foreshadowed the great eighteenth-century furniture of France. These are the later Louis XIV characteristics which are so basic a part of the later styles:

1. The legs of earlier pieces had been characteristically straight. This was the style of legs used on most seventeenth-century furniture throughout Europe. It was also the characteristic design of the Renaissance. Gradually a curve was introduced which became more emphasized as time went on.

Louis XIV carved and gilded console table.   *Courtesy of Dalva Brothers, New York.*

This developed into the characteristic leg of Louis XV furniture: the cabriole or double-curved leg.

2. Under Louis XIV the chair stretchers and other stretchers were in some cases eliminated. While the structure was probably weakened by this elimination, the beauty was increased. This elimination is characteristic of the later Louis XV style.

3. The curve began to be used elsewhere, as in the top member of chair backs, and the curve became completely characteristic of Louis XV furniture.

4. Color in furniture was achieved through gilding and parcel gilding (the gilding of parts or of portions of the ornamentation). The use of inlaid woods, painting and lacquering came in to add color toward the end of the Louis XIV Period. Colors in general became lighter toward the end of the period, a characteristic of both Louis XV and Louis XVI furniture.

5. Rococo ornamentation was developed in this period, although it is one of the chief identifying elements of the later style. This is the shell motif plus the rock, and in its most elaborately developed form water appears to be flowing over the rock and shell.

The Furniture Makers of Louis XIV

Chief among furnituremakers of the era of Louis XIV is André-Charles Boulle (1642–1732). His is the most prominent name in French furniture history. At the age of thirty Boulle was selected as the most capable furnituremaker in the country by Colbert, Louis XIV's chief minister. He was given quarters in the Louvre. By this time (1672) the guild system had been developed in Paris, but because of Boulle's prominence, he was not required to keep solely to his own craft and stay out of all other crafts. (This specialization was a strict guild regulation, but one which did not apply to "makers to the king.") Boulle thus worked in both wood and bronze. His staff included twenty cabinetmakers as well as bronziers. He made chandeliers, girandoles, cabinets, commodes, desks, cupboards and clock cases for the royal lodgings. He even made chairs, and the separation of cabinetmakers and chairmakers under the guild system was a most definite one. He constructed furniture not only for the French royal court but for other royal courts as well. By the end of the century the well-to-do banking and business classes could afford the best, and they, too, bought his products.

The characteristic Boulle work by which the world knows him was not invented by him, but he developed it to a high degree of perfection—inlays of brass, horn and tortoiseshell. Temperature and humidity changes are very destructive to this delicate inlay work, and a Boulle table which we bought cost three times as much to repair as to purchase.

In addition to Boulle's workmen, who obviously worked in his style, his four sons worked in the same style. But far more people worked in the popular Boulle style than ever bore the name of Boulle, and "Boulle" furniture continued to be made even in the nineteenth century. This style of furniture is therefore far from a rarity. Since at the time of Boulle, Sr., no maker signed furniture (although in the reign of Louis XV signatures or stamps were usually required), it is difficult to determine what of the early Boulle-type furniture remaining in the world today is actually the work of André-Charles Boulle himself.

The most outstanding bronze work of the era of Louis XIV was that of Jean-Jacques Caffiéri, founder of the eminent line of metalworkers bearing that name. In fact, Caffiéri became the leading name in the profession of bronziers under Louis XV.

Prices of Louis XIV Furniture

Should a piece of furniture known beyond doubt to have been made by André-Charles Boulle appear on the market, one can only guess the sum it might bring. It is possible that the price might break all previous records. Aside from such an unlikely appearance, Louis XIV furniture does not command high prices as French antique furniture goes, nor has it commanded high prices for a number of decades.

At the Hamilton Palace sale in 1882, a grand *armoire* of ebony inlaid with brass made by Boulle from a design by LeBrun brought 11,500 guineas—almost $60,000 in 1882 dollars! A Boulle pedestal cabinet inlaid with brass and white metal with shell ormolu brought 2,200 guineas ($10,000), and a writing table and *cartonniere* was bought for £3,202 ($15,500).

Grand *armoire* of ebony by Boulle from a design by LeBrun. The Hamilton Palace sale, 1882, $60,000.

Louis XIV pedestal cabinet by Boulle. Christie's Hamilton Palace sale, 1882, $10,000.

In 1901, which is the earliest date we use for the start of most antique price indexes, a suite covered in old needlework consisting of couch, two armchairs and twelve side chairs brought £714 (about $3,500). It is possible that the frames were English or Flemish and not French. On November 16, 1901, a Boulle writing table was sold in Dublin for £140 ($680). We can use this year 1901 as a base equal to 100 percent.

By 1905 prices seem to have collapsed. In May Christie's sold a Boulle marquetry table inlaid with tortoiseshell and brass similar to one at Windsor Castle for £110/5 (about $535). The price index now stood at about 30 percent of the 1901 level. Five years later the price index still stood at about the same level. Bruton, Knowles and Company of Gloucester sold a Boulle oblong kneehole table inlaid with brass and tortoiseshell for £92/8 (about $450).

If these prices were low in comparison to past prices of Louis XIV furniture, they still had not bottomed out. In 1914, the year England entered World War I, prices were halved and were down to the 15 percent level. At the turn of the year, from 1913 into 1914, a Boulle writing table with brass and tortoiseshell brought £46/4 ($225).

This was only a resting place for prices on the way down. Prices in 1920, just after the war finished, were at the 10 percent level. Sotheby's on April 30 sold a walnut high-back armchair with scrolled arms and carved legs for £21 (about $75).

But the furniture boom of the 1920's caught up Louis XIV furniture as it caught up most of the heavy older styles of antiques; in 1926, the big boom year, two needlepoint *fauteuils* brought the relatively enormous sum of $3,100. A matching pair brought the same price, and a third matching pair brought the same—$9,300 for six matching *fauteuils*. Prices for Louis XIV furniture had increased ten times in six years!

From 1926 to 1929 there was no increase in the price of this furniture. It had realized its increase by 1926 and the index stood at 100 percent.

From the peak prosperity year of 1929 prices fell, and for Louis XIV furniture they have never recovered. In 1965 prices were at the 33 percent level, down two-thirds from 1929 (and from 1901). In 1965 Christie's sold a Boulle kneehole writing desk with a glass top, curved drawers and stretchers for $1,000. On May 15, 1965, the Parke-Bernet Galleries sold a *lit de repos*, an elaborately carved and gilded piece (but with repairs and a restored seat rail) for $500.

In the fall of 1966 several very fine pieces of Boulle furniture were offered by Paris dealers. Each dealer claimed the piece was made by André-Charles Boulle himself, but this was an optimistic attribution. Each piece was offered in the $25,000 range. One of these items was a *bureau plat* priced at 120,000 francs ($24,000). A pair of Boulle desks was priced at $25,000, and another *bureau plat* at $8,000. In London prices of Louis XIV furniture seemed lower. A leading dealer offered a Boulle commode for $7,000 and a small Boulle kneehole desk for $4,200. The art and antique magazines in the fall of 1966 seemed to feature an unusual number of Louis XIV items, mostly of the finer variety that usually do not appear on the market. This featuring of such furniture may be part of the "forward and backward movement" described earlier. When a type of furniture rises in price to a very high figure and becomes scarcer, buyers turn both to later periods and earlier periods.

A few very good Louis XIV pieces were offered for sale in the year 1966 by the London and New York auctions. In the enormous Helena Rubinstein sale of April 22 and 23, 1966, four Louis XIV items were sold. The first was a bracket clock sold with the bracket on which it sits. The clock, which had an ormolu dial, was 26 inches high and the bracket 12 inches. It brought $750. The next Louis XIV piece to be sold was a pair of Boulle marriage caskets. These storage pieces were 23 inches long and sat on stands. Only one of the stands was original, however.

One of a pair Louis XIV Boulle marriage caskets (one with contemporary stand). Parke-Bernet, April 23, 1966, $14,500.

Despite this fact the pair brought $14,500, a high price for Louis XIV antiques without much useful purpose. The final Louis XIV antique was a Boulle cabinet four feet nine inches high and four feet wide with a marble top. It brought $6,000.

When Louis XIV antiques are well proportioned, well designed and ornamental they tend to bring good sums. But when they have little to recommend them other than the fact that they date from the Louis XIV era, they tend to be ignored by the market.

Louis XIV furniture is not a significant factor in the market. It is not offered in sufficient quantities to be significant, and what is offered does not bring high enough prices to be featured and illustrated in the auction catalogues. It is more or less in

Louis XIV Boulle cabinet.   Parke-Bernet, April 23, 1966, $6,000.

the same category with Renaissance Italian furniture, earlier French furniture and Jacobean furniture, all of which are not in vogue at the present time. Nonetheless, these styles are participating to some extent in the heavy increase in demand for antiques and may be gradually coming out from under the cloud of obscurity which has covered them for a number of decades.

Louis XIV Prices

Date	1901 Equals 100%	1926 Equals 100%
1901	100%	
1905	30	
1910	30	
1914	15	
1916	10	
1926	100	100%
1929	100	100
1965	33	33

Louis XIV carved oak commode. Parke-Bernet, April 29, 1966, $2,400.   (*Photo: Taylor & Dull*)

LOUIS XV SALON.   The Beauvais-covered *fauteuils* are from a set of six with a
sofa, signed by Bauve. The cream colored and gilt carved paneling is from the
house of LaFayette in Paris.   *Courtesy of French & Company, New York.*

CHAPTER SIX

From Régence Through Louis XV
1715–1774

FRENCH FURNITURE IS CURRENTLY THE preferred furniture in the entire international antique market, and the French furniture that holds this high position in the market is that which was produced in the eighteenth century. It is known as the furniture of the Louis', and it was produced at or about the time of the reign of Louis XV and Louis XVI.

The type of furniture known as Louis XV was actually originated prior to the time of Louis XV—during the reign of Louis XIV. Louis XVI furniture was produced well past the death of Louis XVI and up to the end of the eighteenth century.

It is all too easy to note the prices of the furniture of the Louis', see who buys it, note the grand homes filled with it and then proceed to explain how and why it is the best furniture of any country and era.

To a considerable extent this is false reasoning. In the late 1930's such furniture was far down on the preference lists of antique buyers, and prices reflected this indifference. If we go back to the Albert Figdor sale in Vienna in June 1930, we can take note of one chair in the sale—a three-cornered stool with some carving around the seat and on the legs, and a rather simple back containing some carving. It was made in 1490. It brought $23,500. If excellence were determined by prices paid, it would be a little difficult to explain the intrinsic merits of this piece of furniture which would warrant such a price. It was a vastly different, far older and much more primitive piece than an eighteenth-century French chair.

The appreciation of beauty in anything—paintings, furniture and even women —to a great degree is a matter of fashion.

Furniture of the "Age of Elegance"

While beauty may be a thing of fashion and a product of the times, there *is* possibly such a thing as absolute beauty, a quality that anyone can recognize without reference to the standards of the age and without a detailed education as to "what constitutes beauty." Eighteenth-century French furniture is most certainly furniture of beauty if any furniture possesses beauty. The lines of the furniture are perfection. The use of decoration—including lacquer, inlay, carving and metal mounts—is in keeping with each piece of furniture, yet adds to its pleasing appearance; the woods are varied and suited in color to the furniture, and finally the fabrics and tapestry originally used for upholstering (and often still intact) are of the finest pattern, quality and workmanship.

The furniture is ornate. Of that there can be no doubt. And it is particularly suited to the opulence and love of grandeur of the late 1960's, or, for that matter, the entire postwar period.

Possibly the low point of French eighteenth-century furniture occurred in the secondary depression of 1938 just prior to the advent of World War II, a second period of austerity following the Great Depression, when elegance was not at a premium. As prosperity progressed, ornate furniture of the Louis' came to be preferred.

FRENCH RÉGENCE GROUP.   The *fauteuil* is upholstered with silk brocade of the period and the high-back, carved and gilded armchair is covered with fine needlework. Over the console table is Jean-Marc Nattier's portrait of Mme. de Ceran. *Courtesy of French & Company, New York.*

The Régence *and Its Furniture*

Louis XIV, the Sun King, died in 1715. The period from his death to the coming of age of Louis XV is known as the *Régence* (or Regency). During this period the Duc d'Orleans ruled France in the name of Louis XV.

In this period Europe achieved a degree of prosperity never before realized. And it is a by-product of great prosperity that people emphasize luxury and ease, with the cost of these objectives in a secondary position.

The *Régence* was a transition period, a bridge between the heavy, dark, rectangular furniture of Louis XIV and the extravagant but beautiful furniture of Louis XV. The new developments in furniture style from the Louis XIV period are, generally:

1. The use of the cabriole leg
2. Less emphasis on the rectangle and more on the curve (a) for chair back top rails, (b) for all sides of the chair back, and (c) for the overall shape of commodes
3. Smaller-sized pieces with less bulk
4. More use of surface decoration including ornamental metal

THE RÉGENCE PERIOD.   Exemplified by a bronze doré and marquetry commode said to have been made for the Dauphin.   *Courtesy of Dalva Brothers, New York.*

It was during this period that the tremendous influence of J. A. Meissonier was developing. Two years after the *Régence* ended and Louis XV began to rule in his own name, Meissonier was appointed Designer to the King. He has become known as the originator of the Rococo style. While the term "Rococo" has come to mean in the ordinary sense "highly ornamented," in actuality it is a motif which combines the seashell with rocks as an element of architectural and furniture design. (The shell motif was extensively used on eighteenth-century English and American furniture.) So important and influential was Meissonier not only in France but in all Europe, that an English historian stated that every single one of Thomas Chippendale's designs for furniture came directly from Meissonier, and that Chippendale had not one original idea of his own!

The greatest furnituremaker in the *Régence* Period (1715–1723) was Charles Cressent, and his name affixed to *Régence* pieces generally means that they are the finest of the period.

The Guild: Assurance of Excellence

The guild system which developed at this time was probably more responsible for the excellence of the furniture of the Louis' than any other single factor. The chief guild was the *Corporation des Menuisiers-Ebénistes*. A *menuisier* worked in solid

Louis XV parquetry double-desk by B.V.R.B., valued at $250,000.   *Courtesy of the J. Paul Getty Museum, Malibu, California.*

wood, including decorative elements. An *ébéniste* was a cabinetmaker particularly skilled in veneer. Usually a *menuisier* is considered a chairmaker and an *ébéniste* a cabinetmaker.

The *Corporation* was made up of a group of masters (*maîtres*) who were the senior members of the organization. In 1723, the year the *Régence* ended and Louis XV assumed the reins of government, there were 985 members (maîtres). In 1790, the year the guilds were dissolved, there were still only 985 members. The guild was a very closed corporation, partly because it was in the interest of the members to keep it closed (like the holders of taxicab medallions in New York City); but the restrictions and regulations were government-imposed and were intended to keep standards at top levels.

An apprentice was taken on by a *maître* at age twelve or fourteen, and he served for six years without pay. Then, if his work was satisfactory, he became a *compagnon*, or assistant, with pay. If the apprentice who graduated to the rank of *compagnon* came from Paris, he served three years as *compagnon*; but if he came from outside Paris or from abroad he had to serve six.

After his term as *compagnon* was complete, he could become a *maître* in his own right on submitting a piece of furniture constructed by him to the control committee of the guild. This piece of furniture was known as his *chef d'oeuvre*, and the control committee was known as the *juré*. If the piece he submitted passed the examination of the *juré*, the *compagnon* then presented silver tokens to the *juré* of *maîtres* who passed on his piece, and he presented silver tokens to the *syndic* (president) of the guild. This control committee was composed of *maîtres* having at least ten years of experience.

Fees were charged by the guild. The son of a *juré* had to pay 121 livres for his training, a livre being the value of a pound of silver. The son of a *maître* who had not been a *juré* paid 180 livres for his training. A close relative of the *maître* paid the same as did the second husband of the *maître's* widow. Foreigners paid a

Commode by Charles Cressent. The Hamilton Palace sale, 1882, £6,247/10. Now at Wadeston Manor, England.

much higher fee for the training—536 livres. If they wanted to shorten the training period they might do so by paying an additional 100 livres.

Besides the woodworking guild (*Corporation des Menuisiers-Ebénistes*) there were the following:

> *Fondeurs-Doreurs*—makers of gilt and bronze mounts
>
> *Marbriers*—cutters of marble tops
>
> *Mecaniciens*—makers of the various mechanical devices found in many of the pieces of furniture of this era, some of which are highly interesting and will be described later on
>
> *Sculpteurs*—carvers of the chair frames
>
> *Doreurs*—those who applied gilt
>
> *Tapissiers*—upholsterers

There were few shortcuts in the making of the furniture of this period. The *ébénistes* and *menuisiers* who made the basic wood furniture rarely did the carving, whether or not they had the ability to do so. They were not permitted to do such work. The great Cressent was hauled into court and fined three times for making mounts for the furniture he had made.

The guild system's method of assuring excellent workmanship extended much further than seeing that only those with the proven ability to make fine furniture were permitted to do so. The *jurés* inspected the shop of every *maître* four times a year. They examined every piece of furniture in the shop that was completed and stamped it JME or ME with their stamp, the JME probably meaning *Jurande des Menuisiers-Ebénistes*.

If the piece did not pass the inspection it was confiscated and sold for the benefit of the *Corporation*, or destroyed. In either case a fine was imposed on the *maître* for producing a poor piece of furniture.

When French furniture is sold today one of the most valuable attributes is the stamp of the maker. The auction houses proudly state "stamped Dubois twice on the seat rail." The implication is that if the stamp is put on the piece it is an authentic work by the particular furnituremaker. This is in effect his signature, and sometimes the description reads "signed by Tilliard" rather than "stamped Tilliard."

The purpose of the stamp was somewhat different, however. The guild *required* that the stamp be placed on the furniture. The master did *not* place the stamp on the furniture because he considered his work so fine that he wanted to sign it to advertise himself to the world of furniture users.

The stamp was a control device of the guild. There were several groups of furnituremakers who did not come under guild regulations and who did not belong to the guilds. A very large group worked in religious institutions. These did not stamp their pieces any more than a carpenter of today feels it is necessary to sign his name to built-in bookcases that he makes. The stamp requirement was intended to place the piece of furniture in a higher category than that produced by makers outside the guild system. To a great extent the regulation was placed in effect as a weapon against the excellent German furnituremakers who were becoming important in the mid-eighteenth century. It was promulgated by guild statutes passed from 1744 to 1751.

There were many exceptions to the stamp rule, and while it is nice to have a stamped piece of furniture, the stamp is not the assurance that the piece is necessarily in the highest and most exclusive category. For instance, fragile pieces could be marked in ink or paint, and these marks may now be gone.

Also, the most important makers—those manufacturing for the king himself—did not have to meet the guild regulation which required stamping. They were "above the stamp." In consequence Gilles Joubert, who was the president of the guild from 1740 to 1750, never had to stamp his pieces because they were made for the king. Thus few of his pieces bear his stamp.

Sons were permitted to use the stamps of their deceased fathers. Thus J. B. Tilliard, Jr., used the stamp of J. B. Tilliard, Sr. The stamp thus covers pieces of furniture made by two different men. In the same way René Dubois used the stamp of his father, Jacques Dubois. Francis J. B. Watson, the eminent Director of the Wallace Collection in London, states that a cabinet in that collection bears the stamps of Dubois, Levasseur and Montigny. Repairers of furniture were expected to stamp their jobs; and in the case of this cabinet it is difficult to tell who did what.

One of the finest pieces of furniture in the world is the famous *Bureau du Roi* now located in Versailles Palace. This is a desk made for Louis XV—it took at least nine years to complete. For the two years prior to his death, Oeben worked on it. But Oeben's stamp is not on the piece. After Oeben's death in 1763 the work on the desk was taken up by Riesener. His stamp is on the desk. Wynant Stylen also worked on the wood part of the desk, but his stamp does not appear. Duplessis and Hervieux made the bronzes, but their work is not recognized by any stamp. There is a double-faced clock built into the desk, and the complicated mechanism to operate both dials was made by Lepine. His name appears nowhere.

When Oeben died in 1763 his wife continued to operate the shop, and his stamp appears on many pieces turned out by the shop between the years 1763 and 1768. Thus these pieces not done by him bear his stamp, and the great work of his life, which occupied most of his time for two years—the *Bureau du Roi*—does not bear his stamp.

A stamp is a very easy thing to make. It is not a signature. It is made of lead and can change its conformation with use. Thus the forgery of stamps does not require a high degree of artistry. We sometimes have the paradoxical use of forged stamps applied to genuine eighteenth-century furniture. The application of the stamp apparently was intended to "help things along." Its use is similar to the forged Rembrandt signature which was sometimes applied to *genuine works* by Rembrandt.

Francis J. B. Watson further describes a set of thirty chairs, a sofa and a screen made in 1786 for the King's *salon de jeu* at Fontainebleau. Nine of the chairs are still in existence—six in the Wallace Collection and three in the Metropolitan Museum of Art.

The frames were made by the *menuisier* J. B. Boulard.

The carving was done by Vallois and Charney.

The gilding was put on by Chatard, Guintrange and Julliac.

The upholstery was the product of Capin.

The gilt-headed nails were made by Wafflars.

The only name which appears on the chairs, and this name appears not as a stamp but as a label, is Chatard, one of the three gilders. Boulard, who produced the frames, did not have to use a stamp since he was working for the king.

By 1776 the struggle toward democracy was being felt in France as it was in England, and the king's minister, Turgot, issued decrees abolishing the ranks of *juré* and *maître*. The decrees were suppressed by the king on the day they were to go into effect. But in 1790, the year after the Bastille was stormed, the Revolution dissolved the guilds. From then on there were no formal standards that a furnituremaker had to meet to be able to practice. His pieces did not have to be approved; and when the generation trained to these standards died out, the skills were lost and the quality of furniture went downhill.

Price History of Régence Furniture

From both a stylistic and a market point of view, *Régence* furniture occupies a position between Louis XIV and Louis XV, but it leans very much more toward Louis XV than Louis XIV. In the present market Louis XIV furniture is not preferred. In style certain *Régence* pieces closely resemble Louis XIV while others resemble Louis XV. The latter tend to be worth more than the former. Even if the style were very close to Louis XV and uniformly elegant, *Régence* furniture would not be a major factor in the antique market. There is not enough of it on the market to make it so, and it was not made over a sufficiently long period.

On July 19, 1905, Christie's sold a small commode of kingwood with ormolu mounts and a marble top for the low price of £89/18 ($195). Earlier in the year a slant-top bureau with ormolu mounts and parquetry was sold by the same gallery for £220/10 (a little over $1,000).

If we take the year 1905 as the base period equal to 100 percent, we find that by 1914, the year in which World War I broke out, prices had risen appreciably. On April 23 Christie's sold a shaped-front commode with two drawers, in tulipwood and kingwood, for £630 ($3,068). But as a result of the war the prices of antique furniture dropped in general in 1915, and on April 12 of that year Christie's sold a three-drawer tulipwood-and-kingwood commode to the dealer M. Harris for the low price of £45/3 ($220). Prices were again at the level of 1905 —100 percent.

Ten years later, in 1925, prices had not risen any appreciable degree, and it will be remembered that by 1925 the furniture boom was on, especially the American phase of the boom. On February 14 the Anderson Galleries sold a pair of needlepoint armchairs for $300. On the same day the American Art Association sold a *bombé* commode with *cuivre doré*, of inlaid kingwood, for $190. Another one (of not quite certain period) sold for $240. Also on the same day the same gallery sold two Aubusson-covered, carved and gilded state chairs of the early eighteenth century for $600, and on March 28 the same gallery sold two Aubusson-covered carved walnut armchairs for the very moderate price of $70.

In part *Régence* furniture partook of the 1926 boom in antiques. A Beauvais tapestry-covered carved and gilded *canapé*, 46 inches long, was sold for $650 at the American Art Association Galleries. It had come from Duveen.

By the boom year of 1929 prices were up to the 400 percent level, but it must be pointed out that they started at the 100 percent level *which represented very few dollars*, and a rise to 400 percent still did not put *Régence* furniture in the luxury class. On April 26 the Anderson Galleries sold a needlepoint *fauteuil* with the rear leg repaired for $425, and on May 4 a walnut *fauteuil* with parts of it restored for $725.

By the Depression bottom of 1932 prices had been halved, and on December 3 the American Art Association sold a pair of needlepoint shield-back side chairs, *c.*1725, for $340.

On November 3 and 4, 1933, at the Mrs. Morris Murray sale in New York, an elaborate palissandre commode of *bombé* shape, with *bronze doré* and a marble top, was sold for $150.

By 1939 prices were near the vanishing point. On May 5 at the Dalva sale of excellent period French furniture, a pair of carved walnut side chairs in petit point brought $160. At the same sale two matching carved walnut *fauteuils* brought $60 each. The next day a pair of carved walnut and blue silk *fauteuils* brought $130. Prices in 1939 were at the level of 50 percent with 1905 as the base.

Two years later the Della V. Chrysler sale was held at the Parke-Bernet Galleries. A pair of carved walnut and needlepoint side chairs brought $460, a vastly higher price than the prevailing levels of 1939.

By 1942 prices were again at the 400 percent level. Although a palissandre marquetry commode brought $325, three pairs of *fauteuils* and a wing chair were sold at the Parke-Bernet Galleries on October 17 for $4,200, no small price in view of past prices of *Régence* furniture. On January 10 the same gallery sold a pair of carved fruitwood and green damask *fauteuils* for $1,600 and a matching pair for the same price.

Régence kingwood commode, stamped P. A. Foullet.   Christie's, 1955, $2,115.

By the war's end, however, the Parke-Bernet Galleries sold a carved beechwood and needlepoint *fauteuil* for $170. Prices were halved as compared with 1942. But by 1950 they were back up again. Early in the year the Parke-Bernet Galleries sold an inlaid kingwood and acajou commode of *bombé* design with *bronze doré* for $800 and another later in the year, this one of serpentine design, for $1,000. A pair of walnut *fauteuils* was sold for $575 and $500, while Christie's on June 22 sold a splendid serpentine commode with ormolu mounts, *bronze doré* and Chinese decorations for £1732/10 ($4,850).

By 1955 prices had increased 50 percent and were now up to 600 percent. On February 11 the Parke-Bernet Galleries sold a pair of *grands fauteuils* for $700 and a matching pair for the same price, plus a matching *canapé* for $425. On March 5 they sold a pair of carved side chairs with some restorations for $1,400 and a matching pair for the same price. Christie's on March 10 sold a rosewood *bombé* commode with elaborate bronzes for £252 ($706).

On March 20, 1958, a fine commode was sold in Nice, France, for $1,680 and on May 14, 1960, the Parke-Bernet Galleries sold an inlaid kingwood *bombé* commode for $1,100. Prices in 1960 were at the 800 percent level.

While Louis XV *bureau plats* in the 1960's were some of the most sought after and highest priced of all antiques, a *Régence bureau plat* was sold in May 1961 at the Palais Galliera in Paris for 180,000 new francs ($3,600), a good price but not of the level of Louis XV. Three years later Sotheby's sold a gilt side table with

Pair of *Régence fauteuils* à la Reine.   Sotheby's, 1966, $7,280.   Purchased by F. Partridge.

fluted legs and ram's masks for £2,500 ($7,000), a very high price for a *Régence* piece of furniture.

In early 1964 the Parke-Bernet Galleries sold a beautiful serpentine-carved beechwood *canapé*, seven feet two inches long, for $900, a good price even for *canapés* of the era of the Louis'. A little later in the year they sold two serpentine-front commodes for $2,500 and $900. Prices were now at 1,000 percent level.

In early 1965 the Parke-Bernet Galleries sold two commodes of the *Régence* Period for $1,700 and $1,500. In the same year a *bureau plat* in the manner of Migeon brought the equivalent of $4,704. Late in 1965 prices were certainly not weakening, and commodes were selling for between $2,000 and $3,000. While prices of *Régence* furniture were rising dollar-wise and percentage-wise, they were generally not of the level of Louis XV and Louis XVI, but were very much above the level of Louis XIV.

At the notable Sotheby's sale of July 1, 1966, three good *Régence* pieces were sold. The first was a kingwood parquetry commode which brought $11,200. A pair of giltwood *fauteuils à la reine* with the backs carved brought $7,280. These items were presumably crown furniture and were intended to stand in the middle of the room instead of against the walls. An ordinary but good pair of beechwood *fauteuils* brought $1,680. In the summer of 1966 a London dealer offered a commode without its original brass for £1,150 ($3,220). In Dublin a dealer offered a commode of the same quality for the equivalent of $2,800.

Régence kingwood parquetry commode.   Sotheby's, 1966, $11,200.

In Paris prices of French *Régence* furniture were higher. A very good commode was priced at $9,000, an armchair at $1,100 and six armchairs at $46,000 —almost $7,700 a chair.

Régence *Prices*

Date	1905 Equals 100%	1950 Equals 100%	1925 Equals 100%
1905	100%		
1914	500		
1915	100		
1925	200		100%
1926	200		100
1929	400		200
1932	200		100
1939	50		25
1942	400		200
1945	200		100
1950	400	100%	200
1955	600	150	300
1960	800	200	400
1965	1000	250	500

One of a pair of *Régence* beechwood *fauteuils.*   Sotheby's, 1966, $1,680.

Characteristics of the Louis XV Style

1. Emphasis on the curve, not on the straight line and the rectangle. The style before (Louis XIV) and the succeeding style (Louis XVI) were both characterized by straight lines and rectangles, although the rectangular style was much more characteristic of Louis XIV and earlier styles than of the later Louis XVI style. From across the room a piece of Louis XV furniture can be identified, mainly by its curving legs and curved back members.

2. The use of the cabriole leg (the double-curved leg). While the double-curved leg was certainly characteristic of the furniture of other countries, and was certainly used in the earlier Queen Anne Period in England, it is a primary characteristic of the Louis XV style. It was actually developed under Louis XIV, was used increasingly on the furniture of the *Régence* (1715–1723) and was *the* leg style of Louis XV.

3. Smaller, lighter in weight and more graceful furniture than that of the preceding Louis XIV style, while the succeeding style was even lighter. It thus in a way represents a step in the adaptation of furniture to the smaller living structures and smaller rooms and to the more intimate, informal manner of living.

4. Disappearance of stretchers and underbracing on the chairs so that the furniture had less of a "structural" look and more of a finished look.

5. Mahogany and walnut as the chief woods used, although the variety of wood used was almost without number, including tulipwood, amaranth and violetwood.

6. Overall light color of the furniture (with the exception of provincial furniture) by using inlays and inlay decoration, gilding, polychroming, painting and light, ornamental fabrics.

7. A high degree of ornamentation, depending mainly on Rococo and naturalistic motifs. Ornamentation was achieved through carving, inlays of wood and metal, metal mounts and painting.

8. Innovation—a characteristic of prime importance at this time and a distinct characteristic of the Louis XV Period. The further back in time we go, the simpler the furniture and the more limited the variety of pieces. In this period a whole new group of pieces was invented, or, if not actually invented, then made for the first time in quantity. We are used to seeing all of these pieces on the market today, and we do not think of them as having been "first made" in any particular era.

One of the finest collections of French furniture is the Costantino Collection, and Ruth T. Costantino has performed the invaluable service of illustrating a good many of her pieces in a detailed publication. The collection illustrates most, if not all, of the innovations in this period, as well as those which took place under Louis XVI.

Innovations were numerous. At the end of the reign of Louis XIV the commode was developed. The modern equivalent is the bureau which is found in almost every bedroom today. But it was not until the reign of Louis XV that this highly important and necessary item was made in great quantity.

Sofas, called *canapés*, now appeared. In addition, what is now called the daybed made its appearance. It was called the *lit de repos*.

One of the most sought after of all French antiques also made its appearance just at the start of the reign of Louis XV—the *bergère*. This is a large armchair, deep and upholstered heavily on seat and back, with closed arms. The part between the arm rail and the seat is completely filled in with upholstery.

A very useful piece of furniture which somehow did not become popular made its appearance in the reign of Louis XV. It was in essence a lunch table and was called a *servante* or *rafraîchissoir*.

While the *bureau plat* or table desk was developed earlier, its manufacture was greatly expanded at this time. It is one of the best possible executive desks for use today, and there is hardly a better designed one manufactured now.

The drop-leaf desk or *bureau à dos d'ane* now made its appearance. It is essentially a slant-top desk, but without drawers beneath the slant top. It thus does not have the usefulness of the English and American slant tops, but is of some use as a writing desk and is very ornamental. The *"dos d'ane,"* incidentally, means jackass's back, which it is supposed to resemble.

The *semainier* was first introduced in this era, and as far as usefulness is concerned this article ranks with the commode. It is a tall, narrow chest of drawers. (*"Semainier"* refers to the number of drawers—seven: one for each day of the week.) Ladies' *tables à coiffer* also first appeared in this era. This table was a most necessary part of the boudoir, for it was a dressing table with drawers for cosmetics and other items and it opened to reveal a mirror.

A great variety of tables for games were made at this time. A common kind was the triangular folding card table. A second type of table for games was the tric-trac (backgammon) table.

The entire objective of furniture design and construction was based on (1) a love of elegance and a desire on the part of each person to outdo others, (2) a cultivated social life which included parties and much entertaining so the furniture could be on display, (3) leisure and freedom from the threat of war which allowed relaxation and pleasures, (4) informality and meeting in small groups and (5) a far greater emphasis on women as a definite part of society and a part of the social activities of men. It must be reemphasized that the furniture to a great degree catered to women and was designed with women's comfort in mind.

Elements of Value in Louis XV Furniture

It is next to impossible for anyone but an expert to judge a horse show or a dog show. The physical characteristics of a prize winner are so numerous and so technical that it takes years to learn them all and then be able to grade each entrant. The characteristics of Louis XV furniture that spell the difference between a good and a bad piece are equally numerous and just as hard to judge correctly. In a day of looking at Louis XV furniture under the tutelage of an expert, the layman can get a small idea of what in general is good and bad. He will be considerably more proficient after a year of constant study, yet not an expert. But after some patient study he can judge whether he is looking at a $2,000 piece or a $10,000 piece.

These are some of the value-creating characteristics of Louis XV furniture:

1. Rarity. In the first place Louis XV furniture is much rarer than Louis XVI, and this fact alone tends to give it a value in the marketplace that Louis XVI furniture does not have. If the demand for the two types were equal, the price of the rarer type (Louis XV) would be higher because there are fewer pieces to fill the same demand.

2. Size. To a great degree small pieces are preferred because they can fit anywhere. A buyer can always find a corner for a little table 14 inches wide. But he cannot always find a place for the clock attributed to David Roentgen that was sold at the Parke-Bernet Galleries in early 1965. It was ten feet eight inches tall! It brought a price far lower than its intrinsic merit would suggest.

It has been suggested by one collector of the furniture of the Louis' that the little tables are high in price because they are rare; and they are rare because the legs were so spindly that they were broken over the centuries and the tables discarded, leaving a smaller and smaller number in existence. The fact of the matter is that the more superbly executed little pieces do bring the highest prices. The little oval or circular tables with galleried tops are at a tremendous premium.

One of a set of twelve Gobelins-tapestry-covered Louis XV *fauteuils*. The Hamilton Palace sale, 1882, £892/10. Purchased by P. and D. Colnaghi.

Other things being equal, a small *bergère* will bring a higher price than a large *bergère*. My wife and I collect Louis XV Italian furniture, principally that made in Venice in the eighteenth century. This furniture is very rare, and we buy all we can that is of good quality. But we will not buy the very large chairs that were used in the Venetian Palaces and we will not buy large, although extremely beautiful, chairs like the ones in the Metropolitan Museum of Art. They are too large and too out of place in a modern house—at least in America—and certainly in a modern apartment.

3. Fashion and preference. At the very top of the list of preference come *bergères* rather than *fauteuils* (armchairs with closed arms rather than open arms). *Bergères* in some cases bring 50 percent more than *fauteuils*. If *bergères* are in pairs the price is always very high. *Fauteuils*, however, are next in chair preference.

Bombé, or bulging front, commodes are always wanted and always bring high prices. Writing desks (*bureau plats*) are similarly always in tremendous demand. In the past ten years their price has risen more than that of any other piece of furniture.

Items which are not preferred are:

A. Cylinder desks. These are probably the best buy in Louis XV furniture.

B. Clocks. While a David Roentgen commode recently brought $176,000, the tall Roentgen clock previously mentioned brought only $2,200.

C. Lean-to secretaries. These are the equivalent of the English and American slant-top secretary of the eighteenth century, but whereas English and American slant tops are always in great demand, the French equivalents are not. Yet they are useful, graceful, of small size and a generally beautiful item of furniture.

D. Small bookcases. This is certainly an exception to the rule that the smaller pieces bring the higher prices. A small bookcase does not have the strict use-value that large bookcases have. This conclusion is borne out by the fact that the enormous eighteenth-century English bookcases always bring relatively enormous prices.

4. Carving. It seems strange that quality of carving should be placed ahead of excellence of structural design, but on the international market, particularly the large market in Paris, this conclusion seems warranted. A well-shaped piece with poor carving tends to bring less money than a poorer designed piece with excellent carving.

5. General design. While one has to become used to the design of Louis XV furniture in order to appreciate its beauty, the eye becomes trained to recognize good and bad design. The better proportioned pieces are in greater demand, and the poorer proportioned pieces are less in demand. The New York art market is flooded with late nineteenth-century and early twentieth-century paintings, particularly landscapes. The well-painted ones bring higher prices than the poorly painted ones. What is a

well-painted one and what is a poorly painted one? The buyers in the market must judge. And they do—in the prices they pay! The same for Louis XV furniture.

6. Condition. It is a general rule in antique furniture that the more the piece is original the more it is worth, and the more it is restored the less it is worth.

7. Covering. A few years ago a set of Louis XV furniture was offered by one of the leading art and antique dealers in the world in his New York showroom. The suite of settee and chairs was a large one, but the outstanding feature was the *original* tapestry covering of the eighteenth century. The suite was offered for about $50,000. An examination showed that the wood structure was entirely reproduction. The dealer did not require me to point out this fact to him. It was obvious to him and to everyone else. What he was selling was the original tapestry in excellent condition, and for this covering he felt that $50,000 was a reasonable price. Of course, if the tapestry were removed or if it wore out—and it most certainly will wear out in time—the actual pieces of furniture would be worth no more than reproductions.

8. Value characteristics of chairs. There is a whole complex of characteristics which give value to a Louis XV *chair*.

The first and most important quality of chairs in the world market, and especially in the Paris market, is comfort. That is the one essential element of chair design upon which collectors place the greatest premium. Much antique furniture is not comfortable, especially chairs of the Italian Renaissance. Louis XV chairs are comfortable and were designed with comfort in mind. The able designer made the chairs more comfortable than the lesser designers, and there is little evidence that our increased knowledge of human structure and function has resulted in chairs which are more comfortable than those produced in eighteenth century France.

Strange as it may seem, comfort is one of the tests applied by collectors in order to determine the authenticity of eighteenth-century French chairs. If a chair purportedly of the period is uncomfortable, suspicion is created in the mind of the prospective buyer as to whether it is a later reproduction or an outright fake!

The seats must be low, the arms placed at the right level for comfort, and the cushions must be thick. The seats must be broad and the chairs generally deep. The back must be inclined and should not curve. The legs should be straight and not slope inward or outward. Chairs should be in sets. The price *per chair* is greater for a pair than for a single chair; still greater if there are four chairs, and so on. In the last ten years, with new emphasis on dining rooms, large sets of side chairs are bringing far higher prices.

9. Value characteristics of commodes. The chair is the item of French furniture offered in the greatest numbers on the market, but the item that generally brings the highest price is the commode. This can be used as a bureau in the bedroom or as an ornamental cabinet in the living room.

The most valued commodes are generally the small ones. Next, the finest commodes have two drawers rather than three. The bottom of the top drawer and the top of the bottom drawer should line up so closely when the both are closed that the front of the commode appears to be almost one solid piece. If there is a space between these two drawers so that one sees the wood of the carcass and not just the wood of the two drawers, the piece is less desirable. Also, the gilt mounts should be slender and fit into the overall pattern of the front as well as into the design of the entire commode.

The finest commodes are often lacquered, and the lacquering should be Chinese* rather than European. The lacquer itself determines value to a considerable extent in the following descending order:

A. Pale yellow-white lacquer—most valuable
B. Red lacquer—less valuable
C. Black lacquer—least valuable

The wood inlay should be complex, not simple, and it should be of fine quality. These are the types of inlay in descending order, from the most valuable:

A. Floral marquetry
B. Still life marquetry
C. Landscape marquetry
D. Repetitive cube marquetry

10. The former home of the furniture. On April 30, 1965, a very special commode was offered for sale at Sotheby's in London. It was written up extensively with color illustrations in *Connaissance* for April 1965. It brought £20,000 ($56,000). One reason for this high sale price was that it came from Versailles Palace and bore the Versailles inventory number—"1965." In the same way Mme. Du Barry's bed brought a remarkably high price in England several years ago, particularly when one considers that at that time French furniture was not in demand.
11. Mechanical fittings. The eighteenth century was a time of innovation in furniture and of experimenting with mechanical elements. Many of the pieces could be adjusted in various ways, and many could be converted from one use to another. A table in the Metropolitan Museum of Art has a handle which can be used to raise or lower the top to the desired height. A section of the top also lifts up so that the piece converts into a lady's dressing table. Still other adjustments can be made so that the table is converted into a series of available cubbyholes for placing writing materials as well as items of food. It is thus obvious that the piece can be used as a small dining table (although there were no real dining tables in the Louis XV Period), a library table, a desk, a boudoir table and a breakfast or lunch table for the person who finds it difficult to leave his work for a meal. Mechanical furniture brings premium prices on the present market.
12. Stamp of the maker. This value characteristic of eighteenth-century

*There are several types of lacquer. The Chinese (including the coromandel panels) and the Japanese lacquers are valued equally. There are imitations which are excellent and often indistinguishable. The Western style is usually cheaper, except in cases of exceptional quality, such as *vernis Martin*.

furniture has been left till last, not because it belongs at the bottom of the list, but because it requires special emphasis. In some ways it is the most important of all of the value elements, and on today's antique market it alone increases the price obtainable for a piece of furniture by at least 50 percent. The more important the stamp (the maker) the more valuable the piece. While it is certainly true that a piece of furniture must stand on its own feet, and to a great degree advertise its own value to the prospective buyer, the stamp of a prominent maker helps things along.

It has been previously indicated that the stamp applied to a part of a piece of eighteenth-century French furniture does not necessarily mean that the maker whose name appears on the stamp made the piece and then "signed it" as an artist would sign a painting. The stamp could also be used by the maker's son after the passing of the maker. Or it could be used by his widow or by the new husband of the widow of the deceased maker. Ruth T. Costantino points out that David Roentgen, the maker of the famous "$176,000 commode," employed one hundred cabinetmakers and marquetry specialists, a dozen bronzeworkers, a dozen locksmiths and mechanics, plus clockmakers. François-Honoré Jacob at one time had at least fifteen shops operating.

Prior to 1780 Roentgen was not a *maître* of the *Corporation* and presumably did not stamp his pieces. Anyway, he was a German who manufactured furniture in the French style and sold it to the Russian as well as other courts in Europe. But after becoming a *maître* he *could* have affixed his stamp to all of the furniture turned out by his workmen. Jacob could have done the same thing with the output of his shops.

The stamp of any maker raises the price of a piece of eighteenth-century French furniture over what it would have been had there been no stamp, but a stamp of a leading maker affixed to a piece of furniture of artistic and structural excellence, and a piece characteristic of that maker, often puts the piece in the masterpiece category so that the price is very high. These are some of the great makers of the Louis XV era:

> Bernard van Riesen Burgh (BVRB)—especially Bernard II
> Jacques Dubois
> Roger Vandercruse (RVLC)—Lacroix
> Jean-François Oeben
> Jean-Henri Riesener
> Georges Jacob
> Jean-François Leleu
> Jean-Baptiste Tilliard
> Antoine Robert Gaudreau (made primarily for the Crown. No signed
>   pieces by him are apparently in existence. He was also President of
>   the Control Committee of the Guild in 1744).
> Gilles Joubert

Various attempts have been made to indicate the importance of these masters (and only a small percentage of them have been included here). There is some feeling in France that the most prominent is perhaps Bernard van Riesen Burgh II, and the second most prominent is Dubois. Oeben, however, started the masterpiece, the *Bureau du Roi*, and Riesener continued the cabinetwork.

The furniture of these top workers is the very best example of furniture turned out by top-grade, highly trained masters whose work was rigidly supervised by the guild. The work of these *maîtres* is the cream-of-the-cream. These are the Raphaels, Michelangelos and Leonardos of furnituremaking. And like the artists, the furnituremakers often worked directly for the king. The main goals in life for Louis XIV seemed to be (1) winning wars and (2) building Versailles into the finest palace in Europe. All other objectives seemed secondary. Louis XV and Louis XVI were intent on perfecting Versailles and furnishing it and other royal residences with the finest decorations of all kinds. *Thus primary governmental emphasis was on furniture.* The king placed excellent furniture near the top of his "want list" and he was willing to pay for the best. The result was the elevation of furnituremaking to a highly paid and important function carrying immense social prestige. Significant people went into furnituremaking, were willing to undergo training for a long period of time, meet rigid standards, and then hope for the patronage of the king and all the prerequisites that went with it.

Prices of Louis XV Furniture

A simple starting point to take is the year 1901. Not only was this the beginning of the twentieth century, but price rises started in this general era. It can thus be considered as 100 percent, and price movements since that time can be expressed as percentages which relate back to this base period.

On November 29, 1901, Christie's sold a parquetry commode with a shaped front and four drawers with ormolu, stamped I. Dubois (an excellent *ébéniste*) for £26 ($126), a tiny sum even for a four-drawer commode (two-drawer commodes are the ones most in demand at the present time). Christie's on December 13 sold a Louis XV shaped-front marquetry commode with two drawers, ormolu and marble top, stamped P. Roussel (a very much wanted *ébéniste*), for £120 ($583).

In Paris the Hotel Drouot on December 19 sold eighteen carved chairs for the equivalent of $291. These were side chairs. The price was the equivalent of Victorian side chairs on the market today.

Let us turn back for a moment to the great Hamilton Palace sale of 1882. At this sale a *bombé* commode with bronzes *perhaps* by Caffiéri brought no less than £6,247/10 (the equivalent of $30,235). A very fine massive parquetry commode with shaped front and sides with ormolu chasings and large figures brought 5,950 guineas ($29,000). Such items were the preferred ones in this sale. If we adjust for the higher modern-price level, these items in 1882 brought much more than they would bring if offered on the market today!

It is entirely probable, however, that at the time of the American Civil War, prices of Louis XV furniture were at an almost all-time low, just as prices of

Louis XVI furniture were as we shall see from an analysis of the results of the Page Turner sale of 1903. For this sale we have exact prices paid in the 1860's as against what some of the pieces brought in 1903 at auction.

In its first issue, September–December 1901, *Connoisseur* magazine states: "The high price of £15,000 paid by Mr. Charles Wertheimer at Christie's on the 28th June for a pair of Louis XV commodes has caused a flutter in the press and people ask who it is that can give such absurd prices for pieces of furniture? To those whose business it is to deal in such things there is nothing extraordinary in the price." It should be pointed out that £15,000 equals $73,000, a tremendous price even for today, without adjusting for the decreased purchasing power of money.

In 1903 a small *bonheur-du-jour secrétaire*, 21½ inches in diameter, sold in London for £1,680 ($8,165). Although no earlier purchase date was given for this piece, it was purchased sometime earlier for £21 (about $100). It had appreciated in value eighty times!

At Christie's on December 18, 1903, an oblong table with ormolu and Japanese lacquered panels from the collection of Baron Lepic brought £1,900 ($9,234). For this piece of furniture the price was high because of the maker—Bernard van Riesen Burgh II, who is simply designated BVRB. (Until the late 1950's all that was known about him were his initials; his name was not even identified until that time. Pieces by BVRB will be identified as they appear at auction in this price history in order to indicate how the *ébéniste* was consistently preferred and brought consistently high prices whenever pieces by him appeared on the market.)

Between 1901 and 1905 prices of Louis XV furniture doubled, but most of the doubling took place in the lesser items. The commode, which is in such huge demand today, was not especially preferred at this time, and on May 12, 1905, Christie's sold a small marquetry commode, with two drawers (the preferred number), with ormolu and a marble top, stamped C. Chevallier for £60/8 (about $300). Today this piece would easily bring about twenty times this figure.

In the following year, 1906, Christie's sold a pair of settees and five *fauteuils* for £900 ($4,374). They sold a suite of two white and gold settees and five *fauteuils* for £660 ($3,210). Conceivably, these two suites might not bring any more than this figure in Paris today (without making any adjustment for the decline in the purchasing power of the currency). To put it in reverse, suites of chairs and settees were very much preferred pieces of furniture early in the century.

If the year 1901 is the base—100 percent—then by 1905 prices of Louis XV furniture had risen to 200 percent. By 1910 prices were 300 percent. On February 26, 1910, Christie's sold a fall-front *secrétaire* with folding doors, ormolu corner mounts and a marble top for £210 (over $1,000). Today this piece of furniture is not preferred, and in a poor sale it might bring no more than $1,000 ($1,500 to $2,000 in a good sale).

In 1910 a pair of *encoignures* was sold for £2,600 ($12,636), a very high price were it not for the fact that they had mounts by the greatest bronzeworker of the period—Caffiéri—and were stamped Joseph. This pair formerly went with a pair of commodes, the property of the Duke of Leeds, which were sold in 1901. This was undoubtedly the pair that earlier brought £15,000 ($73,000). These *encoignures* were oak veneered with kingwood and tulipwood with inlaid parquetry.

Another fall-front *secrétaire* brought £1,627 ($7,900). The high price was justified by the maker—Roger Vandercruse (Lacroix). This was a marquetry piece with three open shelves, a small drawer in the frieze, an ormolu gallery and a marble top. It came from the Waller Collection. This association helped to raise the price, which was substantial and probably at least as high as the piece would bring today.

By 1914 prices of Louis XV furniture had not risen appreciably, and they did not rise in 1915. In June Christie's sold a marquetry commode with a slightly shaped front and two drawers, stamped P. Roussel, for £252 ($1,224), a tiny sum when compared with today's prices. But a similar commode also stamped P. Roussel was sold in 1901 for only £120 ($583), and another commode was sold in the same year for just £26.

On March 5, 1915, the Anderson Galleries in New York sold a sofa and four *fauteuils* for $1,100. In this era the American auction houses were not the establishments that the London and Paris auctions were. They did not have the elaborate organization of the English and French auctions; they did not have the prestige; they did not attract the quality of buyer, and they did not handle the volume of business. Their prices tended to lag seriously behind those of the world's leading auction houses located in Europe.

In 1910 prices were 300 percent of the 100 percent base of 1901. They remained the same in 1915 and 1920. On October 28, 1920, Sotheby's sold a cylinder writing table with five drawers and ormolu for £440 ($2,128). It had come from a good dealer, M. Harris, and this somewhat assured its quality. On today's market the cylinder desk is almost unwanted, and $2,000 would be a good price. At the Parke-Bernet sale in New York on October 22, 1965, a beautiful cylinder desk of walnut with amaranth marquetry brought just $1,770. Another cylinder desk with three large drawers, ormolu, a metal gilt gallery and parquetry brought even more in 1920—£544 ($2,644). In the same year a commode stamped D. Dorat brought just £230 ($1,118). Tastes change, and it is difficult to imagine any cylinder desk today bringing anywhere near the price of a signed commode.

In 1919 the American Art Association in New York sold the Emil Pares Collection, and in this sale a few relatively high prices were achieved. A pair of walnut *fauteuils* brought $1,300, and a carved walnut *bergère* covered in petit point brought $1,225. These would not be ridiculously low prices on today's market. An inlaid tulipwood commode with a serpentine front brought only $1,100, however.

By 1925 there was still no rise in prices of Louis XV furniture; the index still stood at 300 percent. A small rosewood commode attributed to Pierre Roussel brought only $375 at the Anderson Galleries in November 1926, but the American

Art Association Galleries in April 1926 sold a stamped marquetry commode with bronze mounts from the William K. Vanderbilt Collection for $1,500. It was a most elegant piece of furniture and would bring ten times this sum if sold on today's market.

We now move forward to the year of the stock market boom—1929. Prices of Louis XV furniture still had not risen. They were still at the 300 percent level— the level achieved in 1910. Were it not for a few high prices, the year 1929 might have shown a price weakening. In March the Anderson Galleries sold a serpentine-front marquetry commode for $310. The Burnet-Clark Sale held at the Anderson Galleries in April 1929 certainly did not bring high prices. An average carved walnut *fauteuil* brought $210, and a kingwood marquetry *secrétaire à abattant* brought $650.

By the Depression low of 1932 the price index of Louis XV furniture was off. It stood at 200 percent. In December of that year the American-Anderson Galleries in New York sold a *fauteuil* signed by Jean-François Oeben, a maker whose name adds to the price of even badly damaged pieces of Louis XV furniture. This piece brought only $350. A day earlier the same gallery sold a pair of *fauteuils* by Jean-Baptiste LeRouge for $160. In the same sale a shield-back chair attributed to Etienne Meunier brought just $60. In England prices were much better. On June 10, 1932, Sotheby's sold a superb cylinder bureau stamped Riesener for £1,300 ($6,300), a high price for the time and a very high price by today's standards for any cylinder bureau, even one by Riesener.

Louis XV *bureau a cylindre*, stamped: Riesener. Sotheby's, June 10, 1932, $6,300. Exhibited Burlington Fine Arts Club, 1919.

One of a pair of Louis XV *Bergères* covered in contemporary needlework. Sotheby's, at Cam House, July, 1939, £58 the pair. Purchased by J. Paul Getty.

Now let us examine prices in 1939. This was the year immediately preceding World War II, and almost three years before the United States entered the war.

Although production started to move up after the low of 1932 and employment rose after 1934 and continued to rise generally to 1939 (with the exception of the one-year depression of 1938), the prices of Louis XV furniture continued to drop. In 1939 they were at the 100 percent mark—about what they had been at the turn of the twentieth century. On February 25, 1939, the Parke-Bernet Galleries in New York sold an acajou and kingwood petit commode with a marble top stamped Jean Stumpf for $100, and a tulipwood and harewood commode with *bronze doré* and marble top for $100. The same gallery secured $550 for a signed P. Bernard amaranth and tulipwood marquetry commode with *bronze doré* in March 1939. In May they sold a *bombé* commode for $200, and in October they sold a fine commode stamped I. Bircklé for $150 and one by the excellent maker I. Boudin for $260.

In England some interesting sales were made at this time. On July 24, 1939, Sotheby's sold a pair of carved gilt *fauteuils* in contemporary Italian needlepoint for £58 the pair ($233). The important thing about this sale, aside from the excellence of the chairs, was the buyer—J. Paul Getty, America's billionaire. On the same day a pair of *bergères* in contemporary needlework was sold for a little less—£58—to the same buyer. A beautiful small kingwood commode, three feet six inches long with a marble top and stamped D. F., was sold at the same time for £110 ($433)—to Getty. Finally, a suite consisting of a tapestry-covered *canapé* and four *fauteuils* was sold to the same buyer for £145/5 ($580).

This sale indicates that this was the bottom of the market for Louis XV furniture. Besides a review of the prices, this low point is attested to by the fact that J. Paul Getty was buying, and he has been unusually successful in buying at the

Louis XV commode, stamped: D. F. (Jean des Forges). Sotheby's, at Cam House, 1939, £110. Purchased by J. Paul Getty.

Louis XV marquetry occasional table, stamped: C. Topino. Parke-Bernet, 1940, $950.

bottom—the Hotel Pierre in the Depression and stocks in the severe market break of 1962. He has a phenomenal capacity for forecasting. As a result of his furniture buying his homes are now filled with Louis XV furniture, as well as other antiques of top quality, much of it bought at a time when such furniture was not in vogue. He placed the furniture in his home in England—he had bought the home in 1959 just before the tremendous appreciation of large English estates started.

The following year, 1940, saw the dispersal of a remarkably fine collection of furniture in New York—the Dalva sale of the collection of M. deBonniere—on March 9. A pair of carved walnut *fauteuils* stamped Nadal brought $540. When this pair reappeared in 1963, my wife and I bid $1,500 for them—and did not get them. Another pair of *fauteuils* brought $350 in 1940; and a *poudreuse*, a much wanted piece of furniture today, brought $145.

A fine collection was sold the next year—1941—at the Parke-Bernet Galleries in New York. Another BVRB piece went—a tulipwood center table with mother-of-pearl inlay and *bronze doré*. It brought the large sum for the time of $13,200.* A kingwood and tulipwood marquetry commode with *bronze doré*, stamped Joseph Baumhauer, brought the then large sum of $3,500. A stamped Topino commode that had been exhibited at the Metropolitan Museum of Art in New York brought $1,700, and a stamped Nicholas Petit commode brought $2,600. This sale represented a new and higher price level for Louis XV commodes.

In this sale a small table went at a high price for the time, perhaps foreshadowing today's high prices for these small Louis XV tables. An inlaid harewood and tulipwood marquetry occasional table of 27 inch diameter, originally sold by Duveen, brought $1,200.

*Sold at the Galerie Charpentier, Paris, 1956, for 17,000,000 francs, and is now in the Charles B. Wrightsman Collection.

Louis XV inlaid kingwood *poudreuse*. Parke-Bernet, 1940, $145.

One of a pair Louis XV carved walnut *fauteuils*, stamped: I. Nadal. Parke-Bernet, 1940, $540; 1963, $2,600 the pair.

The general price index which stood at 100 percent in 1939 stood at 250 percent in 1942. The prices of French Louis XV furniture are like the flight of a swarm of bees. Some bees are moving up in the swarm while others are moving down, but the entire swarm appears to move in one general direction as a group.

At the height of the war there was a marked difference in prices between America and England. Furniture could not be shipped to a safer and a higher-priced market so as to equalize prices. With England on the verge of being invaded, the ownership of furniture was less desirable than in peacetime, and bombings meant that furniture was as much a liability as an asset. There were fewer people at home to buy and use furniture of any sort, and there were many other things in the spending scale that came ahead of antique furniture. In America there was still a good deal of the "business-as-usual" attitude, and there was still buying of Louis XV and other antique furniture.

On January 30, 1942, a tulipwood-and-kingwood commode with marble top, two feet seven inches long and stamped Fromageau brought exactly £31 ($125). The sale took place at Christie's in London. On April 10 the same auction house sold a pair of small parquetry commodes from Partridge, a leading dealer, for £199/10 ($800). Six side chairs were sold at Sotheby's for £91 ($367 for the lot). Early in the year Christie's sold three of the little tables that are so popular now, all with the stamps of good *ébénistes*, for £73/10, £131/5 and £110/5 respectively. The highest-priced one brought $528. In the Parke-Bernet sale of October 23, 1965, two little tables, both unsigned, brought $8,000 and $3,200.

The year 1942 saw some high prices for Louis XV furniture—certainly high for the times. On April 29, 1942, the Parke-Bernet Galleries sold a suite consisting

Louis XV kingwood writing table, mounted in *bronze doré*, stamped: J. C. Ellaume. Parke-Bernet, 1945, $2,600; 1955, $5,250. From French & Company.

Small Louis XV black lacquer commode, stamped: C. Topino M. E. Christie's, 1955, $4,116.

of seven pairs of carved and gilded *fauteuils*, two *canapés*, a pair of *bergères* and one screen. The strange thing about this large suite is that only one pair of chairs had original frames. The value lay in the Beauvais tapestry after François Boucher. The suite was from Duveen Brothers and brought $26,000. I have seen this suite, and in appearance it is the last word in elegance; but, of course, the furniture for the most part is not antique.

By 1945, the last year of the war, prices were firmer, even in England. A marquetry commode stamped Roussel with *bronze doré* brought $1,950. These Roussel commodes alone can be used to trace prices in a summary way. They are excellent in quality and are plentiful enough in the market to be used as a kind of quick price index. A stamped Topino acajou and tulipwood commode with *bronze doré* brought a higher price—$2,600.

The writing table that is so popular now began to show price strength in 1945. An inlaid kingwood writing table from French and Company, 45½ inches long, brought $2,600 at the Parke-Bernet Galleries on October 27.

Prices by the end of the war were double those obtaining in 1942—the middle of the war. In 1942 they stood at 250 percent, and in 1945 they were 500 percent of prices at the beginning of the century.

Between 1945 and 1950 there was essentially no change in the price of Louis XV furniture.

Certainly English auction prices for Louis XV furniture rose substantially between 1945 and 1950, but this was more of a "back-to-normalcy" movement than a genuine rise. What really happened to prices can better be gauged by American prices, and these did not show any significant movement in the period between 1945 and 1950. The index in 1950 still stood at 500 percent.

Louis XV marquetry *bureau plat*, mounted in *bronze doré*, stamped: G. Coulon.   Parke-Bernet, 1955, $8,000.

Louis XV marquetry petite commode *à ecran*.   Parke-Bernet, 1952, $1,000.

In 1955 the Faucigny-Lucinge Collection was sold by the Parke-Bernet Galleries in New York. The only spectacular price in this sale was achieved by an acajou and kingwood writing table 38½ inches long and stamped BVRB. It achieved $6,000. It is almost axiomatic that a piece stamped BVRB brings a high price regardless of the time or the place. In the same sale an acajou marquetry petit commode brought only $400, and another one brought $550.

A number of commodes were sold in 1955. During the year the Parke-Bernet Galleries sold an inlaid tulipwood and palissandre small serpentine commode for $1,100, and an important harewood and amaranth marquetry commode with *bronze doré* and an elaborately designed front for $1,300. On December 10 of that year two commodes sold for different prices, however. A pair of acajou and tulipwood marquetry commodes with *bronze doré*, of *bombé* shape, brought the much higher price of $8,000 each. One of the chief elements of value is the fact that there was a pair. This is extremely rare.

English prices for commodes in 1955 were higher. A kingwood serpentine commode stamped Petit brought £483 ($1,354) at Christie's in May. A black lacquer commode stamped Topino brought £1,470 ($4,116), and an elegant kingwood commode with Rococo design and *bronze doré* brought £750 ($2,115).

Louis XV marquetry table by J. F. Oeben.   Christie's, 1958, $100,000.

In October Sotheby's sold a small writing and toilet table two feet nine inches long for £2,800 ($7,840), a price comparable to today's market but very much higher than the market had been up to that point for small tables. It was an elegant piece of furniture.

On November 24 Christie's sold a large giltwood *bergère* in Beauvais tapestry for a record price—£1,890 ($5,290). This *bergère* acquired value simply because it had belonged to the Empress Eugénie.

The presently very popular and very high-priced *bureau plat* showed a remarkably changed price pattern during 1955. In February the Parke-Bernet Galleries sold an inlaid acajou and kingwood *bureau plat*, 48 inches long, with *bronze doré*, for $700. In March they sold a fine inlaid and kingwood *bureau plat* with black leather and *bronze doré*, five feet two inches long, for $1,700. In December, however, they sold an elegant acajou and kingwood *bureau plat* stamped G. Coulon for $8,000, a vastly higher price than *bureau plats* had gone for up to that time.

The year 1955 can probably be broken into two parts. The first part shows no rise as against 1950, and perhaps shows some price weakening. The second part shows such price strengthening that it can almost be used to forecast the future. Since, however, we are working by years and not by six-month periods, the average for the year is considered to be the average of the lows and the highs. There is thus no higher index figure as compared with immediately preceding years.

For contrast with any previous sale we have summarized to date, let us go to the Thelma Chrysler Foy sale held at the Parke-Bernet Galleries May 13 to May 16, 1959. First, a pair of average carved and gilded *fauteuils* in beechwood brought the high price of $3,200. A second pair of *fauteuils*, with oval backs and stamped Tilliard, brought $6,000. Still a third pair was sold. These were carved and gilded and were exhibited at the 1939 World's Fair. They brought $18,000.

In this sale little tables finally came into their own. An inlaid tulipwood and acajou occasional table, 12¾ inches in diameter, with Sèvres porcelain, brought $21,000. A small average inlaid acajou and tulipwood writing table brought $7,500. A tulipwood marquetry triangular game table with *bronze doré*, 42½ inches in diameter, brought $26,000.

Commodes at this sale finally "arrived," and their prices rose to about present levels. An inlaid kingwood serpentine-front commode with *bronze doré* (from Wildenstein) by Charles Cressent, but unsigned, brought $24,000. In the same sale another stamped P. Roussel commode, black and gold and of serpentine shape, brought $11,000—a far higher price than earlier Roussel commodes had brought. This one, however, was of top quality. In fact, the price was so good that two of our friends in Washington were induced to sell their Roussel commode for exactly the same figure a short time later. A dealer bought it and resold it for $12,000.

By 1957 the Paris market for Louis XV furniture, which was not high up to that point in relation to the past market or in relation to London and New York, started to move up. A commode stamped Mondon was sold at the Hotel Drouot in June 1957 for $868, and a stamped H. Armand commode was sold at Versailles in December for $1,232. The Hotel Drouot in December also sold a commode

One of a pair Louis XV *bergères*, stamped: I Pothier. Parke-Bernet, 1959, $8,500 the pair.

One of six Louis XV painted *fauteuils*, stamped Lebas. Christie's, 1960, $21,600 the set. Purchased by Partridge.

One of a pair Louis XV *fauteuils*, richly carved and gilded. Parke-Bernet, 1959, $18,000.

Pair Louis XV *fauteuils*, stamped Tillard. Christie's, 1960, $4,095. Purchased by Partridge.

for a relatively low price—$1,453. A fine and much sought after black and gold lacquer commode was sold in December at the Hotel Drouot for the equivalent of $7,015.

Fauteuils remained low in France. During the year the Hotel Drouot sold a fine single *fauteuil* for $285. The Charpentier Galleries on June 18 sold four armchairs stamped Lelarge for $2,688.

Prices of Louis XV furniture in 1955 were about 500 percent of their level at the turn of the century. By 1960 they were 1,500 percent of that level—three times as high as they had been five years earlier! Small tables headed the list for price appreciation. On October 29, 1960, the Parke-Bernet Galleries sold a tulip-wood and sycamore oval occasional table, 28½ by 26 inches, from Dalva Brothers —skillfully reconditioned—for $5,000, a very high price for a restored piece of furniture. Christie's on March 17 sold a marquetry work table 13 inches in diameter and stamped J. F. Oeben, for 13,000 guineas (nearly $40,000). On June 30 Christie's sold a marquetry *bonheur-du-jour* for 6,500 guineas (about $19,500). Sotheby's on October 14 sold two more small tables, the latter stamped Boudin, for £4,400 and £4,600 ($12,300 and $12,900).

In 1960 *fauteuils* also rose significantly in price. On June 30 Christie's sold a pair of giltwood *fauteuils* for 1,365 guineas ($4,095), a high price even though they were stamped Tilliard. In the same sale they secured 7,200 guineas (about $21,500) for six painted *fauteuils* with shell carvings on the skirt, stamped Lebas. On October 14 Sotheby's sold a Lebas suite of six armchairs, a pair of corner armchairs and a pair of settees from Frank Partridge for £3,600 ($10,000).

During the year *bureau plats* were uniformly much higher in price. Those sold at the Parke-Bernet Galleries brought $4,000, $4,250, $6,000 and $6,500. In England a stamped Migeon, 23 inches deep and 44 inches long, brought 8,000 guineas ($24,000), and a second Migeon brought 2,800 guineas ($8,400). A stamped I. P. Latz *bureau plat* brought £2,900 ($8,120).

Louis XV marquetry occasional table. Parke-Bernet, 1960, $5,000. From Dalva Brothers.

Commodes did not show as great a price increase, and a Migeon kingwood serpentine commode brought £1,850 ($5,180) at Sotheby's in October. The Parke-Bernet Galleries sold a tulipwood and harewood marquetry commode with marble top and *bronze doré* for $21,000, a Saunier commode for $4,500, a Delorme commode for $4,750 and an elegant Grevenich commode for $8,500.

Prices on the Continent were not especially spectacular as compared with London and New York prices.

In 1962 the Palais Galliera sold a BVRB drop-front secretary. This type of piece is not in the greatest demand but the maker is, and the price achieved was $63,500, an enormous amount for any drop-front secretary.

By 1964 prices of Louis XV furniture, which had reached 1,500 percent by 1960, were now 2,000 percent. On June 26 Sotheby's sold two outstanding items. The first was a small marquetry commode with ormolu and a marble top, a beautiful stamped BVRB piece. It brought £4,000 ($11,200). The second outstanding item was a fine late parquetry *guéridon* with beautiful inlay. It was stamped RVLC. It sold for the great sum of £12,500 ($35,000).

On October 24 the Parke-Bernet Galleries sold a kingwood marquetry occasional table with *bronze dorè*, stamped RVLC, for $10,500.

The *bergère* became very easily the most sought after item of all seat furniture. In 1964 the Parke-Bernet Galleries sold three pairs of *bergères* for $4,200, $2,800 and $3,100.

The July 1964 issue of *Connaissance* magazine had a few highly interesting items on the value of Louis XV furniture. The issue cited a writing table stamped Joseph Baumhauer that had been sold in Paris. The article described the piece as being "in its own gravy," which presumably meant that it was unrestored and in perfect original condition throughout. The selling price was $78,400. The article

Late Louis XV parquetry *guéridon*, signed R.V.L.C. and R. Lacroix. Sotheby's, 1964, $35,000.

Louis XV marquetry occasional table, stamped: R.V.L.C. Parke-Bernet, 1964, $10,500.

also generalized on price and stated categorically that an authentic Louis XV writing table was worth between $20,000 and $40,000, adding that at this price it could possibly be a restored piece in contradistinction to one in original condition throughout. This simply points up the tremendous demand for Louis XV writing tables. The article described the writing table that brought $26,000 at the Parke-Bernet Galleries on October 31, 1963, as possibly being reveneered. It stated that the bronze mounts were ill-adapted to the piece, that the frames were too isolated, that the pendant corner mounts were too bold, and that in summary the table was "redressed."

Had these comments been read by prospective buyers of this table prior to its sale, one wonders if a price of $2,600 could have been reached, much less $26,000!

In 1964 a commode in coromandel lacquer was sold in Paris for the equivalent of $52,800, a high price. It was a beautifully colored and highly decorative piece of furniture with yellow predominating. *Connaissance* commented, after the sale, that the price might easily have been reached by a veneered commode of equal quality.

The July 1, 1966, sale of French furniture by Sotheby's in London was one of the leading sales of furniture of this type to be held in recent years. An ormolu mounted black lacquer commode was bought by Frank Partridge for $40,600, and a small ormolu mounted kingwood *bureau plat*, signed BVRB, brought $57,400. A suite consisting of six *fauteuils* and covered in Aubusson tapestry brought $14,000—$2,000 per item.

In Paris dealer prices showed no weakness despite some complaints that in the summer American dealers were notable by their absence. A Dubois *bureau à dos d'ane* was priced at $48,000, a Migeon *guéridon* at $30,000 and a small black Dubois commode at $7,000, all items being owned by the same dealer, one of

Louis XV painted commode by Joubert and the Martin Brothers, carrying the Versailles inventory number. Sotheby's, 1964, $52,800.

Louis XV *vernis martin* commode, signed Delorme. Parke-Bernet, 1966, $23,000.

the best in Paris. Finally, after much talking, the dealer showed us what appeared to be his finest items, two *secrétaires à abattante* by BVRB, priced at $250,000 the pair.

Another dealer offered a Boudin square salon table for 110,000 francs ($22,000), and six *fauteuils* for $12,000. One London dealer had two commodes for sale at what appeared to be lower prices than obtained in Paris in the same season—£975 and £800. These were small commodes and not of the finest quality, but the prices were not high.

Louis XV Prices (1901 Base)

Date	1901 Equals 100%
1901	100%
1905	200
1910	300
1914	300
1920	300
1925	300
1929	300
1932	200
1939	100
1942	250
1945	500
1950	500
1955	500
1960	1,500
1965	2,000

Six Louis XV giltwood *fauteuils*, three stamped: L. Lebas.   Sotheby's, 1966, $5,320.   Purchased by Frank Partridge.

Louis XV, Aubusson tapestry covered, giltwood seat furniture, signed: G. Jacob. Six *fauteuils* and a *canapé* en suite.   Sotheby's, 1966, $14,000 the set.

Louis XV ormolo mounted, black lacquer commode.   Sotheby's, 1966, $40,600. Bought by Frank Partridge.

Louis XV *canapé*, stamped: G. Jacob, en suite with *fauteuils* on page 91.

Louis XV Marquetry *bombé* commode, signed: P. Roussel.   Sotheby's, 1966, $6,160.

Two other comparative price tables have been prepared. The first considers the period just prior to World War I (1914) to be 100 percent, so that we have a 50-year span to 1965 for price comparison. The second considers the American Civil War period as 100 percent. Civil War prices of Louis XV furniture were 5 percent of 1914 prices.

Louis XV Prices (Civil War and 1914–1915 Bases)

Date	Civil War (1861–1865) Equals 100%	1914–1915 Equals 100%
Civil War (1861–1865)	100%	5%
1901	700	34
1905	1,400	67
1910	2,100	100
1914 (beginning of World War I)	2,100	100
1920	2,100	100
1925	2,100	100
1929 (boom year, peak of stock market)	2,100	100
1932 (bottom of Depression)	1,400	67
1939 (beginning of World War II)	700	34
1942 (U.S. in World War II)	1,750	83
1945 (end of World War II)	3,500	166
1950	3,500	166
1955	3,500	166
1960	10,500	500
1965	14,000	700

Small Louis XV ormolu mounted kingwood *bureau plat*, signed B.V.R.B. Sotheby's, 1966, $57,400.

SALON LOUIS XVI, from the Hôtel de Tessé, Paris, circa 1775. The mahogany writing table with gilt bronze mounts is signed by Jean Francois Leleu and is lent by Mr. and Mrs. Charles Wrightsman. The chairs at the desk are signed by Georges Jacob, and the armchairs against the wall are from a set signed by Louis Delanois and S. Brizard. *Courtesy of The Metropolitan Museum of Art.*

CHAPTER SEVEN

From Transition Through Louis XVI
1774–1789 (1794)

I T IS ALMOST INVARIABLY A RULE OF NATURE that organisms tend to become more elaborate and more complex as time goes on until they are so complex and have such rigid requirements for their existence that they can no longer adapt to their environment. Then they are supplanted by a new species, one better able to exist.

In the Louis XV Period furniture buyers demanded more and more. The structure and ornamentation of the furniture became ever more elaborate and the lines more extreme. Meissonnier, probably the greatest innovator of the Louis XV Period, and Caffiéri, the leading designer and maker of ornamental metal mounts and fittings, knew good design; but the pressure of the buyers in the market was too great. The nobles vied with one another in building elegant homes and furnishing them in the most elaborate manner. Many pieces of furniture tended to be over-elaborate, to be disquieting and in poor taste (by today's standards). The stage was set for the furniture known as Louis XVI.

In the period of Louis XVI (1774–1789) life became still more intimate and less formal, and it was conducted more and more in smaller rooms. Under Louis XV there really were no banquet tables as such. When it was time to eat, crossed legs supported by stretchers were brought in, planks were placed across them, a covering was placed over the planks and the meal was served. A Louis XV dining table is thus a rare thing indeed. Under Louis XVI dining tables made their formal debut.

The furniture of Louis XVI, like most other furniture in other countries, reflected the needs and mood of the times. It became smaller and less elaborate.

The main contributing element, if not the causal element, in the furniture of the style known as Louis XVI was Classicism, and in this respect the Louis XVI style is unique.

Classicism, Basis of the Louis XVI Style

In 1709 the ruins of Herculaneum were uncovered in the region of Naples, Italy. This discovery was followed by Stabiae and Pompeii in 1748 and by Paestum in 1750. The Pompeian discovery was and is the most significant one as far as the general public is concerned, and it remains the most important archeological spot

95

in Italy for the visiting foreign tourist. The most important thing to bear in mind as far as these excavations are concerned is that the architectural and artistic styles are *Greek*, not Roman. The entire style and cultural elements of the city were Greek. In fact, all Roman sculpture of the period about the turn of the Christian era is Greek in its form, so much so that in many ways it amounts to a Roman copy of the Greek. On the sculpture market the high prices are brought by the earlier Greek originals and not by these later Roman pieces made in the Greek manner.

The year following the discovery of Pompeii, the French Marquis de Marigny, brother of Mme. de Pompadour, returned from Italy (this was in the reign of Louis XV and well before Louis XVI came to the throne in 1774). Through Mme. de Pompadour's efforts he had been appointed Director of Buildings. This is the actual beginning of what is known as the Louis XVI style. In actuality the style began under Louis XV and continued past the Revolution and the death of Louis XVI.

The uncovering of some ruins in the early eighteenth century in Italy might not seem to be of vital significance to French art, architecture and decoration. In fact it might not seem to us to merit much news in the papers. The excavations and discoveries would seem to be of primary interest to archeologists. But one has only to go back as far as the 1920's to see the immense impact of archeological finds on people in general. The discovery of the tomb of King Tutankhamen in Egypt was the chief topic of conversation of the majority of American families for weeks.

It is not hard to understand, then, that the discovery of the ancient ruins in Italy created a great impact on Europeans. Many books were written in the mid-1700's about these Italian discoveries.

We are concerned here with the impact these Etruscan discoveries in Italy had on furniture design, and it must again be emphasized that this Etruscan art goes back to the Greek.

To a degree the Louis XVI furniture designs are based on original Greek motifs. The furniture *forms* are not essentially Greek, but the ornamentations were most heavily Greek in their antecedents. Some of the transplanted motifs include:

> Laurel wreaths
> Figures of Victory
> Trophies of war and of the chase
> Horns of plenty
> Symbols of the sun
> Shepherds with crooks
> Shepherdesses
> Scythes
> Rakes
> Watering cans wreathed with flowers
> Caryatids
> Crouching sphinxes

The straight line, which was one of the key elements of Louis XVI furniture (a sharp contrast to the curves of the Louis XV style), was probably also of Greek derivation. And certainly the fluted, tapering legs were characteristic of Greece. Finally, there were direct copies of the Greek furniture style: The tripod table and the Roman curule seat.

Essentials of the Louis XVI Style

1. Smaller size. The size of Louis XVI furniture is generally smaller than that of Louis XV, to suit the smaller rooms and the greater intimacy that developed during the Louis XVI Period.
2. Less elaborate ornamentation. This was a reaction against the over-flowering of the Louis XV style.
3. Straight lines as against the eternal curve of the Louis XV style. These straight lines were the most noticeable on legs. The cabriole leg was largely out, and it was replaced by the tapering, straight, fluted leg. Backs were also characterized by straighter lines as compared with the Louis XV style.
4. Rectangular shape. The rectangle returned, to some extent, for the back, for the general shape of chairs and for commodes and cabinets.
5. Metal mounts usually more subdued. This is, of course, a part of orna-mentation, but it was so important an element of design that it deserves a special handling. The master metal mount and fitting artist Caffiéri was replaced in eminence by Gouthière.
6. Painting of furniture now practiced perhaps more than in any other period.
7. Even more feminine characteristics than the preceding style. Furniture was a little more delicately made and a little more fragile.
8. Innovation. This was very nearly as great as in the Louis XV Period from the point of view of new forms, and is a highly significant character-istic of this period.

Innovations in the Louis XVI Period included the following: A table which is the equivalent of the modern dining table and a small upright desk, much better suited to the use of women than men, called the *bonheur-du-jour*. An item similar to the *bonheur-du-jour* also was developed in this period. It is a jewel cabinet with a drop front on high legs, obviously also an item for the ladies and greatly prized on the antique market today as are almost all small tables.

The *bureau à cylinder* also appeared at this time. It is commonly known as a cylinder desk, and it most resembles the roll-top desk of the nineteenth century. Also in this period the *semainier* of the Louis XV Period became the chiffonier or high chest-of-drawers.

Games which were popular in the Louis XV Period became even more popular under Louis XVI, and tric-trac tables as well as card tables were produced in ever greater quantity. Another game table which has no parallel in furniture construction today but which was produced in the era of Louis XVI is the *bouillotte*. This table is circular and has a marble top with a brass gallery running around the edge. It contains two drawers and two slides.

The *secrétaire* with slant top was also produced in much greater numbers at this time than in the earlier Louis XV Period.

Many mechanical tables and other pieces of furniture were produced in the Louis XVI Period. Some of these were apparently quite useful. Some pieces which are converted into toilets by mechanical means have less use today than when they were originally constructed. The job of designing the mechanical device and making it work in a foolproof manner was not easy. The saving grace was the relatively low cost of labor. Mechanical devices of the grade and of the beauty of construction employed in the time of Louis XVI would today probably cost as much as the entire remainder of the piece of furniture cost, possibly more.

The *rafraîchissoir* or *servante*, a lunch or snack table with places for bottles and a drawer and shelves for food, grew in popularity from the time of Louis XV and was produced in ever greater quantities.

The oval or medallion back was developed for chairs at this time. On the present market this type of chair is not as popular as the rectangular back. It is not of an intrinsically poorer design and it is not expected that the differential in price, which is fairly large, will be maintained in the market in the future. It is probably from this design that the balloon-back chair of the Victorian era was developed, although the specialists on Victorian furniture claim that the balloon back was a strictly Victorian innovation.

(In the preparation of descriptions of specialized and characteristic Louis XVI furniture we are very much indebted to Ruth T. Constantino for the illustrations of her splendid collection of Louis XVI furniture.)

Preeminence of Cabinetworkers and Woodworkers

In the Louis XVI Period we find an even greater emphasis on *ébénistes* and *menuisiers* than in the Louis XV Period, and a great influx of foreign masters into France. Certainly Louis XVI was responsible for the flowering of this art, but the Queen, Marie Antoinette, was almost equally responsible. Her Austrian parentage must have influenced her tremendously in her choice of *ébénistes* and *menuisiers*, for at this time France was almost dominated by foreign craftsmen despite the strictest guild rules limiting membership. These are some of the great names in furniture making in this era:

        Jean-Henri Riesener
        David Roentgen
        Guillaume Beneman
        Adam Weisweiler
        The Jacob family—(chairs)
        The Sené family—(chairs)
        Roger Vandercruse—(Lacroix)
        Martin Carlin
        Charles Topino
        Nicholas Petit

Furniture of the Transition

With the possible exception of Empire furniture, which is in a special category, the furniture of one era is not suddenly cut off and a new style immediately inaugurated. The *Régence* formed a bridge between the dark, heavy, somberly upholstered furniture of Louis XIV and the curved, light-colored, brightly upholstered furniture of Louis XV. In the same way the Louis XV style shades off into Louis XVI, and this "bridge" furniture has certain definite, recognizable characteristics which make it identifiable as "Transition":

> 1. The curved or cabriole leg was still used, but the curve is to a considerable degree straightened out. It was not just made less curved and straighter, but the leg took on its own characteristic shape: much wider at the knee than at the foot, and the inside of the leg tends to approach a straight line while the outside of the leg (the part seen) retains most of the degree of curve developed in the Louis XV era.
> 2. The *bombé* form gave way to the flat rectangular form for commodes and cabinets.

THE TRANSITIONAL PERIOD, LOUIS XV–LOUIS XVI.   A magnificent transitional commode, by Foullet, which was part of the Victor Rothschild collection. *Courtesy of Dalva Brothers, New York*

3. Marquetry, which is so characteristic of the Louis XVI pieces, became well developed.

4. A peculiar type of front for commodes and cabinets is characteristic of this era. It is a kind of block front. The center part of the front of the Transition commode is set forward from the area around the pulls. Sometimes contrasting marquetry is used on the sides, both sides employing the same type of marquetry, while the raised center panel is of a different pattern.

The cabinets and commodes of the Transition Period do not have sharp corners or even rounded ones. They are formed into stiles which are planed flat, and the plane is turned halfway around between the plane of the front and the plane of the sides.

Early Prices of Louis XVI Furniture

When one embarks on a study of the prices of antique furniture, he gradually moves back in time through the auction records and reports of sales. At some point in time he finds where antique prices "started." That is, at some early date antiques had little or no special value.

The study of price trends should ideally start at this base point. But since the records get poorer and poorer as one moves back in history, it becomes increasingly obvious that there was hardly any base or starting point, at least in recent times, when antiques had only utility value and not value as antiques.

The Page Turner Sale

On February 20, 1903, a notable collection of paintings and furniture was sold in England—the collection of the late Sir Edward Page Turner. Many of the items of furniture sold were of the Louis XVI Period and included the following:

Item 1. Louis XVI parquetry writing table, chased ormolu mounts, 52 inches wide	£460
Item 2. Another, nearly similar, 44 inches wide.	85 guineas
Item 3. Louis XVI mahogany console table, chased and pierced ormolu frieze, 41 inches wide	£130
Item 4. Louis XVI console table, veneered with satinwood panels bordered with mahogany, biscuit plaque of Tritons and frieze of ormolu, 31 inches wide	£100
Item 5. Louis XVI oblong mahogany writing table, ormolu beadings, 51 inches wide	370 guineas
Item 6. Louis XVI commode, mahogany and rosewood, chased ormolu mounts, 52 inches wide	220 guineas
Item 7. Pair of upright mahogany Louis XVI cabinets, chased ormolu mounts, 24 inches wide	200 guineas
Item 8. Louis XVI oblong parquetry table, panels in satinwood and mahogany, 31 inches wide	52 guineas

Item 9. Louis XVI upright parquetry *secrétaire*,
panels inlaid in checker design in hare and satinwood,
mounted with chased ormolu, 28 inches wide   480 guineas

Item 10. Oak fire screen, inlaid with panel of old
French crimson silk, 30 inches wide   £90

Item 11. Louis XVI small *bonheur-du-jour secrétaire*,
inlaid with flowers in rosewood on tulipwood field,
21½ inches wide   1,600 guineas

Item 12. Louis XVI marquetry commode, panels
inlaid with flowers in colored wood, chased ormolu
mounts, 52 inches wide   330 guineas

Item 13. Louis XVI parquetry commode, panels
inlaid with simple parquetry of satinwood and mahogany, chased ormolu mounts, 40 inches wide (by J. H.
Riesener)   680 guineas

Fortunately, the original purchase price and purchase date of these items are
available for comparison with prices achieved at the Page Turner sale:

	Price Paid			*Price Realized, 1903*
Item 1	March	1858	£45	£460
Item 2	March	1858	£28	85 guineas
Item 3	March	1858	£25	£130
Item 4	Feb.	1866	£35	£100
Item 5	Jan.	1863	£70	370 guineas
Item 6	Jan.	1864	£30	220 guineas
Item 7		1867	£37	200 guineas
Item 8		1868	£18	52 guineas
Item 9	Sept.	1863	£20	480 guineas
Item 10	Oct.	1869	£10	£90
Item 11	April	1868	£21	1,600 guineas
Item 12	March	1868	£60	330 guineas
Item 13	Sept.	1863	£50	680 guineas

Most of the items were purchased during or shortly after the American Civil
War, and all were sold again shortly after the turn of the twentieth century. The
item which rose the least (Item 4) achieved 300 percent of the base of 100 percent in 1866. The *bonheur-du-jour* (Item 11) rose to 7,600 percent of the 100
percent base of the year 1868. The price of the Riesener commode (Item 13)
was, of course, low. In a period of a little over four decades, the rise in these
pieces of Louis XVI furniture was substantial, and there is no need to go back
further in order to determine just when the rise in Louis XVI furniture began.

The Hamilton Palace Sale

It did not require the forty or fifty years between the date of purchase and the
date of sale of the Page Turner Collection for Louis XVI furniture to achieve

extremely high prices, however. In 1882 the "sale of the century" took place and required seventeen days—the Hamilton Palace sale in England.

The first item of importance was a Louis XVI upright *secrétaire*, stamped P. H. Pasquier. This desk was formerly the property of Mme. Du Barry. It brought 410 guineas (about $2,000). An upright *secrétaire*, a considerably more important piece, made by Riesener (and stamped with his name) for Marie Antoinette, with a center oval chasing by Gouthière, realized 4,400 guineas (well over $20,000). A matching Riesener commode realized 4,100 guineas. When purchasing power in 1882 is compared with that in the middle 1960's, it is quickly realized that the price was a high one, even by modern standards.

An oblong writing table to match the Riesener commode, also made for Marie Antoinette, brought 6,000 guineas, certainly not a bad price today. This table was bought by S. Wertheimer, who also bought a parquetry commode with marble top for 2,200 guineas. An upright marquetry *secrétaire* brought 1,575 guineas.

All of these items would now be in the museum class, both from the point of view of maker and former owner. There were, however, some lesser items that brought lesser prices. A Louis XVI carved and gilded sofa brought 75 guineas and six *fauteuils* brought 80 guineas, prices which would be far under today's prices; they were also far under the prices of the other Louis XVI items in the Hamilton Palace sale. Apparently a great premium was placed on the high status of the original owners.

Wertheimer was also the successful bidder on an ebony cabinet on high legs, lacquered in black and gold with an ormolu center oval by Gouthière. It brought 5,200 guineas. But the next item brought even more. It was an ebony *secrétaire* with black and gold lacquer with ormolu by Gouthiere and bearing the monogram of Marie Antoinette. It reached 9,000 guineas (about $45,000).

The next item, an ebony commode with ormolu by Gouthière made for Marie

Louis XVI writing table (part of a suite made for Marie Antoinette, 1784), stamped: J. Riesener, the bronze mounts are by Gouthière. The Hamilton Palace sale, 1882, £6,000.

Antoinette, was sold to Wertheimer for the same sum—9,000 guineas.

A large sofa made for Versailles with Gobelins tapestry brought 1,120 guineas. A set of six carved and gilded *fauteuils* to match the sofa brought 420 guineas. Both of these items would have achieved far greater prices today, possibly ten times as much.

Nevertheless, by any standards the Hamilton Palace Collection of Louis XVI furniture achieved extremely high prices—both for the time and in comparison with later prices for furniture of the same type. This sale should be remembered as a high point in the price of Louis XVI furniture.

Antique Prices vs. Furniture Prices

A question that always intrigues analytical writers in the field of antique furniture is, "When did the buyers in the market first begin to pay high prices simply because the piece of furniture was old—an antique—rather than just a piece of well-designed and well-made furniture?"

In the report "Christie's Since the War," chronicler Denys Sutton writes:

Louis XVI *secrétaire* by Jean Henri Riesener, with gilt bronze mounts by Pierre Gouthière. (This is part of the suite made for Marie Antoinette's apartments at the Chateau de Saint Cloud, 1784.) Branded: Garde Meuble de la Reine. The Hamilton Palace Sale, 1882, £9,450.   The Metropolitan Museum of Art, bequest of William K. Vanderbilt, 1920.

The taste for French furniture was evidently widespread and in the early part of the last century, the banker Edward Wheler Mills assembled an attractive group of pieces . . . while later the 4th Marquess of Hertford and the Rothschilds were avid buyers of major works by the French *maîtres ébénistes*. From quite early in the 1850's Christie's kept Lord Hertford supplied with photographs of important pieces that were about to appear at auction. The appreciation of the eighteenth century and its art, in fact, was rather more widespread at this era than is sometimes acknowledged.

Prices of Louis XVI Furniture in the Twentieth Century

If we consider that prices of Louis XVI furniture were 100 percent at the time of the American Civil War (1861–1865), they had risen to about 700 percent by 1903 when Sir Edward Page Turner's Collection was sold. It is fortunate that we have original Civil War purchase prices on the thirteen items sold in 1903; but we have not made a strict statistical average of price rise. Such a strict analysis would show 1903 prices at fourteen times the level obtaining at the time of the Civil War. This rise has been statistically lowered to seven because the tremendous rise in a few items tends to influence the average unduly. If the years 1861 to 1865 are 100 percent, then 1901 to 1903 might reasonably be considered 700 percent.

On May 12, 1905, a semicircular commode stamped David (presumably for David Roentgen) brought £336 ($1,633) at Christie's, a far cry from the six figures brought in 1964 for a David Roentgen commode. Five years later, a five-drawer commode was sold from the Waller Collection at Christie's (June 7) for about the same price—£357. This was stamped Dubois, one of the greatest of the Louis XVI *ébénistes*. In this same sale, however, a settee and ten *fauteuils* in old Aubusson brought £2,900 ($14,900), which would not be a low price even by today's standards. The conclusion is that commodes at the beginning of this century were not the treasured possessions that they are today, while chairs were very much preferred. (Although simple Louis XVI commodes were available on the market of the middle 1960's at $1,000 or less, the more elaborate ones are a rarity and are often priceless.)

By the start of the first World War (1914) prices had risen to only 750 percent. Prices in the 1929 peak business year still stood at the 750 percent level.

In December 1930—well after the crash of the stock market—the American-Anderson Galleries sold the collection of the Countess de la Beraudiere. A pair of carved and gilded *fauteuils* brought $60 each, and a matching *canapé* brought $125. An inlaid acajou commode with *bronze doré* brought $500, and a pair of carved and lacquered *fauteuils* stamped A. P. Dupain brought $400 for the pair.

By 1932, the economic low point, the index for Louis XVI furniture had fallen to only 650 percent. If we now consider 1929 to be the base point, or 100 percent instead of 750 percent, the Depression represents a drop of only thirteen points—to 87 percent—a small drop indeed considering the magnitude of the drop in almost everything else.

In February 1932 Christie's sold an upright parquetry *secrétaire* stamped by the great maker Boudin for £399 (a little under $1,400). On June 10 of the same year Sotheby's sold what by today's standards can be considered a great piece—a marquetry commode by David Roentgen from the Duke of Saxony's Collection. This fabulous piece went for £2,000 ($7,000). It is the same design as the famous Roentgen commode sold in 1964 for $176,000! The commode which was sold in 1932 was bought by Lady Eckstein.

The Ira Haupt sale conducted by the American-Anderson Galleries on November 16, 1935, saw slightly firmer prices for excellent pieces. A stamped Martin Ohenberg tulipwood marquetry semicircular commode brought $1,400, and a carved beechwood and Aubusson *bergère* and similar *fauteuil* that had formerly been sold by French and Company brought $950 for the two.

The Mrs. Talbot J. Taylor sale saw very low prices on January 29 and 30, 1937, however. A white-lacquered, brocade-covered *bergère* of fair shape brought $200, while a small tulipwood commode stamped Louis Moreau brought $275. An acajou commode with *bronze doré* brought $250, and a kingwood marquetry demi-lune commode brought $425—certainly no princely prices.

On November 26 and 27 of the same year the American-Anderson Galleries sold the Fonda Collection, and the prices were certainly no better. A pair of carved walnut *fauteuils* covered with Aubusson brought $155 for the pair. An

Louis XVI commode by David Roentgen. Christie's, 1932, $7,000. Purchased by Lady Eckstein.

unelaborate tulipwood commode brought $160. A pair of *bergères* brought $95 and a matching settee $90. A carved and painted *fauteuil* brought $50, and an acajou and bronze commode stamped J. P. Dusautoy brought $155. Victorian furniture prices of today are hardly under these.

By 1939, just before the outbreak of the European part of World War II, the prices of French furniture had not only failed to recover from the Depression low, but they had reached a new and lower low—325 percent. Again, if we consider that the 100 percent mark is represented by the peak year of 1929 and the 1932 low was 87 percent, then the 1939 figure was 43 percent. Prices had been more than halved since 1929, with an almost constant slide through the 1930's. French furniture was not in vogue. It was too ornate. It was the direct opposite of the functional furniture that was experiencing a vogue, and it was unsuitable to the austerity of the 1930's and the resultant rehabilitation and reform movements which placed emphasis on the common man, his poverty and his problems.

On April 21, 1939, a fantastic piece of furniture was sold at Sotheby's: a superb *secrétaire* by RVLC—Roger Vandercruse (Lacroix). It brought just £300 ($1,200). The Parke-Bernet Galleries on February 25, 1939, sold a fine pair of carved and lacquered *fauteuils* upholstered in needlepoint for $40 the pair. On March 18 the same auction house sold an inlaid tulipwood semicircular commode

Louis XVI Riesener commode.   Parke-Bernet, 1939, $490.   *Photo: Taylor & Dull.*

stamped J. H. Riesener for $490. There is hardly a higher grade *ébéniste* than Riesener, and it is most difficult to realize that such a piece could bring so low a price. In the same sale a *secrétaire* signed J. Stumpf brought $300.

In the May 5 Leon Dalva sale a commode stamped Avril brought $190. In the same sale the next day a J. F. Leleu stamped commode brought $310, the maker again being one of the greats of the eighteenth century. Today it would bring 25 times $310!

On May 13 of the same year, Parke-Bernet sold a table attributed to David Roentgen for $150. On October 13 the same house sold three carved and painted *fauteuils* for a total of $82.50.

Today, reproductions of these pieces would bring much more money, and second-rate Sheraton pieces would at least equal these prices.

Prices could hardly have fallen much from this low point, even in the war. In the Dalva sale of the collection of M. de Bonniere at the Parke-Bernet Galleries on March 9, 1940, a pair of lacquered *fauteuils* stamped Jacob brought $380 for the pair. Today they would bring about ten times this price, and a pair of Jacob reproductions sold at the Parke-Bernet Galleries would almost certainly do better than $380 for the pair.

Transitional Louis XV–Louis XVI marquetry commode, stamped: J. F. Leleu M. E.   Parke-Bernet, 1939, $310.

In general the year 1942 showed no upward change from the pre-war period and remained at about 325 percent—43 percent of the 1929 prosperity year.

By 1945, however, a change took place and prices of fine French furniture of the eighteenth century rose. On April 14, the Parke-Bernet Galleries sold a carved and lacquered sofa stamped J. B. Sené, one of the two great *menuisiers*, for $1,300. In the same sale a pair of carved and gilded *fauteuils*, in Aubusson and stamped Delaisement, brought $1,800 for the pair. A similar pair in the same sale brought $1,600, and a pair described as being undoubtedly by George Jacob brought $1,700. A sideboard with an undershelf, known as a *desserte*, brought $3,600.

The 1945 prices were about at the 700 percent level, up from 325 percent three years before; and if 1929 is 100 percent, prices were now 93 percent, just 7 points under the 1929 boom year. Strangely enough, however, by 1950 there was no further rise of great significance.

In France prices in the early years of the 1950's showed no spectacular rise.

On June 22, 1952, the Hotel Drouot sold a fair commode for 120,000 francs ($342). The following year the Galerie Charpentier sold a superb fall-front *secrétaire* with marquetry for 328,000 francs ($934). The quality could hardly have been improved upon. And on March 29, 1954, the Hotel Drouot sold a fine pair of *fauteuils* stamped Sené for 265,000 francs ($755). On April 29 of the same year Christie's sold a *bureau plat* by Leleu, an important maker, for $4,630. A similar *bureau plat* was for sale in New York in the fall of 1965 for $28,000.

On the whole, 1954 prices had not risen above those of 1950, and in 1955 prices were still the same—700 percent of the original base figure and 93 percent of the pre-Depression level.

The Parke-Bernet Galleries on February 11, 1955, sold an inlaid tulipwood and amaranth commode for $350; and on March 5, a *bureau plat* for $1,150, a small price for any Louis XVI *bureau plat*, even a very poor one. Sotheby's on February 18 sold a set of a dozen damask-covered *fauteuils* by P. Remy for $3,640—a small price for such a large set.

By the end of the year 1955 there was little determinable rise in the market for Louis XVI furniture.

Transitional Louis XV–Louis XVI marquetry commode by Bircklé.   Sotheby's, 1955, $1,260.

The Boom

On April 2, 1957, the Galerie Charpentier sold four rectangular-back *fauteuils* by Sené for 40,000,000 francs (about $11,400), a very high price for the time, even for chairs by the best maker. But on June 14 the Hotel Drouot sold a good commode stamped d'Avril for 260,000 francs ($741). In Nice on May 23 another commode, but a plain one, brought 140,000 francs ($390). No spectacular rises are shown in these two pieces.

But now small tables began to be featured. Such beautifully made little tables were certainly sold before, but the market was not so insistent on getting them that the prices rose tremendously—as they did in 1965.

The year 1959 saw the sale of the outstanding Thelma Chrysler Foy Collection at the Parke-Bernet Galleries (May 13–16). An occasional table of tulipwood inset with Sèvres plaques brought $24,000. It had *bronze doré* fitments and was stamped Martin Carlin. An elegant ebony and black and gold lacquer marble top table with *bronze doré* stamped A. Weisweiler, one of the great makers, brought $13,000; an occasional table of harewood and marquetry with *bronze doré* brought $3,100. A decorated black and gold lacquered writing table, stamped Martin Carlin, was bought for $25,500, and virtually a companion table was bought for $19,500. A decorated black and gold lacquer serpentine commode with *bronze doré*, stamped F. Rubestuck, brought $12,000. A pair of carved and gilded boudoir chairs with oval backs brought $4,000, and a pair of carved and gilded *fauteuils* stamped Sené brought $6,000.

Transitional Louis XV–Louis XVI occasional table, stamped: Martin Carlin. Parke-Bernet, 1959, $24,000.

One of a pair Louis XVI carved and gilded boudoir chairs covered in Beauvais tapestry. Parke-Bernet, 1959, $4,000 the pair. From French & Company.

One of a set of six Louis XVI lyre-back side chairs, five are stamped: J. B. B. Demay. Parke-Bernet, 1959, $4,500 the set.

Louis XVI lacquer table de Milieu, stamped: A. Weisweiler M. E.   Parke-Bernet, 1959, $13,000.

From the point of view of historical prices for Louis XVI furniture, this Thelma Chrysler Foy sale is important for several reasons:

1. Prices were very much higher than in earlier years.
2. Prices were higher across the board, not just for certain pieces or certain types of furniture.
3. High prices did not depend on what collections the pieces came from or the history of the collection.
4. High prices did not depend on the fact that Marie Antoinette or some other celebrity of the era of Louis XVI once owned the furniture.
5. Small tables brought very high prices as compared with the past.
6. Elaborate commodes brought high prices as compared with the past.

In general, European prices were very much under this level, although a rise was apparent. On June 12, 1959, the Charpentier Galleries sold a cylinder bureau stamped B. Moliter for 17,200 new francs, ($3,440), a high price for this item of furniture.

If we compare 1960 with 1955 (and we are making comparisons by five-year periods), then prices of Louis XVI furniture doubled in this period. On November 11, 1960, the Myron Taylor Collection was sold (Myron Taylor was former head of U.S. Steel and former U.S. Ambassador to the Vatican). A finely carved pair of gilded and polychromed *fauteuils* stamped L. Falconet brought $5,500 for the pair, an extremely high price for 1960. But earlier in the year the same gallery—Parke-Bernet—sold an acajou and tulipwood marquetry writing table with *bronze doré* mounts, 28½ by 37 inches, for $5,500. Another item in the

Louis XVI console, mounted in *bronze doré*, stamped: I. Dubois.   Parke-Bernet, 1959, $13,500.   From French & Company.

Myron Taylor sale, a carved, gilded and polychromed *canapé* stamped N. Q. Foliot, six feet nine inches long, brought the fantastic price (for a *canapé*) of $10,500.

On March 11 Christie's sold a parquetry and Sèvres porcelain small table stamped A. Weisweiler, 31 by 17½ inches, for 9,000 guineas (about $27,000), a seemingly huge price for so small a piece, particularly when one considers the relatively low prices that such pieces had generally brought in the past.

The year 1955 was 700 percent, and 1960 was 1,400 percent, or double. If we make the year 1929 100 percent, then 1955 was 93 percent and 1960 was 186 percent—the high point to date in the price of Louis XVI furniture. (Remember that the analysis was made for periods of five years and that computations for the in-between years were generally not made.)

One thing seems apparent: The finest items moved up in price the most and the fastest, while the lesser items showed relatively little change from the year 1955. This also is the pattern of price change found in the painting market. It will be seen later, however, that in some types of antique furniture in recent years the bottom-level antiques have at times moved the most since the buyers with the least to spend have rather quickly become "antique conscious."

An analysis of prices in the year 1964 indicates the magnitude of the boom. The most outstanding piece of furniture sold in any sale was the David Roentgen commode which Sotheby's sold on April 17 to the Jack Linskys of New York for approximately $176,000. This was the highest price received at auction for a piece of antique furniture.

Other Louis XVI pieces also brought high prices, however. In London a

Table à ecrire, stamped: M. Carlin M.E.   Park-Bernet, 1959, $25,000.   From Rosenberg & Stiebel, New York.

lacquered commode brought $44,800. Sotheby's on June 26 sold a mahogany *demi-lune* commode with marble top, stamped C. Topino, for £2,900 ($8,100), and an important and elaborate parquetry commode with fine ormolu, attributed to Riesener, for £9,000 ($25,200). In earlier years even fine commodes did not reach anything like such heights unless they came directly from Versailles or belonged in the royal apartments of Marie Antoinette.

Still, low prices obtained in the year 1964 for the lesser pieces of furniture. At Versailles a pair of side chairs with square backs brought $680. The Parke-Bernet Galleries on September 24 sold a carved and gilded wood and gesso *demi-lune* console table for $300 (such items were not in the greatest demand), and on September 23 the same galleries sold an inlaid tulipwood cylinder desk for $325. On the other hand, an A. Weisweiler stamped small palissandre *secrétaire* with lacquered panels and *bronze doré* sold at the Parke-Bernet Galleries on October 24 for $10,000.

In the early part of 1965 there were few prices that might be called low except for certain pieces of furniture not in demand, such as very simple commodes and cylinder desks, as well as damaged and over-repaired pieces and pieces of doubtful authenticity. And by 1965 the boom had spread to the little buyers who often settle for antiques at the bottom end of the quality scale.

Highly important Louis XVI commode by David Roentgen.   Sotheby's, 1964, $176,000.   Purchased by Mr. and Mrs. Jack Linsky.

On April 23 Parke-Bernet sold a pair of stamped Nicholas Louis Mariette carved and painted *fauteuils* for $800, and on March 13 the same galleries sold one Sené carved and gilded *fauteuil* for $2,750.

These were the trends discernible in 1965 for Louis XVI furniture:

1. Prices were triple those of five years earlier. They stood at about 4,000 percent, whereas in 1960 they were 1,400 percent. With 1929 equal to 100 percent, 1965 prices were at the 533 percent mark.

2. The signed pieces were in the greatest demand and brought the highest prices, and the greater the reputation of the maker the more the pieces brought.

3. The pieces of the greatest intrinsic quality and beauty tended to bring the highest prices.

4. Chairs of all types which in the early years (1950 and earlier) brought little now tended to bring very high prices.

5. The fancier and finer commodes brought enormous prices, particularly if they were the products of great makers. Plain commodes could at times be obtained for under $1,000, even at retail.

6. Small tables were in greater demand, and a Vernis Martin *bureau de dame* by René Dubois brought $4,500 at the Parke-Bernet Galleries.

7. *Canapés* tended to bring low prices, as did fall-front desks and cylinder desks.

One of a pair Louis XV painted *fauteuils*, stamped: Delanois. Parke-Bernet, 1966, $1,500 the pair.

One of a pair Louis XVI *fauteuils*, stamped: H. Jacob. Parke-Bernet, 1966, $2,600 the pair.

8. There was little distinction as to where a piece brought a high price, and it often seemed that the smaller auctions could get higher (or at least *as* high) prices than the leading auction houses. Smaller auction houses were particularly successful in selling second-rate pieces at high prices, and the main question asked was not "Is it a fine piece?" but "Is it of the period for certain?"

On July 1, 1966, Sotheby's held a highly important sale which included several excellent Louis XVI items. An important pair of early Louis XVI marquetry and parquetry ormolu mounted side cabinets, signed J. H. Riesener, brought $28,000; but a rare porcelain and ormolu mounted console *desserte* by the same maker brought only $3,080. A marquetry and ormolu mounted *secrétaire à abattant* signed L. Gilbert brought only $2,240, a price which illustrates the usual under-

Louis XVI marquetry *demi-lune* commode. Christie's, 1966, $1,617.

valuation of this particular piece of furniture by the market of the middle 1960's.

In London French furniture appeared to be at a discount as compared with prices in Paris. A leading London dealer offered a good commode, not of unusual or very fine appearance, for £1,150 ($3,220). In Paris prices at the retail dealer level were in general much higher. A *bureau plat* made by Canabas was offered for $28,000, a Saunier *secrétaire à abattant* was priced at $16,000, and a little writing table stamped Weisweiler was priced at $9,000. All Paris dealers complained in the summer of 1966 that there was a notable absence of American

Louis XVI ormolu and porcelain *console desserte*, signed: J. H. Riesener. Sotheby's, 1966, $3,080.

dealers who usually came to Paris during the summer to purchase for resale in America. There was an indication that Paris dealers were quite ready to talk price concessions.

A few very good buys were noted. Four painted *fauteuils* stamped Gaillard were priced at 32,000 francs ($6,400), while two *bergères* and four *fauteuils* made by Charpentier were offered at $1,800 for the lot. These were good pieces, although not of the most elegant variety.

One of a pair of Louis XVI ormolu mounted, marquetry and parquetry side cabinets, signed: J. H. Riesener.   Sotheby's, 1966, $28,000.

Louis XVI Prices

Date	Civil War (1861–1865) Equals 100%	1914–1915 Equals 100%
Civil War (1861–1865)	100%	13%
1901	700	93
1914 (beginning of World War I)	750	100
1929 (boom year, peak of stock market)	750	100
1932 (bottom of Depression)	650	87
1939 (beginning of World War II)	325	43
1942 (U.S. in World War II)	325	43
1945 (end of World War II)	700	93
1950	700	93
1955	700	93
1960	1,400	186
1965	4,000	533

Louis XVI Prices

Date	1950 Equals 100%	1925 Equals 100%
1925		100%
1926		100
1929		100
1932		87
1939		43
1942		43
1945		93
1950	100%	93
1955	100	93
1960	200	186
1965	573	533

Prices of Transition Louis XV to Louis XVI Furniture

In comparison with the volume of furniture turned out in the Louis XV style and the Louis XVI style, not much Transition furniture is available. Nor was it ever available. While certain pieces of Louis XV and Louis XVI furniture have reached astronomical heights in price, Transition furniture has rarely achieved very high prices. In many years of activity and high prices in antique furniture, Transition pieces have not merited many illustrations in auction catalogues and have not been considered of great market importance. It is only in the decades of the 1950's and 1960's that Transition furniture has come to be featured.

We may start with the year 1925 as 100 percent (and we have used this year as the base period for most types of furniture in this study). In that year the

Anderson Galleries sold a pair of walnut armchairs from the Eugene Gueron Collection for $410.

Skipping 1925 directly to the Depression year of 1932, the index remains at 100 percent. On December 2 the American Art Association sold a small carved walnut *canapé* by Roussel for $500, not a small price for a *canapé* in this Depression-bottom year.

By 1950 prices had doubled and the index stood at 200 percent. In 1952 two little tambour tables by Boudin *and* Topino sold for $800 and $630; a good commode stamped by the master Oeben sold at the Hotel Drouot on June 6, 1952, for the equivalent of $5,000. The following year the Charpentier Galleries sold a commode stamped RVLC (Roger Vandercruse) for the equivalent of $1,590. The next year (1954) two commodes sold for $1,283 and $1,436.

By 1955 prices were at the 300 percent level. On February 18, 1955, Sotheby's sold a beautiful marquetry commode with elegant front panels and *bronze doré*, stamped J. Bircklé, for £450 ($1,260). On May 12, however, Christie's sold an important commode made by P. A. Foullet for £2,730 ($7,644), and Sotheby's on November 18 sold a kneehole writing table for £1,350 ($3,780). On June 6, 1957, Christie's sold an RVLC *guéridon* for the very high price of $9,500. On June 18, however, the Charpentier Galleries sold a pair of excellent chairs stamped Nadal for 320,000 francs ($912).

Transitional Louis XV–Louis XVI parquetry commode, signed: S. Oeben. Sotheby's, 1966, $7,280.

Three commodes were sold during the year for $2,072, $770 and $570. The following year a stamped Boudin commode was sold at the Versailles auction for the equivalent of $1,842. A market price for Transition commodes as well as most Transition furniture is difficult to estimate. The rule is that unless the piece is of top quality and stamped by a good maker the price is likely to be low; but if it is a fine piece by a good maker the price is likely to be extremely high and near the level of Louis XV furniture.

In the Thelma Chrysler Foy sale held at the Parke-Bernet Galleries on May 13 to 16, 1959, an inlaid acajou and tulipwood occasional table stamped Martin Carlin brought $10,500, while a tulipwood and harewood marquetry occasional table by the same maker, but not stamped, brought $16,500. A stamped Topino commode brought $6,500; a reconditioned companion piece brought only $3,500. A stamped Roussel commode brought $4,000.

One of a pair of *bonheurs du jour* by the great *ébéniste* Martin Carlin. The pair sold in June 1967 at Christie's for 82,000 guineas ($246,000)—a record price for a furniture lot. They were purchased by the Jack Linskys of New York.

In 1960 Sotheby's sold a stamped Stumpf commode of parquetry design with *bronze doré*, an elegant piece, for £1,400 ($3,900). Prices were now at the 500 percent level as compared with 300 percent in 1955.

In 1963 Sotheby's sold an unusual lot—a pair of bow-front marquetry commodes, 56 inches wide, for £10,500 (almost $30,000). In the same year a petit commode with bow front and serpentine sides, of pearwood with ormolu mounts, signed Leclerc and stamped EHB, brought £6,500 ($18,200).

By 1964 prices of Transition furniture were at the 700 percent level. On May 16 the Parke-Bernet Galleries sold a stamped Topino break-front commode, decorated in vermillion and with *bronze doré*, and having two drawers masked as one and a marble top. There were some restorations to the lacquer. It brought $12,000. On February 14 of the same year Sotheby's sold two stamped Cosson commodes for £1,300 and £1,700 ($3,640 and $4,760). Three more Transition commodes were sold during the year for $5,320, $1,800 and $3,300. The rule still seems to be that fine Transition pieces by known and excellent makers bring very high prices, while the average Transition piece brings a low price. There is not this wide a spread in either Louis XV or Louis XVI furniture.

While prices in 1965 were up, they were up only a little for Transition furniture.

In the notable sale held at Sotheby's on July 1, 1966, a fine Transition marquetry and ormolu commode signed J. Tuart and L. Boudin brought $4,200, and an excellent parquetry commode signed by Oeben brought $7,280. In the summer of 1966 a leading London dealer offered a good commode for $7,000, while in Paris two good commodes were offered at $8,200 and $6,000.

While in London during June 1967, we admired a pair of *bonheurs du jour* at Christie's. They were by Martin Carlin in the Transition Louis XV-XVI style and were veneered with exotic woods and inlaid with painted porcelain plaques. One rarely finds a pair of Carlin writing desks, so we were sure that bidding would be high, but we were not prepared for what happened. The next day the pair brought 82,000 guineas ($246,000)—setting a new world auction record for a furniture lot! The purchasers were Mr. and Mrs. Jack Linsky of New York, who set the record for a single piece described earlier.

Transition Louis XV to Louis XVI Prices

Date	1950 Equals 100%	1925 Equals 100%
1925		100%
1932		100
1950	100%	200
1955	150	300
1960	250	500
1965	350	700

FRENCH DIRECTOIRE SALON.   *Courtesy of Dalva Brothers, New York.*

CHAPTER EIGHT

Directoire
1795–1799

THE DIRECTOIRE (DIRECTORY) WAS A political body which governed France from 1795 to 1799. From 1792 to 1795 France was governed by the National Convention, which was then replaced by the *Directoire*. In 1799 Napoleon dispensed with the *Directoire* and established the Consulate with himself as First Consul; he retained that office until 1804 when he was crowned Emperor.

The *Directoire* style, like all other furniture styles in history, did not start on a particular date and did not end with someone's demise or dethronement or the termination of a particular political organization. Styles overlapped and often had their beginnings in an earlier period or continued into a later period. The *Directoire* style of furniture was made between the early 1790's and the time of Napoleon's coronation, except that for a short period (1799–1804) a slightly different style of furniture was fashionable. This was known as Consulate, and was obviously made during the time Napoleon was First Consul.

The Terror began in 1789. The next year the elaborate guild system was abolished, together with its high standards of production, its inspections of furniture produced by the members and its fines and confiscations for poor workmanship. The palaces and châteaux of the nobles were ransacked and much of their contents destroyed. The furniture of Versailles Palace was dumped in the courtyard and a haphazard auction held, an auction which literally lasted months. Most pieces brought little or nothing. Since that time the French government has been engaged in an endless buying program to get back as much of this furniture as still exists. The government has had to pay on the average four hundred times as much as the furniture brought at this Revolutionary auction!

The predominant motif of *Directoire* furniture is Greek. The great excavations in southern Italy—the excavations that had such a profound effect on the design and decoration of the furniture of the period—uncovered Greek objects, for the ancient communities of southern Italy were Greek settlements with Greek culture and Greek art.

Generally, *Directoire* furniture can be distinguished from other French furniture at a glance. It is more austere, more angular, less slender and graceful and

123

ornamented differently from the preceding Louis XVI style. It is probably less well constructed. We have had the task of rebuilding a piece of *Directoire* furniture, a commode with a marble top which had all but collapsed. We were not impressed with the excellence of construction of the piece, and we were able to examine all members and joints carefully.

Characteristics of Directoire *Furniture*

1. The dominant wood is mahogany. It largely replaced the veneers and marquetry of the Louis XVI Period.
2. If it were possible to make comparisons on the basis of average weight, a piece of *Directoire* furniture would weigh more than a similar piece of Louis XVI furniture. The general overall appearance of the *Directoire* furniture is weighty.
3. The tops of chairs curl backwards.
4. A second type of chair has a large concave encompassing back.
5. Under Louis XVI, Greek *ornamentation* had been much used. Under the *Directoire*, Greek *form* became popular. These actual forms included:

    A. Flaring back and concave back
    B. Chairs of curule form with X-shaped supports
    C. Beds with bronze strips and angular pediments
    D. Copies of Greek table and couch legs
    E. Frames for folding seats
    F. Throne chairs based on Greek and Roman designs
    G. Greek and Roman bas reliefs
    H. Concave rear legs of chairs in one piece with the uprights
    I. Chair arms that rose directly above the front legs
    J. Cylindrical, tapering front legs of chairs

6. Simplicity of design throughout except in ornamentation.
7. The use of paint, especially on chairs where natural mahogany was not used.
8. Revolutionary symbols used for ornamentation. This was only one of the types of ornamentation used, and it was used early in the general era of *Directoire* furniture. By the time the political body known as the *Directoire* actually came into existence, the symbols of the Revolution had become somewhat passé as elements of furniture design. These symbols included:

    A. The Liberty cap called the Phrygian bonnet
    B. The tricolor of the Republic
    C. The fasces
    D. The pikes, which were supposed to be the symbol of free men
    F. The clasped hands of *fraternité*

    G. The symbols of the three important classes of the nation: The cross for the clergy, the nobility's sword, and the spade and bonnet for the great mass of citizens.
    H. Griffins
    I. Sphinxes
    J. Tripods
    K. Palmettes

9. Greek motifs used for ornamentation. This use occurred later on in this period and included the:

    Star
    Daisy
    Lyre
    Lozenge
    Vase
    Greek key

10. Egyptian motifs. The *Directoire* style was a transition style just as the *Régence* style was. *Régence* bridged the gap between the angular, dark, heavy, formal furniture of Louis XIV and the curved, light, graceful, informal furniture of Louis XV. It represented an "average" of the two styles. The actual period of the *Directoire* ended before Napoleon's Egyptian campaigns of 1798 and 1799 bore much fruit in the way of Egyptian design. But even before 1789, Egyptian designs were used. (Two Egyptian figures with headcloths are the arm supports on the beautiful painted and gilded walnut *fauteuils* made by Jean-Baptiste-Claude Sené for the *cabinet de toilette* of Marie Antoinette for her Château de St. Cloud. They were made in 1788, a year before the Revolution.)

On the other hand, the full-blown period of Egyptian motifs did not develop under the *Directoire*. Baron Dominique Vivant de Denon was asked by Napoleon to accompany him on his Egyptian campaign. In 1802 the Baron published an exhaustive work on Egyptian art and design entitled *Voyage dans la Basse et la Haute Egypte*. There were two volumes to this work and it contained 141 plates. The Baron was a friend of the all-powerful style creator and friend of Napoleon, Jacques-Louis David, and this one work of Denon's supplied much material that was immediately used in art, architecture and furniture design.

These were some of the motifs of Egyptian origin used on the furniture of this period:

    Lotus flower
    Lily
    Reed
    Palm
    Papyrus flower
    Lion head supports for tables and chairs
    Sphinx

11. Angularity in the legs and in other members of the furniture. The Louis XVI style had curved and rounded legs and corners.

12. A few new items of furniture. The chief new item was the *méridienne*, a kind of sofa which allowed a person to recline halfway.

Furnituremakers of the Directoire

Georges Jacob (1739–1814), the founder of the famous family of *menuisiers*, made furniture for Louis XV. He then became the chief supplier of chairs to Marie Antoinette, Louis XVI's queen. During the Terror he supported the Revolutionists, and through his friendship with the painter David, a Revolutionist of high rank, he was favored. He built the seats for the huge convention hall at the Tuileries.

Etienne Levasseur was born in 1721 and worked with one of the sons of André-Charles Boulle of Louis XIV fame. The family Levasseur made the transition to the new style.

Guillaume Beneman of Louis XVI fame received some orders during the Terror for unpretentious furniture, and he apparently kept busy eliminating from existing pieces of furniture their royal and noble emblems, including crowns and coats of arms.

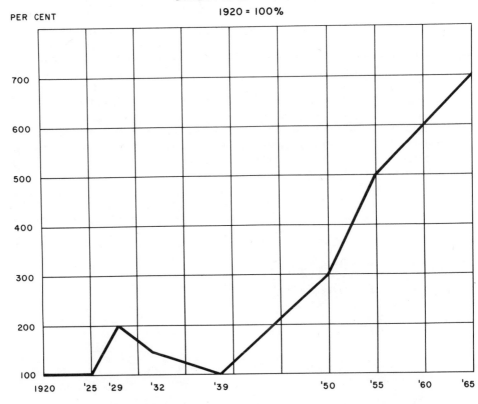

DIRECTOIRE PRICE INDEX

1920 = 100%

Jean-Baptiste Sené, who made furniture for Marie Antoinette, continued to fill orders for furniture up until the time of his death in 1803, one year before Napoleon was crowned Emperor. In like manner the bronzier Gouthière made the transition and continued to turn out quality work even under the drastically altered social conditions.

Prices of Directoire Furniture

Directoire furniture is not and has not been a major factor in the antique market. One reason is that it was not produced over a long period of time, so there is not a great deal of it to change hands. The second reason is that under the *Directoire* and following the Terror, furniture of the highest quality was not made, and what furniture was made was not equal to that of the preceding era— Louis XVI. Neither did it have the distinctive qualities of its successor—Empire. It is actually a somewhat subdued Louis XVI furniture.

In 1920 the leading London dealer M. Harris bought a white and green painted sofa, five feet eight inches long, at Sotheby's for £26 ($95). Five years later, when most other types of antiques were rising in price in the furniture boom, *Directoire* prices were still very low. On March 27, 1925, the American Art Association Galleries sold a satinwood inlaid mahogany upright secretary for $105 and an oval mahogany breakfast table with *cuivre doré* for $12.50. The next day they sold two carved mahogany chairs with Aubusson coverings for $50 and a similar pair for the same price.

In 1929 the same gallery sold an acajou and sycamore commode stamped Savigny for $250. Prices by this time had doubled, but they were still at a low level.

In the Depression bottom of 1932 the same gallery sold a lacquered and carved *bergère* stamped G. Jacob, the leading French chairmaker, for $105. Prices were down to the 150 percent level (1920=100%). Possibly they would have dropped more had there been more room to drop!

Directoire acajou writing table. American-Anderson, 1937, $67.50.

Directoire walnut commode, paneled with brass moldings. Parke-Bernet, 1942, $125.

In the January 29 and 30, 1937, sale of the estate of Mrs. Talbot J. Taylor held at the American-Anderson Galleries in New York, a good pair of carved walnut *fauteuils* brought $240, a matching pair brought the same price, and a matching *canapé* brought $275. At the Fonda sale held at the same auction gallery on November 26 and 27 of the same year, a mahogany writing table 57 inches long brought the extremely low price of $67.50, a pair of white and gold *fauteuils* brought $95 and a walnut commode brought $100.

At the Dalva sale in May 1939 at the Parke-Bernet Galleries, eight mahogany chairs with inlaid brass brought $180—a little over $20 a chair. Prices had declined to the 100 percent level.

By 1950 prices had risen very materially and stood at 300 percent, although it must be remembered that dollar-wise such items did not represent any great investment; and compared with many other types of antiques, *Directoire* furniture was still at an inconsequential level.

At the Count Rochefoucauld sale at the Parke-Bernet Galleries May 16 and 17, 1952, an acajou commode with a marble top brought $350.

By 1955 prices were up a little more. At the April 22 and 23 Faucigny-Lucinge sale in New York, a pair of carved and gilded *fauteuils* attributed to Jacob brought $550, and on November 12 a pair of carved and painted side chairs brought $360. A similar pair brought $300. Prices were now at the 500 percent level. Three years later at a French auction a *canapé*, a pair of small sofas and six *fauteuils* stamped G. Jacob brought 1,850,000 francs (around $4,000).

By 1960 prices were up to 600 percent. At the September 23 sale held at the

Painted *Directoire bergère*.   Parke-Bernet, 1960, $225.

Parke-Bernet Galleries, a painted *bergère* brought $225 and an acajou and ebony tric-trac table brought $500. A pair of *fauteuils* brought $420.

In 1965 the same gallery sold a carved and painted commode of plain design for $250. A good commode could be bought for under $1,000. We bought what amounted to a wreck at about the same time for $350 and restored it at a cost of $150. It was no great work of art, and most of the *Directoire* commodes sold today are in this category. A fine one of Louis XVI quality and excellence of design might bring up to $5,000 in New York. The 1965 index stood at 700 percent.

Directoire Prices

Date	1920 Equals 100%	1925 Equals 100%	1950 Equals 100%
1920	100%		
1925	100	100%	
1929	200	200	
1932	150	150	
1939	100	100	
1950	300	300	100%
1955	500	500	167
1960	600	600	200
1965	700	700	233

FRENCH EMPIRE SALON.   *Courtesy Chicago Art Institute and Mrs. James Ward Thorne.*

CHAPTER NINE

Empire
1804–1815

THE EMPIRE FROM WHICH THIS PERIOD takes its name is the empire of Napoleon Bonaparte who reigned from 1804 to 1815. In actuality the empire did not exist after Napoleon was consigned to the island of Elba in 1814. But, as is well known, he managed to get off the island, return to France, raise armies and very nearly reestablish himself as emperor. In 1815 he and his empire were completely finished when he lost the battle of Waterloo.

The Empire style originated a little earlier than the actual period of the Napoleonic Empire, however. Napoleon had been made First Consul of France in 1799, and he held this office until 1804 when he was crowned Emperor. In this interim period not only he but his style of decoration were becoming dominant.

The Empire style is to a great degree the style that Napoleon ordered the furnituremakers—all of them—to make. It is primarily "furniture style by fiat." The story of the establishment of this style almost by royal command is an interesting one, and it helps tremendously to keep the characteristics of the style in mind.

Interim Furniture—Louis XVI to Empire

The Louis XVI style depended on the ancient Greek motifs for decoration and for some form. The civilized world, including the artistic world, became so impressed with the excavation of objects that were essentially Greek that the entire Louis XVI style was called the Greek or Grecian style. But the style was by no means all Greek in its derivation, not even in the derivation of its ornamentation. It included Roman and even Egyptian motifs and forms.

Just after the middle of the eighteenth century a number of publications on ancient art and decoration appeared. It must always be remembered that the publication of a seemingly authoritative book on a new subject secures a good deal of attention. And these books were more than authoritative and informative. They could be put to a useful purpose—the creation of furniture as well as art and architecture. Such publications contributed to the origins of the Louis XVI style. But they also represent the beginning of the "Egyptian" style since Egyptian motifs were also presented, although the Egyptian styles were certainly not in the majority, and they were not stressed at this time.

Buildings constructed in the late eighteenth century were more like Greek temples than modern buildings of the period. Artists stressed scenes from antiquity and writers used classical themes. Even women's dresses in the later part of the eighteenth century became Grecian. Mme. Recamier was not dressed in diaphanous clothing simply to show off her figure; this was the elegant dress for women of the time. The classical motifs of Greece were greatly overdone, just as the over-ornamentation and extreme styles of the Louis XV Period led to a reaction in the form of the Grecian pattern and the simpler, straight lines and more sober ornamentation of the Louis XVI Period.

The stage was now set for a new style of furniture. The mushrooming of books on the subject of ancient cultures did provide something about ancient Egypt, and these Egyptian forms were used before the Napoleonic conquests:

Half-human and half-animal figures or gods and goddesses
Animal forms
Human feet
Trophies
Swags
Wreaths

The painter Jacques-Louis David was of strategic importance in the development of the Empire style, which to a great degree is synonymous with Egyptian style.

Prior to the storming of the Bastille and the Terror, which began in 1789, David was painting classical subjects, both Greek and Roman. He had the leading *menuisier*, Georges Jacob, copy ancient illustrations in the construction of furniture. David then used this furniture as props in the painting of his pictures with classical subjects. In the Terror David became a political figure, and his paintings came to be identified with the Revolution and the triumph of justice.

In 1786 two prominent French architects, Charles Percier and Pierre Fontaine, visited Rome and studied classical styles. David became impressed with their work and introduced them to Napoleon. By 1799 they had become the leading architects in France. When Napoleon approved their work and the style they advocated, the Empire style was born. Obviously David, Percier, Fontaine and Napoleon all had to be thinking along the same lines.

The entire purpose of the Empire style appears to be the glorification of Napoleon. The emphasis was not entirely spontaneous on the part of the populace or on the part of the furnituremakers. It was the express wish of Napoleon to have "the furniture of glory" built. Jacques-Louis David was thoroughly in accord with this lofty purpose.

Characteristics of the Empire Style

1. The lightness of the Louis XVI furniture disappeared. Empire furniture was predominantly heavy and had a massive appearance that in a way suggested grandeur.

2. Mahogany was the dominant wood and was not used sparingly.

3. Not only was heavy mahogany used, but there were large flat surfaces of mahogany that emphasized the wood rather than the decoration on the wood.

4. In 1810, however, Napoleon banned the use of mahogany for royal furniture. This edict set the style in woods for furniture generally, and the furnituremakers turned to oak, olive, beech, box and lemonwood.

5. The curved leg was used, but the Empire curved legs are not like earlier types of French legs. The rear legs of chairs often curve backwards and the front legs curve frontwards. Sometimes the reverse pattern is used, the front legs curving downwards and the rear legs curving downwards too.

6. The backs of chairs are also curved. The most common is the lateral curve of the back to enclose the sitter. The backs also have a tendency near the tops to flare back in a flourish. On the side chairs the seats are sometimes curved with a high point just under the sitter's knee. There is really a double curve with a low point under his posterior.

7. The legs and arms of chairs are thick. Thus the furniture is not fragile as it often was under the Louis'.

8. A change took place in the construction of furniture. The earlier standard procedure for making joints was to use a dowel, a cylindrical piece of wood running from one member to another to hold both in place. Glue was now substituted for the dowels, resulting in neater construction.

9. Colored marble came into general use. In the earlier eighteenth century white marble had been preferred.

10. Heavy satins were used for upholstering to an increasing extent.

11. Decorative elements were as important as the structure in characterizing the Empire style:

    A. Egyptian heads with headcloths (on legs and supports)

    B. Sphinx heads

    C. Swan heads with curved necks and the heads resting on the breast

    D. The heads of griffins (on legs and supports)

    E. Caryatids (draped female forms) as supports (particularly for the tops of smaller tables)

    F. Wreaths of oak leaves tied with ribbons and garlands

    G. Poppies, clover, pine cones and myrtle

    H. Marine horses

    I. Sirens

    J. Mythological monsters

    K. Horns of plenty

    L. Tripods

    M. Amphorae (long egg-shaped vases with long narrow necks and two long handles rising to the neck)

    N. Palm leaves

    O. Human figures such as Victory with a trumpet or palms, or figures dancing

    P. Lion noses, bees, butterflies, eagles and swans

Q. Winged torches
R. Stars
S. Gorgon heads and heads of Hermes
T. Masks of Bacchus

New Forms of Furniture

In this era the mahogany pedestal-base round table became common. This is an article of furniture made of solid mahogany. It was copied in the Victorian era and made in large volume.

The sleigh bed also came into common use at this time. Both head and foot are very high and flair outward at the top. New York art dealer Spencer Samuels has for many years owned a Napoleon sleigh bed. This type of piece sometimes offers great problems to modern owners because of its size. Auctioneer Edward O'Reilly once offered a fine gilded sleigh bed for sale, but he added (and several times) that the bed was made in one piece. It was apparently of solid wood, and the headboard and footboard would not come off. Mr. O'Reilly warned that the bed would probably not fit through an ordinary door! This type of bed was also made in the Victorian era out of polished mahogany or mahogany veneer.

Empire *acajou fauteuil*, with bronze mounts, by Jacob Frères, with the inventory number of Fontainebleau. *Courtesy of Dalva Brothers, New York.*

A characteristic type of dressing table mirror was made in the Empire Period. It had a drawer beneath the mirror, bronze candle holders and was shield-shaped. Another innovation was the very large floor mirror known as the *Grand Mirror à la Psyche*. It too had bronze candle holders.

Mahogany bookcases with glass doors in the upper part came into vogue. Also, large round tables with three legs became popular, the three legs being in the form of griffins or other animal or human forms.

Furnituremakers of the Empire Period

The history of styles of French furniture from Louis XV through Louis XVI, the *Directoire*, the Consulate and the Empire can be traced in the furniture produced by just one family—that of Georges Jacob.

Georges, Sr., spanned most of the major styles that existed in France. He began under Louis XV and even made furniture for the royal family at this time. He was apparently the chief chairmaker to Louis XVI and Marie Antoinette. Through his friendship with the great painter and Republican Jacques-Louis David, he made the transition to the period of the Terror and went through that and into the *Directoire* Period. He, as much as anyone, carried out the wishes of Napoleon for a characteristic Empire style. These wishes were expressed through David and through the Royal Architects Percier and Fontaine. Just prior to the Empire Period he worked in the Consulate style (from 1799 to 1804 when the Empire was founded).

This is at least one example of a furnituremaker who could make the transition from each dominant style to the next one and at the same time become the dominant figure in the industry, or at least the chairmaking portion of the industry. Such performance is almost never given by anyone in any branch of the arts.

Whereas Caffiéri was the great metalworker of the time of Louis XV and Gouthière occupied this position in the Louis XVI era, the great designer of metal in the Empire Period was Pierre-Philippe Thomire. His bronze work was in no way inferior to that of the earlier bronziers, and it is in great demand on today's market. While one may well criticize the furniture of this period for being too heavy and cumbersome in appearance and perhaps more poorly constructed than the furniture of the Louis', one cannot so criticize the bronze work, which was excellent.

Prices of French Empire Furniture

Prior to the decade of the 1950's, and particularly the late 1950's, Empire furniture was not in demand—even in France. As an interesting sidelight, and nothing more, we can record prices of some Empire pieces sold in the year we have used as a base—1925. On March 17, 1925, the American Art Association sold a dining suite in amboyna wood and *cuivre doré*. It consisted of a circular extension table, a sideboard, a serving table, ten side chairs and two armchairs.

The entire set brought $220. In the same sale a good amboyna wood cabinet with *cuivre doré* brought $70, and on March 21 a mahogany armchair brought $55 (decorated in *cuivre doré*), a mahogany cabinet in *cuivre doré* brought $55, and an Empire *style* cabinet to match brought $50. Apparently the fine appearance of the item was what was worth the price, not the antique character.

Until the 1950's Empire furniture did not attract any consistent market notice. We can thus start the index in 1950 at 100 percent. At the Count Rochefoucauld sale held at the Parke-Bernet Galleries on May 16 and 17, 1952, a pair of Empire acajou *fauteuils* with *bronze doré* and sphinx motifs brought $1,100. Another pair of similar *fauteuils*, but stamped Jacob Frères, brought $1,500. A matching pair brought $950, and a third matching pair brought $400. It is somewhat unusual for the price of successive matching pairs of any kind of chairs to fall off so greatly in price.

By 1955 there was no material rise in the price of Empire furniture. On February 26 the Parke-Bernet Galleries sold a pair of acajou side chairs for $240.

In the February 1957 issue, the French magazine *Connaissance* commented, "In recent years Empire, Restoration and Second Empire (mid-Victorian) have come successively into fashion."

On March 26, 1958, the Charpentier Galleries in Paris sold a commode with the stamp of Heckel for 960,000 francs ($2,240).

By 1960 prices had doubled as compared with 1950 (and there was little price rise between 1950 and 1955).

The June 1961 *Connaissance* comments, "The Murat Sale has raised the prices of Empire furniture. In recent years the rise in price of Nineteenth Century furniture has been commented on. The recent Murat sale has confirmed and indeed emphasized this movement. Certain pieces of Empire furniture of the finest quality

French Empire *bureau plat*. Parke-Bernet, 1960, $1,200.

One of a pair of Empire side chairs. Parke-Bernet, 1955, $240.

One of a pair of French Empire *bergères*.   Parke-Bernet, 1966, $800.   (*Photo: Taylor & Dull*)

Napoleon I *fauteuil de cabinet*, from the Fribourg Collection.   Sotheby's, 1963, $2,800.

fetched prices quite as high as Eighteenth Century pieces of equivalent quality would have done. The rarity of very fine pieces of Empire furniture—the period when they were produced was relatively short—can only contribute to maintaining this situation. At the same time pieces of this period, but of more ordinary quality, are also showing signs of rising in value."

The comment of *Connaissance* was well made. In June 1961 a cabinet veneered with mahogany with gilt bronzes and two plaques, 49 inches wide, sold for $4,910, and a pair of dressers with gilt bronze caryatids brought $6,830 the pair. These were of course the very finest Empire pieces and not the run of the mill type that usually appears on the market.

In October 1963 the Fribourg auction sold a desk with alterations for $1,977. At about the same time a circular *guéridon* with a marble top on a gilt metal trellis brought £1,500 ($4,200), while a pair of mahogany *bergères* with sphinxes of the slightly earlier Consulate period brought £2,300 ($6,440). More ordinary items brought lower prices. On November 26, 1964, Christie's sold a small mahogany console table with human head designs for the equivalent of $442.

In the fall of 1965 an excellent French Empire table was sold privately. It was not elaborately ornamented but was trimmed with bronze and had a circular gray hand-beveled marble top which was original. There was a central column ending in three horizontal legs. It was purchased by the Sheldon Farbers of New York from a collector for under $1,000.

Ordinary Empire furniture is not a rarity on the market, and in New York such furniture appears with some regularity not only in the Parke-Bernet Galleries, but in other auctions as well. Although this furniture is only now coming into vogue —at least the simpler pieces—there is much of it that is definitely *not* of the period and was produced later than the actual Empire Period of the early 1800's. One auction-house official commented about some of these questionable pieces being offered by his firm, "They don't look period to me, but you can be sure the dealer who buys them will offer them as absolutely of the period."

By 1965 the price index had risen to 500 percent as compared with 200 percent

One of a set of four Empire side chairs.   Parke-Bernet, 1966, $640.

in 1960 and 100 percent in 1955 and 1950. Empire furniture was on the way up!

At the notable July 1, 1966, sale held at Sotheby's in London, a fine Empire *fauteuil de cabinet* which was in the Fribourg sales of 1963 brought $2,800. In Paris in the summer of 1966 several good Empire pieces were offered for sale. Ten chairs made by Jacob (four arm and six side) were priced at $6,000—$600 a chair for excellent furniture. A pair of armchairs was offered at $6,500, while six more ordinary chairs were offered at $3,000—$500 a chair.

In Antwerp, Belgium, in the same season a side table was offered at the very low price of $150. Prices of all antiques in Antwerp were lower than in the other major cities, and the dealers explained that the residents did not purchase high-priced furniture.

In one of the earliest sales of the 1966–1967 season, the Parke-Bernet Galleries in New York sold an excellent pair of Empire mahogany *bergères*. They were fairly large and had rollover top rails and turned armrests supported by carved figures of swans. There were gilded bronze appliqués on the seat rails, legs and crest rail. The chairs were covered in green silk taffeta in good condition. The pair brought the low price of $800. One gallery official remarked that for some reason she was hearing a number of remarks that might indicate that Empire furniture was not preferred that season.

French Empire Prices

Date	1950 Equals 100%
1950	100%
1955	100
1960	200
1965	500

FRENCH PROVINCIAL.   *Courtesy of Mr. James Le Pere, New York.*

CHAPTER TEN

French Provincial
1715–1850

ALTHOUGH FRENCH PROVINCIAL FURNITURE is certainly related to the leading furniture styles of France and is based on those styles, it belongs in a class of its own. It forms an extremely large group of items which are more related to each other than to the leading styles. Market-wise it forms a distinctly separate group of furniture. Finally, the appearance of the furniture which we classify as provincial, or country, is considerably different from the leading French styles. The furniture made in the provinces in the exact city style, and which can hardly be told from city furniture, is now considered city furniture and will not be discussed here. We are concerned in this chapter with that charming style of French country furniture made in the provinces in the eighteenth (and into the nineteenth) century.

Louis XIV established the Gobelins plant at the end of the seventeenth century. Foreign workmen were imported to staff this plant, and they had been brought to France even before this time by Cardinal Mazarin, advisor to Louis XIII. But by the end of the seventeenth century the knowledge of furnituremaking as well as of other decorative arts had been absorbed by Frenchmen, and the staff at the Gobelins plant had become almost completely French.

With the guild system centered in Paris, with the Gobelins plant which was under royal sponsorship located in Paris, with discrimination against non-Parisian applicants for membership in the Paris guilds, and with royal orders placed for the most part with the Paris masters, it is to be expected that Paris would quickly become the center of fine furniture manufacture. Even great foreign masters such as David Roentgen became members of the Paris guild.

Origin of the French Provincial Style

French provincial furniture came on the scene at the beginning of the eighteenth century. Before that time the furniture was so simple in design and construction and so limited in variety of pieces that it was not readily distinguishable from primitive furniture of other European countries. It was certainly far removed from what is known today as "French provincial furniture."

The early simple and crudely made items were chiefly stools, beds, chests and tables consisting of saw horses with planks across them. These were known as trestle tables. From the end of the seventeenth century, Italian, Dutch and Flemish furniture was imported into France and was used as a pattern for much of the locally made French furniture for many decades, even as late as the eighteenth century.

The Louis XIII style was a Paris style, as were the later Louis XIV, Louis XV and Louis XVI styles. The Louis XIII style was, however, not a distinctly French style—it was reminiscent of Italian and Flemish furniture of the same period. (The era of Louis XIII was 1601 to 1643.)

Although the Louis XIII style was copied in the provinces, it was copied chiefly for the homes of the more well-to-do and not for the great mass of population, the peasants. Toward the end of the seventeenth century, cupboards and wardrobes based on Louis XIII designs began to make their appearance in peasant cottages. Chairs, stools, benches and tables in the Louis XIII style followed.

While the Louis XIV style was certainly known by provincial furnituremakers,

Section of French provincial room. *Courtesy of Mr. James Le Pere, New York.*

this style was little copied there. It was a pompous furniture, at least in the eyes of the rural dwellers—formal and sumptuous. This style was generally bypassed, and the Louis XIII furniture in the provinces was replaced by the next Paris style —Louis XV.

The Louis XV style quickly took hold in the provinces and became dominant everywhere. The pieces produced by the provincial cabinetmakers were well and sturdily made, the wood was durable, they were fairly graceful, and the decoration was suited to the times and to the provincial location. This was not the furniture of the king, the nobles or the high mercantile classes. It was the adaptation of this fine furniture to rural locations for people of modest means.

Strangely enough, when the Louis XVI style replaced the Louis XV style in Paris, this new style never caught on in the provinces. The cabinetmakers there continued to make furniture in the Louis XV style.

The beginning collector of antique furniture is likely to identify a rural piece as "clearly Louis XV" when it might just as well have been produced in the Louis XVI era or even later. The only concession to the Louis XVI style, as far as provincial furniture is concerned, was slightly fewer curves, reminiscent of the Transition style rather than the Louis XVI style, plus the use of a few classical ornaments. Although a straight line is certainly easier to make than a curved line, the straight lines of the Paris Louis XVI style were supplemented by finely done ornamentation, so that the furniture of the Louis XVI Period looks as elegant as that of Louis XV. But without this fine ornamentation a provincial Louis XVI style would be a retrogression, and the end result would have been less desirable furniture. This is possibly the reason for the indefinite continuation of the Louis XV style in the provinces. Then too, there is the element of inertia, particularly in the country where innovators made their way to the cities. It is easier to keep on making the same old thing than to make something new.

For similar reasons the rural cabinetmakers did not adopt the *Directoire* style and did not even adopt the Empire style. One wonders what improvement in rural furniture, if any, would have taken place if the rural makers of furniture had stopped making the old Louis XV style and made *Directoire* and Empire pieces in the rural style. There is little evidence that the Revolutionary and Napoleonic styles are in any respect superior to the Louis XV and Louis XVI styles. In fact, the later styles are generally inferior. The inertia of the rural makers may thus mean that we have a heritage of many more good antiques than we would have had if they had been more progressive.

Because the Louis XV style was the style of the provinces from the era of Louis XV through the *Directoire*, through the Empire and into the Restoration Period, it is extremely difficult to date this furniture when it appears on the market. Eighteenth-century furniture in general is worth more than nineteenth-century furniture, but French provincial is in something of a class by itself—a simple, rural eighteenth- nineteenth-century style, and its value tends to be pulled down because it was made well into the latter century.

Characteristics of French Provincial Furniture

1. The color was predominantly dark. This is in contradistinction to the light colors of the natural woods, inlaid woods and painted pieces of the Paris styles of the eighteenth century.
2. The woods used were often elm, walnut, beech and wild cherry. Some fruitwoods were also used, such as pear, plum, apricot and cherry. Mahogany was used only in the finer rural furniture.
3. The pieces were, for the most part, solid and not veneered.
4. Upholstery was little used on chairs and settees. Tie-on cushions for seats and backs were used.
5. Fabrics were simple—wool, silk plus wool, printed and painted cottons and linen, and gros point needlework on canvas.
6. The furniture was vastly more comfortable than the peasant furniture which it replaced and the Louis XIII provincial items.
7. The chief decoration was moldings. In the latter part of the eighteenth century wood-carving became more popular.
8. One of the most characteristic elements of the French provincial style was the more restrained curve than that found in the Paris Louis XV furniture.
9. As compared with the Paris furniture, the rural furniture was larger and much heavier in appearance. These elements also made for greater utility.
10. Entirely new pieces were offered in more or less abundance:

    A. *Canapés* with loose cushions
    B. Capuchine chaises (a simple open armchair or side chair with an open back and straw or rush seat)
    C. Buffets

French Provincial fruitwood game table. Parke-Bernet, 1965, $500.

French Provincial walnut commode. Parke-Bernet, 1965, $700.

Late Louis XV provincial oak commode.   Parke-Bernet, 1966, $750.   (*Photo: Taylor & Dull*)

Mid-eighteenth-century French Provincial commode of *bombé* form.   Parke-Bernet, 1966, $700.   (*Photo: Taylor & Dull*)

    D. *Armoires*
    E. *Dressoirs*
    F. Hanging wall shelves
    G. Small tables
    H. Corner cupboards
    I. Secretary slant-front commodes
    J. Provincial simpler forms of the city commodes
    K. Tall clocks

11. Steel and brass mounts were used, and fret-pierced escutcheon plates and buttress hinges were made of wrought steel.

Price History of French Provincial Furniture

One of the most poorly recorded price histories is that of French provincial furniture. The reason, of course, is that this furniture has never in recent times been popular enough to command prices which would make the furniture worthy of being illustrated in the auction house sales catalogues, and while the leading dealers sometimes carry such pieces, they are not featured and they do not bring prices comparable with "prime merchandise."

French provincial furniture has in general not sold in the thousands of dollars. It is characteristically in the hundreds. If we go back to the peak year prior to the Depression—1929—we find a fruitwood shaped commode, 38 inches high and

French Provincial *bureau plat* of the eighteenth century. Parke-Bernet, 1966, $2,300. (*Photo: Taylor & Dull*)

50 inches long, selling for $210 in New York. In the same year a cerisier* wood serpentine-shaped commode sold for $200, and a mahogany and kingwood commode of block and serpentine form brought $135. An eighteenth-century lady's secretary with slant top and cabriole legs of merisier** wood brought $115.

If we jump from 1929 to 1950, well past the end of the war, we find a walnut and oak commode, 48 inches long, selling for $200. Prices had not changed much overall in 21 years, and the prices were so low as to be of little significance in the international antique market, or in the leading auction houses of any city for that matter.

By 1955 prices had doubled as compared with 1950 (and 1929), and in New York a carved walnut and beech commode brought $500.

By 1960 prices had risen only a little and were now at the 250 percent level compared with 200 percent in 1955 (based on the year 1950 as 100 percent). A walnut serpentine-front commode sold in New York for $750, but a restored one sold the next month for $275.

By 1965 prices had risen to 300 percent. On April 23, 1965, the Parke-Bernet Galleries sold a walnut serpentine-shaped commode, 52½ inches long, with imperfections, for $700. A fruitwood game table brought $500.

In the fall of 1966 (the beginning of the 1966–1967 season) a few indications of a rise in French provincial prices were noted. On September 24, 1966, the Parke-Bernet Galleries offered a late Louis XV provincial oak commode for sale. It was not a fine piece of furniture but it realized $750, a high price in light of earlier prices for such pieces. The next week the same gallery offered a mid-eighteenth century commode of *bombé* shape. It realized $700, and a dealer bought it. The price was a little on the high side in comparison with prices of the preceeding season. One item was a real surprise, however. It was a very plainly designed provincial *bureau plat*, five feet long, with restorations. The Parke-Bernet price estimate on it was $600 to $800. It realized $2,300!

The 1966–1967 early season prices compared to the 1965–1966 prices indicates that the trend to French provincial is continuing and that prices are consequently up materially. But while there is some demand for French provincial furniture, it is demand at a low price. The furniture is securing some popularity with recent converts to antiques, and this demand will no doubt grow in the future.

French Provincial Prices

Date	1950 Equals 100%
1929	100%
1950	100
1955	200
1960	250
1965	300

*Cultivated cherry.
**Wild cherry.

CHAPTER ELEVEN

Renaissance Italian
1400–1700

RENAISSANCE TECHNICALLY MEANS REBIRTH. While an entire chapter could be devoted to a description of the Renaissance and its significance for the future of Europe and the world, it will not be necessary in a book on antique furniture to go very deeply into the scientific and philosophical implications of this great movement. It is enough to point out that in the Middle Ages which preceded the Renaissance (lasting from about 400 A.D., the approximate date of the fall of the Roman Empire, to the beginning of the Renaissance) there was very little progress of any sort. Few frontiers were being pushed forward along any line until a few hundred years before the Renaissance began. But with the beginning of the Renaissance, progress went into high gear—scientific, exploratory and geographic, astronomical, philosophical and artistic progress, including innovations in furniture. Considering the length of the Middle Ages and the almost total lack of progress in those centuries, the Renaissance represents an unbelievable rate of change.

The artistic changes that took place in the Renaissance are divided into pictorial art (or simply art), sculpture and architecture (including furniture and decoration). The most significant progress took place in art; but all of these artistic categories developed *pari passu* and were to a great extent interdependent.

No country pioneered in art throughout the entire Renaissance as did Italy. Every major forward step was taken by Italy; and although other countries certainly produced top quality artists and paintings and most certainly did pioneer, the most consistent pioneer from the time of Giotto to the nineteenth century was Italy.

Technically, the Renaissance covers the fourteenth through the sixteenth centuries, but fourteenth-century furniture is all but nonexistent, and the same type furniture was made through the seventeenth century.

As was stated previously, fine furniture usually accompanies fine times. There must be an excess of wealth, a wealthy class, and relative freedom from fear of war and invasion for the amenities of living, including fine furniture, to receive emphasis. Renaissance furniture was no exception.

ITALIAN RENAISSANCE ROOM. *Courtesy of French & Company, New York.*

Probably the type of Renaissance furniture closest to Italian is Spanish, and after the Battle of Pavia in 1525 when Spain defeated Italy and began a period of domination of Italy, there was much reason for the art and furniture of the two countries to be even more alike. But the furniture of France during the Renaissance was also much like Italian Renaissance furniture. We actually once purchased a beautiful bambocci cabinet (cabinet-on-cabinet) without knowing positively whether it was French or Italian. The dealer, who had handled antique furniture for over fifty years, was not quite certain either.

Emphasis on Italian Renaissance Furniture

The emphasis on Renaissance furniture in this book will be on Italian furniture, because Italian is essentially the pioneering furniture of the Renaissance and it is by far the most traded Renaissance furniture on the international market.

The quality of construction and carving on the furniture of the Italian Renaissance is the equal of the art and architecture of the period. It is the finest and most artistic furniture that could be made at that time. While it is true that in the eighteenth century a high degree of beauty and ornamentation was secured while comfort was all important, and while light colors and gay rich fabrics were used, the furniture of the Italian Renaissance still holds its own artistically, even though it was made as early as the fifteenth century.

Italian Renaissance furniture is based on classical motifs of Roman origin. This is not the Rome of the Renaissance, but the Rome of the beginning of the Christian era as interpreted by Renaissance artisans from ancient buildings and excavations. It is also based on Greek motifs of the Pre-Christian era. Renaissance furniture-makers used Greek motifs because they were the basis of antique Roman art and architecture, and because many of the items unearthed in the diggings were actually Greek items made by Greek colonies in Italy. In the eighteenth century these Italian diggings which unearthed Herculaneum and Pompeii as well as other communities were so significant for all of Europe that they formed the basis of the dominant furniture style of Europe known as the Louis XVI style. Thus we have Renaissance Italian furniture based on the antique style, and the much later Louis XVI French furniture based on the same style. Furnituremaking, like so many other things, did not develop in a straight line from the primitive to the highly developed, but rather moved in a cycle that to a great extent was a recurring one.

Characteristics of Renaissance Furniture

The Renaissance covers an extremely long period, and it is to be expected that during this period characteristic Renaissance furniture designs changed. They did. Yet the changes were hardly so great that the Renaissance furniture cannot be categorized.

A further fact of tremendous importance is that there was no Italy as such until after the middle of the nineteenth century. The area that is now Italy was composed of a number of independent countries which often fought each other. The leading countries (city-states) were Venice, Florence, Rome, Siena, Perugia, Milan and Naples.

The Renaissance started in Florence, and most early artistic strides were made there, but the highest degree of magnificence in all branches of art was probably achieved by Venice. It is important to realize that Venetian art is different from Florentine art, and both are different from, say, Sienese art. An antique furniture specialist can fairly easily and accurately identify the city of origin of a piece of Italian Renaissance furniture. Yet all Italian furniture, regardless of city of origin, has a good number of common characteristics:

1. Dark walnut wood.
2. Rectangular pieces of furniture. With the exception of some chests (*cassoni*) and some folding chairs, the pattern of the furniture of the Renaissance is almost all starkly rectangular and generally unrelieved by curves.
3. Architectural design. The predominant architecture of the Renaissance is based on classical motifs, mainly early Roman and Greek. If one took the Greek Parthenon, scaled it down and converted it into walnut, this model might well have been used for Renaissance furniture. The fronts of pieces of furniture look like the fronts of classical buildings, and this is certainly one of the most characteristic features and identifying elements of Renaissance furniture. Of enormous importance in Renaissance architecture was Andrea Palladio (1518–1580). His architectural designs were used as the basis of much of the furniture of the period, and it was natural that it took on a certain architectural quality. In the Queen Anne Period (1702–1714) and in the era of George I (1714–1727), Andrea Palladio again became the dominant element in architectural design—this time in England. The finest mansions and much of the furniture of this later period again took on the character of architecture. Thus furniture design moved in a cycle.
4. Carving as the primary ornamental element.
5. Upholstery, often silk—velvet of cut silk, satin brocades and silk embroidery. Upholstery was generally thick and extremely rich and elaborate in appearance.
6. Generally large and extremely impressive pieces. Very few items are inconspicuous or unobtrusive. Even the smaller pieces have a certain magnificence suggesting the "throne room."
7. Horizontal effect of the furniture. Some of the design elements which contribute to this effect are pilasters, cornices, pediments and moldings.
8. Simplicity of design and classic proportions.
9. Intricate decoration:

> A. Intarsia. This is inlay work in woods of several colors and was a major element of furniture design introduced at this time. This is much more than a simple inlay to provide contrast and relief. The inlays are extremely elaborate and in the form of garden scenes, landscapes, figures, etc.

B. Certosina work. This is inlay work in ivory and bone designed to make a variety of patterns. This work probably originated in Cairo and is still used in furniture, boxes, etc. imported from the East.

C. *Pietra dura*. This is a form of inlay work of cut and polished semiprecious stones set directly in dark wood.

D. Pastiglia work. This is a paste very much like the gesso used on paintings, and it is a good medium for carving.

E. Painting. This method of modification of the surface of the wood tends to relieve the very dark heaviness of the aged walnut.

F. Gilding. This process also relieves the dark wood, and it was sometimes used along with paint to liven up the otherwise heavy pieces.

G. Inlays of mother-of-pearl, exotic woods, tortoiseshell, metals and gilded bronze appliqués.

H. Moldings. As the Renaissance progressed these moldings came into greater use and became much more prominent.

I. Turnings. These too progressed along with the Renaissance and continued to develop in the century following the Renaissance.

10. Decorative motifs. Some of these are flowers, rosettes, scrolls and festoons, as well as figures such as cupids, dolphins and satyrs.

The Gamut of Renaissance Pieces

The most important piece of Renaissance furniture was the *cassone*. Throughout the Renaissance the importance of this piece gradually diminished, and by the end of the Renaissance it was not in such great demand. Essentially this is the forerunner of the cedar chest or hope chest of early American history. A smaller version of the *cassone* is called the *cassette*. This is a rather old piece of furniture going back to the Middle Ages and is not found much in today's antique market.

Probably the next most important piece of Renaissance furniture is the *credenza*. This is a rectangular-shaped, horizontal piece of furniture in which the length exceeds the height. The top is flat and underneath is a row of two or three drawers. Under the drawers are two or three doors, the number of doors being the same as the number of drawers. Inside the doors is storage space and the *credenza* makes an excellent sideboard for a dining room today. The carving on the face or front of a good *credenza* is often a work of art, and the later the *credenza* the more elaborate the carving, as a general rule.

The *credenzina* is a small *credenza*, as the name implies. It has either one or two cupboard doors. For modern homes and apartments a piece of this size is an excellent item of furniture. Such pieces do appear on the market—almost always bringing more money than the larger *credenza*.

Certainly what would be considered the most important piece of furniture from today's point of view is the chest-of-drawers, which appeared toward the end of the sixteenth century. This is almost exactly the same as its counterpart today, and a typical chest of drawers of the Renaissance Period has two small top drawers over three long bottom ones.

The typical table which was of greatest use in the Renaissance is called a refectory table because it was originally used in the refectory or dining room of a monastery. In form it is a typical dining table of trestle design. It is most surprising that tables of such beauty, usefulness and durability are no more in demand than they are—they can often be purchased at minor auctions for less than $200.

An excellent variation of this refectory table was developed in this period. It was known as the draw-top table, and it is the forerunner of the dining table with leaves. When the ends are pulled apart the leaves slide into place on runners and the size of the table is greatly increased. This principle of attached leaves has been used again and again by the mass production furniture industry.

Late in the fifteenth century the center table (occasional table) was developed. This is generally a smaller table than the refectory table and is not of the long variety. The top is round, square, hexagonal or octagonal. One type of occasional table has a center shaft from which radiate elaborately carved and heavy supports. This is a good design and quite elaborate, but it has the appearance of being very heavy and sometimes cumbersome. An alternate design has four legs and still another has eight, all joined at the bottom by a runner extending completely around the bottom of the legs.

Although the slant-front desk was certainly characteristic of England in the eighteenth century, the Renaissance had its own slant-front design. The front panel opened to reveal writing compartments, and in the main body of the desk were drawers. This piece evolved into the beautiful Italian lacquered desk of the eighteenth century.

The Renaissance had its own form of writing table known as the *bancone*. The rectangular top is placed over two drawers, and under these is a recessed part containing more drawers. It was a very useful piece of furniture at the time and still has use, although few such pieces are available today.

Another piece of writing furniture that is often one of the greatest works of art is the writing cabinet. This is the forerunner of the secretary bureau of eighteenth-century England. It is a tall piece of furniture and consists of two halves. The upper half has a panel which opens to form a writing surface, revealing drawers and doors for writing materials, letter storage, etc. Under the writing panel are doors revealing an interior which can be used for storage.

One weakness of the early Renaissance furniture is that there were few chairs; stools, cassoni and benches had to serve the purpose as well as they could. The only real early chairs were those which resembled thrones and were used by top dignitaries of the time. The earliest chairs for common use were, strangely enough, a variety of folding chair. One type was called a Savonarola chair, after the Florentine monk of the same name, and the other was called a Dante chair after the poet.

A second type of chair in common use in the Renaissance, and one reproduced in later periods in great numbers, is the sgabello chair. This was essentially a small stool with a triangular or fan-shaped back made from one piece of wood. The seat is extremely small, and the legs are peculiar in that there are only two, a front one and a back one, but each leg is essentially a wide board. The front board slants forward and the back one backward. Sometimes between the seat and the "legs" is a space which may be used for a drawer. This chair is one of the most uncomfortable items of furniture to bear the name "chair," although it is of ornamental value.

The panchetto is even more primitive than the sgabello chair. It has three legs like a milking stool. The famous Strozzi chair that was sold in 1930 from the Albert Figdor Collection was a panchetto. It brought $23,500! *Antiques* magazine states (September 1930): "A much published item. Since it is a purely ceremonial piece, it must not be judged from the standpoint of comfort. Its beauty was hardly appreciated by the general public. . . ."

In the Renaissance another type of chair was developed that was more like chairs of later centuries except that it was more stark. The seat is square and absolutely flat. There are four conventional legs, and the two back rails rise straight up or else slant backward slightly. They are joined by one or more cross members which are often elaborately carved. We owned one of these chairs for many years, but it was so uninviting as far as comfort was concerned that we sold it.

In the sixteenth century an excellent modification of this general design was developed. Instead of the flat wooden seat there was a deep upholstered seat with the fabric and stuffing covering the front seat rail. Instead of cross members which join the back rails there was a large upholstered panel. There was also a folding armless chair called a monastery chair. Besides interlacing legs and side members, the seat was formed of such interlacing wooden pieces. This is the nearest thing to the folding chair of modern times that was probably ever produced in early eras. In addition, there were metal chairs in the Renaissance which with a little modification would resemble modern metal chairs. There are four iron legs which cross over at the seat, or beneath the seat, and form the side members. On top of the side members are brass knobs, and sometimes beneath these brass knobs are short turned brass rods. This chair is called a *faldistorium* or folding chair.

Wall mirrors were developed in the Renaissance, the mirror part being of polished metal. The mirror was covered with two doors when not in use, since the surface was not considered to be pleasing in appearance. The shape is nearly square, although round shapes are not unknown. The mercury mirror was developed in the sixteenth century, and this was an enormous improvement over the earlier metal mirrors which actually originated in the Middle Ages.

Renaissance beds are not much different from present-day beds. Prior to the sixteenth century beds were designed without legs, but in that century legs were added. The beds have a headboard and footboard, and considerable use was made of carving and other ornamentation. Posts were used as a design element; sometimes a tester was added, and often canopies were used.

All in all, Renaissance furniture is beautiful and often comfortable. The artisans who worked on the best furniture designed and carved with as much skill as the painters and sculptors of the time. Most of the furniture (except a few ornamental pieces) could be used today.

Unique Position of Renaissance Italian Furniture

Renaissance Italian furniture occupies a unique position in the antique world for several reasons. First, the price trend of this furniture is very different from that of antique furniture in general. Renaissance furniture had a particular vogue which started in the early part of this century and ended with the 1929 boom. One highly important sale in 1930 postponed not only the crash in this furniture but also the change in style away from it. The second reason is that Renaissance furniture has considerable value in certain markets and very little in others. In Italy it is treasured and brings very high prices. The same pieces in New York bring much less, despite the fact that Italian dealers buy in New York for shipment to their home country.

The third reason is that there is a vast difference between fine Italian Renaissance furniture and the run-of-the-mill Renaissance furniture that generally appears on the American market. The typical piece that usually appears is rather dark in color; of an awkward size; and has been replaced to the point of either being a fake or else is a reconstruction of several pieces, which of course amounts to a fake.

A really fine Dante or Savonarola chair is worth in four figures, but such chairs do not often appear in any market. The chairs of this type which do appear are either poor in design or else greatly restored.

Prices of Renaissance Furniture

The Hamilton Palace sale held in England in 1882 was noted for the excellence of the French pieces of furniture offered as well as for the tremendously high prices which these pieces fetched. Along with the French pieces, however, some Italian items were sold at reasonably high prices.

A most elegant Renaissance ebony architectural cabinet was sold for 860 guineas ($4,300). A companion piece brought $8,600.

From this date until 1916 few Renaissance pieces were featured in auctions, although they were certainly being bought by the great American industrialists to furnish their enormous mansions.

The Hotel Drouot in Paris on December 10, 1901, sold a carved walnut table that was said to have belonged to the Duke of Burgundy for the equivalent of $1,030.

In 1905 a seventeenth-century carved *cassone*, six feet six inches long, realized, £42 ($204). On February 9, 1911, Christie's sold two excellent *cassoni* for £94/10 and £73/10 ($458 and $357).

On June 22, 1914, Christie's sold a rather elaborate *cassone* for £15 ($73). The next year they sold a small walnut cabinet made in the seventeenth century for £13/2/6 (less than $65), and on March 5, 1915, the Anderson Galleries in New York sold two *cassoni* for $160 and $155.

If there was a trend up to this time it was not very noticeable, and since most of the pieces were low it was not very significant. However, in 1916 an event took place which placed an entirely different complexion on Renaissance Italian furniture and on the collecting of antiques in general. On November 21 to 27, 1916, the American Art Association Galleries in New York held the Elia Volpi sale of the furnishings of the Davanzati Palace in Florence.

The first item of note in this Volpi or Davanzati Palace sale was a large Tuscan center table of the sixteenth century. It realized $11,100. Two Dante chairs of the same period brought $5,500 each. A Bolognese walnut table of the sixteenth century brought $5,100, and a superb Bolognese walnut *armoire* brought $1,550. A walnut *credenza* from Lombardy—sixteenth century—brought $1,800, and two sixteenth-century walnut armchairs brought $1,340.

The Davanzati Palace sale is unique for several reasons. First, public auction prices had rarely reached such consistently high levels. Second, Renaissance furniture had not achieved such high prices at public auction before. And third, never before had so large a collection of first-line, museum-quality Renaissance pieces been sold at one time. For the last reason it is most difficult to judge how much prices of such furniture went up at this time. It is perhaps more meaningful to start the price trend at this point (1916) and see what happened to prices later.

Sixteenth-century Tuscan center table.   American Art Association, 1916, $11,100.

In 1919 the American Art Association held the Emil Pares sale. Some of the items sold were Renaissance Italian. Two velour armchairs from the sixteenth century brought $1,250, two seventeenth-century walnut armchairs brought $600, and a sixteenth-century walnut armchair brought $200. These prices were more in line with those prevailing prior to the 1916 Davanzati Palace sale.

During 1925 three Dante chairs were sold in New York for $280, $260 and $400, and a Savonarola chair was sold for $200. A settee and four armchairs brought $1,800, and an early sixteenth-century Tuscan refectory table, eight feet seven inches long, brought $200. An elaborately carved scrolled walnut library table brought $1,000 and two *credenzas* brought $350 each.

The next year saw a rise in prices of most antiques sold in New York, including Italian Renaissance furniture. Two Savonarola chairs brought $750 and $425, a pair of Dante chairs brought $650, and another such chair brought $250. A seventeenth-century carved walnut refectory table brought $725.

On January 20, 21 and 22, 1927, the American Art Association in New York held the Luigi Grassi sale at which a number of significantly high prices for Renaissance pieces was achieved. A beautiful walnut *cassone* from sixteenth-century Rome with carved figures brought $7,500. A Florentine table made in the first half of the sixteenth century, six feet three inches long, brought $6,300 and a

Sixteenth-century Italian walnut "Dante" chair.   American Art Association, 1916, $5,500.

Sienese carved walnut center table, six feet eleven inches long, *c.*1550, brought the same price. An early sixteenth-century Florentine plain carved walnut *credenza* brought $4,500.

Another Volpi sale was held March 31 to April 2, 1927, at the American Art Association. In this sale three Dante chairs brought $2,700, $3,000 and $3,000, and a Savonarola chair brought $2,700. A *credenzina* brought $2,000, and an early sixteenth-century Sienese carved walnut *cassone* brought $2,500.

In 1929 the American Art Association sold the collection of Count Pepoli. Some extremely high prices were realized. A sixteenth-century walnut cabinet table brought $8,200. Two separate pairs of sixteenth-century carved and parcel-gilded walnut side chairs brought $7,000 each. A finely carved walnut armorial *cassone* from Florence, *c.*1550, brought $4,400, and two fifteenth-century Dante chairs brought $2,800 each.

On November 23 of the same year, Christie's in London sold a fantastically fine sixteenth-century walnut *cassone*, elaborately carved, nine feet wide, for £4,620 ($22,453), a tremendous price even for a piece of this quality. On July 9, 1929, Christie's sold a sixteenth-century carved walnut table, 38 inches long, for £945 ($4,593).

By 1930 prices of Renaissance Italian furniture had begun to weaken, unlike the prices of some other antique furniture. At the Ambrose Monell sale held at the American-Anderson Galleries on November 28, 1930, an early sixteenth-century carved walnut and oak refectory table, nine feet long, was estimated by the gallery to bring between $1,500 and $3,000. It brought $325. A sixteenth-century sgabello

Carved walnut and parcel-gilded side chair. American Art Association, 1927, $25.

One of a pair of sixteenth-century Brussels tapestry, carved walnut state chairs. American Art Association, 1926, $2,800 the pair, and another pair at the same price.

chair brought $180, while a good carved walnut octagonal table, 54 inches wide, brought $1,000.

By 1932 prices were extremely low. On January 16, 1932, the American Art Association Galleries sold a late sixteenth-century Tuscan state table, a fine piece, for $325. A sixteenth-century Florentine carved walnut trestle table that had originally been sold by Duveen brought $625, while a Bolognese center table, *c.*1600, from French and Company brought just $170.

Some dismal prices were recorded in 1933 at the Thomas Fortune Ryan sale at the American-Anderson Galleries. A pair of Venetian carved walnut Savonarola chairs of the early sixteenth century brought $300 for the pair. A fine carved walnut *cassone* made in Florence in the sixteenth century brought $275, and a walnut *cassapanca* with an excellent background, from sixteenth-century Florence, brought $250. A sixteenth-century carved walnut *credenza* bearing the arms of the Sforza family brought $300. But a few prices in the sale were higher. An early sixteenth-century Ligurian carved walnut library table, nine feet four inches long, brought $830.

If prices were down in 1932 and 1933 as compared with the 1920's, they were still further down in 1939, after the Depression was passed and as the world embarked on World War II. On March 9, 1939, the Parke-Bernet Galleries sold a carved walnut *credenzina*, 29½ inches wide, for $95. An early sixteenth-century Venetian carved walnut and crimson velvet Dante chair brought $140. This gallery also sold an attractive finely turned walnut refectory table from Liguria (sixteenth century) for $100. Early in the year a Tuscan carved and paneled walnut *credenza*, five feet six inches wide, brought just $25 at the Parke-Bernet Galleries. Prices could not have gone down much after 1939 without completely disappearing.

But 1942 saw a change. On April 18, 1942, the Parke-Bernet Galleries sold a late sixteenth-century walnut bambocci chest from Tuscany, five feet two inches

Carved walnut *credenza*.   Parke-Bernet, 1939, $25.

long, for $250. In the same sale an important carved and parcel-gilded walnut refectory table, nine feet one inch long, made in sixteenth-century Florence and originally sold by French and Company, brought $1,200.

By the war's end in 1945 prices of Renaissance furniture were up a little more, but only a little. By 1950 there was a slight rise in prices, but the general level of prices for Renaissance antiques remained far below the 1920's, and after 1945 Renaissance furniture had almost dropped from the market. It was not featured in the sales catalogues and it was not in any substantial demand.

The Myron Taylor Collection which was sold at the Parke-Bernet Galleries November 12, 1960 saw some quality pieces offered. An elegant sixteenth-century carved walnut *credenza*, seven feet eleven inches wide, brought $900, and an early sixteenth-century walnut carved and parcel-gilded Tuscan octagonal dolphin table brought $800.

On May 2, 1964, a sixteenth-century carved walnut armorial *cassone* of good design but with some restorations brought $725. Prices had risen just a little since 1960.

On November 20, 1965, the Parke-Bernet Galleries had a sale which was unusual in that it stressed Italian Renaissance furniture, but it was not a sale to liquidate any particular estate. A seventeenth-century *credenza* with two doors of carved walnut and two short drawers in the frieze above two cupboards brought $500. The area of origin of the piece was not determined, and the piece was late seventeenth century and not of the more desirable sixteenth century. The next item to be sold was a Roman *cassone* of the second half of the sixteenth century, 21 inches high and 43 inches long. It brought $400. An Italian walnut *credenza* of the sixteenth century, five feet ten inches long, with two frieze drawers and two paneled doors below, fairly elaborately carved, brought $250. A seventeenth-century side chair brought $180, a sixteenth-century armchair brought $130 and a seventeenth-century folding armchair brought $130.

While these items were not of the finest quality, the prices were still uniformly low and did not show any appreciable rise since the war. In 1925 better items in general were sold than in this sale, and prices were a little higher in 1925 than in 1965, so that for this quality furniture sold in 1965 prices were definitely under the level of 1925. In the United States and in England, the two major world markets, Renaissance furniture had hardly started any comeback But there can be little doubt that it will come back if the boom in business keeps up. The furniture is intrinsically of good quality, well constructed and artistic. One has only to look at the furnishings of the Robert Lehman Museum in New York City to realize the artistic merit of furnishing in the Renaissance style. (This museum was formerly the Lehman family home.)

On April 9, 1966, the Parke-Bernet Galleries sold a late sixteenth-century walnut *credenza*, five feet two inches long, for $350. It was a fairly good antique and the price was what might be expected.

One of the first sales of the new season was held in the same gallery on September 24, 1966. In this sale a mid-seventeenth century cupboard of small size,

Italian mid-seventeenth century walnut cupboard. Parke-Bernet, 1966, $625. (*Photo: Taylor & Dull*)

Late sixteenth-century walnut *credenza*. Parke-Bernet, 1966, $350. (*Photo: Taylor & Dull*)

27 inches wide, brought $625, a little more than might have been expected, judging from prices of the previous season.

In the sale the next week there were a few surprises in Renaissance furniture prices. A pair of early seventeenth-century walnut armchairs from the Bardini Collection, but not of great beauty, brought $1,400, a high price in light of recent prices for such chairs. The next item offered in the Renaissance category also achieved a high price. This was an early seventeenth-century walnut *credenza* 51 inches wide. It brought $1,250. The next significant Renaissance item was a very

Pair of early seventeenth-century Italian walnut armchairs from the Bardini Collection, Italy.   Parke-Bernet, 1966, $1,400 the pair.   (*Photo: Taylor & Dull*)

fine and unusual parcel-gilded walnut *cassone*. It was quite early Florentine. It was from the famous Holford Collection and had been exhibited at the Burlington Fine Arts Club in 1921 and 1922. Both its age and provenance made it somewhat unique. It brought $2,400. The price was not high considering the item.

If a price comparison between the 1965 season and the 1966 season were based solely on this one sale (and it statistically cannot be because the sample is too small), one might assume that prices about doubled in Renaissance furniture in one year. In any event it seems clear that they rose materially.

Early seventeenth-century Tuscan walnut *credenza*.   Parke-Bernet, 1966, $1,250. (*Photo: Taylor & Dull*)

Italian Renaissance Prices

Date	1925 Equals 100%
1925	100%
1926	200
1929	300
1932	30
1939	5
1942	30
1945	40
1950	50
1960	60
1964	75
1965	85

Important Renaissance parcel-gilded walnut *cassone,* Florentine, early sixteenth-century. Exhibited Burlington Fine Arts Club, London, 1921–1922. Parke-Bernet, 1966, $2,400. (*Photo: Taylor & Dull*)

Summary of Renaissance Prices

Prior to the Davanzati Palace sale in 1916, prices for Renaissance furniture in general were low as far as the auction market was concerned. Private buyers of great wealth were, however, buying privately and at high prices; but the Davanzati Palace sale established high prices for this type of furniture at public auction. In a sense, too, it pulled up all antique prices regardless of type, and the literature of the period points this fact out again and again. It alone did a tremendous amount for collecting of antiques in general.

After this sale the ordinary items of the Renaissance period came onto the market at lower prices, but the Davanzati sale had its influence and prices were definitely up materially over what they had been.

If we take 1925 as a base, prices tripled between 1925 and 1929, a great part of the rise taking place in 1926 (as it did in many other types of antiques sold in America). But by 1932 Renaissance antiques had lost 90 percent of their value. The Depression had combined with a turn away from the heavy and ornate furniture to wreck the market in Renaissance styles.

But the Depression low of 1932 was not the low for Renaissance antiques. They were definitely out of fashion as few antiques have been in the past. They did not fit smaller homes and apartments. They were dull, and the emphasis in interior decorating began to be on light colors. They were not simple and functional, and functionalism had its day in the 1930's and early 1940's. By 1939 Renaissance furniture had lost 95 percent of its 1925 value.

The war reversed the trend, but not by much dollar-wise. In 1942 the index was where it had been in the 1932 Depression bottom. By 1945 it had gone up slightly, and between 1945 and 1965 it doubled. Yet Renaissance furniture still is not a factor in the antique market and is most certainly not in vogue. The only price-wise direction this furniture can move in the future is up, provided prosperity continues.

VENETIAN ROOM. *The Metropolitan Museum of Art, Rogers Fund, 1906.*

CHAPTER TWELVE

Painted Italian
1680–1820

I N THE EIGHTEENTH CENTURY TWO general types of furniture were produced in Italy—natural wood and painted. The natural wood furniture is generally light in color, well constructed and durable, often veneered in beautifully grained wood and frequently inlaid with lighter woods or those of various colors. Sometimes the inlays take the form of elaborate and beautiful designs. The great advantage in purchasing this furniture today is that it is relatively cheap. There is by far more English eighteenth century furniture of the same general style for sale, but the prices of fine English pieces usually far exceed those of comparable Italian natural wood pieces.

In the United States there are few good unpainted Italian pieces offered for sale. However, in Italy they are in more than ample supply, and in that country there is a definite market price. In Florence a few years ago every dealer had some of this furniture, and some dealers had hundreds of pieces. While generalization on prices is of course difficult, it seemed that a card table, a side table, a rectangular table, a *demi-lune* table, a very plain commode or a cabinet all cost about the same—$250. Such a piece might well sell for $500 to $600 in America. Although this furniture is something of a novelty on the American market, its scarcity does not make it valuable here.

A second type of furniture made in Italy in the eighteenth century is painted furniture, and this furniture is in a class by itself. It is some of the finest in the world, and is some of the most wanted and highest priced. A good eighteenth-century *bombé* commode in *natural wood* should cost about $1,000 in Italy, possibly as much at $2,500 for the very best; but for a painted *bombé* commode of high quality the minimum price would be $15,000, and a few years ago we saw in Venice a superb green *bombé* commode and two small matching commodes for $95,000. In America a fine Italian eighteenth-century painted commode can bring $25,000 to $35,000 and more.

Origin of the Eighteenth Century Italian Style

No country in the world outdid the Italians in art and sculpture from the beginning of the Renaissance through the eighteenth century. Italian art comprises the vast majority of the outstanding paintings of the world, and rightfully so. Likewise, Italian Renaissance furniture was the finest and most original of the era in Europe, and it was the prototype of all European furniture of the time. Even Louis XIV furniture, for the most part, was not an original and novel French design. It was more like Italian, although there were certain innovations, the most notable being the cabriole leg. But the great forward strides in furniture were mainly made by Louis XIV's successor, Louis XV.

Italy was freed from Spanish influence when France defeated Spain in 1659, and French influence thereafter became strong in Italy. But it remained for the elegant Louis XV style to become dominant everywhere on the continent and spread from France down to Italy. In Italy, however, it took on a distinctive Italian form; yet it had all or most of the elements of the French Louis XV style. The French cabriole leg is one of the prominent features of Italian eighteenth-century furniture, but the leg has an Italian personality. It tends to curve out a little more positively and has much less restraint than its French equivalent.

The same is true for the chair arms. They are curved like French arms, but they curve even more. The Italians superimposed their own design for the arm ends: a large flourish and a heavy scroll.

The backs are typically Louis XV in shape, except that they tend to be larger and a good deal wider at the top. They are also higher than French backs. Someone once likened the back to those of Victorian chairs made under the Louis XV influence. While this comparison may have some merit, the Victorian style misses from an artistic point of view and the Italian style does not.

Probably the workmanship of Italian Louis XV chairs is not up to the standard of the French. Certainly the woods are not of French quality. Yet these deficiencies are more than made up by the freedom of design and the excellence of the painting. As a general rule, Italian Louis XV furniture tends to be somewhat larger in size than the French equivalent. The generalization can be made that it is less restrained and more flamboyant than the French furniture of the same era.

There are certain characteristic Italian eighteenth-century colors which predominate. The first is green—a medium shade—and it is so characteristic of Venice (which produced the finest painted furniture of the period) that it might be called Venetian green.

There is also a characteristic yellow that was used for covering the entire outer surface of furniture. This is typical of the furniture of Lucca. Some of the very finest furniture of the period was made in Genoa, and here again we get a characteristic yellow color which was greatly used.

Designs, often in water colors, were superimposed on top of this surface of solid color, and on top of the water colors a varnish was placed to fix the water colors. Very often the motifs are not only natural and in the form of flowers and vines, but are of *chinoiserie* design. Possibly some furniture was sent to the Orient to have the figure work painted. At other times the Italians painted the Oriental figures, gardens, houses, etc., but in their own style. The figures are a caricature of the Oriental figures, but are characteristic of *chinoiserie* furniture of this period.

If anything, the Italian *chinoiserie* is more sought after and more valuable than the real Oriental work.

Much of the furniture is painted in pastel colors, light blues and purples among others. On this base such designs as flowers and bouquets are painted in contrasting colors, and the results are more than pleasing. The furniture is often a work of art from the point of view of color and painting.

It is an ironical fact that the Louis XVI style in Italy was basically a French style, but that the entire style originated in Italy. The Italian excavations at Pompeii and Herculaneum influenced the world of painting, sculpture, architecture, decoration and furniture. The influence amounted very nearly to a revolution, and for a long period all these arts had to be in accordance with these classical discoveries or they were not in fashion.

The classical style was well established in France and even in England before it was adopted by Italy, despite the fact that Giovanni Piranesi, the architect and etcher whose publications so profoundly helped establish the classical style throughout the world, came from Italy. The founding of the Milanese Academy in 1775 also helped a great deal to establish the classical, or Louis XVI, style in Italy.

There is little need to enumerate the Louis XVI characteristics of Italian furniture. It was essentially like Louis XVI French furniture, except that the style tended to be freer and the furniture was often painted. Traditionally, the legs were straight. Curves were at a minimum, although the circle, the oval and the ellipse were used extensively. Gilding was used in addition to painting. Caning was extensive, and fine marquetry work was done.

From the Louis XVI style the Italian furniture moved into *Directoire* and then into Empire. Napoleon saw to it that his style was carried out in Italy by establishing his second palace there and setting up his family as rulers of parts of Italy. His sister Caroline became Queen of Naples. His sister Pauline married an Italian nobleman, and they undertook the remodeling and furnishing of several palaces in Rome. His sister Elsie became Grand Duchess of Tuscany, while other members of his family were established in other parts of Italy. It is to be expected that the Empire style was vigorously executed in that country.

Characteristics of the Eighteenth Century Italian Style

1. Designs similar to French furniture of the period. In the early part of the century a style similar to eighteenth-century Dutch and English was used extensively in Italy. The chairs resembled early Dutch and Queen Anne English. The following style, Louis XV, was similar to French Louis XV and was based upon it. The Louis XVI, *Directoire* and Empire styles were also closely allied to French styles of the period.
2. Beautifully painted surface. (This is, of course, the furniture we are confining ourselves to in this chapter.) One of the reasons for painting is that a cheaper wood like pine could be used. This was covered with gesso to smooth it and to build raised designs, particularly for *chinoiserie* decoration. Color was then applied.
3. Raised designs in gesso.

4. Water color designs and oil color designs.

5. *Découpage* designs. These were similar to decalcomanias in that they were stuck on. By this means quite fine ornamentations could be applied quickly and at little expense since no artistic work was required.

6. Painting in some cases by top artists of the period. (Such pieces are an extreme rarity on the market, and when they do appear the value is dictated more by the artist's painting as a work of art than by the excellence of the piece as an item of furniture.)

7. Use of the shell or rocaille design. This was the favorite motif of eighteenth-century Italy. There was often a large shell in the middle of the top rail of the back, and there might be another on the apron of the seat or the front seat rail. This design was used everywhere in Europe and in almost all periods.

8. Chair backs which are higher than the corresponding French styles.

9. Chair backs which flare out wider at the top than the French chairs of the same period.

10. Extreme curves of arms, legs and arm supports of chairs and sofas.

11. Extreme scrolls at the ends of arms.

12. Shaped chair and sofa skirts, sometimes quite elaborate. These are usually highly decorated, with figures and carving.

13. All manner of feet of decorative design. Some early pieces used the Spanish or paw foot. Later pieces used drake or trifid feet, scroll feet and various other forms.

Venetian painted commode of the *Régence* period. Anderson Galleries, 1926, $110.

14. *Bombé* fronts as a favorite form for commodes and small tables. Sometimes serpentine fronts were made and some concave fronts as well as sides.

15. Wide, angulated corners for case furniture, especially desks and secretaries.

16. Extensive use of *chinoiserie* for painted decoration, much of it done in Italy in the Oriental manner. Flowers and birds were also used extensively for designs.

17. Use of bright colors for painted designs on characteristic Italian greens and yellows or soft pastel colors. This is perhaps the strongest artistic characteristic of the furniture of eighteenth-century Italy.

18. Use of classical decorative motifs including:

> Foliated scrolls
> Cartouches
> "C" and "S" scrolls
> Coats of arms and other elements of heraldry
> Volutes
> Banderoles
> Little figures of children (*putti*)
> Grotesques

One of a set of three Venetian lacquered and gilded armchairs.   American Art Association, 1927, $300 each.

19. General rectilinear shape relieved by extreme curves in backs, arms and legs.

20. Sparing use of ornamental bronze (used often by the French). Metal keyplates and handles, mostly of wrought iron, were used.

21. Use of gilt to great effect to enrich furniture.

22. Extensive use of caning for seats and backs of chairs and sofas.

23. Use of stretchers on early furniture, but the disappearance of stretchers on Louis XV and Louis XVI pieces.

24. Manufacture of some pieces in the later English styles—Adam, Hepplewhite and Sheraton.

Prices of Eighteenth Century Painted Italian Furniture

Painted Italian furniture, including the preferred Venetian, occupies a unique position in the antique market. It is of artistic excellence, and in its way is comparable to eighteenth-century French furniture. Yet until the last ten years painted Italian furniture was never preferred in the market. Its recent tremendous rise in popularity—and in price—is due no doubt to its own artistic merit and to the fact that it resembles French furniture. A third reason for its popularity is that nothing epitomizes the new "Age of Elegance" more than painted Italian furniture. It is ornate, yet artistically tasteful. And it is colorful at a time when colors are the fashion in decorating as well as in art in general.

One of a set of five painted and decorated Venetian chairs of the early eighteenth century. Purchased by the Author from the late Leon Medina, 1959, $1,250.

On May 12, 1905, Christie's sold six carved and gilt armchairs covered in velvet for £157/10 ($765), about $125 a chair.

In 1914, when the European phase of World War I was about to start, an Italian painted cabinet with folding doors and four drawers below, in gold and black, eight feet six inches high, brought £52/10 (about $250). Prices had been halved as compared with 1905.

The next year when England was at war, however, a tapestry-covered Venetian armchair with a gilt frame decorated with shells and scrolls brought £2/5 (a little over $10). Prices were down to about 25 percent of the 1905 100 percent base level.

By 1920 prices had doubled, but they were still below the 1905 level. On November 12, 1920, Sotheby's sold a Venetian cabinet containing eight drawers and a small cupboard for £54 (just under $200). It was a fine piece of furniture with enamel, small plaques and a top of lapis lazuli.

Five years later prices had not moved upward. On April 20, 1926, an eighteenth-century Venetian lacquered commode with a serpentine front brought $110 at the Anderson Galleries in New York, while three *Directoire* Italian painted chairs brought $50 for the lot. On October 11 of the same year, however, the Anderson Galleries sold a carved and gilded Italian *Directoire* lacquered settee with five armchairs and two footstools for $1,300.

Venetian painted *secrétaire*. Sotheby's, 1966, $3,220.

Although 1926 saw a boom in most antique furniture, particularly in the New York market, Venetian furniture prices were for the most part low. On April 20 the Anderson Galleries sold two Venetian lacquered armchairs of Louis XV type for $55 for the two chairs. A matching pair went for the same price and a third matching pair went for $40. In the same sale a Louis XV-type Italian armchair in cream and gold brought $32.50. By the end of the year, however, the American Art Association Galleries sold a pair of red lacquered *fauteuils* for the very high price of $1,450. Prices in 1926 were rising.

In the 1927 Grassi Collection sale at the American Art Association Galleries, three green lacquered and gilded Venetian armchairs of elaborate Rococo design brought $300 each.

Between 1926 and 1929 the painted Italian furniture index doubled. Moreover, there were many offerings, and several of the offerings merited illustrations in the auction catalogues. In the Burnet-Clark sale at the Anderson Galleries on April 25 and 26, 1929, two commodes sold for $550 each, although one Venetian flower-painted commode of Louis XV type brought only $250. Five Venetian lacquered and parcel gilded *fauteuils* of Louis XV type, fine pieces of furniture, brought $1,125, and a matching side chair brought $320 at the Count Pepoli sale at the American Art Association on January 18 and 19.

On December 11 to 13, 1930, the belongings of the Countess de la Beraudiere were sold at the American-Anderson Galleries. A Venetian *Régence* lacquered commode with *chinoiserie* brought $450, a high price for a year after the stock market crash.

In 1932, however, prices of painted Italian furniture had been halved as compared with 1929. A pair of Ligurian Louis XV carved, lacquered and parcel-gilded

Very fine Venetian painted commode. Christie's, 1961, $27,930, purchased by Francesco Genova of Venice.

One of a pair of Venetian small painted commodes (en suite with above) Christie's 1961, $14,112, also purchased by Francesco Genova.

armchairs brought $90. Two matching pairs went for $80 each. A fine Venetian Louis XV decorated lacquer serpentine-front commode with painted flowers and a top of simulated marble brought $280. In 1967 ten times this figure would have been a low price.

In 1937 at the Fonda sale in New York a pair of Louis XVI Italian lacquered and parcel-gilded pier tables brought $300. At the time of the United States entry into World War II, prices were substantially the same.

By the war's end prices had risen about 50 percent, and they stayed at this figure through 1950. On March 16, 1950, the Parke-Bernet Galleries sold three pairs of *fauteuils* (not matching) for $240, $220 and $110. Two days later they sold three *fauteuils* for $390 and a matching *canapé* for $100.

Five years later prices had doubled as compared with 1950. At the Faucigny-Lucinge sale held at the Parke-Bernet Galleries on April 22 to 23, 1955, a Louis XV Italian painted and decorated serpentine-front commode brought $900, and a matching one brought $725. The fact that the commodes were a pair made them somewhat unique, and the price per piece was consequently higher. In the same sale a Genoese Louis XV decorated vermillion-and-gold lacquered serpentine commode 48 inches long brought $500. Today it might bring as much as $10,000.

By 1960 prices were up to 450 percent of the 1905 100 percent base, and they had risen 50 percent since 1955. At the Myron Taylor sale held at the Parke-Bernet Galleries on November 11, a pair of Louis XV carved and gilded *fauteuils* of Italian origin brought $1,200, and a matching pair brought the same price.

From this point on a steady and rapid rise took place in painted Italian furniture. In 1961 a pair of small Venetian commodes sold for $17,640 at Christie's. It is believed that this was the pair which, together with a fine matching serpentine commode, was offered to us for $95,000 in Venice in 1961. These pieces were of

Painted and decorated console. Florence Antiques Fair, 1963, $18,000.

Carved and painted Italian *Régence* armchair. Purchased by the Author's wife at the "on the premises" estate sale of Leon Medina, 1964, $25.

course standouts of superb shape, with the typical green color of Venetian furniture and with only minor restorations to the paint.

Even ordinary furniture was rapidly increasing in price, however. In 1963 a pair of armchairs of Louis XV type, painted with flowers and sprays on a green background, sold for £546 ($1,530). Three Venetian gilt stools sold for £399 ($1,120), and a gilded and painted mirror brought £273 ($764).

In the fall of 1963 the great Antiques Fair was held in Florence. Here a beautiful turquoise side table with slender cabriole legs was offered at $18,000 and a dozen fine green armchairs for $1,000 each.

By 1965 the price index was up to 1,200 percent. It had almost tripled in the five-year period. In Italy, under the impact of inflation and abnormal prosperity together with quick profits for those who had never realized them before, prices rose as much as six times in the five-year period.

Still, prices on the international market did not respond as might have been expected, and often near-prime pieces of Venetian furniture brought less than expected in New York, London, Munich, Cologne and elsewhere. Christie's on March 18, 1965, sold a pair of small *bombé* Venetian commodes, 23 inches long, for $4,410, and on March 12 Sotheby's sold ten late-eighteenth-century North Italian chairs with square backs and fluted legs for $1,176. In late 1965 the Parke-Bernet Galleries sold an excellent green Venetian sofa that had been estimated at $1,000 to $1,200 for $500. The author bought it!

In Europe in the summer of 1966 very few pieces of painted Italian furniture were offered for sale, and outside of Italy there were extremely few pieces of fine quality painted furniture. In Paris a fair set of six Venetian chairs was priced at $7,000. In London a red lacquer bookcase with its original mirror, *c.*1690, was offered for £6,500 ($18,200).

New York City is scoured regularly for painted Italian furniture, particularly Venetian, by Italian dealers (and one dealer in particular). While Italian dealers

Venetian lacquered, carved and gilded bench. Plaza Art Auction, 1966, $350, purchased by the author.

encourage New York dealers to hold such pieces for them, the Italians do not like to pay prices comparable with their Italian retail prices. Thus, while these dealers tend to build the market in painted Italian furniture in America, they do not tend to build it very high; and in America as well as in other major markets outside of Italy, this furniture is not preferred as much as eighteenth-century French. Other things being equal, however, and barring a depression, this furniture in America will experience a considerable rise in public favor and in price.

Painted Italian Prices

Date	1905 Equals 100%	1950 Equals 100%	1925 Equals 100%	1920 Equals 100%
1905	100%			
1914	50			
1915	25			
1920	50			100%
1925	50		100%	100
1926	100		200	200
1929	200		400	400
1932	100		200	200
1939	100		200	200
1942	100		200	200
1945	150		300	300
1950	150	100%	300	300
1955	300	200	600	600
1960	450	300	900	900
1965	1,200	800	2,400	2,400

Venetian *secrétaire*. Parke-Bernet, 1966, $4,000.

One of a pair of painted Italian Louis XVI side chairs, from Sydney Brown, Inc., New York. Plaza Art Auction, 1966, $340.

JACOBEAN ROOM.　*Courtesy of the Victoria and Albert Museum, London.*

CHAPTER THIRTEEN

Jacobean
1603–1689

F URNITURE STYLES IN ITALY CHANGED radically during the Renaissance (the fourteenth, fifteenth and sixteenth centuries). The style was imported into England, but not without great difficulties. England was a century behind Italy in accepting Renaissance styles. The first real Renaissance-styled item was probably the tomb of Henry VII; this was made by the Italian Torrigiano between the years 1512 and 1518 or 1519. In the reign of Henry VIII (1509–1547) England took over the Renaissance styles and grafted them onto the existing English style (Gothic).

The Gothic period began in 1100 and ended in the early 1500's. This was a period in history that was static in almost every way, and certainly in furniture design. The style, the construction and the variety of pieces were all rudimentary.

Henry VIII brought to his court a number of Italian artists who to a certain extent brought Renaissance ideas to England. England possessed the background at this time in which new ideas could breed. The rigid discipline of the church had been thrown off by Henry, and the king himself set the tone of enjoyment and comfort. Furniture design was just one manifestation of the new spirit.

Up until this time Church and State had gone hand in hand as somewhat equal partners (as well as rivals). Now Henry confiscated church lands and sold them inexpensively to the new wealthy merchants who were prospering through England's growing international commerce. These properties were secularized, expanded and furnished in elegant style.

The feudal system, which did not encourage business enterprise, had more or less ended with the War of the Roses (between the two Royal houses of England), and for the first time people other than the Lord of the Manor could look forward to a higher level of living.

Upon the death of Henry VIII in 1547, his son Edward VI became king. In 1553, a relatively short time later, Henry VIII's daughter became Queen Mary I, but five years later Henry's other daughter, Elizabeth, became queen and reigned from 1558 to 1603. It was in this later period that the real progress of English homes and English furniture was made.

Elizabethan Furniture—Forerunner of Jacobean

The Low Countries provided much of the impetus for the changing styles in English furniture, and Flemish pattern books began to arrive in England. One of the most important factors all through the history of furniture styles is the preparation of books of design, as we shall see in the progress of the eighteenth century.

During the reign of Queen Elizabeth, Flemish and German craftsmen came to England. This was to be expected in view of the close commercial ties that existed and in view of the new emphasis in England on houses and furnishings. French craftsmen also appeared in England, paving the way for the dissemination of the French styles which in the later seventeenth and eighteenth centuries were to be prominent in Europe.

The Elizabethan furniture was primarily of oak, the principal furniture wood for centuries. It was available in England; it was cheap and it was durable. A few fine pieces were made of walnut, which became the wood of the famous eighteenth century until replaced by mahogany.

The variety of furniture was not great and consisted primarily of tables, chairs, chests, cupboards, stools, benches and bedsteads.

The furniture was extremely heavy and cumbersome in design. The chief artistic contribution in this period was the profusion of carving. Although not of the highest quality, the carving was there in quantity. While the structure until the time of Elizabeth was essentially Gothic, Renaissance motifs crept in during her reign, along with native English designs. The overall shape of the pieces was simple and rectangular.

One motif is particularly characteristic of the Elizabethan Period. This is the big carved ball found chiefly on legs (somewhere around the middle of the leg) and chiefly on cupboards and tables, not chairs. It looks something like a melon, and it is sometimes referred to as the "cup and cover support." This motif was also used in the seventeenth century, but it became smaller and more in keeping with good design.

Painting and gilding of furniture were used in the era of Henry VIII, but in the latter half of the sixteenth century this decoration gave way to carving (including scrolls, grotesques, caryatids, leaves, vases, human forms and swags) and some inlay (leaves, flowers and simple geometric designs). Some fairly elaborate inlays called bandings were used, the wood being cherry, bog oak, poplar and holy. Very little upholstery was used.

Early Jacobean Furniture

Our review of English furniture starts with the so-called Jacobean Period, which immediately precedes the William and Mary style.

The name "Jacobean" pertains to James I, King of England, "Jacob" being essentially the same as James, and Jacobean being the adjective derived from James. James came to power in 1603 and died in 1625, at which time his son Charles I became king. James I was the first English king of the House of Stuart, and the House of Stuart continued to rule England on and off until 1714.

Technically, the Jacobean Period is confined to the reign of James I (1603–1625), but it is usually stretched to include the reign of Charles I, who ruled until he was ordered beheaded by the House of Commons in 1649.

When Charles I was beheaded and his Anglicans defeated by a combination of Scotch and Puritans who demanded and secured political power through military victory, a unique period began in the rule of England—the Protectorate. Actual power was held by the Protector of the Realm, Oliver Cromwell. This period is also called the Period of the Commonwealth. It lasted from 1649 (the date of the beheading of Charles I) to 1660. Oliver Cromwell died in 1658, whereupon his son Richard became Lord Protector of the Realm. Richard resigned in 1659. The furniture of this period is somewhat distinctive and is known technically as Cromwellian furniture.

The following year (1660) the House of Stuart was restored in the person of Charles II, son of Charles I, and the power of the Anglicans was once again established.

Charles II died in 1685 and Charles I's younger son became king as James II. He remained king until 1688 when he was deposed. The period from the reestablishment of the monarchy in the person of Charles II through the reign of James II is called the Restoration (1660–1689). In 1689 William and Mary from Holland became the rulers of England, and a new style of furniture came into vogue.

It will suit the purposes of this book to call the *entire* period of the House of Stuart (including the Protectorate) the Jacobean Period (1603–1689). This is not technically correct, but if the term Jacobean is derived from James it can be stretched to include James I, the original Stuart, to James II, the last Stuart prior to William and Mary.

It was during the seventeenth century that most of the great manor houses were built in England, and they obviously had to be furnished in the style of the time—Jacobean. One dominating style was the Palladian style, named after Andrea Palladio, the Renaissance architect. The exponent of this style in England was the great English architect Inigo Jones. This Palladian architecture superseded the earlier Elizabethan architecture which, however, was also based on Italian Renaissance design.

Charles I was probably the greatest patron of the arts who ever ruled England. He married the sister of Louis XIII of France and thus the way was paved for some French influence in English design, as well as the appearance in England of French artists and architects. Then, too, it was fashionable for Englishmen to travel in Europe and to absorb European culture along the way. The dominant culture was Renaissance, of course. During the Civil War of 1642 and the Protectorate of the Cromwells (1649–1660), travel was cut off and there was no emphasis on building, architecture, art or furnishings. It was a period of austerity that was reflected in furniture as well as in other elements of living.

Characteristics of the Jacobean Style

Early Jacobean furniture was very similar to the Elizabethan except that in many ways it was less ornate. Few new pieces were added until Charles II came to power following the period of the Protectorate.

Under the Puritanical Protectorate there was a marked simplification of furniture styles. But when Charles II returned to the throne in 1660, the Englishman of greater means was ready for a relief from the long period of austerity. Charles II had a suitable background to help the new demand for elegance: He had spent part of his exile with the court of Louis XIV and the rest in Holland. The level of elegance of living in both of these countries was far above what it was in England in the same period. When the Stuart line was reestablished in England, the atmosphere was thus propitious for the migration of Dutch craftsmen to that country, and the decline of business activity in Holland at this time further promoted their emigration. This is one explanation for the Dutch influence on Jacobean furniture.

In this period another great architect came onto the English scene to dominate fashions, Sir Christopher Wren. He brought both the French and Italian influence to bear on English architecture. He was also by no means unmindful of Dutch interior designs.

The Restoration was a time of such rapid progress in furniture that it amounted to a revolution. (For perhaps five hundred years the static, heavy and simple Gothic style had predominated, while the Elizabethan era simply grafted elaborate ornamentation on this simple style.) Now real ornamentation came in, as well as a whole series of new pieces of furniture that had never been seen before. The predominating influence was foreign, not native English. And of the foreign influences the French and the Dutch were paramount.

These are some of the specific characteristics of the Jacobean style, most particularly that part of the Jacobean called Restoration (1660–1688):

1. Straight lines, rectangles and squares. These basic forms are extremely pronounced.
2. Large size.
3. The use of dark wood.
4. The use of oak as the chief wood. It was produced domestically in England, but there were other and cheaper woods in use—elm, chestnut, beech and deal (pine or fir).
5. The use of framing. In this type of construction the surface does not stand on its own with perhaps some ornamentation. Rather, the surface assumes the aspect of a painting which must be framed, and the frame consists of posts and rails which are joined together by the traditional and best method of joining—a slot and a tongue known as mortice-and-tenon construction. The tongue is held in place by a wooden pin.
6. Applied ornamentation which was not particularly attractive.
7. Scratch carving, a primitive, crude type of carving.
8. Low relief that was little like the attractive low-relief carving developed in the last half of the eighteenth century.
9. Painted designs and some broad inlay work which provided a measure of ornamentation.
10. Turning of legs and stretchers for ornamentation. The wood to be

turned was placed in a fixture which rotated it while a cutting tool was applied to the surface to form various circular shapes. This turned design for legs and stretchers was used on and off up to the present time. It is a form of ornamentation so common that one accepts it after a time as being a part of the basic structure, which it is not.

11. Straight and square feet that gradually yielded to ball feet, and to the flattened variety known as bun feet.

12. Little upholstering, especially prior to the Restoration.

Basic Innovations in the Restoration Period

1. Use of a few curves such as scrolls for arms, legs and stretchers.
2. New decorative elements:

> Bright colored marquetry in floral designs.
> Bright lacquer work.
> Gilding on gesso, a plaster containing glue which was built up in height for surface ornamentation.
> Richer upholstering, including brocaded silks and silk velvets.

3. New elements of surface decoration

> Marquetry, sometimes employing ivory
> Inlays, sometimes employing ivory
> Parquetry in geometric designs with thin wood inserts
> Veneer.

4. Decorative motifs such as fruit, foliage and vases.
5. Use of glass on furniture.
6. Caning of seats and backs.
7. Introduction of walnut as the most fashionable wood. Lime, pear, cedar, chestnut, beech and elm were also used.
8. Use of metal mounts:

> Brass mounts in place of the wrought iron ones used earlier.
> Brass handles of the large drop or pendant type.
> Some silver handles on the finest pieces.
> The use of the acorn or teardrop on the simpler pieces. These forms are very characteristic of this and the following period.

Characteristic Early Jacobean Pieces (1603–1660)

Although a chair would seem to be an obviously necessary piece of furniture, there were relatively few chairs prior to the Commonwealth (1649–1660). The chief pieces of "sit-upon" furniture were stools with no sides or back, and a long tablelike seat called a "long form." Chairs were the possession of the elite. But the Commonwealth was a period of presumed democracy (in addition to being a period of austerity, religious intolerance and seriousness of attitude toward life), and it was felt that the common man, as well as the elite, should have a chair on which to sit. Thus in this period several characteristic types of chairs were made, including the Wainscot chair, the Yorkshire, the Derbyshire and the Cromwellian. Larger seat furniture included the long form, which was essentially a bench, and the settee, which is a long form with arms and a back.

A host of new types of tables were added at this time, including the refectory table (much like the Renaissance refectory table), the gate-leg table and the gaming table.

The chest also appeared at this time, a combination of storage piece and seat. Cupboards also appeared in profusion, including the press cupboard, the court cupboard, the livery cupboard and the Welsh dresser. Two types of chests were made—the chest-of-drawers (essentially the same as today's chest-of-drawers or bureau), and a low chest consisting of a storage compartment plus a drawer or two below this compartment.

The Late Jacobean Period (1660–1689)

The important thing about the return of Charles II to England is the inauguration of a period of elegance and the evolution in furniture.

While the eighteenth century is the century of elegance, this late Jacobean Period did represent a substantial improvement over the earlier era. It is true that all Jacobean furniture can be classed together as dark (mostly made of oak), heavy and rectangular, with a great deal of rudimentary ornamentation; but the later furniture (1660–1689) represents improvement plus the philosophy of change that persisted through the eighteenth century. These new pieces of furniture appeared at this time: the Carolean chair, the banister-back chair, upholstered sofas, daybeds, footstools and a desk consisting of a cabinet set on a frame having the appearance of a table.

While walnut came in as a rival to oak and was a better wood from the point of view of appearance, other woods were used, including ash, birch and maple.

Price History of Jacobean Furniture

Jacobean furniture was once the height of fashion, just as Louis XV furniture is in the late 1960's. It is most difficult to visualize a time when such furniture would have been eagerly sought and bought at fantastic prices. It was, however, in this much desired status position just prior to World War I.

On November 11, 1901, a carved oak hall chest dated 1681 was sold in a Belfast auction for £18/8/6 ($90), a price which indicates that successive bids were in very small amounts. On October 17, a carved oak cabinet was sold for 28 guineas ($140), and an oak cupboard brought £29/8 ($143).

By 1905 prices were rising rapidly. An oak table 85 inches long on carved balluster legs brought £54/12 (about $270). On March 16 of the following year Christie's sold a Charles II oak chair with a rounded back for £152/5 (about $760).

With 1901 as the base equal to 100 percent, prices were at the 1,000 percent level by 1910. On April 19 Christie's sold a Charles I oak buffet with two drawers, an open shelf in the center and with lion and unicorn carving, for £283/10 ($900).

By 1914, the year World War I began, the prices of Jacobean furniture were at boom levels. Christie's on December 2 sold a James II oak side table with an elaborate frieze for £1,050 (about $5,000). A refectory table from Knoll, one of the great English historic houses, brought £241/10 ($1,171), and seven walnut armchairs brought £1,123/10 ($5,460), almost $800 a chair. Prices were about at the 5,000 percent level!

From here prices plunged during the war, and on June 1, 1915, Christie's sold a Charles II oak armchair to Stair and Andrew, dealers of some consequence, for £7/7 (about $35). Another armchair of the same variety was sold in the same sale for £10/10 (about $50), and Stair and Andrew bought a wing armchair at the same time for £8/8 ($39). The Anderson Galleries in New York did better at this time. On March 12, 1915, they sold a pair of armchairs in petit point for $220 each.

As the war progressed and it became increasingly clear to Englishmen that the Kaiser would be defeated, prices of Jacobean furniture began to rise. By 1920 the index stood at 500 percent, whereas in 1915 it had dropped to 100 percent. A pair of James II walnut armchairs now brought £504 (about $1,850). On November 12, 1920, Sotheby's sold a Charles II armchair for £185 ($675).

Between 1920 and 1925 prices did not rise despite the furniture boom that was nearing a peak. In America prices were weak, and two drop-leaf tables sold in New York in 1925 for $145 and $110.

In 1926, however, the American Art Association Galleries sold a Charles II carved walnut armchair for $625 and a pair of Charles II side chairs for $660. Prices were now at the 1,000 percent level.

From here they rose with the boom in general business conditions, and in 1928 two Charles II armchairs and six side chairs brought 1,150 guineas ($5,750) at Christie's.

On April 24 to 27, 1929, the famous Reifsnyder sale was held in New York at the American Art Association Galleries. This was primarily a sale of the finest American antiques, and tremendous prices were realized. While buyers of American antique furniture were at this sale in force (rather than buyers of English Jacobean furniture), the quality of the items and the importance of the buyers tended to raise the price of all furniture offered. A James II walnut caned tall-back armchair c.1685 brought $3,100. Yet a pair of James II side chairs brought only $375 each. Prices were about at the 1,500 percent level, well under the 1914 peak for this type of furniture.

The Depression and the War

On January 9, 1932, the American Art Association sold a pair of James II carved walnut armchairs for $620, and on May 23, 1932, Christie's sold a Jacobean oak chest to the dealer Partridge for £28/7 (about $100). Prices were cut in half as compared with 1929.

Prices seemed a little stronger at the Alfred H. Mulliken sale held in New York on January 7, 1933, and four Charles II turned walnut side chairs with original Mortlake tapestry brought $2,800, while eight Cromwellian side chairs brought $1,040. In 1935 at the Ira Haupt sale in New York a carved oak buffet from French and Company brought $2,100.

By 1939, however, prices had tumbled and they now stood at the 300 percent level. A Cromwellian carved oak wainscot armchair brought $190 at the Parke-Bernet Galleries (on October 27, 1939), and on June 22 Christie's sold a draw-leaf table for the small sum of £38/17 (a little over $150).

By 1942 prices had sunk to 200 percent. Sotheby's on October 9 sold six walnut straight-back chairs for £38 (slightly over $150). Christie's on February 12 sold an oak dresser for £36/15 ($148) and a James I oak table for £55/15 ($224). On the other hand, an earlier Elizabethan table and buffet brought £1,260 ($5,078), but of course they were older than the Jacobean furniture and museum-type items.

Jacobean oak chest.   Christie's, 1932, £28/7, purchased by Frank Partridge.

Postwar Prices

By 1945 prices were back up again. On August 2 Christie's sold eight Charles II armchairs with carved front rails and scrolled arms and legs, illustrated in one of the leading books on antique furniture, for £2,205 ($8,820). On December 20 Christie's sold six Cromwellian oak chairs plus another six illustrated in *Country Life* for £283/10 ($1,062). Prices at this time were about at the 1,000 percent level.

By 1950 prices were down again, and six James II carved and turned walnut tall-back chairs with a carved front stretcher rail brought $250 in New York. The price level now stood at 500 percent.

Jacobean oak buffet.   Christie's, 1964, $720.

Here the price index remained for the next five years. But by 1960 it had risen materially, and Sotheby's sold a late seventeenth-century Japanned cabinet for £720 (over $2,000).

By 1964 prices of Jacobean furniture were firm, but not very much on the rise except for inexpensive pieces. A Commonwealth oak dining table seventy inches long brought 650 guineas ($1,950) at Christie's on April 16, and in the same sale an elaborately carved Charles II open armchair brought 160 guineas ($480). A James II armchair brought 150 guineas ($450) and a James II settee brought 160 guineas ($480). In the same sale an oak buffet illustrated in the May 1957 *Connoisseur* magazine brought 240 guineas ($720).

Between 1960 and 1965 the low-end items of Jacobean furniture moved up more rapidly than the finer items, and a gate-leg table that might have sold for

Charles II open armchair.   Christie's, 1964, $480.

$50 in 1960 sold for $150 to $200 in 1965. In 1963 the author visited a number of English shops looking for Jacobean furniture of good quality, as he had done in 1961 and 1959. Finally, a good buy was made in The Hague, Holland. A small gate-leg table was bought for $150 and shipped to the United States at a cost of about $50. Today the same table would cost about $250, and at auction in New York the medium-good pieces of Jacobean furniture have risen from the $100 level to perhaps $200 or $300 in 1967.

The summer and fall of 1966 saw nothing startling in either the demand for or price of Jacobean furniture. In Paris a few high prices were noted at the dealer level. One dealer offered two rectangular long tables for $2,000 and $2,400 respectively. These were of the finer type.

Jacobean Prices

Date	1901 Equals 100%	1950 Equals 100%	1925 Equals 100%	1920 Equals 100%
1901	100%			
1905	200			
1906	500			
1910	1,000			
1914	5,000			
1915	100			
1916	100			
1920	500			100%
1925	500		100%	100
1926	1,000		200	200
1929	1,500		300	300
1932	750		150	150
1939	300		60	60
1942	200		40	40
1945	1,000		200	200
1950	500	100%	100	100
1955	500	100	100	100
1960	1,500	300	300	300
1965	1,750	350	350	350

WILLIAM AND MARY DINING ROOM. Featuring an outstanding set of English William and Mary side chairs, shown with a fine Charles II table. *Courtesy of Frank Partridge, New York.*

CHAPTER FOURTEEN

William and Mary
1689–1702

THE WILLIAM AND MARY STYLE was an innovation. It represents not only an extremely sharp break with the past, but it is the earliest furniture made in England which has general liveability. It is the first furniture made which can be used to furnish modern houses and apartments completely. In that sense it was the first "modern" furniture produced in England.

King William III was the son of the Dutch William of Orange, and William and Queen Mary came to England from Holland with a Dutch background and with Dutch interests. William's mother was the daughter of King Charles I of England, the great art collector who was beheaded in 1649. William's Queen was Mary II, eldest daughter of King James II of England who was deposed in 1688. William and Mary came to the throne in 1689, and William died in 1702 at which time this era came to an end.

The William and Mary style, as might be expected, is to a great extent a Dutch style. When William and Mary came to England a group of tradesmen and artisans accompanied them. More came in following years. But the fact that William and Mary came over to rule England did not mean that a Dutch style of furniture suddenly came into vogue. As early as the sixteenth century there were social, commercial and political relationships between England and Holland. Prior to the era of William and Mary, Dutch craftsmen had been attracted to England by the prosperity of that country. The great cabinetmaker Gerreit Jensen came to England from the Low Countries, and his work for the Royal House spanned the reigns of Charles II (predecessor of William and Mary), William and Mary, and their successor, Queen Anne.

In 1685, four years before William and Mary began ruling, an event took place which was of great importance to English furniture design: The Edict of Nantes, which guaranteed religious freedom for Protestants living in France, was revoked. As a result, a number of skilled Huguenot craftsmen fled to England and set up shop. Among these refugees was perhaps the greatest cabinetmaker of the era, Daniel Marot. He was also an architect, furniture designer and engraver of ornaments. Marot fled to Holland where he became the head architect to William of Orange, later to become William III, ruler of England. Marot followed William and Mary from Holland to England.

191

This French infiltration of workmen and top furniture designers meant French influence on English furniture design. Furniture of this period is often considered to be purely Dutch in origin, but it is not. It is a blend of Dutch and French, the French being primarily of the Louis XIV style.

All furniture is evolutionary, and William and Mary furniture is no exception to this rule of evolution in design rather than revolution. In a sense it is an average of the preceding styles—late Jacobean (Carolean) and the subsequent Queen Anne style.

Characteristics of William and Mary Furniture

If one characteristic of William and Mary furniture had to be chosen to typify that furniture as compared with the late Jacobean style which immediately preceded it, it would be that William and Mary is smaller furniture. It is smaller in every sense, particularly from the point of view of being vastly less formal and less imposing. This is the primary reason for the importance of William and Mary furniture in the antique market today as compared with the Jacobean styles which generally are not in demand.

In a sense the William and Mary style of furniture can be considered in one of two ways, either (1) that it is an evolutionary style which progressed rapidly from the elegant formality of the Jacobean style to the practical middle-class furniture that is so much on the market these days, or (2) that there were two styles of William and Mary—the style for kings, nobles and other top aristocracy; and the style for the "sub-aristocracy," the "well-to-do" layer of the population.

Marot's furniture was made primarily for the elite classes. It was made in the style of Louis XIV and is of great elegance. Elaborately carved and gilded, it has an air of magnificence. Silk velvets and damasks were used for upholstering. The decorations are often marquetry and take the form of seaweed and arabesque. Some of the furniture is lacquered. (Most was lacquered in England but some was imported from the East.)

In this furniture of the high aristocracy the backs of chairs are high, the pieces are large, and the shape is still definitely rectilinear, as one would expect of furniture based on the style of Louis XIV.

The characteristics of the more popular and more "democratic" furniture include:

> 1. Turned legs in the form of trumpets or similar shapes. This is one of the most dominant characteristics of William and Mary furniture, and one that makes it almost immediately recognizable. The furnituremakers of this period became intrigued with the operation of wood lathes and turned out very large and elaborate forms. The descriptive word "trumpet turning" simply means that the form looks something like the blasting end of a trumpet. A variation of this trumpet form is the inverted cup form. The blasting end of the "trumpet" usually points upward from the floor and toward the base of the carcass of the furniture. If one placed an inverted cup over the blasting end, he would have this inverted cup design. It also

looks something like the mutes that are used on trumpets to muffle and refine the tone.

2. X-shaped stretchers. These were more simple than the scroll-shaped stretchers used on Louis XIV furniture or the elaborately turned and carved stretchers used on Jacobean furniture.

3. Frequent use of finials at the center of the stretcher. This little ornament gave a finished look to the stretchers.

4. Predominantly rectilinear shape which gradually gave way to more curves. In this respect William and Mary furniture is like Louis XIV furniture which gradually developed the curvilinear element later elaborated in the Louis XV Period.

5. Hooded and double-hooded tops on cabinets of various types. This is a distinct William and Mary characteristic. This same top is used on chairs and sofas.

6. A double curved back for sofas. Sofas of this period have a highly characteristic appearance. They look like two chairs fastened together to make a bigger piece of furniture. There are double backs.

7. Ball feet and bun feet. These are distinct characteristics of this style. The bun foot looks as though the weight of the piece of furniture was so great that the ball feet became flattened. Both types came into general use in this period, and they quickly yielded to different types of feet in the succeeding period.

8. Use of multiple legs. Very often William and Mary furniture has four legs in the front and two in back, whereas the usual design in furniture is to have two and two.

9. Prominently molded cornices on the tops of cabinets, etc., to outline the hooded or double-hooded tops.

10. Well-shaped aprons on cabinets and similar pieces which add to the ornamentation and to the finished look.

11. The use of finials facing downward on such aprons as an added element of ornamentation and to create a finished appearance.

12. The innovation of the straight leg instead of the scroll-shaped leg of the preceding style. The straight line was the most common basic shape, although the trumpet turnings, inverted cups, baluster turnings and columnar turnings obscured the essentially straight *line* of the characteristic leg of this period.

13. The cabriole leg. This was of tremendous importance in later English and French styles. While this type of leg probably originated in China, it was most highly developed under Louis XV and is the most important single style element of that era. In actuality it was developed under Louis XIV. In England it was originated in the William and Mary era, but it did not develop until the next era in furniture. A hoof foot was used.

14. Veneered walnut surfaces richly figured.

15. The use of more subdued baroque ornamentation than in the Jacobean era.

16. The introduction of the all-important shell motif. This was much used in later styles in England and in the United States, but was also

characteristic of the furniture of the Louis'.

17. The use of such motifs as acanthus leaves, husks, female masks, scrolls, foliage, vase forms and drapes.

18. The spoon-back chair. This was shaped to fit a person's back, in contradistinction to the straight back chairs of the preceeding period. The center part of the back or splat was shaped and extended nearly to the seat.

19. Use of veneered and solid walnut and oak.

20. Large, unbroken surfaces.

Innovations in Furniture

Although the William and Mary style was not of long duration in England (1688–1702) and certainly does not represent the best developed or most beautiful English furniture style, this era was responsible for the development, if not the origination, of some of the most characteristic English pieces of later date and some of the most useful ones.

The slant-top desk originated in the William and Mary Period. In succeeding periods the desk part was placed over drawers, but in the William and Mary Period there were legs which extended from the writing compartment to the floor, thus offering no storage drawers. The style is somewhat similar to the cabinets which have elaborately turned legs instead of drawers in the bottom half.

The secretary-cabinet or bureau-cabinet was also originated. This is the fully developed slant-top desk with long drawers and a cabinet above, an extremely useful piece of furniture which was well developed in succeeding periods. In addition, the kneehole desk was developed. This is the basic form of desk in use today in most offices. It has room for a person's legs in the center of the desk and a set of drawers on each side.

Another innovation was the chest-of-drawers mounted on a stand. This useful piece of furniture later developed into the chest-on-frame. The top part was used for drawer storage, but the bottom was strictly ornamental with the characteristic turned legs. The chest-on-chest also was developed. This is the same as the chest-on-frame except that the bottom part consists of more drawers instead of legs. One part sits on the other part and can be separated for moving. Intact it provides enormous storage capacity. It was used for many generations after the William and Mary style went out and was a basic piece of American furniture.

Other items which originated during this period included a dressing table mirror that combined mirror, frame and a base with drawers; a detachable wall bracket to hold such items as clocks and vases, and carved and gilded wood sconces. Also, the hanging shelf for books, etc., was popularized, although such shelves were certainly known, but not much used, in earlier times.

The toilet table, a small table with one row of drawers, was also developed. This item is called a lowboy in America and is one of the most desired of all William and Mary pieces. In order to meet the demand for such tables, adaptations are often made from one section of larger pieces of furniture by adding a new top or a top made out of old wood.

William and Mary Price History

From approximately the beginning of this century until the end of World War I, William and Mary furniture was not at an elevated price level. Moreover, the price level was static. Using this period to start the index at 100 percent, we find that the index remained static until the 1920 recordings.

In 1910 a walnut china cabinet with glazed doors sold for £36 ($175). On December 17, 1915, Christie's sold a marquetry chest of drawers for £25 ($120). By 1920, however, prices were far up. In November of that year six walnut chairs with cabriole legs brought £300 ($1,098), and six other chairs brought £390 ($1,428). The index stood at 500 percent.

In 1925, five years later, the index still remained high, but had made no appreciable advance in this period of furniture boom. William and Mary furniture did not show any appreciable rise in price even in the boom year of 1929. although English furniture in general did show such a rise.

A unique fact about William and Mary furniture is that it did not experience a severe drop in price in the Depression. On January 29, 1932, the American Art Association auctioned a finely turned gate-leg table (once sold by the leading dealer Frank Partridge) for $600, and a walnut and needlepoint wing armchair,

William and Mary gate-leg table.   American Art Association, 1932, $600.

*c.*1700, for $1,500. Later in the year another group of items once owned by
Frank Partridge was sold—four walnut side chairs, *c.*1690, brought $800, not a
low Depression price. An inlaid six-leg tallboy brought $270, while in London
a walnut bureau on six legs with elaborate marquetry brought £467/5 ($1,635)
—a very high Depression-year price.

In November 1935 the Ira Haupt sale was held at the American-Anderson
Galleries in New York. A walnut tall-back side chair, designed by Daniel Marot
and having an elaborately carved back, brought $3,600, a high price for any chair
today, even of Louis XV design.

On March 21, 1936, at the J. Henry Lancashire sale at the American-Anderson
Galleries, a very important set of six carved walnut side chairs after Daniel Marot,
with slight repairs, brought only $1,140, despite the fact that they were once
owned by dealer Frank Partridge. Prices were off.

By 1939 prices were only half of what they had been in the Depression year of
1932. On October 28 of that year, the Parke-Bernet Galleries sold five finely
carved walnut side chairs with stretchered legs for $100 apiece.

In November 1942, the first full year of American entry into the war, the
Rosenbach Company sale was held at the Parke-Bernet Galleries. A carved walnut
tall-back side chair of the late seventeenth century brought $200; and at the
Charles E. T. McCann sale held a few days later in the same gallery, another such
chair, this one after Marot and once sold by French and Company, brought only
$125.

One of four William and Mary side chairs.   Christie's, 1964, $480.

By 1950 prices of William and Mary furniture had slipped again, and the index stood at the 250 percent mark, where it had been in 1929 and in 1942.

Most types of antique furniture were starting their rise in 1955, but not William and Mary furniture. It declined to 200 percent. On December 21 Christie's sold a pair of walnut chairs for £6/6 (about $17). The same gallery on December 8 had sold a walnut bureau for £42 ($117), and on November 3 they had sold a walnut and oak side table for £29/8 ($78).

Prices were rising by 1958, and in April of that year the Parke-Bernet Galleries sold a rare turned walnut lowboy (the lowboy in general being a most sought after item in the antique market) for $4,400.

In May 1960 Christie's sold eight side chairs of walnut with elaborately carved backs and Spanish feet for £320 (just under $900). Prices were at the 500 per-cent level where they had been for so long in the 1920's and in the early 1930's.

By 1964 and 1965 prices were still rising, but not at so great a rate as they had been and not as fast as many other types of antique furniture. On April 16, 1964, Christie's sold four William and Mary chairs in the style of Daniel Marot for 160 guineas ($480), but in the same sale an important small cabinet on turned and

English William and Mary wing armchair, covered with needlework.   Sotheby's, 1966, $952.

spiral legs with ball feet that had been exhibited and written up by *Connoisseur* magazine brought 750 guineas ($2,250).

Although the index now stood at 600 percent, it was only a little above the level of the 1920's and even of the early 1930's. William and Mary furniture is not in vogue and does not have the refinement of line or the small size to fit modern concepts of home interiors.

On June 24, 1966, Sotheby's sold a rather rare William and Mary wing armchair covered in needlepoint. It brought the equivalent of $952, a rather low price in relation to the quality of the chair.

In one of the early sales of the 1966–1967 season, the Parke-Bernet Galleries sold a wing chair covered in good contemporary needlepoint, originally sold by French and Company, for $1,700. The next lot was a pair of small settees 55 inches long covered in seventeenth-century Flemish tapestry. They realized $2,500 for the two. Prices in this sale were not unduly high when one considers the quality of these offerings.

In late 1966 an unusual piece of William and Mary furniture was sold by Christie's for an unusual price. It was a William and Mary walnut card table on six hexagonal legs. The piece was 36 inches wide and had a foldover top which was contoured. The body of the table included one drawer in the front and was fairly elaborately shaped. The stretcher was large and prominent. The piece brought the high price of 1,600 guineas ($4,800). It was a fine item and merited a high price, but the price nevertheless seemed to be out of line with the immediately prior market for William and Mary antiques, perhaps presaging a return to fashion.

English William and Mary wing chair, covered in contemporary needlepoint, from French & Company.   Parke-Bernet, 1966, $1,700.   (*Photo: Taylor & Dull*)

William and Mary Prices

Date	1910 Equals 100%	1950 Equals 100%	1925 Equals 100%	1920 Equals 100%
1910	100%			
1915	100			
1920	500			100%
1925	500		100%	100
1926	500		100	100
1929	500		100	100
1932	500		100	100
1939	250		50	50
1942	250		50	50
1945	350		70	70
1950	250	100%	50	50
1955	200	80	40	40
1960	500	200	100	100
1965	600	240	120	120

One of a pair of William and Mary settees, covered in seventeenth-century Flemish tapestry.   Parke-Bernet, 1966, $2,500 the pair.   (*Photo: Taylor & Dull*)

QUEEN ANN ROOM. A special exhibition featuring Queen Anne furniture. *Courtesy of Frank Partridge, New York.*

CHAPTER FIFTEEN

Queen Anne
1702–1714

W HEN WE ARRIVE AT THE QUEEN ANNE PERIOD in furniture history we enter the era of perhaps the finest English furniture ever made —that of the eighteenth century.

In the eighteenth century furniture began to be designed primarily for use combined with beauty. Very few people, if any, would entirely furnish a house today with early seventeenth-century furniture. They could use William and Mary furniture; much of it is both beautiful and comfortable. But this period is a transitional era to furniture which is even more beautiful and more comfortable.

When we move from the William and Mary era (1689–1702) to the Queen Anne era (1702–1714), we enter a more refined period of development in furnituremaking. If it were possible today for a fortunate collector to secure enough fine Queen Anne pieces of furniture, an entire house could be furnished in this style to create a home of exceptional charm and elegance. Right now we seem to be beginning a Queen Anne vogue. Many more people are becoming "Queen Anne conscious," and collectors are watching the sales rooms of auction houses and dealers for fine pieces.

Characteristics of Queen Anne Furniture

Historically, Queen Anne furniture is the logical development of the William and Mary style, with more beauty, more usefulness and more refinement. It is graceful in the extreme. Like William and Mary before it, it is essentially a Dutch style, but a more refined Dutch style. In fact, eighteenth-century Dutch pieces are sometimes so close in style to English Queen Anne that distinguishing between Dutch and English requires some study. Yet the curves of Queen Anne furniture (especially the typical curve of the legs) are considered French in origin.

Detailed characteristics of Queen Anne furniture include:

1. Emphasis on curves, especially for chair backs, legs and seats.
2. Extension of the use of the cabriole leg. This leg was developed in England at the end of the seventeenth century, and at about the same time or a little earlier under Louis XIV. But it was not until the eighteenth

century that it came into its own. It is certainly not characteristic of
William and Mary pieces, although this is the immediately preceding style.
The cabriole leg came into general use on chairs and on various types of
bureaus and highboys. The leg is a double curve or cyma curve, and it was
developed in the short Queen Anne era into an extremely beautiful element of furniture design. In this era it reached the ultimate. No later style
improved upon this particular element of design.

3. Elimination of stretchers. There is little question that stretchers add
to structural strength. (These are the braces part way down the legs of
chairs and other pieces of furniture which offset weights on the legs and
in effect tie the legs together.) Stretchers were eliminated by constructing
strong legs firmly fastened to the body. Yet the legs were not so thick as
to detract from the beauty of the furniture. Certainly this elimination of
stretchers represents one of the chief forward advances in furniture styling
in the Queen Anne Period.

4. Retention of the rectangular structure.

5. Bonnet tops, and broken arches, which technically are broken pediments. The obvious top for highboys, tallboys, etc., is a flat one, especially
since these pieces are generally so tall that one cannot see the flat surface
of the top. But the bonnet top is a form of ornamentation which is so
elaborate as to form a basic element of the structure of such pieces in this
period.

While the double arch is characteristic of William and Mary furniture,
the broken arch is characteristic of the more elaborate pieces of the Queen

Section of Queen Anne room. *Courtesy of Frank Partridge, New York.*

Anne Period. It is a somewhat unique style, and one which might seem so different as to have limited interest. But it was accepted in this period and continues to enjoy extreme popularity.

6. Spoon chair backs. This style was developed in the William and Mary era, but became extremely well developed and popular in the Queen Anne era.

7. Curved or horseshoe-shaped seats. This style is an excellent complement to the spoon back and provides a unity of design with the back. In addition it is very comfortable.

8. Shaped aprons carried to a degree of beauty generally not achieved in the William and Mary era. The aprons give a finished appearance to larger pieces of furniture. In this era it was not considered necessary to have pendant finials to finish off the aprons.

9. The great use of the shell which corresponds to the Rococo ornamentation of the furniture of the Louis'. This shell embellishment is found all over Queen Anne furniture. It was used on aprons, chair leg knees, tops and drawers of tall pieces, desk drawers, and on slant-top desks in the writing compartment. The shell is considered a most important and fine element of design, and the more shells the better. While such shells are certainly a value element that may have run wild, the design is excellent.

10. Vase-shaped chair splats. This is the wooden back support used where there are unupholstered backs.

11. Use of walnut. This is *the* wood of the Queen Anne era.

12. The use of veneer, a thin layer of wood (walnut in the Queen Anne era) glued onto a carcass of oak or other wood. While solid walnut was used in the Queen Anne era, the use of veneer resulted in a finer selection of woods for the visible surface and an extremely fine finish. This veneer sometimes replaced marquetry of earlier eras, as well as the elaborate carving of those eras. Figured veneers are characteristic. At this time there was more use of veneer for ornamentation than at any time in the history of English furniture. (Figured veneers are also characteristic of Dutch furniture of approximately the same era. The Dutch, however, made greater general use of veneers and carried designs in veneers to a great extreme.)

13. Upholstery of a permanent nature for seats and backs of many dining chairs, wing chairs and settees.

14. Club feet. They are a logical development of the ball and bun foot of the preceding era, but are far more beautiful and in proportion to the rest of the furniture. In the later Queen Anne Period this foot was sometimes combined with the so-called broken cabriole leg which curved like the true cabriole leg as far as the knee and then went straight down, flaring into the foot.

15. Ball-and-claw feet. Although the ball-and-claw foot is considered characteristic of Chippendale, a later style, it came in in this earlier period and seems to have been unrecognized by Thomas Chippendale as an important element of design. Since it has been used so much in later periods in both England and America, it is significant to point out that it was introduced in the early part of the eighteenth century—in the Queen Anne era.

New Forms of Furniture

"Two-stage" pieces of furniture were developed during the Queen Anne Period. The base was either a frame on which sat the drawers or cabinet, or a kind of small bureau on which sat another bureau or cabinet. These pieces have two great advantages which probably have not been exceeded by any later pieces of furniture. First they were designed to hold the maximum volume; the drawers start near the floor and continue up so high that on the tallest pieces not even a tall man can see in the drawers without a stepladder. Such pieces have immense storage capacity. The second great advantage is that the pieces can be taken apart for moving. These pieces were highly elaborated in broken arches, cabriole legs, aprons, finials on the top and shell designs.

The card table was developed in England in this general period simply because some such piece was required to meet the demand for card playing. This new pastime was growing by leaps and bounds. The card table is small, with a fold-over top and often with indentations for chips.

Many types of chairs became prominent in the Queen Anne era. The winged armchair was developed and continues to be one of the most sought after and valuable pieces of furniture on the market today. The most obvious characteristic of this chair is the wings that extend outward around the sitter's shoulders. The top of this chair is flat or arched. The arms turn outward in scrolls. The legs are of the cabriole variety and end in club feet, so that the whole chair has a somewhat lighter and more graceful appearance than some of the later chairs that have ball-and-claw feet. Sometimes the cabriole legs have shell-carved knees. A similar chair was also developed, but it had a lower back that was either flat, rolled over or serpentine in shape.

Another most peculiar type of chair was known as the reading chair. The seat is almost triangular, one point of the triangle being at the back where the seat joins the back. The shape is something like a bicycle seat, but the "rider" faces the back.

Another unusual variety of chair developed at this time was the so-called burgo-master chair. Essentially it is a circular stool with six legs and stretchers. The sides of the chair above the stool flare outward and consist of three oval panels held in place by four turned uprights.

Still another new type of chair of this era is a four-legged stool with one of the legs directly in front of the sitter, one behind and one on either side. The shape is essentially square. At the back are three uprights and two typical Queen Anne-shaped splats, plus a kind of serpentine top rail extending past the uprights. It is called a corner chair.

Two other new types of chairs introduced at this time were the hall chair in which the servants waited to see the master, and the porter or page chair which is about what the name implies. Both were elaborate pieces of hall furniture for the great manors of the period.

In the realm of chairs, a great innovation was made in this period as far as popularity is concerned—the Windsor chair. This chair became extremely popular in later years in the United States. The Windsor chair was just as popular in England and continues to be made there even now. It has been little developed or modified with the passing years.

The Windsor chair is an all-wooden chair with saddle-shaped seat. It has splayed turned legs joined by an H-type stretcher. The back is formed of thin, turned spindles sloping outward. Sometimes there is another higher back formed of narrower spindles coming out of the top rail of the "first back."

The Home in the Early Eighteenth Century

What happened to furniture in the eighteenth century is more than simply a natural development and a gradual evolutionary process. To a great extent it is the product of the social developments which took place in this era.

There are really two types of furniture in the Queen Anne era, as there are in other eras: The elegant furniture of large size and elaborate design, and the furniture for the larger group of people who represented as much of a "mass market" as there was at that time.

Somewhere toward the end of the Queen Anne era and at about the time the Georgian era began, the influence of the sixteenth-century Italian architect Andrea Palladio (1518–1580) began to be felt in England in construction, decoration and furniture. His books on architecture were more or less the bibles of English architecture of the period, at least as far as the houses of greatest elegance were concerned. These houses were extremely large, with ceilings and columns both on the exterior and interior. They were stuccoed in the manner of Venetian palaces. The furniture for these homes was specifically designed for them. It was large and elaborate, although far more comfortable than that of the seventeenth century.

In England at this time, the economy was in good condition, and an important by-product of a healthy national economy is the prosperity of a substantial section of the population. A large group of prosperous businessmen was developing—not a group which could generally afford Palladian mansions, but one which wanted excellent homes filled with fine, comfortable furniture.

There was thus a new emphasis on fine houses that did not exist even as late as the William and Mary era. The demand for furniture to fill these homes was a by-product of the demand for homes, and the furniture had to be of excellent but comfortable design. While such furnituremakers as John Gumley, John Pelletier and James Moore were supplying furniture to the Crown, the lesser cabinetmakers were kept busy supplying the nobles and the merchant classes. Cabinetmaking now became a dignified paying business enterprise, not just an activity for the carpenter in overalls. This increased demand from a large group of well-to-do resulted in the furniture known as Queen Anne and the subsequent design of George I.

Overall Prices of Queen Anne Furniture

Market-wise, Queen Anne furniture occupies a unique position among antiques. In the twentieth century, even in the early years; it was in demand at substantial prices, whereas other antique furniture at that time was sold at prices roughly comparable to "secondhand" furniture today (and secondhand furniture prices are among the few prices which have not been materially affected by inflation).

Throughout the twentieth century, furthermore, there was never an era in which Queen Anne furniture was passé; while in Louis XV and Renaissance furniture, among many other types of antiques, there were periods of rock-bottom prices—when such antiques were priced at very little above reproductions, if any above!

The next distinguishing market feature of Queen Anne furniture is that to a great degree its ups and downs corresponded with the ups and downs of general business. Many types of antiques hit a peak in the middle 1920's, especially in 1926. Queen Anne furniture is distinguished by setting price records in the *late* 1920's.

In boom times Queen Anne furniture is very near—or at—the peak in price, taking into consideration all types of antiques. Ordinary pieces of Queen Anne furniture, as distinguished from masterpieces, bring very high average prices in times such as the present, and there is little indication that these prices will be lowered, at least in the near future.

Twentieth Century Prices to the Depression

On January 31, 1902, Christie's sold four Queen Anne chairs with open backs, cabriole legs, ball-and-claw feet (brass claws) and eagles' heads at the ends of the arm rails. They brought £157/10 ($763), a little less than $200 a chair. In these early years of the present century, $200 a chair was not a low price.

If 1901 and 1902 are used as the 100 percent price base, prices were up 50 percent by 1905. But just prior to the start of World War I prices lost their 50 percent increase, and by 1915 they were down to 20 percent. On June 1, 1915, a walnut chest of drawers brought £3/13/6 ($15), a price which indicates bids in extremely small amounts. The chest was bought by the eminent firm of Stair and Andrew—for the equivalent of a little over $15. In April Christie's sold a walnut table for £11/11 (a little over $50).

The progress of the war and the success of the Allies had little uplifting effect on prices, and in 1918 Sotheby's sold two high-back chairs with cabriole legs for £18/10. In the same sale the dealer Harris bought an armchair for £15. Later in the year Sotheby's sold a fine walnut armchair to the dealer Speelman for £22 (a little over $100).

The war ended in 1918, and by 1919 a great boom was on in antiques. To a considerable extent, it expressed itself in Queen Anne furniture. On May 29, a ten-piece walnut suite from Cambridge College brought £1,050 ($5,000). Another suite brought 1,600 guineas ($8,000), and a William Kent table brought 620 guineas (over $3,000). The price index in 1919 stood at 500 percent.

By 1920 prices were at boom levels. One armchair brought £2,016 (almost $7,500), the price of a fine Royal Louis XV chair today. Of course, the more ordinary items brought lower prices. Prices stood at about the 1,000 percent level.

By 1925 when the boom was gathering force, particularly in America, Queen

Anne prices were at about this same level. In America they did not rise as rapidly or as greatly.

New records for Queen Anne furniture were being established by 1928, even for the less illustrious pieces. At Christie's a red lacquer secretary brought 1,950 guineas ($10,000). Six marquetry chairs brought 1,650 guineas ($8,250, or almost $1,500 a chair).

On March 14, 1929, Christie's sold a walnut sofa and six chairs for £8,400 (about $40,000), a headline price even today. In the same year, another suite was sold for 10,000 guineas ($50,000). Prices were at the phenomenal level of roughly 10,000 percent!

Even in the faltering year of 1930, after several important banking failures and after the crash of the stock market in America, Christie's sold six armchairs in old needlepoint for 4,200 guineas ($21,000, or $3,500 a chair). In its annual report Christie's commented that 1930 was the third year in which they had received the highest prices for Queen Anne furniture of any antique furniture sold.

Depression and Recovery

By 1932 prices were sadly reduced. On May 26, 1932, the American Art Association sold a walnut and needlepoint armchair for $750 and a pair of side chairs (that Partridge had once sold) for $900. On November 5 they sold a wing chair for $415. While these prices are low in comparison with pre-Depression

English Queen Anne walnut sofa (en suite with six chairs). Christie's, 1929, $40,000.

prices, it must be remembered that brand new cars could sometimes be bought for $400, the tuition at a top college was $400 a year, and wages of 10¢ an hour were not unknown. Prices were down to about the 4,000 percent level—off 60 percent from the peak.

Still Queen Anne was the preferred furniture. At the Alfred H. Mulliken sale held on January 7, 1933, at the American-Anderson Galleries in New York, a carved and inlaid card table with a needlepoint top brought $2,900, and at the Ira Haupt sale on November 16, 1935, at the same galleries a carved walnut love seat with ball-and-claw feet and original needlepoint (from French and Company) brought the extremely high price of $5,200.

In 1939, a period of doldrums for the antique market in general, Queen Anne prices were at an extremely low level, having fallen rapidly from the year 1932. In fact, Queen Anne prices were almost back to the level of the beginning of the twentieth century. On October 14, 1939, the Parke-Bernet Galleries sold a pair of claw-foot side chairs with needlepoint upholstery for $760, but a wing armchair was sold on November 25 with leaf carvings and cabriole legs, a chair once sold by French and Company, for $150. On June 22 Christie's sold a black

English Queen Anne walnut and needlepoint armchair.   American Art Association, 1932, $750.   (*Photo: Taylor & Dull*)

lacquer secretary with mirror panels, *chinoiserie* decoration and bracket feet for £46/4 ($185).

The War and Postwar Eras

By 1942 a material price recovery in Queen Anne furniture had taken place, at least as compared with 1939.

On the other hand, Christie's on February 5, 1942, sold an enormous set consisting of 26 chairs for £252 (about $1,000). On June 26 some high prices were received when Sotheby's sold eight needlepoint chairs with carved club feet and cabriole legs from Queen Mary's room in Roxton Abbey for £900 ($3,600). Prices were at about the 400 percent level, but were rising rapidly. At the Wadsworth R. Lewis sale held at the Parke-Bernet Galleries in New York on April 1 to 3, 1943, a *demi-lune* card table went for the astonishingly high price of $3,400, while six carved walnut side chairs with carved knees brought $2,100.

By 1945 prices were back at about boom levels. On November 16 Sotheby's sold eight chairs, two settees and two screens for £3,300 ($13,000). Christie's on August 7, sold a set consisting of sixteen chairs and two settees illustrated in the *History of English Furniture*—a superb suite—for £4,095 (over $16,000).

Pair of Queen Anne walnut and needlepoint side chairs.   American-Anderson Galleries, 1932, $900.

On December 1 the Parke-Bernet Galleries sold a wing chair for $2,100. Prices were booming, although they were still at about one-half the 1929 peak.

Prices in the 1950's and 1960's

By 1950 the price level attained in 1945 had been cut in half, but from this point a steady rise began, a rise which has continued to the late 1960's. On January 7, 1955, the Parke-Bernet Galleries sold four shell-carved walnut side chairs with ball-and-claw feet and eagles' head designs for $3,000—$750 a chair. In the same sale a walnut shell-carved settee with some repairs brought $900. On November 18 a rare small wing settee was sold by Sotheby's. It had a covering of fine St. Cyr needlework and brought £1,150 ($3,220). The level of 1945 had again been reached.

By 1960 some records of past sales of Queen Anne furniture began to be approached. At the Walter P. Chrysler sale at the Parke-Bernet Galleries held on April 29 and 30, 1960, two settees and eight side chairs with a good background, including ownership by the dealer Partridge, brought $17,000. Even ordinary Queen Anne pieces were bringing high prices by 1960. Six side chairs brought $2,700, a matching wing armchair brought $900, and a love seat brought $2,300. Prices were about at the 7,000 percent level.

By 1964 they were at the 8,000 percent level and showed no signs of weakening. While sets of chairs were still in demand, they were replaced in popularity by high

English Queen Anne chair and screen, from a suite of eight chairs, two settees and two screens.   Sotheby's, 1945, $13,000.

English Queen Anne suite, part of the set that included two small sofas and eight side chairs.   Parke-Bernet, 1960, $17,000.   (*Photo: Taylor & Dull*)

case furniture (fine examples almost never appear on the auction market), and by that ultra-prestige piece, the Queen Anne lowboy. A good lowboy will easily bring in five figures. In a secondary auction in December 1965, the *bottom* part of a highboy with an added top, a piece far too large ever to be a Queen Anne lowboy, brought almost $1,000.

In Queen Anne furniture, more than in any other, the extremities of boom and depression are expressed, while changing tastes are not so much reflected. Queen Anne furniture seems always in demand if anyone has the money to buy antique furniture.

Queen Anne lowboy.   Sotheby's, 1966, $840.

English Queen Anne Prices

Date	1950 Equals 100%	1925 Equals 100%	1920 Equals 100%	1901 Equals 100%
1901				100%
1905				100
1910				150
1914				100
1915				20
1916				75
1920			100%	1,000
1925		100%	100	1,000
1926		500	500	5,000
1929		1,000	1,000	10,000
1932		400	400	4,000
1939		20	20	200
1942		40	40	400
1945		500	500	5,000
1950	100%	250	250	2,500
1955	200	500	500	5,000
1960	280	700	700	7,000
1965	320	800	800	8,000

CHIPPENDALE ROOM—special loan exhibition. *Courtesy of Frank Partridge, New York. (Photo: Champeau)*

CHAPTER SIXTEEN

Chippendale
1749–1779

Thomas Chippendale (1718–1779) is unique among furnituremakers for many reasons. One reason is that he was the first furnituremaker of any country whose name is given to the entire style. His style was in vogue between 1749 and 1779. The prior English style was Queen Anne (1702–1714), and the contemporary French styles were Louis XVI (1774–1789) and Louis XV (1715–1774).

Technically, Chippendale furniture is a division of Georgian furniture (1750–1800). Early Georgian runs from 1714 to 1750. But the furniture known as Chippendale is of a rather distinct style as compared with what is usually known as Georgian, and the market knows this type of furniture as Chippendale rather than Georgian.

In the summer of 1965 a desk from Harewood House, Yorkshire, England, was sold for 41,000 guineas ($123,000) at Christie's in London. This was the highest price ever paid for a piece of English furniture. It was probably made by Chippendale's employees working under his direction from a design by Robert Adam. From the same source and in the same sale, a mirror whose frame was made by Chippendale brought 10,000 guineas ($30,000), no small sum for any kind of mirror! This was a particular kind, however, in that the mirror was painted. There was a river landscape in the background and two terrace scenes in the foreground. These high prices are typical of Chippendale furniture of top quality.

An immense number of antique collectors, including the author, would like to own a set of Chippendale dining chairs, say ten side chairs and two armchairs. But although many of these sets were made in England, there are pitifully few sets, or even single chairs, for sale in the United States, while a large set is almost unobtainable. Sometimes second-rate chairs or country Chippendale chairs come up for sale, but almost no fine ones.

Probably the publication in 1754 by Thomas Chippendale of his book *The Gentleman and Cabinet Maker's Director* did more to establish his own preeminence and that of the Chippendale style than any other single contributory element. A second edition of this work was published in 1755 and a third in 1762. The importance of this book on furniture design is that it contained a series of illustrations of furniture of the mode. The first two editions had 160 plates each, and the third and final edition had 200.

For a long time it was thought that this book contained exclusive creations of Thomas Chippendale. But further research led to the conclusion that, in addition to some original designs, it was a catalogue or summation of existing designs of the period.

The process of "putting Chippendale in his place" is an interesting one and often a highly amusing one. One researcher, who need not be quoted verbatim with source and page, states that Thomas Chippendale created nothing, that he stole everything he ever used in the way of design from the French designer Meissonnier. Two other researchers, publishing their findings through the Metropolitan Museum of Art in 1929, concluded that Chippendale retained furniture designers Matthias Lock and Henry Copland, and that these two were primarily responsible for Chippendale's designs.

Franklin H. Gottshall in his book *Period Furniture* (New York: Bonanza Books, 1937) states, "He was a versatile designer, a master wood carver, and a skilled cabinetmaker." But Louise Ade Boger in *Complete Guide to Furniture Styles* (New York: Charles Scribner's Sons, 1959) says, ". . . there is no evidence that he himself carved at all."

Who is technically right is of little importance. When we buy a Chippendale sofa we do not ask if the piece was made by Thomas Chippendale, or even in the shop of Thomas Chippendale. Such pieces are in the Harewood House price range. All we ask is that the piece be in the Chippendale style and of the period

A pair of Georgian chairs. *Courtesy of Mr. James LePere, New York.*

in which Chippendale made furniture. This is what Chippendale furniture is from a market point of view.

We do know that Chippendale at least corralled the best designs of his period in his *Director* and that he had a large and successful furniture shop. There is no dispute that he ran the shop and that he was a good business administrator. His only major shortcoming seems to be that he got too much favorable publicity—so favorable that an entire style was named after him. Such prominence gets criticism. Poor Chippendale is still getting his share of the criticism, even from the excellent English publication *Country Life*, which says in the July 22, 1965, issue about the *Director* of Chippendale, ". . . that famous pioneering volume of dignified advertising which has tended to obscure the fact that Chippendale was not so much an inspired original designer as a good craftsman and business man perfectly willing to work to the instructions of others."

Now that we have contributed to putting Thomas Chippendale in his rightful historical place, let us go on to say that Chippendale furniture is some of the most wanted and most valuable of all English furniture, as must be obvious from the sales records previously cited. Just the day prior to the writing of this chapter, my wife and I were asked whether we would be interested in a set of Chippendale dining chairs. We thought enough of them to drive to Connecticut from New York City to look them over. As always seems to be the case, they were not Chippendale chairs of the period, but were turned out about one hundred years later when there was a rebirth of the Chippendale style.

EARLY GEORGIAN ROOM.   *Courtesy Chicago Art Institute and Mrs. James Ward Thorne.*

One Chippendale item that we did miss, and it was like the "fish that got away," was an original edition of the *Director* which an art and antique dealer in Cologne, Germany, had several years ago. The price was $500, and we will always regret that we did not buy it.

The furniture of Chippendale design, like so much other furniture, represents a normal evolution of the furniture of preceding periods. It is not difficult to point out that much of the Chippendale style can be traced back to Holland through the furniture of the Queen Anne and the William and Mary eras. But in the Chippendale period the influence of France is felt even more directly than in the two earlier English styles. This is partly because of the French carry-over from these two styles, but it is also because of the cultural dominance of France and French furniture in the Chippendale era.

The Chippendale era is also the era of the Louis', and the impact of this French furniture design and workmanship on the English aristocracy was immense. Shortly after the Terror began in 1789, important Englishmen were in France buying up French furniture because they liked its design, not because such furniture was "antique," which it was not. Then, too, they were able to get furniture which belonged to the dominant and most cultured monarchs on the Continent, and the possession of such items was always interesting. Besides, some of the royal nature of such pieces might "rub off" on the new English owners!

The French furniture designers of the era of the Louis' made patterns which were combined into pattern books, and these books became the basis of provincial as well as sophisticated city designs in France. They were also exported to England where they were studied and used. Chippendale was undoubtedly one of these users of French furniture patterns.

Characteristics of the Chippendale Style

1. Ball-and-claw foot. This design was certainly not invented by Thomas Chippendale—it was used in the Queen Anne Period (1702–1714) and was probably of Chinese origin—but it is the hallmark of Chippendale furniture. The ball-and-claw foot almost involuntarily evokes the conclusion, "Chippendale." But Chippendale's famous original *Director* contained not one design with a ball-and-claw foot! Yet there is little question that today the furniture of the Chippendale style that is the most wanted is that furniture that has the ball-and-claw foot.

Just as Queen Anne furniture was made in the United States, so was Chippendale furniture, and no one has to demonstrate that this furniture is Chippendale, yet not made by his hand or in his shop. Much of this American furniture does not have the ball-and-claw foot. Much of it, too, has square, straight legs and is much more conservative than English Chippendale.

2. Cabriole leg. In the Chippendale Period this leg was hooked to the ball-and-claw foot to give an excellent design.

3. Straight legs on some of the later pieces of furniture. These are either carved or molded on the outside.

4. Dark color. This is due to the almost exclusive use of mahogany.

5. Absence of stretchers on cabriole leg pieces. This was also the practice on the cabriole legs of Louis XV furniture.

6. Stretchers on straight leg pieces. These stretchers are carved, fret-sawed or flat and are not of heavy design.

7. Carving. In contrast to other periods and certainly other countries of the same period, Chippendale furniture uses carving as almost its only source of ornamentation.

8. The use of the pierced and carved splat. The splat reached a high degree of use and development in the Queen Anne Period, but it was in general a simple splat, often of vase-shaped design. It was neither pierced nor carved. In the Chippendale Period the splat was pierced in order to provide some indirect ornamentation. Some of the piercings are very intricately done and of great value to the pleasing appearance of the piece. Carving is sometimes totally absent on the splat. On the other hand, carving can be extremely intricate, so much so that the chairs have the appearance of being over-ornate. Strangely enough, the more the piercings and carvings on the splat, the greater tends to be the value of the chair and the demand.

9. The use of three "rungs" for the back. This is the ladder-back design which was greatly used. The contour of the rungs is often undulating and is very pleasing. The ladder-back design is a popular one which never tends to be over-ornate. The splats are joined directly to the seat rails.

10. Upholstered seats for the chairs. This design was either slip-seat, in which the whole seat slips out to reveal the seat rails, or upholstered over the front seat rail.

11. Broken pediment design. While this design is characteristic of Queen Anne furniture, it was used as well on Chippendale furniture—and with great effect. Pediments are often carved and ornamented with finials and other devices.

12. Carved aprons and skirts on chairs, cabinets and tables. These are often carved in elaborate ways.

13. Quarter columns or pilasters actually cut out of the corners of desks, cabinets, tall pieces, etc.

14. Use of serpentine contour, or the bow or the kettle base. Such forms were used on commodes of the highest quality made in the period.

15. A Chinese style which had wood cut to simulate bamboo. There was also fret-work carving and straight lines to simulate the Oriental.

16. A Gothic style which had a few key Gothic structural elements conveying the origin of the style.

17. Upholstery in needlework, tapestry, Spanish leather, damask and brocade.

18. Chippendale also used other surfaces and other ornamental work, which should be mentioned, although they are not strictly Chippendale. They included:

A. Marquetry of light woods in floral patterns set in veneers of mahogany, satinwood and harewood.

B. Veneered satinwood.

C. Veneered panels.

D. Parcel gildings.

E. Moldings which sometimes are extremely elaborate and were placed on the edges of tables and tall pieces and on sofas and settees.

F. Lacquered and painted surfaces.

G. Chinoiserie

Typical Chippendale Furniture

The chair is the most typical of the Chippendale pieces. Design features included a pierced splat, often highly carved, attached to the back seat rail; ball-and-claw feet (used in some cases but by no means all) and a cabriole leg of somewhat heavy construction.

Variations on the chair included the ladder-back with three parallel rungs in place of the splat; the Chinese with straight members and wood cut to look like bamboo, and the Gothic with a few key elements of the Gothic period such as the arch. Another variation was the double or triple chair settee. This is not a new design and was made in the Queen Anne Period. The Chippendale multi-chair design looks like two or three typical Chippendale chairs stuck together.

The so-called great armchair is characterized by an upholstered back with gently curved top rail and with arms which start out from the back parallel to the seat rails and then have a sharply sloping concave portion which drops off abruptly to join the front of the seat rail.

Another chair variation was wing chairs which are extremely popular today and in tremendous demand at very high prices. An extremely elaborate wing chair will sometimes bring thousands of dollars. The wings around the sitter are very much the same in design as in the Queen Anne wing chair, while the upholstered arms roll outward.

Adam-style chairs were produced by Chippendale later in his career. These chairs are really more Adam than Chippendale. It is sufficient to state that many in this style were made by Chippendale, but the designs will be discussed under the Adam style.

A "French" armchair was another Chippendale variation. This is the English attempt to produce a chair in the Louis XV style. (In actuality, most chairmaking countries of Europe produced chairs in this period which were based on the highly developed and highly fashionable Louis XV design.) There is often a serpentine shape to the back and it slopes backward. It has cabriole legs which end in French whorl feet of beautiful design rather than in the heavier ball-and-claw feet. The carving on such chairs is in the Rococo style and restrained rather than over-elaborate, as are some of the splat-back chairs. There is often an apron of valanced design. Finally, gilding was sometimes employed. In many ways this chair may be considered the equal of Louis XV chairs, and certainly Chippendale's chairs in the French style are of finer design than many Louis XV French ones.

There was hardly a more beautiful chair ever made than a really fine "French" Chippendale chair.

The multi-use three-part dining table is another typical piece of Chippendale furniture. It actually consists of three tables pushed together to form one large dining table. The central portion is a double drop-leaf table—there is a drop-leaf on each side of the center portion. On each side of this main table is a semi-circular end table. These end tables can be placed against the wall for independent use when the main table is not in use; and, of course, the moving of three small tables is very much easier than moving one large table.

The tripod tea table was very popular in the Chippendale era and remains one of the most popular and sought after tables today. This table was developed along with tea drinking in England. This became a great social institution in the eighteenth century and apparently required some ceremony and fine equipment, like the tilt-top tea table. The table's scalloped edge inspired the name "piecrust." These tables usually have a diameter of 25 to 30 inches.

While the tilt-top was the earliest table developed in this period, smaller tables were developed later in the century so that each tea guest could have his own table.

Just before mid-century a table was developed which can be considered an elaboration of the tilt-top tea table. This is the so called dumbwaiter. Instead of one circular top, it has three, each one above the other and the higher ones of progressively lesser diameters.

At about mid-century the supper table was developed. This is based on the tilt-top tea table but is modified with circular sections carved in the upper side of the top to hold plates. These tables are about thirty inches wide and have eight and sometimes ten carved-out indentations for dishes.

Along with these innovations came a dressing table that was also developed at about mid-century. This is of kneehole shape. The top drawer has a hinged mirror and is compartmented to hold toilet articles. Sometimes the top lifts up, and under it is a hinged mirror which can be lifted up for use. Under the top, too, are compartments. Although mahogany is the wood of Chippendale, these were made of walnut as well as mahogany and were sometimes lacquered. A smaller variety is the shaving table.

Whether the lowboy is a table or a truncated highboy depends upon one's classification and method of thinking. At any rate, the lowboy was and is one of the finest of all Chippendale pieces of furniture. It is more highly developed than lowboys of the Queen Anne era and is in tremendous demand. Sometimes the bottom sections of highboys have remained when the top section went somewhere else. A new top has been fitted and the piece sold as a lowboy. Such pieces have only a fraction of the value of a genuine lowboy.

Mid-century also was the time of the development of a somewhat unique table called a rent table. The top is hexagonal, and under the top are six drawers (designed to hold papers) which are pulled out from the periphery of the table. The table is a large one, about 52 inches in diameter.

The Pembroke table was developed in this era. It is a small table with small drop leaves and one long drawer. It has innumerable uses today, is of convenient size and is easily moved. Whether it got its name from the Countess of Pembroke (1737–1831), who first ordered one, is not certain. But such a table is known as a Pembroke table today. Some of the most beautiful Chippendale Pembroke tables have shaped drop leaves and fret-work carving around the edge of the leaves.

Probably the most important single piece of French furniture in the eighteenth century was the commode. We know it was extremely popular and was made by nearly every *ébéniste*. Although many of these come on the market each year, they always bring high prices and, in the case of the very finest ones, prices that seem fantastic.

The commode was just as popular in eighteenth-century England as it was in eighteenth-century France. It is a drawing room piece based directly on designs of the Louis', but with adaptations to the English taste. It is richly ornamented and often has a marble top like the French pieces. The characteristic French piece has two or three long drawers. The English commode has drawers, or else drawers and also doors enclosing a cupboard. These English pieces often have applied ormolu mounts like French pieces.

These commodes are sometimes made of satinwood and some are lacquered, often in *chinoiserie*. Such lacquered pieces were generally used in bedrooms. Marquetry was also used. Some of the later Chippendale commodes show the influence of Adam, and some are of *bombé* design like their French prototypes. A *bombé* satinwood commode with marquetry and ormolu mounts is today an almost priceless piece of furniture.

Prices of English Chippendale Furniture

If one were asked to select just one kind of furniture that is the best representative of "antique" or that best embodies the meaning of "antique," he might well select Chippendale. He would not have to describe this furniture as English Chippendale. Chippendale is synonymous with England in the antique field, and American Chippendale is, of course, based on it. (However, since this is an American book designed for American readers, and since American Chippendale is certainly available on the market, it will be discussed as a separate section in Chapter XXII).

From the point of view of pure volume of antique furniture, Chippendale (English) probably dominates the market. Nevertheless, there have been ups and downs of demand for Chippendale furniture and wide variations in price at various times. Price is often a measure of economic conditions and the vogue of collecting antiques.

The English magazine *Connoisseur,* organized in 1901 to serve the rising group of collectors, states in its September–December 1901 issue, ". . . while the prices of fine old French mounted furniture . . . quite hold their own . . . there has been a more rapid appreciation lately of really high class English furniture of the 18th century."

The January–April 1903 *Connoisseur* says, "Now-a-days almost anyone who owns a fairly good article of furniture, the date of which may be anything between 1740 and 1800, vaguely tells his admiring friends it is 'a Chippendale,' probably adding 'and it is very valuable.' " *The Connoisseur* continues, "His [Chippendale's] work is now, after a considerable period of more or less neglect, again appreciated . . . as the prices realized in the sale rooms, not only for exquisite, but even doubtful or second-rate specimens testify."

Prices of Chippendale Furniture in the Early Twentieth Century

The first issue of *The Connoisseur* states that twenty or thirty years prior to the turn of the century Chippendale chairs were banished to the housekeeper's room, but high prices for such chairs by 1901 made the owners realize that they had treasures. Thus the chairs were restored to a place of honor. The "high prices" of the year 1901 were, however, low by today's standards or even by the standards of the early 1930's at the bottom of the Depression!

At a Belfast auction on November 11, 1901, seven Chippendale carved mahogany chairs brought £29/15 (about $145). At a little over $20 a chair, the price of Chippendale furniture at this time seemed to be near the vanishing point. In the same month, Christie's sold a pair of mahogany armchairs with open backs and a carved shell on the top rail, cabriole legs and ball-and-claw feet, for £35/14 ($173). Almost throughout the history of antique collecting, the Chippendale armchair has been one of the most sought after and highest priced pieces. On December 16, 1901, Christie's sold a mahogany armchair with ball-and-claw feet and carved legs for £18/7/6 (about $89).

Two years later, on February 27, 1903, Christie's sold a large armchair for £42 ($203) and one for £54/12 ($265). A settee to match with six legs of cabriole design brought £105 ($510), while one of double chair back design, five feet wide, brought £294 ($1,436).

Prices had tripled in two years' time! Were it not for eight chairs which went for £204/15 ($993), eight for £168 ($816) and six for £283/10 ($1,378), the index might even have risen above 300 percent in 1903 with 1901 the 100 percent base.

In 1904 one chair brought £336 ($1,630). The index stood at 500 percent.

By 1905 the index was up to 600 percent. It was at this approximate figure in 1906. Large sets of chairs were going at higher prices. The index continued to climb. By 1910 it stood at 750 percent. On December 9, 1909, Christie's sold a mahogany wing armchair in English needlework, with carved cabriole legs and ball-and-claw feet, for £162/5 ($785). Conceivably, such a piece might sell for the same price today, not considering the decline in the value of English and American currencies. In 1910 large sets of chairs—ten each—sold for £304, £262 and £241 ($1,474, $,1271 and $1,169).

In the United States, prices of English Chippendale furniture were definitely lower than in England. At the American Art Association sale of the Thomas B. Clarke Collection under the auspices of the Tiffany Studios, December 1 to 3,

1910, a pretty mahogany side chair with ball-and-claw feet, carved knees and Chinese fret-work brought $320. A mahogany ladder-back armchair brought $255, and a mahogany upholstered armchair with straight legs went for $220. It should be noted that early in American auctioning (prior to the late 1920's) there was often no designation of origin as to English or American Chippendale. For this reason, many Chippendale items sold in American auction houses and advertised for sale in American magazines were not used in this price analysis, because it was not clear from the description or the appearance in the advertisement whether they were American or English. For that matter, many dealers today sell Chippendale pieces that they are not quite sure are American or English.

The World War I Debacle

At the outbreak of World War I—at least the European phase of it—prices of furniture dropped almost catastrophically. On June 2, 1915, Christie's sold a pair of Chippendale mahogany chairs with cabriole legs for £31/10 ($145).

The leading London dealers bought at this sale, so the items were of some importance. Yet prices were at the level of the turn of the century, and the price index again stood at 100 percent. The most spectacular boom had taken place between the opening of the century (it actually started before the turn) and the outbreak of World War I.

Prices of Chippendale furniture remained at a low level throughout the war. In the last year of the war, 1918, Sotheby's sold a handsome commode of serpentine shape, with four drawers and bracket feet, for £35 ($166). On July 31, 1918, Sotheby's sold a mahogany bureau bookcase with original brass for £43 ($204). This is one of the high-priced and most sought after items in the present antique market. The price index still stood at 100 percent.

The Rise in the 1920's

By 1920 the price index stood at about 200 percent. At least one Chippendale item of museum quality was sold during the year—a remarkably fine mahogany commode with serpentine front, elaborately carved corners, scroll feet, gilded original brass handles, and two small and two long drawers. The piece was four feet long and was a work of art. It brought £2,400 (just under $9,000). This illustrates that a work of art, a piece of museum quality, will bring a high price by almost any standard, even though sold in a period of relatively low prices in the general antique market. The height of that market is not judged by these superior or supreme pieces of furniture.

By 1925 the antique boom of the 1920's was developing rapidly. Many more fine items were offered on the market and these were featured through illustrations in English and American auction houses alike.

During the early months of 1925 two tilt-top tables brought $360 and $250. The first was an elegant galleried-top piece. Prices stood at 1000 percent.

The year 1926 saw a boom in the field of antique furniture, particularly in America. On January 9, 1926, the American Art Association Galleries sold a mahogany side chair with beautiful carving and ball-and-claw feet for $375 and another for $275. On May 5 they sold an elegant "master's chair" in the French taste for $1,000. Five side chairs and one armchair were sold for $750, and a set of eight ladder-backs brought $1,760. During 1926 Christie's sold six chairs for £924 ($4,481—about $750 a chair). At the same time the American Galleries sold a superb carved mahogany tripod tea table with a tilt top and a fretted octagonal gallery for $1,700.

Prices now stood at the 1,500 percent level.

Between 1926 and the boom year of 1929, prices of English Chippendale furniture did not rise appreciably. They had already risen in a boom that peaked out earlier. This was the second run-up since the turn of the century.

Prices in the Depression

The next year chosen for recording prices is 1932, which represents the bottom of industrial production in the United States. At the same time most of Europe was in a deep depression, including England, so the effects of depression can be determined in connection with London as well as New York auction prices.

In *Christie's Season 1930* the depression in general business was carefully noted, and then the statement was made, ". . . it was soon evident that values were to be maintained at a very high level."

Christie's Season 1931 states, "If the greater proportion of investments have shown a falling tendency, fine Works of Art have suffered little if anything in comparison." Both reports state, however, that American buying support in the art and antique market was weak, but British prices were not weak. During the year, 2,300 guineas ($11,500) was secured for a Chippendale writing table; 960 guineas ($4,800) for a Chippendale settee; 820 guineas ($4,100) for a tripod table, and £2,415 (almost $11,000) for a mahogany writing table.

While America was suffering from the Depression, the prices of Chippendale furniture in New York in 1932 did not reflect much of this suffering. A piecrust table sold for $575, a console table for $1,400, a tea table for $1,500, a superb tilt-top table for $2,650 and a dining table consisting of five parts for $4,000. In general prices were off very little, and certainly the index was not below 1,000 percent, even considering American prices. In fact, a good case can be made that English prices did not go down at all!

The Rise Out of the Depression

There were a few important sales of Chippendale furniture between 1932 and 1939 which should be noted.

The first is the Alfred H. Mulliken sale held in New York at the American-Anderson Galleries on January 7, 1933. At this sale an excellent carved armchair with ball-and-claw feet brought $650. A finely carved mahogany ball-and-claw foot card table brought $450, and an upholstered armchair of carved mahogany with ball-and-claw feet brought $1,025. These were by no means low prices.

In 1936 Chippendale prices were still high. At the Marsden J. Parry sale held at the American-Anderson Galleries, April 3 and 4, 1936, a carved mahogany table in the French taste brought $4,750; twelve elaborately carved side chairs brought $6,600; a finely carved mahogany commode of French type brought $2,950; a pair of elaborately carved armorial armchairs of English or Irish origin brought $1,550, and a pair of beautifully carved mahogany ribbon-back armchairs with straight legs brought $1,300.

The War

By 1939 prices were down to 300 percent. On February 7 Christie's sold a mahogany armchair of Chinese design with straight legs and a laced splat for £46 (about $185). On June 29, Christie's sold a suite of four armchairs, two settees, two window seats and two stools for £304 ($1,216)—an extremely low price for such a suite. The Parke-Bernet Galleries on February 4 sold five ladder-backs with straight legs for $324 the lot.

Sotheby's on March 3 sold a pair of serpentine commodes with original gilt Rococo handles and escutcheons and with canted and decorated angle ogee feet for £310 ($1,240). Christie's sold another serpentine commode for £48/6 ($194).

Tables seemed to bring almost nothing. A circular birdcage table brought £17 ($68)—even with a scalloped top. A superb heavily carved giltwood side table with scrolls brought £18/18 (about $75). A piecrust table brought $80 in New York.

By 1942 prices had improved a bit. The price index stood at 500 percent, about the level of the middle of the first decade of the present century.

One of a pair of English Chippendale serpentine commodes. Sotheby's, 1939, $1,240, purchased by Mallett.

One of a pair of English Chippendale "ribband-back" side chairs, from Frank Partridge, New York. Parke-Bernet, 1955, $7,000 the pair.

The Postwar Years

By 1945, the war's end, prices had again risen materially. Tripod tables are a good measure of prices of Chippendale furniture. Two galleried tripod tables sold for £560 and £310 ($2,240 and $1,240) at Sotheby's on November 9. On December 1 the Parke-Bernet Galleries sold a similar table for $1,500.

Armchairs were up markedly. On November 9, 1945, Sotheby's sold a mahogany elbow chair referred to in Macquoid and Edwards' *Dictionary of English Furniture*. It had carved knees, a carved splat and dolphin feet and brought £420 ($1,640).

A very fine eighteenth-century walnut and parcel-gilt Gainsborough chair, circa 1750. Price—$3,080. *Courtesy of Mallett & Son, London.*

Nine mahogany armchairs of French character upholstered in needlepoint and of fine design brought £6,090 (just under $25,000) at Christie's on August 2. Prices were now at the 3,000 percent level.

Prices of English Chippendale furniture had again slumped by 1950. The index stood at 1,000 percent.

By 1955 Chippendale prices started the rise which has continued to the present time. The Parke-Bernet Galleries on April 30, 1955, sold a finely carved mahogany ribbon-back side chair of elegant design, once sold by Partridge, for the high price of $7,000.

Some rather spectacularly high prices were realized in 1955. On November 17 Christie's sold a small upright French-type cabinet, 29 inches wide, to Partridge for £3,780 ($10,584). On May 12 Christie's sold to Partridge a French-type marquetry commode 60 inches wide for £5,460 ($15,290). On April 30 the Parke-Bernet Galleries sold a carved mahogany and green leather library desk for $5,900. Prices had tripled in five years and the index stood at 3,000 percent again.

The 1960's

On April 29 and 30, 1960, the Walter P. Chrysler sale of English furniture was held in New York City at the Parke-Bernet Galleries. This was one of the finest

One of a pair of Chippendale open armchairs.   Parke-Bernet, 1960, $7,000.

English Chippendale bow-front commode.   Parke-Bernet, 1960, $6,500.   (*Photo: Taylor & Dull*)

George II carved mahogany kneehole desk, attributed to Kent.   Parke-Bernet, 1960, $6,000.   (*Photo: Taylor & Dull*)

offerings of English furniture in recent history. At this sale, a pair of carved mahogany and old gold damask open-arm easy chairs brought $7,000. A fantastically fine bow-front carved mahogany commode from French and Company realized $6,500. The House of Lords armchair of open design, once sold by Partridge and shown at the Art Treasures Exhibition of 1955 in New York (from the Hearst Collection) brought $5,000.

At Christie's on March 24, fourteen Gothic mahogany chairs brought 600 guineas ($1,800)—not a high price.

If prices rose between 1955 and 1960, they did not do so materially and overall. For the lesser items an on-the-spot survey was made in late 1959. In Canterbury, England, a set of fine Chippendale chairs could have been purchased for $50 a chair. The index still stood at 3,000 percent.

One of a set of fourteen English Chippendale chairs in the gothic taste.   Christie's, 1960, $1,800.

In 1961 a record was established for a piece of Chippendale furniture when a commode was sold in New York for $70,000!

The middle of the 1960 decade saw some record prices for English Chippendale furniture, but these were items of museum quality. On January 31, 1964, Sotheby's sold a late marquetry commode of serpentine design in the French taste, with *bronze doré* mounts, for £2,200 ($6,160). On June 24, 1965, Christie's sold an important mahogany commode, 41½ inches wide, in the French taste, *by Thomas Chippendale*, for the equivalent of $26,460.

In the summer of 1965 a new Chippendale record was established. The Harewood House desk brought 41,000 guineas—over $120,000!

Some other contents of Harewood House were also by Thomas Chippendale and were said to be based on Robert Adam's designs. A mirror brought the surprising sum of 10,000 guineas ($30,000). Four giltwood open armchairs in the French manner brought 3,200 guineas ($9,600); and a marquetry and giltwood side table on six tapered legs, with square capitals and lions' heads in relief,

Commode by Thomas Chippendale. Christie's, 1965, $26,460.

a veneered top panel of mahogany and satinwood, and inlaid with draperies and musical ornaments, brought 6,000 guineas ($18,000).

The less-than-museum-quality items still did not bring materially higher prices than they had brought earlier in the 1960's. In the fall of 1965 a set of four mahogany chairs of fine design in the French style brought 750 guineas ($2,250).

In the October 30, 1965, Parke-Bernet sale, an excellent carved commode with a shaped top and gadrooned border, with two short and three long drawers, with shaped sides and elaborately carved canted angles, brought $600. It was estimated to bring $2,000. On January 8, 1965, the Parke-Bernet Galleries sold a fine armchair of wing design with ball-and-claw feet, cabriole legs and leaf carving for $675.

It is true that museum quality pieces probably rose in price between 1960 and 1965, as did the low price furniture. But the in-between furniture did not show any appreciable rise, and in the fall of 1965 several excellent Chippendale items sold perceptibly under the Parke-Bernet estimates. They were neither poor items nor museum quality items. If it were possible to divide the 1965 price index, the fine items would probably show a rise, the very inexpensive items would show a considerable rise, and the in-between items would show little or no rise, in some cases possibly a falling off in price.

The Harewood House Chippendale desk. Christie's, 1965, $120,540.

One of a set of four George I walnut dining chairs, circa 1720, covered in old needlework. Parke-Bernet, 1966, $6,800 the set.

One of four giltwood open-arm chairs, in the French Style, by Thomas Chippendale after an Adam Design. Christie's, 1965, $9,400 the set.

English Chippendale wing armchair. Parke-Bernet, 1965, $675.

One of a pair of George II walnut armchairs. Parke-Bernet, 1966, $900.

On July 15, 1966, Sotheby's sold two important lots of Chippendale furniture. The first was a mahogany library table which brought the equivalent of $3,360. The next was a set of ten Thomas Chippendale mahogany dining chairs, including a pair of armchairs. The total price was $14,560, almost $1,500 a chair.

In the summer of 1966 the author visited a number of London dealers, including the leading antique houses. One of these dealers offered one of the finest Chippendale pieces ever to come onto the market, a gilt wood display cabinet, c.1765, in perfect condition. It was fairly priced at £45,000 ($126,000).

Another dealer offered a truly fine pair of Chippendale chairs in the French style, one was the equal of an excellent Louis XV chair. They were gilded, and the gilding looked in excellent condition. The price was £5,000 ($14,000). In the same super-fine category was a *bombé* commode for £9,500 ($26,600)

From an important set of eighteen Georgian walnut chairs and a settee made by William Hallett in 1735. Sotheby's, 1966, $7,000 (with original bill of sale—18 chairs £20/14, 2 settees £4/18).

One of a pair of George III *bombé* commodes.   Sotheby's, 1963, $900.

Serpentine marquetry commode, attributed to Thomas Chippendale.   Sotheby's, 1966, $13,440.

From the sublime we go to the ridiculous. A Dublin painting dealer was moving to London where he felt business would be better. We visited his shop and greatly admired a Chippendale mahogany slant-top desk that was obviously one of his personal possessions in which he kept his belongings. While we were in the shop two moving men came in, removed the drawers which the dealer emptied, and carried the desk to a waiting moving van. "A pity I had to let that go," the dealer told us, "and I got only £40 for it, but I couldn't take it with me." The price equivalent in dollars was $112! In New York at a secondary auction it would have brought perhaps $750.

Although Chippendale chairs in the French style are in the all-but-priceless category, some other pieces in that style are not. A table in the French style was offered in London for £675 ($1,890). At the same time in London, one of the large dealers offered a top-grade card table for £825 ($2,310). The establishment of this dealer is somewhat unique. In addition to offering high grade antiques, the store also carries men's and women's clothing and delicatessen products. In fact, the delicatessen department is the main one and occupies almost the entire

From a set of George II walnut chairs, six side chairs and one armchair.   Sotheby's, 1966, $8,960.

George II gilt side table in the manner of William Kent.   Sotheby's, 1966, $2,240.

Thomas Chippendale mahogany library table.   Sotheby's, 1966, $3,360.

ground floor. Incidentally, all delicatessen products are sold by salesmen in striped trousers and cutaway coats!

All markets have preferences or biases in antiques, and one dealer in London offered a pair of fold-over tables for the very reasonable price of £800 ($2,240). On the other hand, a New York auction house in 1965 realized $1,500 for a fold-over card table with needlepoint top. In the summer of 1966 this same table was offered in London for $7,500! In America the pair of tables would bring more than they were offered for in London, but the table with the needlepoint top was vastly preferred in London.

One of a set of ten Thomas Chippendale mahogany dining chairs, including a pair of armchairs.   Sotheby's, 1966, $14,560.

English Chippendale Prices

Date	1901 Equals 100%	1925 Equals 100%	1920 Equals 100%	1950 Equals 100%
1901	100%			
1903	300			
1904	400			
1905	600			
1906	600			
1910	750			
1914	750			
1915	100			
1918	100			
1920	200	20%	100%	
1925	1,000	100	500	
1926	1,500	150	750	
1929	1,500	150	750	
1932	1,000	100	500	
1939	300	30	150	
1942	500	50	250	
1945	3,000	300	1,500	
1950	1,000	100	500	100%
1955	3,000	300	1,500	300
1960	4,000	400	2,000	400
1965	5,000	500	250	500

One of a pair of early George I walnut dining chairs, circa 1720.   Parke-Bernet, 1966, $1,350 the pair.

Georgian Furniture

There is a large group of English furniture which appears regularly on the antique market and has appeared on that market for many decades. It is often called simply "Georgian." While it is very close to Chippendale, the category "Georgian" is a catch-all. The term is used to include the furniture of George I, George II and George III. Sometimes a piece is simply designated "Georgian." At other times, it is designated by the particular monarch.

It is hardly possible to group this furniture into the summary category of "Georgian" even though the sales catalogues sometimes do so. The combined "Georgian" period of reigns covered over one hundred years—from 1714 until 1820—and there is only limited similarity between George I and George III furniture. Sometimes the term "Georgian" is used to cover Chippendale as well as what is commonly known as Georgian. To include a price index designated "Georgian" confuses not only George I, II and III, but Chippendale as well.

A superb Chinese Chippendale gilt and padouk display cabinet, circa 1765.   Price $126,000.   *Courtesy of Mallett & Son, London.*

Prices of this so-called Georgian furniture were traced from the early years of the century until the present time. Not enough is found to include separate categories for each of the three Georges, and it is not entirely certain that such designations have meaning or that the assignment of a particular piece of furniture to one of the three Georges by the cataloguers at the auction houses was always correct. In any event, a price index was *estimated* for this composite group of furniture. It rose from 100 percent in 1916 to 4,000 percent in 1965. If 1925 is used as the 100 percent base, then in 1965 the index stood at 800 percent. With 1950 equal to 100 percent, the 1965 figure was 500 percent.

At the Walter P. Chrysler sale held at the Parke-Bernet Galleries on April 29 and 30, 1960, a curved mahogany kneehole desk attributed to William Kent brought $6,000. It was designated as George I.

A pair of important Chippendale carved and gilded open armchairs. Price—$15,000 the pair. *Courtesy of Spink & Son, London.*

From a suite of Chippendale seat furniture in the classic Louis XVI style, consisting of two sets of six armchairs, six side chairs, and a pair of settees. Sotheby's 1966, $11,200 the suite.

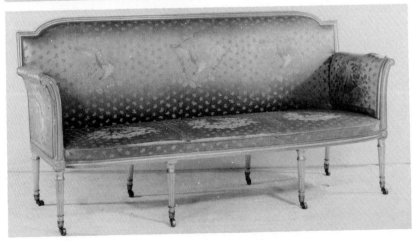

In the 1963 season Sotheby's sold a pair of George III *bombé* commodes in the Louis XV style for £3,200 (about $9,000).

In the October 30, 1964, sale held at Sotheby's in London, a small George II mahogany dining room side table in the manner of Matthias Lock, 44 inches wide, was sold to dealer Frank Partridge for $7,000. The same dealer in the same sale bought seventeen early George III mahogany chairs with scroll feet for $5,600. The catalogue states that these chairs were in the Chippendale manner. On April 10 Sotheby's had sold a George II mahogany serpentine-front kneehole desk for £2,100 ($5,880), while in the same season the Parke-Bernet Galleries sold a pair of George II carved and gilded walnut armchairs, with eagles' head decorations, for $3,550 the pair. They had cabriole legs, ball-and-claw feet and a solid splat.

On February 11, 1966, Sotheby's sold a fine George II giltwood side table, five feet wide, in the manner of William Kent, for $2,240. In the June 24 sale they sold two good Georgian lots. The first was a set of eighteen walnut chairs and a settee made by William Hallett in 1735. The lot brought $7,000—only $368 per item for an extremely large set of seat furniture of superb quality. Incidentally, the original bill of sale was offered along with the furniture. The price when made for the eighteen chairs was £20/14 (about $58) and two settees (not just one) cost £4/18!

When this composite index of George I, II and III was compared with the Chippendale price index, the correlation was very close. It was decided not to place such a composite index in the final Antique Price Index.

Georgian Prices

Date	1916 Equals 100%	1950 Equals 100%	1925 Equals 100%	1920 Equals 100%
1916	100%		20%	20%
1920	500		100	100%
1925	500		100%	100
1932	50		10	10
1939	500		100	100
1942	500		100	100
1945	1,000		200	200
1950	800	100%	160	160
1955	800	100	160	160
1960	2,500	310	500	500
1965	4,000	500	800	800

CHAPTER SEVENTEEN

Adam
1760–1793

E DWARD WENHAM IN HIS BOOK *Old Furniture* (London: Spring Books, original publication date 1939, recent edition 1965) says, "Robert Adam may have been the supreme dictator of the fashionable world of this time in matters of architecture, decoration, furniture, and the various other phases of the correct interior treatment of the large houses, but little if any of the furniture made from his designs would be suitable in any average home."

H. Avray Tipping in *The Dictionary of English Furniture*, edited by Percy Macquoid and Ralph Edwards (London: 1954), says, ". . . the conception is ceremonial, not domestic. The eclectic refinement of design and delicate splendour of execution of the thoughtfully appointed and deliberately placed pieces of furniture banish the sense of easy homeliness." To which Mr. Wenham in *Old Furniture* adds, "And that well defines the frigid and formal designs which this clever Scottish architect successfully made fashionable."

In the year 1774, when the Adam style was in full vogue, Samuel Johnson said, ". . . the grandeur was all below . . . the bedchambers were small, low and dark, and fitter for a prison than for a house of splendour."

If I myself had to rank Adam furniture with other furniture made throughout history and in all countries, I would rank it near the top. Three of our finest items of furnishing are a matched set of urn-shaped knife boxes made about 1775. They are strict Adam in design, and one sits on the desk in my office where I can admire it from time to time.

Opinions vary, and while some think the furniture based on designs by Robert Adam is unsuitable today, and some even think it was unsuitable at the time it was made, others like myself think it is some of the most superb furniture ever made.

Origins of Adam Furniture

Robert Adam (1728–1792) went to Italy in 1754 and stayed there for four years. Upon his return to England in 1758 he published a work entitled *The Ruins of the Palace of Diocletian at Spalatro*. The essence of this publication was Adam's proposed restoration of what remained of the Emperor Diocletian's palace which

AN ADAM ROOM, with furniture, furnishings, rug, and architectural detail of Adam design, giving classic unity to the whole interior. *Courtesy of The Victoria and Albert Museum, London.*

was built at the end of the third century A.D. The publication of this work and the theme of antiquity took hold in England, and in 1762 Robert Adam was appointed Architect to the King. Robert's brother, James, was also a designer of furniture. While James was a good draftsman and later on took Robert's place as Architect to the King, Robert was the innovator.

Robert Adam was only incidentally a furniture designer. His main profession was to design, or preferably redesign, houses, principally the interiors, from top to bottom. He designed the walls and the wall decorations, stairways, and furniture. He commissioned such artists as Angelica Kauffman, Cipriani and Zucchi to paint wall and ceiling decorations. We saw one such piece in 1961 in a house in Slough, near London. The owner of the house apparently guessed what was in our minds, for he stated, "The painting can never be removed, and when it is in need of cleaning or restoration, funds are provided by the government."

While one of the disputed points about Thomas Chippendale is whether he himself was a good carver, there is little question whether Adam was a carver or even a furnituremaker. He was a *designer* of the interior of the finest homes in England, and he commissioned craftsmen to carry out his designs. He employed such eminent cabinetmakers as Samuel Norman, William France, William Beckwith and John Linnell. The great desk from Harewood House was built by Thomas Chippendale, but was based on the designs of Robert Adam. It reached the record price of about $123,000 as mentioned earlier. Whether the desk is a Chippendale desk or an Adam desk is a matter of viewpoint. Adam designed it, and Chippendale made it in his shop with his (Chippendale's) workmen. Chippendale, while he certainly had his own designs, also made use of Adam's designs. Was such furniture Adam furniture or Chippendale furniture? We can call it Adam if we wish because the design was Adam, and that is what we are doing in this chapter.

Characteristics of the Adam Style

The primary characteristic of the Adam style is that it is "antique" in the sense of the Louis XVI style. Both styles were tremendously influenced by the remains of the classical civilization discovered in Italy. At first Adam confined himself, as far as furniture is concerned, to altering the Rococo design of Louis XV. He used the curved lines and the cabriole leg and scrolled and other curved feet of the Louis XV style. Possibly because Adam furniture depends so heavily on Louis XV, it is not given as much credit design-wise as it should get. Adam is a French design taken by an Englishman and modified.

If Adam had been a member of the Paris guild that made fine furniture in the style of the era, he would have been one of the greatest French designers. He introduced into the Louis XV style (at least in his earlier period) something of the heaviness of the Chippendale style, but he has a certain restraint in design, whereas the later Louis XV designs sometimes tended to go overboard in curves and over-elaborate ornamentations.

On this Rococo furniture (Rococo from a structural point of view), he placed classical ornamentation. But later on in his career he changed the entire form of the furniture; and, while it is true that he then designed furniture in the Louis XVI style, in this style too he would have been a leader had he belonged to the Paris guild. In addition, he made furniture that was distinct and apart from Louis XVI furniture and was distinctly "Adam":

1. Architectural quality. In 1773 Adam and his brother, James, published *Works in Architecture* which contained engravings and design descriptions. His reconstruction of Diocletian's palace had brought him wide acclaim. This new work was also of an architectural nature. Adam's acquaintance with Piranesi, the engraver of ancient Roman architectural scenes, undoubtedly influenced Adam in his architectural career and helped to stress architectural design elements in all of his work.

Without the *demand* for the designs and the products based on the designs that Adam turned out, Adam and his works would not have succeeded, and the factors contributing to the awakening of the demand for English designs based on antiquity are highly interesting.

Beginning in the early Georgian era (around 1725), it became fashionable to make the Grand Tour of Europe, and especially Italy. The Tour often lasted for years and was a part of the upbringing of wealthy young men. It was considered a vital part of their cultural education to absorb Old World arts and antiquities. And it was natural that the Grand Tour should include a visit to the early Greek ruins.

At the same time, the prosperity of England allowed more and more people to have fine homes finely furnished, and an ever greater emphasis was placed on the home and what it contained. The splendor of France and the building of Versailles, as well as other royal and noble palaces with their lavish interiors, was felt in England. The stage was thus set for innovations in furniture design (as well as in architecture, construction and interiors in general) and for furniture of excellence.

The pieces of furniture, particularly the larger ones made by Adam, often looked liked scaled-down buildings. The cornices and friezes sometimes had the appearance of elaborately ornamented Greek temples, and often the tops of large pieces had the roof line of large buildings of antiquity. The classical decorations helped to create this feeling of ancient architecture.

2. Ornamentation with classical motifs. The small ornamentation on Adam pieces was in many ways like that used on Renaissance Italian furniture, and to these designs were added the truly classical motifs of ancient Italy. Some of these were paterae, festoons and honeysuckle.

3. Rectangular construction. This carried out the architectural theme on many large pieces of furniture. This pattern was used on tables, cabinets and even chairs.

4. Use of straight lines in the fully developed Adam style. It was pointed out that the structure of the earlier Adam pieces was essentially Rococo and based on Louis XV design with classical motifs sometimes superimposed. The later style of Adam was definitely Louis XVI with emphasis on the straight line. The legs were square, tapered and slender and sometimes ended in spade feet.

5. Underbracing often absent. This was one of the improvements that made Louis XV furniture more beautiful. It also added to the beauty of Adam furniture compared with some of the earlier styles. It is particularly useful where the legs are slender and the piece is intended to have something of a fragile appearance.

6. Mahogany as the principal wood. Some of the highly ornamental pieces were made in other and more costly lighter woods, and some of these pieces are of great beauty and command high prices today. Some of the rare woods used were tulipwood, harewood, thuja, ebony, holly, amboyna, rosewood and satinwood.

7. Fine moldings of small scale.

8. Use of painted panels done by top-grade artists of the period.

9. Upholstery materials such as silk damask and light fabrics.

10. Flat surface ornamentation of great variety. While Adam used all manner of carving and most of the motifs from the antique, one of his distinctive features lies in his flat surface ornamentation which included the following:

> A. Satinwood. The age of Adam has sometimes been called the "Age of Satinwood," particularly the late eighteenth century. Adam liked mahogany and it offered a good medium for his carving; but in many ways he is known for his light colored satinwood pieces, including chairs and commodes. Satinwood was used as a veneer, and there were contrasting veneers of some of the exotic woods already mentioned, in addition to mahogany. Satinwood has a very distinctive deep mustard color of considerable beauty.
>
> B. Bandings of veneered wood.
>
> C. Stringing. The use of very narrow bands like strips. (This is a form of wood inlay.)
>
> D. Gilding. This process used on chairs results in a most beautiful piece of furniture.
>
> E. Parcel gilding in conjunction with painted furniture.
>
> F. Paint.
>
> G. Fluting (or very flat carving) on legs, pilasters and friezes and
>
> H. Marquetry. This was set in satinwood or harewood veneer used in the 1760's and later. It was much like French marquetry and employed a number of classical motifs. In the last decade of the eighteenth century painting replaced marquetry.

Characteristic Adam Furniture

Adam was not an innovator insofar as the creation of new pieces of furniture is concerned. Nor was the Adam Period a period of innovation. He did, however, make certain modifications of design and make certain arrangements of several pieces of furniture which resulted in a new idea. Nor was he an actual cabinetmaker. He simply designed furniture of new and elegant style, with heavy emphasis on the classical. So important were his classical motifs that they are often used to identify a piece of furniture as Adam.

The commode was one of Adam's most characteristic pieces. This article was in great demand for the living rooms of eighteenth-century England. The Adam commode is as ornate a piece of furniture as the commode of the Louis'. The satinwood marquetry commode designed by Adam has in general a straight front while each side curves inward, a novel design and not in the manner of the Louis'. The front often has a top drawer over two doors. There are short carved feet and ormolu mounts.

Another type of commode is of different design but just as typical of Adam. This is made in satinwood and harewood and is of semicircular design. These were usually designed in pairs. There is also marquetry in this type of commode, and later painted decoration was used instead of marquetry. There is either one or two doors, and sometimes there are doors on the side. There are short legs ending in plinth feet. Sometimes not only the decoration is painted but the entire ground is painted and the decoration painted on top of this.

During this era the old standby, the slant-top desk, went out of fashion. The desk of the new era was essentially in two pieces. The top part contains two doors. The lower portion looks as though it contains three drawers, but the top drawer conceals the writing part. This is a particularly beautiful piece of furniture, well-proportioned and of considerable ornamental value.

The Adam bookcase is also vastly more graceful and refined in appearance than similar pieces of the preceding era. It is smaller than earlier pieces, and it has architectural elements which are not so prominent as to give the piece a clumsy appearance. When the bookcase is made of light wood such as satinwood, it becomes a piece of furniture which, while it has to be big to hold books, is an ornamental asset. China cabinets were made along the same lines and have a similar grace and beauty.

Two types of chairs have been mentioned. The early one is of the Louis XV type, yet characteristically English. The later style is Louis XVI, and at first glance one can mistake an Adam chair for a Louis XVI chair.

The innovation in arrangement mentioned earlier had to do with the Adam sideboard table. On each side of this table is a pedestal on which an urn sits. This was a "must" in the age of Adam, and unless the furniture was placed thus, one was not in fashion! The table itself has a straight, tapered leg and classical ornamentation, and is something of an innovation in itself. The shape of the front can be serpentine, straight or broken, and it is often fitted with a brass gallery. The frieze has the same shape as the front and is often carved or fluted. There are usually six fluted rectangular legs which terminate in plinth feet. The pedestals and urns had to be of the same wood and style as the table. The urns were used for washing the silver and for holding ice water. Sometimes one of them served as a knife box.

While structurally the side table is not unlike its predecessor, the straight tapered leg and the characteristic Adam ornamentation very much altered its appearance. These tables are usually gilded, although some are made of mahogany. The frieze and the legs are the same as those of the sideboard. The tops are often marble.

Another form of side table is semicircular or semioval, and these were often made in pairs. There are four legs. These tables are usually made of satinwood (inlaid or painted) or of gilded wood. Sometimes they are painted and parcel-gilded. These, too, are some of the most beautiful and most characteristic of all Adam pieces of furniture.

Summarizing Adam furniture through an implied contrast with the furniture of other styles and eras, we may say that Adam:

1. Made the furniture infinitely more graceful and the elements smaller and more beautiful, even though some of his pieces were tremendous, being designed for tremendous rooms in tremendous houses.

2. Lightened and beautified furniture through the use of light woods, marquetry, painting, gilding and other means, including novel uses of veneers in different woods.

3. Made use in both design and ornamentation of classical motifs which came out of the discoveries of the civilizations uncovered in Italy, and used these elements most artistically.

4. Made furniture in the Louis XV and especially Louis XVI style with a distinct English flavor.

5. Designed the interior of the house and the rooms for the furniture as a part of the whole interior decorating scheme.

6. Emphasized the straight line.

Price History of Adam Furniture

Throughout the twentieth century Adam furniture has always been a preferred antique. It has rarely sold at giveaway prices as have many other types of furniture. The main reason is that it is generally of superb design and excellent construction. The same general purchasers buy Adam furniture who buy French furniture of the era of the Louis'.

The rise in the price of Adam furniture has been phenomenal in recent years. It is admirably suited to the new Age of Elegance. It is ornate, small, admirably proportioned and colorful, much of it being gilded. It is also in short supply. It was not turned out in the quantities that Louis XV and Louis XVI furniture was, and far less of it appears on the market.

Even in the early part of this century when much antique furniture sold at extremely low prices, Adam furniture was relatively high in price. On November 24, 1905, Christie's sold a mahogany sideboard containing three drawers, together with a pair of urns on pedestals, for £246/15 ($1,200). On December 1 of the same year they sold an Adam commode of Louis XVI design with three drawers in the frieze and three drawers below, and with inlay work. The sale price was £420 ($2,040). On the other hand, on November 17 the same gallery sold four partly gilded mahogany chairs for £19/9 (about $100). At that time, this much sought after item on today's market was not in demand.

In 1910, five years later, prices were about at the same level, and Burton and Knowles of Gloucester sold a hall table with marble top and six supports, decorated in rams' heads and husks, for £117/12 ($570). In 1914 an elaborate commode given by the Duke of Wellington to the Reverend Thomas Cooke of Brighton brought the prestige price of £693 ($3,368). Yet in the same year, sixteen side chairs of lyre-back design plus two armchairs (an unusually large set) brought only £367/10 ($1,783)—less than $100 a chair.

While prices in 1905, 1910 and 1914 were about the same—100 percent—in 1915 they dropped to 30 percent. The price of many other antiques also fell in the early part of World War I.

On June 2, 1915, the dealer Jacobs bought a pair of Adam settees, six feet six inches long, for the extremely low price of £33/12 ($152). Even in the last year of the war (1918) Sotheby's sold four small mahogany chairs with open lattice-work backs for £8 ($38).

In 1920 Sotheby's sold a serpentine-shaped mahogany card table with carved legs for the same price, $38, and the Anderson Galleries in New York sold a pair of painted mahogany console tables for $160. Prices had not risen from the 30 percent war level.

But the antique craze of the 1920's caught up Adam furniture along with most other antiques, and the Anderson Galleries in April 1925 sold a carved mahogany console table, seven feet eight inches long, for $350. On May 2, 1926, the American Art Association sold a pair of armchairs for $700, and in the same year the Anderson Galleries sold a pair for $600. Prices were back to the 100 percent level.

In 1928 Christie's sold a mahogany sideboard for 205 guineas ($1,000). Prices in 1929 were about at the 200 percent level.

Even in the low Depression year of 1932, however, Adam furniture was selling at fairly high prices. The American Art Association on January 29 sold a painted and carved beechwood sofa with upholstery, five feet six inches long, for $300; and on May 26 the same gallery sold a satinwood marquetry half-moon commode that had been owned by Partridge for $900. Prices were about at the 150 percent level.

Adam carved beechwood settee.   Parke-Bernet, 1939, $185.   (*Photo: Taylor & Dull*)

From a suite of eight Adam open armchairs and a pair of settees.   Christie's, 1960, $10,000 the suite.

Original Adam design for the settee.

Armchair from the "Arlington Suite."

Settee from an Adam design, part of the "Arlington Suite," consisting of a settee and three armchairs.   Sotheby's, 1963, $19,600 the suite.

Prices were on the decline, however. On November 3 and 4, 1933, four flower-painted and caned beechwood armchairs were sold in the sale of the belongings of Mrs. Morris Murray in New York for $140, and in the same sale a pair of painted and parcel-gilded half-round console tables brought $270.

In 1939 prices of Adam furniture were cut in half as compared with the Depression low of 1932. On April 21 the Parke-Bernet Galleries sold a beautiful carved beechwood and damask settee for $185, while on February 7 Christie's sold a mahogany side table with serpentine front and spade feet for £24 (about $100).

By 1942 the price of Adam furniture had gone up 50 percent, as compared with 1939. A pair of carved mahogany oval armchairs was sold in New York for $580. The same gallery (Parke-Bernet) sold eight carved lyre-back mahogany dining chairs, including two armchairs (listed in the *Dictionary of English Furniture*), chairs of identical design being in the Victoria and Albert Museum, for $800. On the other hand, Christie's sold four gilt armchairs plus two window seats, illustrated in a 1912 issue of *Country Life* magazine, for £84/6 ($339), and in the same sale four more chairs illustrated in *Country Life* brought £42/4 ($170).

By 1945, the year the war ended, prices had increased 50 percent, and during the year the Parke-Bernet Galleries sold a carved mahogany upholstered sofa, 48 inches long, for $675—by no means a low price for the general level of antiques at the time.

Five years later the general level of prices of Adam furniture had not risen appreciably. During 1950 the Parke-Bernet Galleries sold one armchair for $520, a pair of armchairs for $450 and another armchair for $210. A carved, painted and inlaid mahogany *demi-lune* commode was sold for $300, and a beautiful carved and gilded settee brought $300.

One of a pair of Adam carved and gilded armchairs.   Parke-Bernet, 1966, $2,900.

One of a set of six giltwood armchairs.   Sotheby's, 1966, $3,220 the set.

Tambour covered marquetry writing table.   Sotheby's, 1966, $4,480.

Detail of the painted floral garlands and classic motifs.

One of a pair of giltwood and satinwood side tables (see detail). Sotheby's, 1966, $7,560.

By 1955 prices had risen a little and stood at the 200 percent level (1905 base). In New York a pair of armchairs brought $580 and another matching pair brought the same price. They were of beautiful design and were carved, painted and gilded. Christie's on November 17 sold a pair of mahogany open armchairs with fancy backs similar to six in the Victoria and Albert Museum for the very high price of £1,312/10 ($3,675). This was an indication of the rise to come.

In 1958 the Parke-Bernet Galleries sold a pair of harewood and satinwood marquetry side tables for $3,000.

In 1960 high prices were the rule in Adam furniture. At the Walter P. Chrysler sale held at the Parke-Bernet Galleries on April 29 and 30, a carved mahogany breakfront writing and china closet from Stair and Company brought $3,000, and a carved and parcel gilded *demi-lune* console table with painted decorations attributed to Cipriani and Pergolesi brought $1,300.

On May 19, 1960, Christie's in London achieved a very high price for Adam furniture. A set of eight open armchairs and a pair of settees brought 3,600 guineas (about $10,000). The trend had been reversed, and the seat furniture that was so little in demand in the 1920's was now in tremendous demand.

In the 1962–1963 season this level was surpassed, however. Sotheby's sold a suite consisting of a settee and three armchairs (the fourth armchair being in the

Fine Adam satinwood and marquetry semicircular commode. Sotheby's, 1966, $16,800, bought by Frank Partridge.

Victoria and Albert Museum). The price realized was £7,000 ($19,600). A
significant aspect of this suite is that in 1947 Sotheby's realized £700 for it—10
percent of the 1962–1963 season price!

Yet in 1961 a world record had been set by a piece of Adam furniture, and
this £1,700 only represented the general price level for fine Adam furniture. In
1961 the Parke-Bernet Galleries in New York sold a satinwood and mahogany
commode with ormolu for $70,000.

As compared with 1960, the price level of Adam furniture had doubled by 1965.
It stood at 1,200 percent of the 1905 level. On May 27, 1965, Christie's sold a
fine pair of satinwood commodes, 32¾ inches wide, from the Leverhulme Collection, for the equivalent of $15,876.

These later prices are for museum-quality antiques of the Adam Period. In 1964
a fine quality set of eight chairs was offered to the author by a firm in England.
There were two armchairs and six side chairs, of excellent design and gilded. The
offering price was $5,500. This represents a fair market price at retail for a fine
set of Adam furniture neither strictly of museum quality nor with important historical associations.

An Adam carved giltwood settee with shaped back, circa 1770.   Price, $3,780.
Courtesy of Mallett & Son, London.

Very few really fine Adam items come onto the market, either the dealer or the auction market, and still fewer of the gilded variety. On June 24, 1966, Sotheby's offered a fine satinwood and marquetry semicircular commode. It realized $16,800.

In the summer of 1966 the London dealers were offering a few good Adam pieces. Thirteen natural wood chairs made by John Cobb were offered at under £5,000 ($14,000). There were no arm chairs in the lot, and only eleven of the chairs were original. A pair of semicircular side tables with repaired tops were offered for $15,400. Twelve chairs plus a settee in giltwood and *églomisé* (glass decorations) were offered for £8,500 ($23,800). Finally, a finely shaped gilt settee with carved back, made in about 1770, was priced at £1,350 ($3,750).

Adam Prices

Date	1905 Equals 100%	1950 Equals 100%	1925 Equals 100%	1920 Equals 100%
1905	100%			
1910	100			
1914	100			
1915	30			
1920	30			100%
1925	100		100%	330
1926	150		150	495
1929	200		200	660
1932	150		150	495
1939	75		75	247
1942	100		100	330
1945	150		150	495
1950	150	100%	150	495
1955	200	133	200	660
1960	600	400	600	2,000
1965	1,200	800	1,200	4,000

ENGLISH HEPPLEWHITE ROOM.   Rooms in Miniature by Narcissa Thorne.

CHAPTER EIGHTEEN

Hepplewhite
1780–1795

GEORGE HEPPLEWHITE WAS THE third man after whom an entire style of furniture was named—the others were Thomas Chippendale and Robert Adam. It will be recalled that there was considerable opinion that Chippendale was not as brilliant a designer and craftsman as some claim he was. The same opinion was voiced about Robert Adam. His designs, said one critic, were entirely unsuitable to today's living, and one contemporary of Adam stated that Adam's bedrooms looked like the interiors of prisons.

One analyst on the construction of antique furniture has this to say about Hepplewhite:

> George Hepplewhite was the originator of a style that ranks with that of Chippendale—a style so meritorious that it remains to this day a fitting monument to the gentleman cabinetmaker who brought it into being. Little is known of his life, and little need be known, other than that he was one of the four greatest designers of furniture and the first one to give the world a style having consistent refinements of line, of proportion, and of scale. At the same time, he did not lose sight of utility requirements, nor of practical structural qualities. . . . Hepplewhite conducted a shop in London, and he achieved a reputation of sufficient prominence to gain as his client the Prince of Wales himself.

But a leading present-day compendium of furniture styles states:

> Ten designs signed "Hepplewhite" appeared in the second edition of the *Cabinet Makers' London Book of Prices* published in 1788. These ten signed designs were similar to the designs of the other contemporary contributors and revealed that Hepplewhite did not introduce any innovations in design. The designs in the *Guide* were not signed and it is probable that they were drawings by several contemporary contributors. . . . The character of the Hepplewhite style is based on the designs in the *Guide*. These designs were not the creation of any one particular person, but represented collectively the prevailing taste in furniture design. . . . In fact there has never been a single piece of furniture which has been definitely known to have been made by Hepplewhite.

The September–December 1904 issue of *The Connoisseur*, in an article by H. S. Clouston entitled "The Hepplewhite Period," states:

> . . . in his list of cabinet-makers in and around London in 1803, the name (Hepplewhite) does not appear. From this and other facts, it has been argued not only that there was no such firm, but that there was no designer of the name, the book being the joint production of two or more of the cabinet-makers of the time, who used the signature as a *nom-de-plume*.

Thus, there may never have been a George Hepplewhite!

It is obvious that the easiest way to secure devastating criticism is to have one's name attached to a style of furniture!

After a review of source materials on the subject, it seems a logical conclusion that a person by the name of George Hepplewhite did live, that he did design furniture, that he did operate a shop, and that he was something of an innovator in addition to being a reflector of the prevailing styles in furniture.

Hepplewhite's book, *The Cabinet Maker and Upholsterer's Guide*, was published in 1788, two years after his death. It contained about three hundred designs for pieces of furniture that were apparently used by his firm, A. Hepplewhite and Co., Cabinetmakers.

Whether or not Hepplewhite ever lived and whether or not he was a furniture innovator or even a furniture maker, the antique market recognizes a style of furniture known as "Hepplewhite" and uses this designation. While the appellation "Hepplewhite" may be a bit arbitrary at times, as will be made clearer later on, most of the furniture sold as "Hepplewhite" is relatively easy to identify by those familiar with furniture styles.

The style came into vogue in the latter part of the eighteenth century and was in top position from about 1780 to 1795. Certainly Hepplewhite used the ideas of Adam. Much of his furniture is clearly based on Adam's designs, and some furniture cannot easily be classified into Adam or Hepplewhite. But most of it can be.

Characteristics of the Hepplewhite Style

1. Small size and graceful design. If we consider Robert Adam to be primarily a designer of interiors to whom furniture design was incidental, and if we consider that the furniture style at the time (at least the style in which most pieces of furniture were made) was Hepplewhite, then it is logical to compare Hepplewhite with the immediately preceding dominant style—Chippendale. Hepplewhite furniture is not heavy. It is not bulky. The members are small in diameter and the overall dimensions of the pieces are not as great as Chippendale.

2. Use of straight lines. This is the predominant line, although by no means the only line. It is the general line of the overall piece and is also the predominant line of the legs and the feet. The legs are not only straight, but they are slender and in the Louis XVI style. The feet are not curved but are typically of the spade type and tapered. Sometimes no feet are used. The legs themselves are often square.

3. Use of curves with the straight lines. When we come to Sheraton we will see that on top of the Hepplewhite straight lines there are imposed other straight lines to give the Sheraton piece a look of straightness. But in the Hepplewhite style, the straight elements are relieved by curved ones. The typical backs of chairs in the Hepplewhite style are of shield, oval or hoop shape. All these elements are of course curved. The seats of chairs also have a curved aspect in the front—a swelling somewhat like the top of the shield-back chair, but less pronounced. The gently swelling front also appears on cabinet furniture, on tables, on settees and on other forms of furniture.

On cabinets and chests, curved bracket feet are used, very much in the French style.

The commode, a principal piece of furniture in the Hepplewhite Period, is often basically semicircular and is very much like the semicircular Adam commode. Tables have a similar curved top—of oval shape. Elaborate curved fronts were used on sideboards, particularly the serpentine front. Bow fronts were used on chests-of-drawers, and the cabriole leg was sometimes employed—all curvilinear forms.

4. Dependence on classical design. Classicism was predominant in furniture design in the last half of the eighteenth century in France, England and most other parts of Europe. The Hepplewhite style in this respect borrowed from Adam; but often the classical motifs that were so greatly emphasized in Adam designs were played down, frequently by reducing the size of ornaments. One can go through the classical Adam motifs and practically recopy the list to indicate the motifs used by Hepplewhite.

5. Mahogany as the dominant wood, although lighter and more fancy woods were also used, as will be outlined later.

6. General absence of stretchers on chairs. This added to the elegance of design. When stretchers are used on chairs they are of a straight, rectangular variety.

7. Small-scale, finely executed, moldings.

8. Fine flat surface decoration which included using satinwood and other exotic woods, usually in veneered form and using marquetry on the more elaborate pieces such as commodes, often set in the light wood veneer. In the last quarter of the eighteenth century, painting replaced marquetry to a great extent as a decorative element. Floral designs and medallions were favorite forms of decoration in this period.

The Hepplewhite style is also noted for its gilt furniture. Some of it is the most beautiful produced by any style setter in any period. The gilt chairs are especially graceful and well designed. Settees, mirrors and pier tables are also often gilded. In addition, the carving on painted or natural wood furniture was sometimes parcel gilded with considerable beautifying effect.

Bandings of exotic wood were also used. This is a form of veneer using satinwood, harewood, rosewood and kingwood. Paneling was used as a form of banding in which entire panels of a different wood were set in the main wood for decorative purposes. In form these panels are rectangular, circular or oval. Stringing was also employed. This process involves placing very narrow strings of veneer in the main wood of the piece of furniture so that the string gives the appearance of a fine contrasting line.

9. Fine carving. Carving in the Hepplewhite style was not the important element that it was in the earlier styles. It was less used, less prominent in size and in depth, but is fine in workmanship. It often hardly stands out from the surface of the furniture.

10. Backing plates and French mounts on the more elaborate pieces such as the commodes. These pieces were designed to compete with the elegant French commodes of the period.

11. Fine upholstery. Hepplewhite upholstery was dominated by French styles and tapestries. Silks and satins were used, plain or striped. There were also materials of plainer varieties such as leather, linen and horsehair.

Typical Hepplewhite Furniture

The most typical piece of Hepplewhite furniture is the chair. Of all the chair types of the Hepplewhite style, the so-called shield back is the one most identified by the public with this style. The back, which is outlined by a wooden frame, is in the form of a large shield which forms the entire back. The center of the back top rail forms an upward curve. The back is joined to the seat by a post rising on either side of the back seat rail. From the middle of the back side rails, the arms come down to join the seat side rails. Sometimes the post which connects the back to the shield is really an extension of the rear legs, and sometimes this post forms a continuous piece with the side rails of the back.

There is another type of chair which is also typical of Hepplewhite, although the shield back is the Hepplewhite trademark. This second type of chair has an oval back. The oval is joined to the seat in the same way as the shield back; and, if there are arms (there need be no arms on the shield back or oval back), they are joined in the same way to back and seat. This is one of the finest patterns of duced in equally beautiful designs. There is also a back which is just a little off from circular.

chair in the Hepplewhite style, and one which is the rival of any chair of any period.

A modification of the oval-back chair is the circular-back chair which was pro-

The heart-shaped chair-back style was less popular. The heart part is modified by a center circular addition, but the heart form is clear. Still another form of back is the cartouche-shaped back. The shape of the back is generally of the "square" French type with slightly undulating back rails. There are three high points in the top rail—the two ends and the middle—and the top rail curves gently into these points.

The camel-back chair is essentially a simplification of this elaborate design. The chief and most obvious curve is in the middle of the top rail where it reaches a high point.

Still another type of chair was made which Americans call a Martha Washington chair. This has a high sloping back which is upholstered and of rectangular

design. The curved arms are not very long and are joined by reverse curve members to the seat rails behind the front legs. This is a relatively large easy chair.

Finally, there are Hepplewhite wing chairs. This chair is much like the Chippendale wing chair, except for the arms, which are smaller and do not scroll outward as prominently, and the legs and stretcher which are square and not curved or elaborately carved like the Chippendale chairs. These chairs, although perhaps not as good looking as their Chippendale counterparts, are nevertheless much in demand and at high prices.

The elements inside the outer back rails are equally characteristic of the Hepplewhite style, perhaps more so:

> 1. Banister backs. This type of chair has as a back filler several upright elements or bars known as balusters, banisters or simply bars.
> 2. Radiating backs. Here the bars run from an oval in the center of the back to the outside rails.
> 3. Prince of Wales backs. This is a particularly elegant design which uses the typical Prince of Wales feathers as the interior element of the back. This is the back form of one of the most famous sets of chairs in the United States—the Elias Hasket Derby chairs. The set originally comprised 24 chairs, most of which are now in leading museums, where chairs of this fineness and rarity belong.
> 4. Urn backs. This is one of the principal motifs of Robert Adam and it was used by Hepplewhite.
> 5. Medallion backs.
> 6. Drapery backs which suggest the anthemion, ears of wheat, a heart or honeysuckle.
> 7. Upholstered backs.

The settee designs are essentially like the chair designs. Settees generally rest on eight legs. Multiple chair designs are found on some settees.

The typical Hepplewhite leg is a square leg which tapers and ends in a spade foot or no foot at all. Sometimes the leg is cylindrical, and sometimes it has a bulge near the top called a ring, which adds considerable beauty to the chair, particularly to the gilt variety. The cabriole leg was also used—particularly on chairs made in the French style.

Mahogany was still a favorite wood, but satinwood was also used, and sometimes painted or gilded wood.

The sideboard was an innovation in the last quarter of the eighteeenth century. This is ordinarily a relatively large dining room piece of veneered mahogany resting on four front legs and two back ones. The front is either straight or curved, and the common curved form is serpentine. This is one of the largest and most beautifully designed, finished and decorated pieces of the entire style gamut.

Tambour furniture was a great innovation in this period and is particularly beautiful as well as practical. The tambour part consists of a series of strips of finished and polished wood fastened to a canvas (or other fabric) back, so that the tambour part will do what the roll part of the roll-top desk will do—disappear.

A circular tambour element was often placed over a flat desk to cover up the work in progress. It was also used on the upper cabinet or bookcase part of a desk. This upper part is often set back from the desk part and is most attractive.

China cabinets and bookcases are of essentially the same design, large enough to accommodate the books or other things to be stowed away but not as large and bulky as the corresponding Chippendale pieces. Such Hepplewnite pieces were often made in light, ornamental woods such as satinwood, and are some of the most beautiful and desired pieces on the market today. They are very similar to the Adam pieces designed for the same purpose.

The commode is a most typical Hepplewhite piece of furniture and one which was worked on most carefully since it was a showpiece. The semicircular shape was the one most wanted later in the eighteenth century. Commodes are usually veneered pieces of light woods, such as satinwood; various inlaid designs are set in the veneer, many of them the characteristic Adam motifs.

A related piece of furniture, but one which is much simpler and less a work of art, is the chest-of-four-drawers. The front can be straight, but it is often bowed or serpentine in form. French bracket feet are used or the feet may be straight brackets.

The secretary-cabinet is essentially in two pieces. The top contains two doors behind which is a cabinet. This top part is set back or recessed from the bottom part. The bottom contains a "drawer" that hinges outward to reveal a desk. Under this are either three real drawers or two cabinet doors enclosing a storage cabinet.

There are a number of types of Hepplewhite tables of smaller size. There is a sideboard table which has no drawers. The frieze is carved, inlaid or painted with classical motifs, or it is fluted. Pier tables, over which hung mirrors, were often made in pairs and are frequently of light woods or completely painted, although some are of mahogany. They are decorated by inlays, painting or carving.

The Pembroke table was turned out in great numbers and is particularly well made and handsomely decorated. For ornamentation it has inlays or painting, and the table itself is frequently of light wood. The shape is usually rectangular, although the oval shape was also employed. The legs are square and often the spade foot was used.

A fitted dressing table was popular in this period. The top is of the hinged variety so that it can be folded flat. When the top is lifted it reveals a mirror which can be folded out like the top. There are compartments under this mirror for various toilet items.

Still another type of table is the so-called work table, which is really a sewing table. It is small and has either one or two drawers, or else the top lifts up and underneath the top is a well. Sometimes a bag is suspended under the top for needlework. These tables are often of light woods and carefully ornamented. The square, tapering leg is usual in such pieces.

Not one of the pieces of furniture described here is a rarity on the market and, as antiques go, an immense amount of Hepplewhite furniture is available for sale. It is in considerable demand because of its useful size as well as its beauty.

Price History of Hepplewhite Furniture

Hepplewhite furniture is one of the most important elements in the antique market and is sold in great quantities both in England and the United States. It is reasonably high in price, although it is not in the class of French furniture of the eighteenth century. The finest pieces are not as spectacular as the finest Chippendale pieces. The swings in price over the years have not been as violent as, say, those in Jacobean furniture. Hepplewhite furniture went well in homes fifty years ago and it goes well in the smaller homes and apartments of today. It has been no great price performer in the past, and it will probably not be so in the near future.

Early Price History of Hepplewhite Furniture

Like so many other types of antique furniture, a base of 100 percent at the opening of the twentieth century may be used. To us in the middle 1960's the early years seem like the all-time low; but to those living in 1901 the world was experiencing an antique boom, particularly England.

In December 1901 Christie's sold six Hepplewhite chairs with open rail backs for £21 (about $100). On October 15 of the same year, Phillips and Neale sold six armchairs of wheel pattern with oval backs and in white enamel for £32/10 (about $158).

With 1901 as the base equal to 100 percent, prices by 1905 had increased 50 percent. Although there was a rise in this five-year period, the prices were so low as to make the furniture of little consequence market-wise.

By 1910 prices had doubled over 1905 prices, and the index now stood at 300 percent. Although seven chairs were sold for £50/8 ($245) and six were sold for £68/5 ($321) nine mahogany shield-back chairs of somewhat illustrious background, lightly carved with foliage and inlaid with satinwood, brought the relatively high price of £162/15 ($790). At the American Art Association sale in New York of the Thomas B. Clarke estate, a mahogany sideboard c.1790–1800 brought $210.

In 1914, just prior to the outbreak of World War I, two armchairs and six side chairs with shield backs and lyre centers brought £126 ($613)—not a low price.

The war, however, had a devastating effect on the prices of Hepplewhite furniture, as it did on most antique prices. In June 1915 Christie's sold a mahogany armchair plus two side chairs for £22/1 ($102). Four chairs sold for £15/15 ($71) in the same sale, and a few weeks later Christie's sold a pair of armchairs to the dealer Partridge for £50/8 ($235). The price index was down again to 200 percent.

But by 1920 the index was back up to 300 percent. During the year, Sotheby's sold five chairs for £100 ($366), and another set of five for £112 ($409).

Prices remained at this approximate level for the next five years. At the April 24 and 25, 1925, sale held at the Anderson Galleries in New York, a carved mahogany sofa brought $355, and the following year the same gallery sold a pair of three-feather shield-back mahogany chairs for $600. A mahogany armchair brought to America by Francis Scott Key brought $460. Eight chairs from the same set were sold in 1903 for $8,000. This, of course, was a large suite from an illustrious owner.

By 1928 prices were still on the rise, and Christie's sold a mahogany sofa during the season for 270 guineas ($810). In 1929 at the A. Rubin sale at the Anderson Galleries in New York, a mahogany armchair brought $500, a very high price for Hepplewhite furniture.

On January 13 the Anderson Galleries sold a mahogany settee for $950. While in the year 1929 the price index stood at 600 percent or six times that of the turn of the century, the level of a single piece of good Hepplewhite furniture was below $1,000. Peak prices in five figures were being achieved by Queen Anne furniture, but Hepplewhite did not seem to be in the same league.

Hepplewhite Prices in the Depression and the War

While the prices of Hepplewhite furniture declined in the Depression, they did not decline spectacularly by any means. A pair of decorated shield-back side chairs painted on the back was sold at the American Art Association on January 29, 1932, for $200, and on January 30 the same gallery sold a fine pair of decorated beech-wood armchairs for $700—$350 a chair. On May 26 the same gallery sold a serpentine inlaid mahogany sideboard for $925. In the same sale, six beautifully carved and inlaid armchairs that had been sold originally by Frank Partridge

English Hepplewhite mahogany settee.   Anderson, 1929, $950.

brought the high price of $3,300—$550 a chair. While prices in 1932 were down to 400 percent from 600 percent in 1929, they did not rise with the increasing prosperity in the late 1930's.

In the Marsden J. Perry sale at the American-Anderson Galleries on April 3 and 4, 1936, a carved mahogany upholstered sofa with a beautiful serpentine back, an illustrated piece, brought $400.

In 1939 the Parke-Bernet Galleries sold a carved mahogany settee with fluted legs for $210, a very low price for a settee and a price which indicates a downtrend. The price of chairs was sharply down in 1939 also. During the year, the Parke-Bernet Galleries sold a pair for $140, another pair for $180 and six for $450. Christie's sold eight chairs for £44 ($176) and five for £46 ($185). Prices in 1939 stood at the 200 percent level.

The war did not seem to have a tremendously significant effect on the prices of Hepplewhite furniture. A pair of side chairs that had once been sold by Mallett of London sold at the Parke-Bernet Galleries for $75. In England, Sotheby's sold a pair of elbow chairs for £70 ($280). On February 26 Christie's sold a pair of wheel-back armchairs for £99/15 (about $400), while on December 23 they sold a mahogany cabinet with a writing slide for £252 (about $1,000). The Parke-Bernet Galleries on January 23 sold a pair of carved oval armchairs in green silk for $800, a high price. Prices were 50 percent over the prewar period, but the index was far below the 1929 peak.

By 1945, the war's end, prices were at the 400 percent level. A set of nine chairs sold for $1,080, a set of ten for £183/15 (about $750) and a set of twelve for £173/5 (just under $700). An inlaid mahogany serpentine-front sideboard brought $600, and on October 19 Sotheby's sold a rare mahogany settee for £850 ($3,400)—a very high price for any piece of Hepplewhite furniture.

English mahogany sideboard. American Art Association, 1932, $925.   (*Photo: Taylor & Dull*)

The Postwar Period in Hepplewhite Furniture

By 1950 prices were very far off in Hepplewhite furniture, as they were in many other types of antiques. On January 6 the Parke-Bernet Galleries sold a pair of carved mahogany heart- and shield-back side chairs for $160, a very low price compared with 1945. An inlaid mahogany serpentine-front sideboard table brought $350.

The year 1955 represented the first recording period (we have used five-year intervals throughout a good deal of this study) in which the present antique boom was present. On January 6 the Parke-Bernet Galleries sold five shield-back chairs, including one armchair, for $700. In the same sale, a carved mahogany settee brought $900, a mahogany and satinwood marquetry serpentine-front commode brought $1,800 and another with delicate inlay work but with some repairs brought $1,800. Prices in 1955 were double 1950.

By 1960 prices had doubled as compared with 1955, and they were four times what they were in 1950. On November 5, the Parke-Bernet Galleries sold a pair of carved and gilded armchairs for $1,000 each. A short time earlier it was difficult for any one piece of Hepplewhite furniture to reach $1,000, but now a single chair achieved this figure. On June 23 Christie's sold four open armchairs of Louis XV style for 1,250 guineas ($3,750)—almost $1,000 a chair. Sotheby's on May 13 sold twelve armchairs and a settee for £3,700 (over $10,000), certainly a very high total figure that would tend to limit the number of buyers with sufficient funds.

Hepplewhite is one type of furniture that can be divided into top quality items and run-of-the-mill items. A lacquered chest with fine carving, for instance (and relatively many of these were made), will bring a very high price—in the thousands of dollars. So will a fine set of gilded chairs if the quality is high. On the other

English Hepplewhite carved and painted settee, circa 1770.   Parke-Bernet, 1966, $1,050.   (*Photo: Taylor & Dull*)

hand, a Hepplewhite bow-front commode of ordinary design may go for $200.

On May 1, 1965, the Parke-Bernet Galleries sold an inlaid mahogany swell-front sideboard for $925. It was an above-average piece, but no standout. On May 7 they sold a mahogany settee, with imperfections, for $575, and Christie's on April 29 sold a fair set of mahogany shield-back chairs for the equivalent of $2,794. At retail, a fair pair of armchairs was offered for sale by a Madison Avenue shop for $3,500—$1,750 apiece.

The price index at the end of 1965 was up to 1,200 percent as compared with 800 percent in 1960, 400 percent in 1955 and 200 percent in 1950.

On January 29, 1966, the Parke-Bernet Galleries sold a top grade mahogany break-front bookcase, nine feet high and nine feet two inches long, for $2,700. On February 12 they sold a mahogany *bergère* in the French taste, c.1770, for $600. A week later they sold a mahogany armchair, c.1770, for $500, and in the same sale a carved and painted settee, c.1770, for $1,050.

In the summer of 1966 a Dublin, Ireland dealer offered six side chairs and two armchairs of fairly good quality for £450 ($1,260)—a little over $150 a chair. In the same season a leading London dealer offered a semicircular table with cabriole legs for £725 ($2,030).

Pair of carved mahogany English Hepplewhite side chairs.   Parke-Bernet, 1966, $250.   (*Photo: Taylor & Dull*)

English Hepplewhite Prices

Date	1901 Equals 100%	1950 Equals 100%	1925 Equals 100%	1920 Equals 100%
1901	100%			
1905	150			
1910	300			
1915	200			
1920	300			100%
1925	300		100%	100
1926	450		150	150
1929	600		200	200
1932	400		133	133
1939	200		67	67
1942	300		100	100
1945	400		133	133
1950	200	100%	67	67
1955	400	200	133	133
1960	800	400	267	267
1965	1,200	600	400	400

English Hepplewhite mahogany *bergère* in the French taste.   Parke-Bernet, 1966, $600.   (*Photo: Taylor & Dull*)

English Hepplewhite mahogany armchair, circa 1770.   Parke-Bernet, 1966, $500. (*Photo: Taylor & Dull*)

English Hepplewhite mahogany breakfront bookcase. Parke-Bernet, 1966, $2,700.   (*Photo: Taylor & Dull*)

ENGLISH SHERATON ROOM.   Rooms in Miniature by Narcissa Thorne.

CHAPTER NINETEEN

Sheraton
1795–1810

THE WILLIAM AND MARY STYLE of furniture was an innovation in England, although it was based primarily on already existing Dutch styles with infusions of the French. For England, it was a revolutionary style as compared with the preceding Jacobean style which was dark, heavy and rectangular. The Queen Anne style was a progression of the William and Mary style, a refinement and an improvement. It, too, was based on the Dutch style with French elements. Chippendale was certainly a style of its own, but in many ways it was also a natural progression.

Hepplewhite was a different style. It did not represent the natural evolutionary path from Chippendale. Rather, it represented a kind of revolt against Chippendale with its heaviness and massive qualities. Of course, Chippendale was vastly more livable than the old Jacobean style.

The Sheraton style was a logical development from Hepplewhite, which had its heyday from 1780 to about 1795. The Sheraton style then reigned from 1795 to 1806 or perhaps even to 1810.

It is worth noting one authority's explanation of why the Sheraton style came into being. First, he says that Chippendale's designs "are now wholly antiquated and laid aside." Of the furnituremaker Manwaring, he says that his book has nothing ". . . but what an apprentice boy may be taught by seven hours of proper instruction. . . ." And finally, he says of Hepplewhite, ". . . . If we compare some of the designs, particularly the chairs, with the newest taste, we shall find that this work has already caught the decline and perhaps, in a little while, will suddenly die in the disorder."

This same critic had this to say about French furniture of the late eighteenth century (Louis XVI):

> . . . a clumsy fourfooted stool from France will be admired by our connoisseurs in preference to a first-rate cabinet of English production. . . . When our tradesmen are desirous to draw the best customers to their ware-rooms they hasten over to Paris, or otherwise pretend to go there, plainly indicating at our defects in cabinet-making, or extreme ignorance, that we must be pleased and attracted by the mere sound of the French taste.

The authority who made all of these criticisms leading up to full approval of the Sheraton style as the latest and the best was—Thomas Sheraton himself!

Sheraton is far from being alone in approving of the Sheraton style as the last word in excellence. Franklin H. Gottschall in *Period Furniture* (New York: Bonanza Books, 1938), states: "Thomas Sheraton was the last of the great English designers and cabinetmakers. . . . From his designs in *The Cabinet-Maker and Upholsterer's Drawing Book,* . . . he was a designer of exceptional ability. His actual knowledge of the laws governing design and construction, as it pertained to furniture, was superior to that of any of his predecessors or contemporaries, so far as we know. He developed a style, which at its best has been unsurpassed for perfect proportions, simplicity, restraint, and good taste in ornament and structural soundness."

The Connoisseur for May–August 1905 states, "I do not see how a careful comparison of Hepplewhite designs for chairs with those given in the *Drawing Book* (by Thomas Sheraton) can lead to any other conclusion than that Sheraton's are vastly superior."

On the other hand, Edward Wenham in *Old Furniture* (London: Spring Books, 1939), says, "As the designs published in George Hepplewhite's *Cabinet-Maker and Upholsterer's Guide* and those in Thomas Sheraton's *The Cabinet-Maker and Upholsterer's Drawing Book* are so closely correlated and intermingled, it is convenient to regard furniture styles which bear their names as that of the Hepplewhite-Sheraton school."

Mr. Wenham does not even recognize a Sheraton style!

He adds:

> Any noticeable differences between the designs of Hepplewhite and Sheraton are, to a very large extent, confined to the chairs; other furniture such as wardrobes, cabinets, sideboards, and tables being so closely similar that the applications of the name of either man to denote the style of any particular piece is, at the best, arbitrary.

Wenham then continues,

> It is highly probable that this book [Sheraton's *Cabinet-Maker and Upholsterer's Drawing Book*] was at least well on the way to being ready for publication before Sheraton came to London; and although he alludes to Hepplewhite's *Guide* as already being on the decline, there is little doubt that he had derived considerable 'inspiration' from the drawings in that book, and even from the title.

Mr. R. S. Clouston writing in *The Connoisseur*, May–August 1905 says:

> The evidence is so strong as to be overwhelming, and it is almost out of the question that any so-called "Sheraton" furniture was either made by, or produced under the direction of the man himself. It is occasionally possible with the other cabinet makers of the century to be certain that some

particular piece is by the man whose style it resembles; but in Sheraton's furniture we arrive at the somewhat paradoxical conclusion that the more an object is in accordance with his recognized treatment the more certain it is that he had nothing whatever to do with its construction. . . . He had no workshop, and if anyone who reads his book had taken trouble to hunt for the squalid shop in the dingy back street, there was not even furniture for sale, only books, stationery and sermons.

The only thing Mr. Clouston apparently left out of this criticism is how poorly Sheraton's clothes fit, even if they were pressed (which they never were), and how he walked with a perpetual slouch!

Thomas Sheraton was born about 1751 at Stockton-on-Tees, England. His occupation was apparently preacher and religious writer. In 1791 he came to London and immediately he issued his most important book, *The Cabinet-Maker and Upholsterer's Drawing Book.* It seems obvious that this was supposed to be of the same nature as Hepplewhite's *Cabinet Maker and Upholsterer's Guide* published in 1788. A second edition of Sheraton's book was published in 1793 and a third in 1802.

Sheraton also published the *Cabinet Dictionary.* In 1805, he published Part 1 of the *Cabinet-Maker, Upholsterer and General Artist's Encyclopaedia.* No more parts were published. (Sheraton died in 1806.) After his death, still another of his publications appeared, *Designs for Household Furniture.*

While it seems to be a popular pastime of students of antiques to deflate the reputations of the "greats" of furnituremaking just as it is often popular to deflate the greats of history, it is a fact that there is such a thing as Hepplewhite furniture and there is such a thing as Sheraton furniture. The market recognizes these designations; and, although there are certainly incorrect appellations and certain pieces are of doubtful style classification, most pieces can be recognized as Hepplewhite or Sheraton—or something else.

Importance of Sheraton Style

The Sheraton style is a particularly important style from the market point of view for several reasons. In the first place, it is furniture of pleasing design and of excellent construction. It was the fashionable furniture of the period, regardless of who designed it and who made it; and the furniture design and construction in England at the end, or toward the latter part, of the eighteenth century had reached a high point.

In addition to being furniture of the highest quality design and the best construction, Sheraton furniture is available on the market today in some quantity. It is thus unlike, let us say, Louis XV furniture or Venetian furniture, which is scarce. We are talking about a very substantial portion of antiques currently available when we talk about Sheraton.

Yet Sheraton furniture is by no means poorer furniture just because it is available. There are several reasons for this availability. One is that the original demand for eighteenth-century English furniture was much greater than for the Louis XV furniture. Many people were ordering Sheraton pieces and the prices were low enough so that a number of families could afford to buy the furniture. There was thus a great deal produced that is still available.

Sheraton furniture was produced as late as the end of the eighteenth century and the beginning of the nineteenth century. There has been much less time for it to deteriorate and to be destroyed. (The French Terror of 1789 and 1790, for instance, eliminated much fine Louis XV and Louis XVI furniture in a very short period of time.)

This large supply, which is on the market or potentially available, means that prices are not high. Antique furniture is certainly no exception to the law of supply and demand which states simply that price varies directly with demand and inversely with supply.

Even taking into consideration these facts, the low price of this furniture is still not entirely explained. Sheraton is distinctly lower in price than Hepplewhite, although Hepplewhite is most certainly a closely related furniture style. A further explanation is that Sheraton furniture represents the turning point into the nineteenth century, and the nineteenth century is anathema to furniture historians as well as to furniture dealers. It is the least wanted of all eras of furniture making, largely because later furniture is not as good in design or construction as that of the Golden Age of Furniture—the eighteenth century.

Sheraton himself turned the corner and began to design in the "new and modern" style which was poorer than his earlier style. He produced these designs at the turn of the century and into the nineteenth century. He and his name are thus identified with what is known as the "beginning of the decline."

But there are further reasons for the low prices and lack of popularity. Sheraton in the past has been a style so popular that it was reproduced in great quantities, some of these reproductions being very faithful. Rather than popularizing the originals, these later pieces have tended to drag them down.

Finally, the style elements of Sheraton have been used by furnituremakers who do not even pretend to make reproductions, but who simply use some of the good designs of Sheraton furniture for, say, a leg, a part of a leg, a design motif or the shape of a front. Thus the antique buyer does not have much really new when he gets a Sheraton antique, and it does not stand out as something novel.

Sheraton furniture is near a low point in the antique market; and, because it is at this point and yet is top quality furniture, it represents one of the greatest of all antique buys, if not *the* greatest. The situation will not always be as it is today, and in all probability Sheraton will rise very rapidly each year from now on.

Characteristics of the Sheraton Style

1. Smaller structural members than in the preceding style. It must be repeated for emphasis that the Sheraton style is closely related to the Hepplewhite style. The latter was essentially a new style and was not simply a development of the Chippendale style. Hepplewhite furniture was lighter and much more graceful. Hepplewhite depended to a great degree on the

style of the Louis'. Probably both Hepplewhite and Sheraton got their inspiration, their basic style and ornamental motifs from Robert Adam.

The Sheraton style can be considered a logical development of the Hepplewhite and a refinement of that style. The pieces were often less bulky and more graceful than their Hepplewhite counterparts. In fact, if we used a scale to weigh the various pieces of furniture, we might well find that the "average" Sheraton side chair would weigh less than its Hepplewhite counterpart. The same for Pembroke tables, etc.

2. Far greater use of the straight line. Certainly Hepplewhite made chair backs which had flat top rails, and Sheraton made top rails that curved. But in general the Hepplewhite top rails are curved, with the high point in the center of the top rail, while Sheraton made flat (horizontal) top rails. This was his characteristic style. Sometimes he seemed to pay lip service to the curve of the top rail by placing a rectangle in its center which was raised above the line of the top rail to give the impression of curvature.

3. Excellent proportion or the impression of proportion. Large pieces of furniture frequently look massive (many of the Renaissance pieces do) and sometimes bulky. The large pieces of Sheraton furniture do not have this appearance, thanks to the genius of Thomas Sheraton. If the piece was naturally very tall, as a china cabinet or bookcase, he made it narrow in order to reduce its overwhelming appearance. The Chippendale bookcase is often a monumental, overpowering piece of furniture that appears most at home in a king's drawing room.

Through the breaking up of masses which are naturally great, the impression of lightness and small size is created, and this is an important achievement in furniture.

4. Turned legs, either reeded or fluted, which taper toward the floor and have small turned feet. The earlier Hepplewhite leg is usually square and ends in spade feet, a fine design, but not quite as refined as the Sheraton leg and foot.

5. The impression of rectangularity in furniture without the feeling of angularity found in Jacobean furniture or similar early pieces. The backs give the distinct impression of being a rectangle. The entire piece has the feeling that the cubistic furniture designers of the 1920's were trying to achieve. Sheraton has a less strident quality and far more refinement. Needless to say, cubist furniture was a fleeting style which never quite took hold.

6. The use of veneers and inlays for ornamentation.

7. The use of mahogany, but often in conjunction with light ornamental woods.

8. Classical ornamentation like the earlier Adam and Hepplewhite.

9. Modified pediment tops of tall pieces of furniture to give a finished appearance.

10. The use of striped materials for upholstering.

Price History of Sheraton Furniture

Of all eighteenth-century furniture on the market, the largest group is Sheraton, both English and American. That is probably the principal reason for the relatively low price of the ordinary pieces. When a fine piece appears, one of museum quality, it commands a disproportionately high price.

The rule in Sheraton is, however, low price; and even though the price of Sheraton has recently been rising fairly rapidly, prices are still low; of all the types of eighteenth-century furniture made in England, France or the United States, Sheraton remains the lowest priced overall.

In style Sheraton is closest to Hepplewhite. Market-wise, it behaves to a degree like Hepplewhite. It is a kind of younger brother and, in a sense, it sells at a "discount" from Hepplewhite.

Early Prices of Sheraton Furniture

Prices of Sheraton furniture were not at rock bottom in 1901 as they were for some other types of furniture. At the Edward James Carter auction in Tunbridge Wells, near London, a Sheraton mahogany and inlaid satinwood wardrobe was sold on November 1, 1901, for £95 ($462).

By 1902 the antique boom was well under way, certainly for Sheraton furniture. On January 14, 1902, Powell and Powell of Bath sold an inlaid satinwood secretary-cabinet with silver handles for £250 ($1,215). This price was no exception for good Sheraton furniture in this period. On January 31 Christie's sold a pair of settees and six armchairs in painted satinwood with caned seats for £162/15 ($790). In the same sale, two painted and inlaid satinwood settees and four armchairs brought 155 guineas ($775). In 1905 a beautiful sideboard with pedestals and knife boxes was offered for £550 ($2,673), a good price even for today.

When inlay, satinwood, painting or gilding are mentioned in connection with Sheraton furniture, the piece offered is generally a preferred one and brings a higher price than ordinary items. Where these attributes are not present, prices are very much lower.

On June 19, 1905, the Chesterton auction in England sold an inlaid commode of satinwood with brass handles for £70, ($340) and Dew and Son of Bangor, England, sold a Pembroke table for £32 ($155). None of these was a giveaway price, especially considering the low general level of antique prices at the turn of the century as compared with those of recent years.

Between 1901 and 1905 Sheraton prices tripled, but they did not move up materially in the next five years. In America, the Thomas B. Clarke sale was held at the American Art Association Galleries from December 1 to 3, 1910. In this sale, a late Sheraton mahogany extension dining table, c.1810, brought the low price of $120. Six mahogany side chairs with reeded legs brought $70 apiece, while a plain sideboard brought $115.

By 1914, the year of England's entry into the war, prices still had not moved upward—or downward either. On July 9 Christie's sold a small mahogany satinwood cylinder secretary with an ormolu gallery, an attractive piece of furniture, for £60/18 (just under $300). On July 16 the same auction house sold a pair of card tables, a pair of side tables and a commode for £262/10 ($1,276).

The prices of Sheraton furniture fell to pieces by 1915. Christie's on June 16 sold a mahogany five-drawer chest with a slightly rounded front and satinwood banding—not the ordinary plain type of Sheraton commode—for £7/7 ($34). A mahogany miniature cylinder-front secretary of satinwood and tulipwood, plus another similar one, went for £10/10 ($48) during the year. In the same sale a mahogany table with folding leaves and of inlaid satinwood brought £5/15/6 ($27). The degree of detail in the price indicates that the auction house was struggling to get the last penny. A pair of semicircular side tables of inlaid satinwood brought £9/19/6—about double the price of the mahogany table. On December 19 Sotheby's sold a sideboard with a convex front and concave sides for £29/10 ($136). Prices in 1915 were at the 50 percent level (with prices in the immediate prewar period 300 percent).

The war ended in 1918, and in the following year the prices of Sheraton furniture, and of much other antique furniture, were far different. On May 29, 1919, a pair of satinwood tables 41 inches long brought £1,470 ($7,000), a fantastically high price in light of Sheraton price history.

The next year a cabinet from a well-known English house brought £504 ($1,845). Still, some prices were low, and Sotheby's on February 4 sold a pair of painted armchairs with caned seats for £20 ($73) and a painted settee for £15 ($55). On November 12 the dealer Harris bought a semicircular side table at Sotheby's for £210 ($768). Prices were at a level of 200 percent again. They remained there for the next five years.

By the boom year of 1929 Sheraton prices had risen another 50 percent and the price index stood at 300 percent—the 1905 level. At the famous Reifsnyder sale held April 24 to 27, 1929, at the American Art Association Galleries in New York, an inlaid mahogany swell-front sideboard, made about 1790, brought $2,200. The high level of this price was most certainly influenced by the high level of the other prices in this sale, several of them in five figures.

From a set of five Sheraton painted and caned chairs. Anderson, 1929, $130 the set.

At the Burnet-Clark sale held at the Anderson Galleries in New York April 25 to 26, 1929, a mahogany inlaid drum table, 39 inches long, brought $725. Other prices during the year were lower; and at the A. Rubin sale held on February 1 and 2 at the same gallery, four painted and caned side chairs and one armchair brought the small sum of $130 for the lot. During the year fourteen carved mahogany chairs (two arm and twelve side) from Duveen brought $2,520.

Prices During the Depression and the War

Christie's in its 1930–1931 season managed to secure an extremely high price for a piece of Sheraton furniture with an illustrious background. A pair of Sheraton marquetry commodes once owned by the Prince Regent brought 1,550 guineas ($7,363).

In the Depression low of 1932, however, Sheraton prices held up well in comparison with other types of antique furniture and compared with things in general. On January 29 the American Art Association sold a pair of black-and-gold caned beechwood armchairs of fine quality for $350 the pair. On June 9, however, the same gallery sold fourteen inlaid mahogany oval-back chairs (two arm and twelve side) for $770.

In 1933 at the sale of the belongings of Dr. and Mrs. Morris Murray in New York, an inlaid mahogany and satinwood sideboard of convex and concave shape brought $400.

Sheraton marquetry commode.   Christie's, 1939, £16/16.

By 1939 the Depression was well past and Europe had just plunged into war. Sheraton prices were not up. On February 23 Christie's sold a beautiful marquetry commode for £16/16 ($66). It was forty inches wide and contained ormolu plaques. At the Parke-Bernet Galleries during the year, a satinwood marquetry *demi-lune* commode brought $80, and eight inlaid mahogany dining chairs brought $360. An inlaid mahogany sideboard with shaped feet brought $420, but an illustrious sideboard of inlaid mahogany and satinwood, belonging at one time to Lord Nelson, brought $900.

In 1939 Sheraton prices were at the 200 precent level. They had changed little by 1942. But by 1945 they were up materially. During the year, the Parke-Bernet Galleries sold an inlaid serpentine-front sideboard for the large sum of $2,400, and a mahogany three-pedestal dining table for $1,400. Still, very ordinary Sheraton items brought lower prices, and the Parke-Bernet Galleries during the year sold a mahogany sideboard for $400.

The Rising Market of the 1950's and 1960's

Five years later—1950—prices had not moved upward from the 300 percent level of 1945. By 1955 they had moved slowly upward to the 350 percent level, and by 1960 to 450 percent. During the year, Christie's sold eight reeded-leg open

One of a pair of English Sheraton satinwood and marquetry commodes.   Christie's, 1965, $3,381.

armchairs for £1,470 ($4,116). An English dealer, Frank Bly of Tring, reported a considerable demand for sets of Sheraton chairs, a demand which, he said, drove sets of six side chairs and two armchairs from a December 1959 level of £180 to £190 ($504 to $532), to a level of £250 ($700) in the winter of 1960.

By the early and middle 1960's, Sheraton prices were definitely rising, although certainly not as rapidly as the leaders in the antique field. Sotheby's in December 1962 sold ten mahogany dining chairs for £800 ($2,240). In 1964 Sotheby's sold a semicircular writing table for £1,400 (nearly $4,000). They also sold a mahogany and tulipwood commode for £1,100 (over $3,000), and a set of two arm and twelve side chairs for £1,250 ($3,500). During the year the Parke-Bernet Galleries sold an inlaid mahogany and rosewood bookcase for $2,400.

In 1962 prices were still rising, and on January 9 the Parke-Bernet Galleries sold a three-pedestal mahogany extension table for $1,850, and on February 20 a similar table in mahogany and rosewood for $2,700. Christie's on May 27 sold a pair of satinwood and marquetry commodes, 65½ inches long, for $3,381.

Although some high prices were recorded at the major auctions in the middle 1960's some good Sheraton prices still went low. At the Plaza Art Galleries, auctioneers, in New York in the summer of 1965, the author bought an excellent

One of a set of four English Sheraton decorated chairs. Parke-Bernet, 1967, $2,700.

swell-front sideboard for $160. Its only fault, aside from requiring an expenditure of $55 to put it in perfect condition, was the fact that it was large—7½ feet long. In the fall of the same year the author made a second Sheraton purchase, this one privately—a faded mahogany inlaid folding card table with two movable legs. All legs were tapered and reeded. The price was $225.

Thus the price index has to be adjusted downward a little from what it might appear to be from a study of reported auction prices alone. Still, in 1965 it stood at 600 percent.

On February 11, 1966, Sotheby's sold a set of eight mahogany dining chairs, including a pair of armchairs, c.1795, for $6,720. On May 20 of the same year the Parke-Bernet Galleries sold two armchairs and six side chairs of a later period (c.1820) for $640—under $100 a chair.

Sotheby's on June 24, 1966, sold a pair of rosewood card tables for $1,680, a fair price for excellent tables, and a pair is not the most common thing on the market. In the same sale, a set of eight armchairs and a settee brought $1,904.

In the summer of 1966 the London dealers were offering a few good Sheraton items, although not as many as might be expected. A fine painted side table was offered for $7,000. This illustrates the high prices most painted and gilded furniture brings, almost regardless of era or country of origin. A pair of semicircular tables was offered at £850 ($2,380). This relatively low price for a pair of fine tables indicates the market bias of England—not placing a premium on a pair of tables of convenient size. A sideboard, on the other hand, was offered at £620 ($1,736), at least 50 percent more than such an item would be offered for in New York.

English Sheraton Prices

Date	1901 Equals 100%	1950 Equals 100%	1925 Equals 100%	1920 Equals 100%
1901	100%			
1905	300			
1910	300			
1914	300			
1915	50			
1920	200			100%
1925	200		100%	100
1926	200		100	100
1929	300		150	150
1932	200		100	100
1939	200		100	100
1942	200		100	100
1945	300		150	150
1950	300	100%	150	150
1955	350	117	168	168
1960	450	150	225	225
1965	600	200	300	300

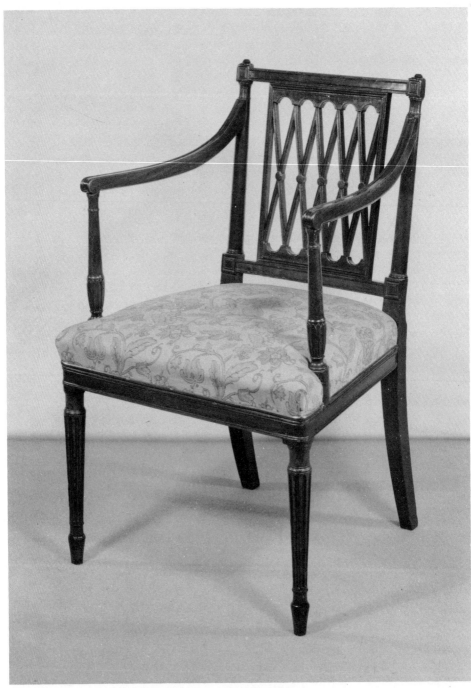

From a set of fine English Sheraton mahogany dining chairs, including a pair of armchairs, circa, 1795.   Sotheby's, 1966, $6,720.

From a set of eight English Sheraton chairs, two armchairs and six side chairs, circa 1820. Parke-Bernet, 1966, $640. *(Photo: Taylor & Dull)*

From a suite of English Sheraton mahogany seat furniture, a settee and eight armchairs.   Sotheby's, 1966, $1,904 the suite.

REGENCY ROOM, the south drawing room of the Royal Pavilion. *Courtesy of the Royal Pavilion Museum, Brighton, England.*

CHAPTER TWENTY

Regency
1795–1830

IN 1810 GEORGE III'S MENTAL CONDITION made necessary the appointment of a Regent to act in his place. His son George IV, then Prince of Wales, became the Regent, and in 1820 George IV assumed the throne. This ten years was the period of the Regency, although what is called the Regency style of furniture actually dates from perhaps 1795 when the Prince of Wales married Caroline of Brunswick. A furniture style usually does not start with a specific historical event and end with another; and, although the Regency ended with the assumption of the throne by George IV in 1820, that style continued until perhaps 1830.

The Regency style is also known as the English Empire style, and it was long known as Empire without any reference to the Regency. (The Empire was the *French* Empire, not the English.) To a degree the English Empire style is based on the French Empire style, and to secure the background of English Empire furniture one must study the background on the French Empire style.

The Regency or English Empire style is, however, somewhat unique and not simply an English version of a continental style. It is usually not hard to look at a piece of furniture and determine that it is a Regency piece and not a French one, and this determination does not rest on superficialities. The style is distinctly English.

The Louis XVI style (1774–1789) was called the Greek or Grecian style because most decorative motifs and a few basic shapes were influenced by the Herculaneum and Pompeii excavations. When Napoleon came to power, a new and invigorated classical style was developed, invigorated because everything possible of a classical nature was added, both basic classical forms of the furniture itself and as many decorative motifs as could be used.

Henry Holland (1745–1806) was perhaps the first architect and designer to promulgate the Regency style in England. In his furniture designed for the Prince of Wales and for Samuel Whitbread he used British versions of the French Empire style.

The successor to Holland as a furniture designer was Thomas Hope. In 1807 he published *Household Furniture and Interior Decoration*, and for his own home at Deepdene he made furniture in the style now known as Regency. Henry Holland, significantly, was a friend of Charles Percier, and Hope's statements on the objectives of his furniture styles reflect exactly the ideas of both Percier and Fontaine, architects supreme to the Emperor Napoleon.

Thomas Sheraton's *Drawing Book* (1791–1794) and *Cabinet Dictionary* include drawings which are clearly in the Regency style, as is much of the later furniture produced from these designs.

In 1798 Dominique Denon accompanied Napoelon on his Egyptian campaign. Denon, who later became Director-General of French Museums, published *Voyage dans la Basse et la Haute Egypte* in 1801. This contained a number of illustrations of Egyptian ornament. It was translated into English and influenced English furniture design. Thomas Hope's book *Household Furniture* illustrates Egyptian designs, and in 1804 and 1805 Thomas Chippendale, Jr., used Egyptian designs for some of his furniture.

Other factors were also responsible for the rise of the English style. The Industrial (Economic) Revolution had begun about 1795 and was well underway by 1815. One result was the enrichment of the middle class. At the same time, the war with France had made "gracious living" much more difficult and expensive. The control of furniture design, insofar as the buyer could control it, passed to a great degree from the upper class to the middle class. And, while the middle class had the wherewithal to buy, it did not have the educated tastes to demand the kind of furniture (and at the price) produced by hand labor in the eighteenth century.

The formality and elegance of the stately homes appeared to be in a state of decline, probably because (1) it cost too much in relation to rising prices to keep them in orderly condition and, no doubt, because (2) the time-consuming occupation of gracious living was going out of fashion. It is to be expected that with less attention to the home and less interest in it and its amenities, the furniture might show a similar decline, which it did.

A final factor in the transfer of the Empire style to England was the migration of cabinetmakers to England from France because of the unsettled conditions caused by the Terror in 1789, the Directorate and the wars of Napoleon. Obviously, French workers tended to produce in the French style.

Characteristics of Regency Furniture

1. Simpler form and decoration. Elaborate and highly decorated pieces of furniture were out of fashion and there was a return to simpler line, simpler construction and simpler finish.
2. The use of flat surfaces. These were often unrelieved and were considered beautiful simply because they were large and of fine wood.
3. Minimizing of decoration.
4. Use of dark woods. The two woods used most were mahogany and rosewood. Sometimes other woods were stained dark, and sometimes they were first filled where the grain was not smooth and then stained. The emphasis was clearly on the dark, although light wood was occasionally used. In addition to rosewood and mahogany, zebrawood, amboyna, calamander and kingwood were used.

5. Influence of French Empire furniture.

6. Absence of carved decoration. This was not only passé, it was expensive since it was the product of hand labor.

7. Use of brass for decoration. This is certainly one of the chief, as well as one of the best, features of Regency furniture; it is also a novel form of decoration. Brass decorations included:

A. Inlays of delicate lines, often on the tops of tables.

B. Scrolls on table tops and in other conspicuous places.

C. Floral designs.

D. Classical motifs.

E. Galleries for tables and sideboards.

F. Beading for ornamental purposes as on mirrors.

G. Gallery and shelf supports called "colonettes."

H. Wire trellises in the doors of cabinets, bookcases and cub-boards. This use was similar to that in Adam, Hepplewhite and Sheraton designs.

I. Casters on chairs and tables.

J. Lions' feet.

8. Use of chased ormolu.

9. Boulle work—inlay of brass and tortoiseshell in the manner of André-Charles Boulle of the Louis XIV era. An entire factory was established in England at this time to turn out this work.

10. Absence of inlaid wood for decoration. The trend to simplicity and the high cost of wood inlay resulted in the elimination of this popular and beautiful eighteenth-century decorative style.

11. Classical decorations such as swans, dolphins and scrolls.

12. Some use of veneered surfaces for decorative purposes—bandings, borders and lines set in other veneers.

13. Absence of comfort. One of the primary objectives of eighteenth-century French and English furniture makers was comfort. But Regency furniture was not particularly comfortable, and the desire for disciplined classical austerity too often conflicted with the equally important objective of making furniture usable.

14. A Gothic style. This style appeared to the English to be an English style; and, in fact, some of the oldest structures in England, as well as some of the most primitive wood furniture, appear to be of a Gothic nature. However, they are actually French in style. The style was dominant from the twelfth to the sixteenth centuries and spread from France to other parts of Europe. But the new Gothic style of the early nineteenth century paid only lip service to that ancient style by using some key motifs such as the curved arch and window traceries.

15. A Chinese style. Here, too, some details of the Chinese were incorporated in furniture, but not the spirit or the workmanship. Imitation bamboo was used and such motifs as pagodas, dragons and mandarins.

16. An Egyptian style. This style was dominant after Napoleon's 1798

Egyptian campaign and particularly after the Egyptian motifs were publicized by Denon's book translated into English. Here again the symbols
or motifs of Egypt were stressed such as sphinx heads, serpents, crocodiles,
lion supports and lotus leaves.

17. Imitation or copy of furniture in the classical style. Great care was
taken to determine just what kinds of furniture were used in Greece, Egypt
and early Rome. Wall pictures, pottery and the reconstructed remains of
pieces of furniture were studied to get the original contours and construction of antique pieces. Fairly true reproductions of the ancient klismos,
the tripod and the X-form stool were made. The great modern recon-
structor of this ancient furniture, Robsjohn-Gibbings, might not agree that
these old Regency pieces were faithful to the originals, but there is certainly a resemblance.

18. Rapidly changing styles. While the William and Mary style was succeeded by the Queen Anne style, and this in turn was succeeded by the
Chippendale style which gave way to the styles founded by Adam (including Hepplewhite and Sheraton), all these styles came in and went out
gradually. But the Regency style was essentially a new style and not an
evolutionary one. It was marked by styles *within* the general style. These
substyles were not by any means evolutionary; they were simply changes
for the sake of change. A parallel with automobile body styling is not a
good one, because there is some general tendency for automobile body
styling to get more beautiful and there was not that tendency in Regency
furniture.

Chippendale conceived the idea in his *Director* of publishing a style
compendium. Hepplewhite and Sheraton published their style books. So
did everyone in the Regency period, and there were more style manuals
put out in that period by far than in the entire eighteenth century!

19. Proliferation of "novelty furniture." Many of these new items were
patented, and this production of new and novel designs illustrates both the
restlessness of the era and the onset of the Industrial Revolution with its
emphasis on mechanical development. A few of these new pieces will be
described in the next section.

In actuality, the Regency style is a combination of Empire, *Directoire* and a
simplified eighteenth-century style. In its simpler forms it is extremely attractive
and not bulky. Of special interest are the side chairs, often with brass inlaid designs on the top rail of the back. On the other hand, the larger pieces are often
bulky and unsuitable in today's smaller home or apartment.

Regency furniture is in great demand on the market of the late 1960's, and
the particular pieces in the greatest demand are the smaller, more graceful ones.
The inlaid brass on table tops and chair top rails, as well as elsewhere, is highly
ornamental and not at all out of place in the homes of today. Some of the chairs
of smaller dimensions are made with small-diameter arms and legs. These are
relatively graceful pieces and some of them bring extremely high prices even when
compared with good eighteenth-century pieces.

Regency furniture, in the eyes of most experts and connoisseurs, is not the equal
in construction, design or ornamentation of that made in the eighteenth century.

On the other hand, there is no general feeling that furnituremaking in the Regency era reached an all-time low. Rather, it seems to be the general consensus that furniture in this era was on the way down, but certain items were good. The market reflects this discriminating taste. The poor items are not wanted and bring very low prices, while the very good items bring prices in line with Adam, Hepplewhite and Sheraton.

Regency Prices

Until the postwar period, prices of Regency furniture were not high enough for the furniture to command much interest in the market, and auction catalogues rarely illustrated such pieces. On February 3, 1939, the Parke-Bernet Galleries sold eight Regency dining chairs of carved mahogany (two armchairs and six straight chairs), made in about 1815, for $280—less than $40 a chair. On September 30 the same gallery sold a work table, a common Regency item, for $75; but this one was of inlaid rosewood with inlaid brass borders on the top and front. It had ring-turned legs and was 29 inches high and 23 inches long. In the same sale a drum table was sold for $210, and on December 16 six dining chairs (including one armchair) were sold for $180—$30 a chair.

By 1942 prices had, in general, not risen. On November 12, Christie's sold four armchairs and four straight chairs plus a settee. This set was illustrated in *The English Chair*, a prominent English book on furniture. The entire set brought

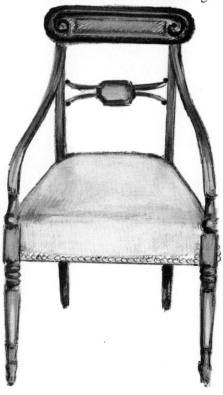

Regency inlaid rosewood work table, circa 1815. Parke-Bernet, 1939, $75.

From a set of eight Regency dining chairs. Parke-Bernet, 1939, $280.

£ 89/5 (about $360). A month later the Parke-Bernet Galleries sold eleven dining chairs made around 1815 (two arm and nine side) for $247.50—a little over $20 a chair. At the Charles E. T. McCann sale in November, however, the Parke-Bernet Galleries sold four painted and elaborately decorated side chairs, *c.*1810, for $1,200.

By 1950 prices had risen to 150 percent (1939 base). At the sale of the belongings of Mrs. Henry Ford at the Parke-Bernet Galleries, eight brass inlaid mahogany and rosewood dining chairs (two arm and six side), *c.*1815, brought $1,360.

By 1960 prices had risen only a little more—to 187 percent. The rise in price in ten years was only about 25 percent. In February 1960 the Parke-Bernet Galleries sold one of the very popular sofa tables of brass inlaid rosewood and kingwood for $350. This was one of the few Regency items that was illustrated in any Parke-Bernet sales catalogue in 1960. In the same sale, four carved and inlaid mahogany side chairs brought $240, while on January 15 a small mahogany bowfront sideboard brought $300. On February 12 another sideboard of bow-front design brought $185. The following day a pair of carved and inlaid beechwood and fruitwood armchairs brought $175.

Prices of Regency furniture had risen materially by 1964. On November 26 Christie's sold six ebonized and painted open armchairs for $1,529—about $250 a chair. In the same sale, twelve lacquered open armchairs brought $8,232—almost $700 a chair. Earlier in the year, Sotheby's had sold six painted armchairs and two

Regency drum table.   Parke-Bernet, 1939, $210.   (*Photo: Taylor & Dull*)

single chairs (one armchair being of a later date) for £440 ($1,232). In the same year, the Parke-Bernet Galleries sold six carved and painted side chairs for $1,440. Sotheby's sold a rosewood settee table for £300 ($840) and Christie's sold a mahogany bookcase-cabinet of Thomas Hope general design for £577 ($1,615). The Parke-Bernet Galleries also sold items for four figures—a pedestal desk for $1,050 and a Récamier sofa for $1,000.

On April 29, 1965, Christie's sold a Chinese lacquered writing table for the equivalent of $1,029, and on June 24 ten ebonized and gilt open armchairs made by Charles Elliott for the Tufnell family sold for $2,647—$265 a chair.

On occasion, however, sets of Regency chairs could still be bought for $100 a chair, and a fine work table was priced at retail at $225. Another was sold by one of the leading department stores to a friend of the author for $650. While prices were rising rapidly, Regency furniture still was not attracting wide attention. Prices in 1965 were about at the 500 percent level, as compared with 125 percent in 1960 and 100 percent in 1950.

On March 18, 1966, Sotheby's in London sold an excellent rosewood center writing table for $4,900. In the same sale they sold a fine secretary-cabinet three feet five inches wide for $952. In the May 14, 1966 sale the Parke-Bernet Galleries sold a small rosewood secretary-cabinet, 54 inches wide, for $2,000.

In the summer of 1966, London dealers offered surprisingly few good Regency items. An early nineteenth-century circular rosewood table was offered for £1,250 ($3,500), and a pair of armchairs was offered for $2,100.

One of six ebonized and painted Regency open-arm chairs. Christie's, 1964, $1,529 the set.

One of a set of twelve lacquered Regency open-arm chairs. Christie's, 1964, $8,232 the set.

Regency Prices

Date	1939 Equals 100%	1950 Equals 100%
1939	100%	
1942	100	
1950	150	100%
1955	150	100
1960	187	125
1965	750	500

Regency writing table in the Chinese manner.   Christie's, 1965, $1,029.

Very fine Regency rosewood center writing table.   Sotheby's, 1966, $4,900, bought by Frank Partridge.

Small Regency *secrétaire* cabinet.   Parke-Bernet, 1966, $2,000.   (*Photo: Taylor & Dull*)

Regency *secrétaire* cabinet.   Sotheby's, 1966, $952.

A VICTORIAN ROOM, the Rockefeller bedroom. *Courtesy of the Museum of New York.*

CHAPTER TWENTY-ONE

Victorian
1830–1900

F EW, IF ANY, FURNITURE HISTORIANS or antiquarians, museum directors or first-grade antique dealers consider Victorian furniture to be antique at all. Queen Victoria did not come to the throne until 1837, and she reigned until 1901—64 years, but the furniture known as Victorian began to appear a little before Victoria's time, and it continued to be made past her death.

The literature on Victorian furniture is highly interesting. Most of the books and articles start out objectively by stating that in some ways Victorian furniture is to be criticized, but in some ways it has artistic merit. This is the open-minded or objective approach for which scholars are supposedly noted. But then, almost without fail, the real feelings of the writers come through, and it becomes clear that most believe Victorian furniture is monstrous and hardly to be tolerated.

Like the Victorian houses, the "finest" Victorian furniture was very large and very thoroughly decorated. This gave an air of permanence and solidity to the furniture, and the "antique" motifs connected it with the splendors of the past.

Fortunately, there were other popular styles of furniture. The second group is well decorated but smaller furniture, and includes products of J. H. Belter and Co., whose designs will be discussed later. Suffice it to say here that very large surfaces were used on which large and deep designs such as grapes were carved. This furniture is in some demand today, and that demand is growing. If any part of Victorian furniture comes to be prized, it will probably be Belter and other pieces similar to this style.

There is a third type of Victorian furniture. This is the simple, largely undecorated furniture of a certain heavy design. It is fairly well made of rosewood or mahogany; the proportions are not bad; and it is not only serviceable, but is not detrimental in appearance to a room or a home. Probably its chief appeal at the present time is that it is cheap. For the most part, few people seem to want it, and a good bureau or desk or chair can usually be purchased for under $50. It is significant to note that $50 would buy a good piece of Victorian furniture in the *mid*-1960's, but $15 would have bought the same piece in 1960. Purely second-hand furniture declines in price as time goes by. Antiques in general go up. And Victorian furniture follows antique furniture in its price pattern.

A very significant reason for including Victorian furniture in this book is that it is fitting more and more into the category of antiques. When another one hundred years goes by, perhaps we shall get a different perspective on Victorian items. Perhaps we are too close to them to realize that they do have merits from an antique design point of view. But probably the overwhelming reason for including them as antiques is that they are now offered as antiques—and in tremendous quantities.

While neither Victorian nor Country American is strictly antique, both border on being so. Both are sold as antiques, and a very large group of the buying public thinks of them as antiques and can afford to buy them. For all these reasons, these two categories have been included in this book.

Characteristics of the Victorian Style

To summarize so far, there are three general types of Victorian furniture:

1. Very large and very highly decorated (carved)
2. Smaller but highly decorated (carved)
3. Smaller and almost completely undecorated

The first category rarely appears on the market. It was often designed for a particular house and often was sold with the house to a new owner, primarily because it was too heavy to move. It does not often appear at auction or even in dealers' establishments because it is too hard to move and occupies too much space. Then, too, large pieces have an extremely limited market. Whereas large paintings are often sold to museums, large pieces of Victorian furniture are not generally wanted by museums.

If we combine extra large size, over-decoration and a style that is not only not popular but not even strictly antique, we have what is commonly known as a "white elephant." This to some extent describes these larger Victorian pieces.

The second category not only appears more and more on the market, but it is bringing progressively higher prices. The Parke-Bernet Galleries not only handle this finer Victorian furniture, but now illustrate some of the better pieces.

The third category appears in great volume in auctions and in the shops of the lesser dealers. The best American auctions handle it in tremendous quantity.

Such a classification is arbitrary in the extreme, but it represents in a general way the market classification of Victoriana. The classification is meaningless from a stylistic or historic point of view. Some brief history of the furniture developments in the nineteenth century should be explored so particular pieces can be classified properly.

So-called "purists" recognize few pieces of furniture made after 1800. That is the dividing line between furniture they consider good and what they consider bad.

By the turn of the century—1800—a decline had begun in the quality of furniture. (While it is well to be open-minded, one must make some stylistic judgments if what he is writing is to have any meaning.)

In 1790 the French furniture guilds were disbanded and the control of member-ship disappeared, together with the standards that were constantly enforced by guild inspections. Even more important, The Terror of 1789 destroyed the chief market for fine furniture—the royal court and the nobles. It was no longer fash-ionable, even if the demand had existed, to make the elegant Louis XVI furniture. Under the *Directoire,* a modified form of eigheenth-century furniture was made, but it was not of the quality of Louis XV and Louis XVI.

While Napoleonic furniture had a certain regal look about it, since Napoleon in effect ordered the new regal-looking Empire style, it did not have the delicacy of the furniture of the Louis'. With the end of the Empire and Napoleon's final exile in 1815, the Empire style was clearly finished. Furnituremaking went downhill both in style and in construction.

In England, Sheraton's own designs reflected the changed era. The English equivalent of the Empire style was the Regency style. In many ways this style was heavy and somewhat ungainly like the French Empire style. But when the Regency style came to an end about 1830, furniture quality began to toboggan downhill.

There were many reasons for this decline. Possibly the most important was the Industrial Revolution that started in about 1795 in England and was in full swing by 1815. This was essentially a revolution in the productive process. From a furni-ture point of view it did several things. First it required a large group of people to operate the new factories, and the lowest incomes increased. A new class of busi-ness entrepreneur arose who had a relatively substantial amount of money with which to buy houses and furnish them. The machine process of production began to be applied to furniture instead of the old handmade process, so furniture could be glorified as the essence of progress, and whatever the machine turned out was *ipso facto* good. What was not fully realized was that the new machine-made furni-ture was not as good as handmade furniture. As the individual became more and more divorced from the production of each piece of furniture, individual designs for each piece became divorced, too. More and more "mass production designs" came in, particularly designs which the machine could turn out. This meant simpler designs and less complicated surface processes.

This trend by itself might have resulted in some good simple designs; but there was an opposite tendency to overdecorate, principally through carving. Later in the century machines were designed which could carve, and monstrosities resulted.

Style Trends in the Nineteenth Century

It is certainly incorrect to lump eighteenth century French furniture into one category. The Louis XV style is definitely different from the Louis XVI style. Yet in many ways the styles are similar. To lump Victorian furniture together would be committing the same kind of error through lack of discrimination.

However, nineteenth-century furniture can be broadly divided into furniture of the first half of the century and furniture of the latter half. There were several dis-tinct styles in the early part of the nineteenth century (up until about 1870): Classical, the dominant style; Gothic; Elizabethan, and Rococo revival.

All of these styles tried to revive the past; and, while even the styles of the great eighteenth century looked to the past, they were distinctive in the extreme. The Victorian styles, while they can certainly be distinguished as being Victorian, add much less of their own time and depend very much more slavishly on the past.

As the century progressed, the search of the past and the revivals of the past seemed to grow more and more frantic and, at the same time, more meaningless.

Furniture styles of the later part of the nineteenth century include a version of Louis XVI, Renaissance and Jacobean; Near Eastern, and a new classical revival.

Classical Furniture

From 1800 to 1840 France and England produced a Classical Revival style of furniture, and America followed a little later (1820–1850).

By 1850 the leading cabinetmakers had turned from classical to Rococo. In fact, the trend was evident in 1840 in the products of the best cabinetmakers. But mass production still depended heavily on this overdeveloped style.

Gothic Furniture

At the same time that the classical style was being overelaborated, a parallel style was coming in, not to replace the classical style but to run alongside it—the Gothic style. The style was nothing new, since Chippendale considered it to be of considerable importance, and there are a number of Chippendale chairs still extant with certain elements having a Gothic flavor.

In America the Gothic revival style was introduced around 1830 and it secured almost immediate public acceptance. In 1842 the first published Gothic revival designs were contained in Robert Connor's *Cabinet Maker's Assistant*. By mid-century the Gothic style had run its course.

Elizabethan Furniture

Elizabethan furniture represented still another reversion to the past. In fact, the entire century (with one notable exception) was an attempt, as far as furniture was concerned, to recapture the past—a past which was apparently felt to be glorious, especially by Sir Walter Scott.

The Gothic and Elizabethan styles paralleled in time the classic style. All three were styles of the first half of the nineteenth century. But Gothic and Elizabethan styles never provided much competition for the classical style.

Victorian Rococo Furniture

The Rococo style of Louis XV with its curved and flowing lines was revived in France under Louis Philippe, who came to the throne in 1830. In 1835 the Louis XV chair was revived, and in the 1840's the entire Rococo style became popular. Some items produced are not distinctly inferior to the original Louis XV styles.

At the turn of the mid-century this Rococo revival spread to America, and this vogue is responsible for an immense amount of furniture which was produced at this time and which is presently on the market. Probably the leading name in Victorian furniture in America is John H. Belter. His chairs were some of the best proportioned of the period, and they are characterized by pleasing carvings on the back, particularly at the top of the back. He used vines and flowers, especially roses and grapes, in attractive patterns. The chair backs themselves were often made of laminated wood several layers thick. Such lamination adds enormously to the strength of the piece and provides an excellent surface for carving. It also shows off the grain of the rosewood to great advantage. Marble tops of various colors were also used extensively in this period.

A chair developed at this time and in the Rococo style, which can lay some claim to uniqueness, is the balloon-back chair. This is a chair best described by its name. The back looks something like a balloon being inflated. Many of these balloon backs look like the round-back Louis XVI chairs, but they also have a characteristic Victorian look. They are always on the market in great quantities, and they are sometimes quite attractive.

By this time (1850–1870), machines had been developed which could cut scrolls and frames of irregular design, as well as machines which could carve fairly elaborate ornaments. Mass production techniques could thus be applied to the entire furnituremaking industry, with resultant lower prices to the buying public. Between 1845 and 1865, the volume of furniture produced in the United States doubled.

But furnituremaking was not solely a mass production industry, and the machine is not solely to blame for the decline of design. Machine workmanship is not generally as fine as hand workmanship, but design is something else. There were designers in the Victorian era who executed their designs by hand and charged $250 for a handmade sofa—not a low price even today, and a high price considering the purchasing power of the dollar in the middle 1800's. Still, these designs and the resultant handmade furniture are not, by any means, regarded as highly as those of the eighteenth century.

Louis XVI

In the 1850's and 1860's Empress Eugénie commissioned the German cabinetmaker Grohé to redesign Tuileries, St. Cloud and Compiègne in the style of Louis XVI. (Grohé had promoted that style as early as 1840). In 1860 American furnituremakers began to produce furniture in this style. The style was, of course, like the other styles of the era, a Victorianized version of Louis XVI. This Victorian furniture in some ways also resembled Louis XIV furniture, particularly in its heaviness.

Renaissance

Shortly after the turn of the mid-century, a revival Renaissance furniture appeared. This began in France about 1855. The style spread to England and to the United States.

Jacobean

In England the ornamentation of the Renaissance revival type was applied to chairs of the Carolean (Charles II) type. These were called Jacobean chairs. This furniture was made until almost the close of the century.

Near Eastern

In the late 1800's still another style made its appearance. This was a kind of Moorish furniture, and it went along with such architecture as the Brighton (England) Pavilion of John Nash and P. T. Barnum's Bridgeport, Connecticut, house known as Iranistan. The wealthy decorated entire rooms in this fashion. Furniture designers had to create their own patterns because little Near Eastern furniture of the type needed in England and in the United States was available.

New Classical Revival

In the latter part of the nineteenth century, there was another classical revival which practically amounted to a series of reproductions of the furniture of Robert Adam and his successors (late eighteenth century). Some of the pattern books might well be eighteenth-century publications instead of Victorian ones, so close to the originals are the designs.

Positive Elements of Victorian Furniture

If one does not spend a considerable time studying furniture and furniture design and walking through museum exhibits of French, English and American furniture, Victorian furniture does not look extremely bad. It looks the worst when it is compared with the best. Long exposure to good furniture designs makes one critical. Everyone tends to adapt his tastes to what is considered to be the best taste of his era. The "best" furniture of the middle 1960's is the furniture of the Louis', and the very best English and American furniture of the eighteenth century is just about in this class. Our standards of "best" are those of the eighteenth century, and Victorian furniture does not compare favorably with the work of that century.

Yet some of the smaller pieces of the Victorian era are not poorly designed or poorly made. Some are light and have a certain grace, and the woods are beautiful. When these features are combined with a price which is very low in comparison with earlier pieces, Victorian furniture has a definite place. With the severe limitations of the available stocks of the earlier periods, it becomes a matter of buying "the best of a bad lot."

In the Victorian era there was some realization that the furniture was not as artistic as it might be, and serious attempts were made to improve it. The whole craft of furnituremaking by 1850 had fallen to quite a low level. In the eighteenth century the great French furnituremakers worked directly for the king and queen and knew them personally. One of the greatest objectives of the Louis' was to make Versailles Palace magnificent, and it was a far greater concern to them than the rebuilding of our White House was to the President of the United States, even though that project cost $5,760,000! This rebuilding was most certainly very incidental to his other duties.

By 1850 furnituremaking had become just another industry. The makers were no longer artists but industrialists, yet not of the importance of railroad builders or steelmakers. In fact, the furniture industry was many rungs below the railroads, steel mills, banks and other economic enterprises in the middle nineteenth century. No longer was it an art like painting, but rather a fairly low-level machine-shop operation.

Pre-Raphaelite Furniture

The Pre-Raphaelite furniture was developed by William Morris in partnership with the Pre-Raphaelite painters—Rossetti, Burne-Jones, etc., who in their art went back to the type of art of Benozzo Gozzoli (fifteenth century). The group was organized in the middle of the nineteenth century to improve the "bad taste" and "lack of culture" of the times. It deplored the machine age and what it considered to be its tolerance of a low artistic level. Morris' company designed furniture which went back to the thirteenth century—massive but straightforward, well-proportioned and well-constructed. It was also made by hand, not by machine. The lines were straight and the carving was simple and sharply cut in straight lines. There was some painting of Pre-Raphaelite figures by the artists in the group. There was also some painted decoration in the form of vines and flowers. Polychroming was also used.

Eastlake Furniture

Charles Eastlake was greatly influenced by Morris and his group. Eastlake's book, *Hints on Household Taste*, originally published in 1868, went through many printings. This furniture was based on Morris' designs, but a simplified version. Eastlake used heavy oak with very simple decoration and very prominent hinges which give the pieces a feeling of antiquity. His simpler pieces are characterized by a feeling of horizontal and vertical straight members, the vertical predominating. There is no feeling whatever of curves, and certainly no feeling of the furniture and ornamentation of the Louis'. The color is almost always dark and natural wood, preferably oak. These pieces frequently appear on the market, and until the last few years they almost never brought as much as $100. However, there now seems to be something of a demand for Eastlake. The smaller pieces are not massive and can be used in smaller homes. The furniture is very distinctive, but it still has to overcome a feeling of out-of-dateness. It looks as though it belongs in living rooms of the 1890's where, in reality, it was very much at home.

Japanese Victorian Furniture

Another attempt to produce a furniture which would counter the trend to machine-made furniture of low-level design and poor craftsmanship was Japanese Victorian furniture. It appeared in France in the decade of the 1860's. The ornamentation was the principal feature of this furniture, and in some ways it was similar to English and Italian *chinoiserie* furniture in that it depended on Oriental surface motifs. There were little figures of Oriental flavor, but executed in France. There was an attempt made to use the fine line and asymmetry of Japanese art and architecture. This furniture never became very popular and does not appear on today's market in any quantity.

In summary, not one of the revival schools of furniture, those schools which attempted to improve furniture design and construction, was inherently good, was novel enough to form a new school, or lasted. All of these attempts at improvement fell by the wayside, and the question remains as to whether one day any of the types of furniture produced in Victorian times will secure lasting recognition like the Chippendale or Louis XV style.

The Price of Victorian Furniture

The price history of Victorian furniture is difficult to trace. Very few Victorian items bring a high enough price at auction, or have ever brought a high enough price, for the auction houses to bother to illustrate them. Of late more such items are being illustrated, perhaps in an attempt on the part of the auction firms to stimulate interest in Victorian furniture. Whether the public will become interested in such items is problematical. Certainly, as long as good eighteenth-century furniture remains at roughly present price levels the interest in Victorian will probably not grow, but a vogue for Victorian may develop as it developed for abstract art.

Victorian rosewood sofa with fruit carvings, which belonged to the Author's great-grandmother. This type can usually be purchased, in need of upholstering, for under $200.

The price of Victorian furniture has about doubled in the past five years. In order to check this assumption, several of the lesser auctions in New York where such items are handled were visited in the winter of 1966. In general the good, but not the best, Victorian items all the way from sofa tables to chests-of-drawers to dining tables to armchairs can be purchased for well under $100. The low-end items can sometimes be purchased for $25 or less, and in 1964 the author purchased much of such furniture for $15 an item and less. It was simply a matter of waiting for such items to appear at a time no one was at the auction who wanted them—and there are many such occasions.

On September 25, 1964, the Parke-Bernet Galleries offered for sale five of the best Victorian chairs—those made by the Belter firm of New York. They were of carved rosewood and consisted of one armchair and five side chairs. They were dated 1845. The lot brought $1,050—about $200 a chair. On February 19, 1965, the same gallery sold a pair of Belter chairs. The price was $140 for the pair. In the same sale, an early Belter carved rosewood sofa dated 1845 brought $550. The price depended on a particular person who wanted this particular item.

On October 22, 1960, the Parke-Bernet Galleries sold a set of early Victorian carved rosewood side chairs produced by the Belter firm, c.1845. The price was $725. A pair of armchairs to match brought $525. This one sale, not noted for its high prices in general, might indicate a rise in American Victorian furniture.

Let us go back over twenty years—to 1943—to try to determine whether there is a discernible trend in Victorian furniture. The Juliana Force sale was held at the Parke-Bernet Galleries on April 30, 1943. In this sale a Belter carved rosewood sofa, c.1845, brought $450, approximately the price brought by the same type of sofa in 1965. In the same Force sale, a decorated black lacquer oval breakfast table, c.1850—this one English—brought $675, and a decorated gold and black lacquer tilt-top table thirty inches in diameter brought $330. An English black and gold lacquer chair, elaborately stenciled and dated 1845, brought $130. An elaborate mother-of-pearl inlaid black and gold lacquer gondola chair of English origin, c.1845, brought $210.

These same prices might well be duplicated today item for item.

Victorian sofa, New York, circa 1855.   Parke-Bernet, 1943, $450.

Victorian armchair with fruit carvings, one of a pair matching the sofa on page 307. This type can usually be purchased for under $100 each.

Black lacquered sewing table with mother-of-pearl-inlay. Plaza Art Galleries, 1966, $130.

Victorian black lacquer breakfast table. Parke-Bernet, 1943, $675. (*Photo: Taylor & Dull*)

Victorian inlaid gold and black lacquer gondola chair. Parke-Bernet, 1943, $210.

From a set, Victorian armchair and two side chairs, attributed to Belter. Parke-Bernet, 1964, $1,050.   (*Photo: Taylor & Dull*)

Victorian Belter sofa.   Parke-Bernet, 1965, $550.   (*Photo: Taylor & Dull*)

New England, circa 1710. Room from the Samuel Wentworth House in Portsmouth New Hampshire, paneled about 1710, and furnished with a William and Mary highboy and lowboy and gate-leg table, together with late seventeenth-century chairs. *The Metropolitan Museum of Art.*

AMERICAN QUEEN ANNE. Room from Portsmouth, Rhode Island, before 1765 (the Metcalf Bowler House), furnished with American furniture of the Queen Anne period. *The Metropolitan Museum of Art.*

CHAPTER TWENTY-TWO

American Furniture

William and Mary—1700–1725
Queen Anne—1725–1750
Chippendale—1755–1790

T HE FINEST PIECES OF AMERICAN furniture made in the eighteenth century equal the English furniture of the same period. Basic designs for the most part did not originate in this country. They originated in England and after a time found their way to America.

In the American market, there is a tremendous preference for American furniture. It brings between two and three times what comparable English pieces bring. A few years ago I visited a dealer in Washington, D.C., and asked to see a chest-on-chest. He showed me an English one and quoted a price. "That's fine," I commented, "but I want an American chest." We went into another room and there he showed me an almost identical chest-on-chest, only this one was American. "This is just what I'm looking for," I told him. "What's the price?" When he informed me that he wanted the same price for both chests, I bought the American one on the spot. At the same price the English chest was a fair buy, but the American chest was a great bargain.

The price differential between English and American furniture is not based so much on comparative quality as comparative scarcity. American furniture has value because of its rarity; but, of course, quality must be comparable between the American and the English piece for the American piece to command such a price differential.

Just how good is American furniture of the eighteenth century? This is a matter of opinion. The important American dealer, Albert Sack, said in *Fine Points of Furniture: Early American* (New York: Crown Publishers, 1950), "Two outstanding developments in American furniture are reflected in the highboy and the block-front which reached a height of perfection not equaled in any other country."

In concluding his foreword to the same book, Israel Sack, who had been an antique dealer since 1905, said, "What will happen when more wealthy people will begin to realize that this country produced as fine furniture as any made in any other land?"

On the other hand, Carl W. Dreppard and Lurelle van Arsdale Guild in *New Geography of American Antiques* (New York: Doubleday, 1927) say, "We may speak glibly or we may speak in hushed admiration of cabinetmakers such as

311

Savery, Randolph, Goddard, Gostelowe and Duncan Phyfe. But these men were not demigods. They are not to be classed with Chippendale, Hepplewhite, Sheraton, or the brothers Adam."

Concerning the importance of the art of furnituremaking in the United States in the eighteenth century, *The New York Times* of January 12, 1930 states, "To the end of the 18th century furniture making was the most highly developed of any art in America. Music, literature and painting came behind it."

In any event, good American antiques are as sought after on the present market as good French antiques.. Museum-quality American antiques have about disappeared from the market, and they have been in this state of "almost disappearance" since the 1930's.

The Flow of Style from England to America

The American furniture styles of the eighteenth century are based almost completely on the English styles of the same period; and, although there were published documents like Chippendale's *Director* which some American cabinetmakers must have read, there was not the proliferation of pattern books on English furniture as there was on French furniture. The actual shipment of English furniture was what mainly influenced domestic American styles in furniture.

The spreading of style was not simply a matter of thinking up a new type of slant-top desk, making one of the new models and shipping it on the next boat bound for America where the local cabinetmakers were eagerly waiting at the pier for its arrival. Furniture styles in America did not change that fast. No great premium was put on the latest English style, and the local cabinetmakers were important in their own right.

The style lag in America as compared with England averaged between five and fifteen years! For instance, the Chippendale style in England began in 1749 and lasted until about 1779; the Chippendale style in America started in 1775 and lasted until about 1790. This lag is too often forgotten in authenticating American antiques. A chair may be an authentic Chippendale of the period—but it may have been made ten years after Chippendale's death and at least ten years after the Chippendale Period closed in England.

Roughly, these are the periods in which each style was in vogue in England and in the United States:

Style	In England	In the U.S.
William and Mary	1689–1702	1700–1725
Queen Anne	1702–1714	1725–1750
Chippendale	1749–1779	1755–1790
Hepplewhite	1770–1780	1785–1800
Sheraton	1790–1810	1795–1815
Empire (French)	1804–1814 (France)	1810–1840

Alice Winchester, an authority on American furniture, places the dates in which the styles prevailed *in England* a little later—William and Mary from 1690 to

1710, Queen Anne from 1710 to 1720, Chippendale from 1745 to 1770, Hepplewhite from 1780 to 1790, Sheraton from 1790 to 1810 and English Empire from 1805 to 1820.

The "Greats" of American Antique Furniture

The greatest designers and makers of American furniture of the eighteenth century came from a relatively few areas. Not only are the areas few from the point of view of the present extent of the United States, but they are few from the point of view of the original colonies. These are some of the great names in furnituremaking of the period:

John Goddard I and the Goddard Family	Newport, R.I.
John Townsend and the Townsend Family	Newport, R.I.
The Dunlap Family	New Hampshire
William Savery	Philadelphia, Pa.
Henry Connelly	Philadelphia, Pa.
Ephraim Haines	Philadelphia, Pa.
Jonathon Gostelowe	Philadelphia, Pa.
John Aitken	Philadelphia, Pa.
Benjamin Randolph	Philadelphia, Pa.
Thomas Affleck	Philadelphia, Pa.
Samuel McIntire	Salem, Mass.
Nathan Bowen	Marblehead, Mass.
John Seymour	Boston, Mass.
Thomas Seymour	Boston, Mass.
Benjamin Frothingham	Charlestown, Mass.
Stephen Bedlam	Dorchester Lower Mills, Mass.
Nicholas Disbrowe	Hartford, Conn.
Aaron Chapin	Hartford, Conn.
Eliphalet Chapin	East Windsor, Conn.

American Chippendale Furniture

The study of prices of American furniture can well start with American Chippendale. Through the entire period of price analysis covered by this study, Chippendale has been the leading type of American antique furniture sold, both in volume and in price. American Chippendale is also generally considered to be the most highly developed and most artistically fine furniture produced in this country.

Prices in the 1920's

Early auction offerings were very meager when it came to American antiques, and illustrations of the American items offered were even fewer. On November 13, 1920, the Anderson Galleries in New York sold a straight-leg walnut side chair with a pierced splat, made about 1770, for $50, an extremely low price for any antique chair of any era or country of origin in 1920. As early as 1920 there were definite signs of an antique boom in America, but not for Chippendale furniture of American origin. A similar chair was sold for $60 in the same sale. A walnut chair of the same era with a Gothic splat, pierced, sold for $50. A cherry ladder-back side chair sold for $42.50, while a matching cherry armchair sold for $45.

Two years later, *Antiques* magazine carried one of its earliest advertisements of a priced American antique offered for sale. Katherine N. Loring advertised in the September 1922 issue a block-front bureau at her place of business in Wayland, Massachusetts. The price was $650 for what today would be considered one of the finest and highest priced pieces.

In the following year, 1923, J. K. Beard of Richmond, Virginia, offered something unique in the field of antiques: not one, but a *dozen* gate-leg tables for $3,000. His ad contained a photo of many tables piled on top of each other.

By 1925, prices had risen to 500 percent of the 1920 level for American Chippendale furniture.

In 1926 some fine pieces of furniture were sold. Three Philadelphia side chairs were sold at the American Art Association Galleries on January 9 for $1,575. On

AMERICAN CHIPPENDALE.   Room from the Powell House, Philadelphia, Pennsylvania, 1768, furnished with important American Chippendale pieces.   *The Metropolitan Museum of Art.*

Highly important Chippendale highboy, circa 1770, attributed to Thomas Affleck and from the family of Benjamin Franklin. Price above $75,000. *Courtesy of Ginsberg & Levy, Inc., New York.*

Walnut side chair.   Anderson, 1920, $50.

From a set of six American chairs, circa 1760.   Anderson, 1928, $3,200 the set.

Boston-made Chippendale mahogany kettle-base (*bombé*) desk, circa 1765, (from the Sargent family in Boston). It was sold in the 1920's for under $2,500, and in the 1930's it was resold for approximately $6,000. It was recently purchased by a dealer and sold for $35,000.

January 23 the same gallery sold five ladder-back chairs with straight legs for $1,900. On March 18 the Anderson Galleries sold an elaborately carved lowboy with ball-and-claw feet, by William Savery of Philadelphia and dated about 1760 for $9,000. In December the Anderson Galleries sold a Goddard block-front bureau with three shell carvings for $4,200. In the same sale a similar chest, but not by Goddard, brought $1,300. In the early part of the year, a chest by Goddard had brought $1,350.

This one year—1926—saw a doubling of prices for American Chippendale furniture. The index now stood at about 1,000 percent as compared with 100 percent in 1920.

In the period between 1926 and 1929 prices rose, but by nowhere near so great an amount. They stood at about 1,500 percent in the year of the stock market boom.

The Reifsnyder Sale

In 1929 one of the greatest sales in American furniture history took place—the Howard Reifsnyder sale held at the American Art Association Galleries, April 24 to 27, 1929. It is difficult to conceive of some of the prices achieved in this sale, even in terms of French furniture prices of the late 1960's. A carved mahogany Philadelphia side chair with a carved splat and ball-and-claw feet, made in about 1765 and illustrated in many important books, brought $7,200. The same type chair but with a little more elaborate carving brought $8,700. A third chair, but not quite of the quality of the first one, brought $5,200. A finely carved Philadelphia side chair with ball-and-claw feet brought $8,300, and an elaborate sample side chair brought $9,500. A Philadelphia sample side chair of extraordinary quality, made in 1770, brought no less than $15,000!

Philadelphia Chippendale wing arm-chair. One of the six "Sample" chairs by Benjamin Randolph. Reifsnyder Sale, 1929, $33,000.

Philadelphia Chippendale "Sample" chair by Benjamin Randolph, (illustrated in Wallace Nutting's *Furniture Treasury*). Reifsnyder Sale, 1929, $15,000.

Prices for quality chairs were almost uniformly high in this sale. An important James Gillingham armchair made in Philadelphia in about 1765 brought $8,500, and a fiddleback walnut armchair bearing the original label of William Savery brought $9,000.

As if these prices were not enough, a Benjamin Randolph sample mahogany armchair made in Philadelphia in about 1770 brought the staggering sum of $33,000! No present day price for any chair, even a Louis XV chair, is known to the author to have approached this sensational height.

The slant-top desk which is so popular today was not equally popular in 1929. A Rhode Island mahogany block-front desk of about 1765, with shell interior and bracket feet, fan-carved and of good quality, brought $3,400. (In the A. Rubin sale at the Anderson Galleries, held a few months prior to the Reifsnyder sale, a similar desk brought only $900. The important buyers were at the Reifsnyder sale, and the fine items tended to pull up the prices of the rest of the offerings.)

In the Reifsnyder sale the famous Ormiston sofa made in Philadelphia about 1775 brought $3,000. Sofa prices were not and still are not up to those of other pieces of furniture.

A carved walnut Pennsylvania tall chest made in 1793 in Pennsylvania brought only $2,100. Today such items are in the greatest demand. A similar piece, a famous chest-of-drawers, brought only $1,500.

One chest-on-chest—a carved mahogany piece made in Philadelphia in about 1770—brought an extremely high figure. It had ogee feet and a broken arch top with a basket of carved flowers. It brought $26,100, which seemed high even in this sale for this quality piece.

American Chippendale highboy. Reifsnyder Sale, 1929, $44,000.

American Chippendale chest-on-chest. Reifsnyder Sale, 1929, $26,000.

A card table brought $4,100 and a tray-top table brought $5,000. A beautiful Philadelphia lowboy brought $9,000. Today a lowboy of far inferior quality would bring an equal price.

However, the star performer of the sale was an item known as the Van Pelt highboy, a carved mahogany piece with original brass and exquisite carving. It was made in Philadelphia about 1770. It brought the fantastic price of $44,000!

If one simply used these prices in this one sale and compared them with prices in, say, 1926, he would have to conclude that the rise was in the neighborhood of several thousand percent. But the Reifsnyder sale was one of the standouts in all antique history. It is true that in after years, when the excitement had died down, there was criticism of the sale. Some said the pieces were not the best in America and that their provenance was not the best, but in retrospect only a few sales of American antiques ever approached this sale in quality.

Some other 1929 prices should be quoted, prices for fine items to show that this was a runaway sale and was not strictly representative of 1929 prices for American Chippendale furniture.

On February 1, the Anderson Galleries sold a fine New England block-front desk with a sunburst interior and arched pigeonhole for $900. In the same sale, a block-front kneehole desk of New England origin, made in about 1770, brought $1,350. Two block-front bureaus brought $2,200 and $1,800 on May 4 at the Anderson Galleries. One masterpiece went for $5,400 on April 13 at the Anderson Galleries—a mahogany highboy in the style and period of William Savery of Philadelphia, made in about 1760–1770, with a broken arch top, shells, ball-and-claw feet and cabriole legs, and exhibited at the Metropolitan Museum of Art. Yet, even this fine piece was not up to the general level of the Reifsnyder sale in price.

Chippendale Mahogany tea table by John Goddard, 1763.   American-Anderson, 1930, $29,000.

The Flayderman Sale

The most important sale to take place in 1930, and one of the greatest sales of American furniture in history, was the Philip Flayderman sale which took place January 2, 3, and 4, 1930, at the American-Anderson Galleries in New York. This sale took place well after the stock market crash and when business was definitely headed into a depression. However, the prices achieved did not fully reflect the dark national economic picture. A John Goddard tea table of mahogany with ball-and-claw feet, carved and made for Jabez Bowen of Newport in 1763, brought $29,000. A fan-carved cherry highboy made by Aaron Chapin of Connecticut for Governor Strong somewhere around 1770–1780, with a broken arch top, brought $12,000, and a mahogany carved block-front secretary-cabinet with ball-and-claw feet and three flame finials, made in New England about 1770, brought $13,000.

The Garvan Sale

The third highly important sale of American antique furniture took place January 8 to 10, 1931, at the American-Anderson Galleries. In 1931 there was no question of the permanence of the stock market decline. Nor was there any question that the United States was heading into a deep depression.

The highly significant aspect of the Garvan sale is that many of the items had been bought at the Reifsnyder sale of 1929 and at the Flayderman sale of 1930. We thus can secure at least one definitive measure of the effect of the declining economic conditions on fine antiques. Unfortunately, the very best items in the Reifsnyder and Flayderman sales were not resold in the Garvan sale. But many of the lesser items were, and we must limit our conclusions to the lesser items. (Note: Not all of the items listed in the following comparison are American Chippendale pieces.)

Price Comparison—Items Bought in 1929 and 1930
from the Reifsnyder and Flayderman Sales and
Resold in the Garvan Sale in 1931

Item	Buying Price—1929 or 1930	Selling Price—1931
Mirror	$ 35	$ 70
Maple chair	50	70
Maple desk-on-frame	230	400
Mahogany card table	250	260
Mahogany and maple work table	50	200
Maple chest-of-drawers	150	175
Pembroke table	110	175
Mahogany satinwood card table	275	400
Mahogany gate-leg table	240	500
Mahogany web-foot lowboy	1,500	1,700

PROFIT ON THESE 10 PIECES—$1,060

Maple banister-back chair	180	130
Maple fiddle-back chair	300	180
Mahogany secretary	550	300
Walnut lowboy	1,000	740
Cherry table	150	70
Pine desk-on-frame	400	360
Two slat-back side chairs	540	280
Pair of walnut chairs	260	190
Walnut highboy	1,100	1,000
Maple and mahogany secretary	1,800	1,350

LOSS ON THESE 10 PIECES—$1,680

In summary, ten of the items showed a profit and the other ten showed a loss. The combined profit was $1,060 and the combined loss $1,680, resulting in a net loss of $620. The conclusion from these comparative prices is that the crash and the economic depression did not have a tremendously important effect on antique prices—at least on the prices of the items sold in these sales.

A number of notable items were sold in the Garvan sale. The first was a Savery carved mahogany side chair made in Philadelphia between 1760 and 1775. It was sold to dealer Israel Sack for $5,000. A fabulous walnut scroll-top highboy attributed to Savery, an item which had been exhibited in the notable Girl Scouts Loan Exhibition, brought $11,000. Sack bought this piece and he bought another highboy made by Gostelowe or Savery for $9,000.

Prices In the 1930's

There was an attempt early in the business decline to regard it as of temporary importance only. It was considered to have no effect on antique prices, and the press contained a good many statements that there was no effect whatever on antique prices. Dealers attempted to buy antiques in order to stock for the prosperity which was "just around the corner" and to bolster prices.

On April 14, 1931, the Woman's Club of Hartford, Connecticut, held an antique sale at which the highest prices were received of any antique sale held up to that time in the history of Connecticut.

Toward the end of 1931 the remainder of the Flayderman antiques were sold. They brought 50 percent of their anticipated value.

In January 1932 another notable sale of American furniture was held at the American-Anderson Galleries. The furniture belonged to Israel Sack, the dealer, and was sold at his order. Sack was a pioneer in the field of dealing in American antiques and had been in the business since the beginning of the twentieth century. At the Flayderman sale in early 1930, Sack had purchased a number of fine pieces of furniture. These he sold along with many other items, so that we can determine how much several pieces of furniture brought in January 1930, just after the stock market crash but before the Depression got very deep and before optimism had died. We can then determine prices at the bottom of the depression in 1932 when there was no talk of any "temporary suspension" of antique buying or any "brief pause in American prosperity."

Prices Received for the Same Piece of
Furniture Sold in the Flayderman Sale
(January 1930) and the Israel Sack
Sale (January 1932)

Item	1930 Price	1932 Price	Price Decline
Mahogany slant-top desk—Frothingham	$3,600	$1,500	58%
Mahogany side chair	2,700	1,000	63
Grandfather clock—Philadelphia	3,700	850	77
Cherry secretary-cabinet—Chapin	3,300	675	80
Pair inlaid card tables—Townsend (made in 1790 and classified Sheraton)	5,600	1,700	70
		AVERAGE DECLINE	70%
		1932 as a % of 1930	30%

When the same piece of furniture was sold before the onset of the major Depression and sold again at the bottom of the Depression, it constitutes very persuasive evidence of the exact quantitative nature of the price decline of American Chippendale furniture. It must be stressed that the Flayderman sale and the Sack sale (as well as a few others, such as the Reifsnyder sale and the Garvan sale) can be classified as the greatest ever held in this country, and certainly the greatest sales of American furniture held in the world. Buyers paid prices which bore little relationship to the intrinsic excellence of the pieces of furniture they were buying.

These sales of the most notable American pieces of furniture tended to bring prices that were far above the customary prices for pieces of comparable quality— prices that would strain any buyer, even in boom times. Two factors tended to raise the pre-Depression prices above reality: the optimism engendered by a booming stock market, and the wherewithal to purchase nonnecessities created by the rapidly rising market and economic prosperity. The particular two sales held just before the Depression—the Reifsnyder and the Flayderman—also tended to distort prices. In 1929, for instance, a mahogany block-front slant-top desk with a sunburst and an arched interior, made in about 1770, brought only $600. In the Flayderman sale (1930), this desk would almost certainly have brought more.

Thus, in computing a price trend line we cannot use the Flayderman and Sack sales "as Gospel" even though they represent the prices of the same piece of furniture. The decline was not quite so deep as the figures might lead one to believe.

Although the country began to improve economically by the end of 1934, there was no recovery in the price of American Chippendale furniture. In 1939, just before the start of the European phase of World War II, the price index which had stood at 700 percent in 1932 stood at 500 percent. Prices had been cut drastically since the low point of the Depression! On May 20, 1939, the Parke-Bernet Galleries sold a walnut and mahogany block-front slant-top desk with some restorations for $250. The slant-top desk belonging to Nathaniel Hawthorne brought $175. Other slant-top desks sold during the year for $170, $270, $185 and $135.

On May 29 the Parke-Bernet Galleries sold a rare Philadelphia carved mahogany lowboy in the manner of Savery for $600. Another lowboy was sold by the same gallery on May 20. This one had belonged to General Lewis Morris, signer of the Declaration of Independence. It went for $1,200. In the same sale, a Philadelphia carved mahogany dish-top tripod table with a bird cage and with ball-and-claw feet brought $150. Prices were down tremendously, even for very good items, although these were not in the masterpiece category.

Prices in the War

From the year 1939, prices slid downward during the war. In the Parke-Bernet sale of March 7, 1942, a walnut slant-top desk with blocked interior, bracket feet, a sunburst and a scrolled skirt brought $150. A desk in the masterpiece category was sold November 12 at the Parke-Bernet Galleries. It was a rare New England block-front slant-top desk with ball-and-claw feet and three shells carved in the interior. It brought $425. Other slant-tops sold during the year brought $115, $130, $180 and $280.

American Chippendale slant-top desk belonging to Nathaniel Hawthorne.   Parke-Bernet, 1939, $175.   (*Photo: Taylor & Dull*)

To indicate how much prices of fine American furniture had fallen, on March 7 the Parke-Bernet Galleries sold six Goddard mahogany side chairs from the Van Courtland estate for $480—$80 a chair! These chairs might conceivably have brought $5,000 *each* in the Reifsnyder sale.

One of a set of six side chairs.   Parke-Bernet, 1942, $480 the set.

American Chippendale walnut block-front highboy. Parke-Bernet, 1945, $1,300. (*Photo: Taylor & Dull*)

American Chippendale maple block-front secretary. Parke-Bernet, 1942, $1,050. (*Photo: Taylor & Dull*)

On November 7 a maple block-front two-door secretary with ball-and-claw feet, illustrated in Lockwood's book *Colonial Furniture in America*, brought $1,050. On May 1 a carved maple scroll-top chest-on-chest with a broken arch, three flame finials and unusual carving brought $170. Prices in 1942 were at the 200 percent level as compared with 500 percent in 1939.

This 1942 period represented the low point of American Chippendale furniture. From here, prices started to rise.

In the last year of the war prices achieved a relatively high level. On January 12, 1945, the Parke-Bernet Galleries sold a mahogany slant-top desk with ball-and-claw feet and one shell carved in the interior for $675, a price far above that of slant-top desks three years earlier. In the same month a Rhode Island block-front slant-top desk of mahogany with bracket feet and three shells carved in the interior brought $1,500. Another block front with shells made in Rhode Island or Connecticut brought $2,800.

One very fine item was sold on January 13 at the Parke-Bernet Galleries—a walnut block-front highboy attributed to John Goddard and exhibited in the Metropolitan Museum of Art. It was shell-carved with an elaborately molded deep cornice and was illustrated in Lockwood's book. It brought $1,300, a low price for such a piece.

Whereas prices of American Chippendale furniture were at the 200 percent level in 1942, they had risen to the 500 percent level by 1945.

Rhode Island Chippendale highboy, circa 1765. Plaza Art Auction, 1951, $11,000.

Chippendale kneehole block-front desk by John Goddard, Newport, Massachusetts. Sold in the early 1950's, for close to $30,000. (*Courtesy of Ginsberg & Levy, Inc., New York*).

Prices in the 1950's

In the period immediately following the war, prices did not rise perceptibly. In 1950 the index still stood at 500 percent.

On January 12, 1950, the Parke-Bernet Galleries sold a pair of fret-carved ladder-back armchairs of mahogany with straight legs for $950. In April a side chair owned by President Willard of Harvard was sold for $310. In this same sale a Goddard mahogany block-front writing desk with three shells in the interior was sold for the low price of $2,500. In the same sale a very fine chest-on-chest was sold for $3,750.

By 1955, five years later, prices of American Chippendale had doubled and the index stood at 1,000 percent.

An elegant mahogany lowboy with shell carving and ball-and-claw feet, made in Philadelphia, brought $8,000, a very high price considering prices in general.

On May 13 to 15, 1954, the Parke-Bernet Galleries sold the Luke Vincent Lockwood Collection of antiques. (Lockwood was one of the two great authorities on American furniture.) A carved mahogany piecrust tilt-top table of birdcage design, with ball-and-claw feet, 36 inches in diameter, displayed in the Girl Scouts Loan Exhibition, brought $9,000, a very high price for the times and for the piece of furniture.

In the same sale a carved mahogany block-front secretary-bookcase with ball-and-claw feet and three shells in the interior brought $9,000. A carved mahogany block-front kneehole desk with original brass and made in Massachusetts brought $10,000. A carved and parcel-gilded block-front chest-on-chest of Massachusetts origin with bonnet top brought $15,000. A carved mahogany tassel-back side chair with ball-and-claw feet, made in Philadelphia and shown in the Girl Scouts Loan Exhibition, brought $2,700, and a Philadelphia wing armchair brought $4,750, a high price for one chair no matter how fine.

The March 1956 issue of *Antiques* magazine carried an advertisement of the Irving H. Vogel estate by the Hammer Galleries. Six extremely fine Philadelphia mahogany side chairs were offered that had been in the Prentiss Collection. The offering price was $10,990. Still, the rest of the advertised prices between 1955 and 1960 were not extraordinarily high and did not indicate a growing boom.

Prices in the 1960's

By 1960 prices had again doubled and stood at the 2,000 percent level. Few masterpieces, such as those sold from the earlier collections, were sold in 1960, so we do not have a fair comparison of prices of highest grade Chippendale furniture.

Prices were rising by 1965; the level was about 3,000 percent.

The most important sale of American furniture during 1966 was the Andrew Varick Stout sale held at the Parke-Bernet Galleries in New York on January 22, 1966. (Actually, very few pieces of significant American furniture were auctioned anywhere during 1966). A very good serpentine-shaped slant-top desk in mahogany with ball-and-claw feet and three carved shells under the slant top, but with a few imperfections, brought $1,600. A carved mahogany tilt-top candlestand made in Philadelphia, 18½ inches in diameter, brought $1,300.

One of a pair of New Jersey Chippendale side chairs. Parke-Bernet, 1966, $5,200 the pair.

One of a set of six Philadelphia Chippendale side chairs. Parke-Bernet, 1966, $27,000 the set.

Chippendale armchair in the Chinese taste. Parke-Bernet, 1966, $6,500.

Philadelphia Chippendale wing armchair. Parke-Bernet, 1966, $24,000.

A cherry desk of slant-top design from New England, very much like the serpentine slant top but with no shaped front, brought $1,200. The difference in price is partly attributed to the curvature of the front of the other desk, but this flat-front desk did not have any significant repairs.

A pair of New Jersey carved walnut ball-and-claw side chairs with a central shell and slip seats brought $5,200. They were of good design, but not the very best. The next lot to be sold was a single Philadelphia side chair of similar design but with a solid splat. This brought $2,300.

Other items sold at this time were in the ultra-fine category. Six carved mahogany ball-and-claw side chairs made in Philadelphia brought the very high price of $27,000. The so-called Wharton carved mahogany side table made in Philadelphia by Thomas Affleck, 29 inches high and 36 inches long, with fluted and chamfered Marlborough legs (but straight), brought the extremely high price of $23,000. It was certainly a fine table, but $23,000 was a good amount of money to pay for it.

A carved mahogany wing armchair with ball-and-claw feet made in Philadelphia brought $24,000, a high price for any chair of any variety.

This, then is the index of prices of American Chippendale furniture from 1920 to the middle 1960's. The best recordings are from 1925 on. Before that time, recordings and illustrations of pieces sold were scarce and somewhat unreliable.

American Chippendale Prices

Date	1925 Equals 100%	1920 Equals 100%
1920	20%	100%
1925	100	500
1929	300	1,500
1932	140	700
1939	100	500
1942	40	200
1945	100	500
1950	100	500
1955	200	1,000
1960	400	2,000
1965	600	3,000

American Queen Anne Furniture

Prices in the 1920's

On November 8, 1920, a Queen Anne solid curly maple highboy, made in 1730, with two small drawers and three large ones in the top part and four in the base, sold at the Anderson Galleries in New York for $200. The highboy had cabriole legs and Dutch feet. On the same day at the same gallery, a cherry highboy with two drawers in the base and four in the top sold for $260. It had a carved fan on a lower drawer, cabriole legs and Dutch feet.

While a good deal of furniture in the early 1920's seemed to be high in relation to other products sold at the time and in relation to what antique furniture sells for today, Queen Anne furniture was low in price in 1920 on almost any basis.

By 1925 prices had doubled and were rising rapidly. The same auction house on October 9 and 10, 1925, sold a curly maple highboy with cabriole legs, scrolled top and a sunburst decoration for $355. It was an elaborate piece six feet one inch high. On October 14 the same gallery sold another highboy for $600, a broken arch piece with a center spike and ball finial, two sunburst decorative carvings and cabriole legs. It was seven feet four inches tall and an excellent piece of furniture. In April of the same year, the gallery sold a 1700 highboy for $800. On October 23 they sold still another highboy, this one a fairly elaborate one. It was a hooded highboy of maple with two sunbursts, fluted pilasters, a broken arch on top, cabriole legs and three flame finials, seven feet two inches tall. It brought $460.

These highboys if sold in the late 1960's would bring many times these 1925 figures, and they are among the most sought after pieces of furniture of any kind sold in the United States, regardless of country of origin or historical period.

By 1926 prices of Queen Anne furniture had increased rapidly. Of course, other types of antiques had jumped at about this time too, and the boom in antiques was in full swing. On March 18, 1926, the Anderson Galleries sold a hooded maple highboy 88 inches high, with a broken arch top, two sunbursts, three flame finials and ball-and-claw feet for $2,100—considerably in excess of the average prices of earlier years.

In January 1926 a flat-top highboy was sold by the American Art Association Galleries for $950. Today a sculptured-top highboy is vastly preferred to a flat-top highboy, but in 1926 there was some preference for the flat-top variety. In general in the 1920's, there was a preference for simpler types of antiques, as well as a preference for items of so great antiquity that they looked as though they were falling apart.

On January 2, 1926, the American Art Association sold an early eighteenth-century highboy made of cherry with a flat top and fluted shell ornamentation for just $180. Today this piece would bring in the neighborhood of $3,000.

Early in 1925 the index stood at 200 percent. One year later it stood at 500 percent.

Between 1926 and 1929 the price of Queen Anne furniture did not rise appreciably. Outstanding sales brought outstanding prices, but they brought outstanding prices for almost all types of furniture, not just Queen Anne. This was partly because of the importance of a particular collection and its owner, and partly because of a boom psychology that developed at some sales and which was not typical of all sales held in the era. Highly important sales created peaks that were not entirely representative of prices at the time.

The Reifsnyder sale of 1929 saw very different prices, however. A carved fiddle-back side chair, made in about 1730, was sold for $6,000. Three matching chairs were sold separately in the same sale for $6,100, $6,700 and $9,000. These are enormous prices for a matching set of four chairs, regardless of what kind of chairs they are. A maple armchair was sold in the same sale for $375. In 1929 the simpler varieties of Queen Anne furniture in the ordinary sales seemed to sag while the standouts rose. The level in 1929 was thus the same as it was in 1926—500 percent.

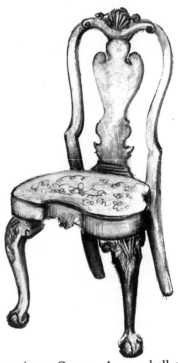

American Queen Anne curly maple highboy.   Anderson, 1925, $355.

American Queen Anne shell-carved side chair.   American, 1929, $6,000.

The Recession

In 1930 the important Flayderman sale was held. The stock market had crashed and things were starting downward, and prices reflected this situation to a degree. A New England highboy with original brass, made about 1730, with shell carving and a bonnet top, brought $5,100. A wing chair made by Job Townsend, with a stretchered base but of plain design, brought $3,600. A wing armchair brought $900. But a carved walnut side chair of Rhode Island origin brought only $200, and a fan-carved walnut lowboy with pad feet, made in New England c.1740, brought $485, an extremely low price in light of present demand for such pieces.

The significant Garvan sale of 1931 also saw low prices for Queen Anne furniture. Two lowboys brought $430 and $475. Three highboys brought $725, $1,050 and $550, and four New England fiddle-back side chairs brought $400 each.

Later in the year at the Clifford Carlisle Kaufman sale, a rare Queen Anne curly maple web-foot armchair made in Philadelphia in 1750 brought $1,000, although it was of plain design. In the same sale a good fiddle-back side chair from New England brought only $110.

A number of the Sack pieces offered for sale in 1932 had been purchased by him at the 1930 Flayderman sale. These are two of the comparative prices of the same piece of furniture sold in both sales:

Comparative Prices of Queen Anne Pieces
Sold in January 1930 at the Flayderman Sale
and in January 1932 at the Sack Sale

Item	1930 Price	1932 Price
Six walnut fiddle-back chairs made by Job Townsend, 1743	$5,400	$2,200
Upholstered walnut wing chair made by Job Townsend, 1743	3,600	875

The first item had declined 60 percent and was down to the 40 percent level with 1930 as 100 percent. The second had declined even further—to 25 percent—a 75 percent drop.

Also in the Sack sale, one wing chair brought $750 and another $535. Two lowboys brought $400 and $275, and a New England highboy brought $400.

The Recovery Phase

For the next seven years—to the outbreak of the European phase of World War II—there was no increase in the prices of Queen Anne furniture. In fact, prices weakened. Prices were now down to the level of 1920—100 percent. They had been cut in half since the economic bottom of 1932!

Even at retail, prices were at an almost rock-bottom level for any kind of an antique. In the March 1939 issue of *Antiques,* the firm of Shreve, Crump and Low advertised on the back cover an American Queen Anne walnut chair for $110. The same firm advertised a walnut lowboy made in 1760–1770 for $285.

The War Years

When Wallace Nutting's collection was sold on October 4, 1941, at the Parke-Bernet Galleries, a Rhode Island walnut serving table, 32 inches long, illustrated in Nutting's book, brought just $230. A rare carved walnut side chair with a cut splat and drake feet, also illustrated in Nutting's book, brought $350.

The next year some of the belongings of Mrs. Luke Vincent Lockwood were sold at the Parke-Bernet Galleries. A pair of maple stretchered side chairs with pad feet brought $200. Two small tables brought $350 and $220. And on February 6, 1942, the Parke-Bernet Galleries sold a curly maple bonnet-top highboy with two carved shells, cabriole legs and pad feet for just $130. (It had some restorations, however.) In 1942 prices had not risen to any appreciable extent from the 1939 level of 100 percent.

On January 12, 1945, the Parke-Bernet Galleries sold a bonnet-top walnut highboy with two shells, cabriole legs, pad feet and three flame finials for $900. On January 26 the same gallery sold a flat-top highboy for $300. The fancy-top highboy was emerging as the one more in demand. Two lowboys were sold during 1945 for $390 and $350, and a chest-on-chest brought $250 while a chest-on-frame brought $370.

Prices between 1942 and 1945 (the war's end) had approximately doubled, and the index stood at 200 percent.

Retail prices were stronger. The January 1945 issue of *Antiques* carried an advertisement for a pair of 1730 Queen Anne chairs in light walnut with pad feet and solid splats for $475; and Carson, Pirie, Scott offered a circular drop-leaf table for $350.

Prices in the 1950's

On January 12, 1950, a fan-carved cherrywood highboy with club feet and a flat top, which originated in New England, brought $575. On May 5 the same gallery, Parke-Bernet, sold a highboy of cherrywood with a scrolled top, one finial and cabriole legs, but somewhat restored, for $825. The preference of the market for fancy-top Queen Anne highboys was apparently maintained. On April 29 the same gallery sold a rare maple slant-top desk with club feet, bandy legs and a shell interior, from Ginsberg and Levy, for $1,075. Prices were up about 50 percent compared with the war's end. The index now stood at 300 percent.

In 1955 the Parke-Bernet Galleries sold a Virginia or South Carolina armchair with a stretcher for $2,000. The next day an excellent walnut shell-carved side chair with drake feet brought $1,600, and a pair of Philadelphia walnut side chairs brought $1,600. These were illustrated in the *Blue Book of American Furniture*.

Earlier in the year, a fine secretary-bookcase from Ginsberg and Levy brought $2,800. It was of carved tiger maple, seven feet four inches high, with bracket feet and a shell-carved interior.

A few items during 1955 were still low in price. On January 22, 1955, the Parke-Bernet Galleries sold a Massachusetts maple and tiger maple bonnet-top highboy, seven feet ten inches high, with three flame finials, hoof feet and two pendants on the skirt, for $325. As the year progressed, however, prices seemed to rise. They had virtually doubled since 1950 and the index stood at 600 percent.

In the December 1957 issue of *Antiques*, John S. Walton of New York offered a New England walnut and maple wing chair, *c*.1740–1750, for $1,500.

Prices in the 1960's

Queen Anne American furniture was offered at auction in considerable volume in 1960. The furniture was not simply offered. It was featured as it had not been for some years, with illustrations and fairly lengthy descriptions of the excellence of each piece. The lowboy had finally come into its own. On January 15, 1960, the Parke-Bernet Galleries offered a good fan-carved walnut lowboy with a shaped apron and two pendants. It brought $2,300. On February 6 the same gallery sold a carved walnut and yellow silk damask covered wing chair with cabriole legs and a stretcher for $1,000. Sets of chairs sold for low prices. During the year a set of seven chairs sold for $1,120, a set of six chairs sold for $1,260, and another set of six chairs brought $1,800. They were all side chairs and are available on the market in fairly large quantities today.

American Queen Anne bonnet-top highboy.   Parke-Bernet, 1955, $325.   (*Photo: Taylor & Dull*)

American Queen Anne tea table.   Parke-Bernet, 1964, $3,500.   (*Photo: Taylor & Dull*)

American Queen Anne, shell-carved, walnut armchair (exhibited: Metropolitan Museum of Art, 1963).   Parke-Bernet, 1966, $27,500.   (*Photo: Taylor & Dull*)

In 1960 highboys continued up in price. On October 22 the Parke-Bernet Galleries offered an important shell-carved walnut bonnet-top highboy with cabriole legs carved on the knees, with shells and three flaming urn finials, from Philadelphia. It brought $3,500. Another elaborate highboy sold during the year for $1,700, and a rare Connecticut secretary-cabinet brought $1,600.

The index in 1955 stood at 600 percent. By 1960 it had risen to 800 percent.

The momentum of price rise had increased tremendously by 1964. On January 24 a tea table made of maple was sold by the Parke-Bernet Galleries. It had a dished top, cabriole legs, pad feet, a shaped apron and was 31 inches long. It brought $3,500.

This price was no exception for such a Queen Anne piece, however. Another tea table was offered by Parke-Bernet the next day. This was a maple and pine dished-top tea table which originated in New England. It had a valanced apron, cabriole legs, pad feet and was painted red. It brought $5,250.

Late in 1964 two pieces of furniture of the Queen Anne variety were sold at prices which were hard to believe in light of the price history of this furniture. A Philadelphia Queen Anne armchair made by Savery brought $15,000, and a New England Queen Anne carved walnut block-front lowboy brought $24,000. This piece, of course, combined two elements in the greatest demand—the block-front characteristics and the piece of furniture known as the lowboy.

By 1965 prices had tripled as against 1960. They had reached a level of 2,400 percent (1920 equal to 100 percent.) With 1925 as the base, they now stood at 1,200 percent. Yet in 1945 the index stood at exactly the same place it had stood in 1925—100 percent. In twenty years the price of Queen Anne furniture had increased twelve times!

With the exception of the Andrew Varick Stout sale held at the Parke-Bernet Galleries in New York on January 22, 1966, very few fine American Queen Anne items were sold at auction during 1966. The most notable item in the Stout sale was a Philadelphia shell-carved walnut armchair with trifid feet, a spoon back and solid vasiform splat. In the middle of the crest rail was a particularly graceful and elaborate scroll. The price realized was $27,500 despite the fact that there were some repairs. But the chair had been exhibited in the Metropolitan Museum of Art, and its mate was in the Henry Ford Museum and appeared in illustrations in two leading books on American furniture.

The next lot was a Philadelphia walnut side chair of generally similar design except that this chair had a carved splat and the back rails were rounded whereas the armchair had angular back rails. Also, the side chair did not have a stretcher whereas the armchair did. The side chair realized $18,000 even though a notation was made that one foot was repaired. But an ordinary Philadelphia walnut side chair with an imperfect foot brought only $900.

A shell-carved Philadelphia walnut armchair with trifid feet and a carved vasiform splat brought only $2,000. Its design was a little awkward, and its back rails were not rounded. This antique for $2,000 cannot be compared with an antique of excellent design described earlier that achieved $27,500, over ten times as much.

A carved cherry dressing table from Connecticut brought $2,100. Here again the item was not in the super-fine category. Finally, a carved walnut desk on frame made in Philadelphia, with cabriole legs ending in trifid feet, but with some restorations, brought $1,400.

It is clear from this sale that ordinary items bring ordinary prices, while very fine items bring prices in the fantastic range.

American Queen Anne Prices

Date	1925 Equals 100%	1920 Equals 100%
1920		100%
1925	100%	200
1926	250	500
1929	250	500
1932	100	200
1939	50	100
1942	50	100
1945	100	200
1950	150	300
1955	300	600
1960	400	800
1965	1,200	2,400

American William and Mary Furniture

Since the 1920's and early 1930's, William and Mary furniture has not been particularly featured in the antique market. While the price has not deteriorated tremendously in poor times, it has not achieved great heights even in great sales such as the Reifsnyder and Sack sales. William and Mary is not the vogue of the 1960's. The 1960's are the beginning of a new Age of Elegance, and William and Mary is not entirely a furniture of elegance. Rather, it represents a transition from the more primitive types of furniture of the 1600's to a more refined Queen Anne furniture of the early eighteenth century (which was followed by the refined and highly popular Chippendale furniture). To a degree, William and Mary is in the same position as Renaissance furniture. While the pendulum may well swing again to more simple and primitive forms of furniture, it has hardly begun this swing.

Prices in the 1920's

Like so much other American antique furniture, prices of William and Mary in the early 1920's were low. In the Jacob Margulis sale of November 16 and 17, 1923, held at the Anderson Galleries in New York, a New England maple six-leg highboy, made in 1710, was sold for $290.

In November 1926 the American Art Association Galleries sold a walnut and ash highboy of about the year 1700 for $400. In January the same gallery sold a walnut lowboy made in 1690 or thereabouts for $900. Prices had approximately doubled between the beginning of the 1920's and the middle of the decade.

Philadelphia Queen Anne side chair. Parke-Bernet, 1966, $18,000.

American William & Mary lowboy. American, 1929, $4,800.

Important American William & Mary highboy. American, 1929, $3,600.

William & Mary New England highboy. Parke-Bernet, 1942, $100.

Two William and Mary pieces worthy of note were sold in the famous Reif-snyder sale of April 24 to 27, 1929. The first was a Pennsylvania trumpet-turned walnut lowboy with bun feet and flat scrolled stretchers. It brought $4,800 and at that time was apparently in the same category as the much wanted Queen Anne lowboy today. In the same Reifsnyder sale, a six-leg William and Mary maple highboy, *c.* 1700, brought $3,600.

At a sale held at the American Art Association Galleries February 9, 1929, an inlaid burl walnut highboy, five feet two inches high, but with the underframe re-stored, sold for $725.

Between 1926 and 1929, prices of Queen Anne furniture had tripled. The index now stood at 300 percent with 1926 equal to 100 percent.

The Depression and the 1930's

Two years later at the notable Francis P. Garvan sale, a William and Mary piece still brought a high price. A walnut six-leg flat-top highboy, made in New England in 1705–1720, brought $1,600.

At the Israel Sack sale held at the Parke-Bernet Galleries April 8, 1932, at the Depression's bottom, an inlaid walnut six-leg highboy made in New England about 1700–1710 brought $2,000. A somewhat similar highboy from New England in burl walnut brought $850, and a New England inlaid walnut lowboy brought $2,000.

The prices of these William and Mary pieces in this sale were high. In the same sale the level of the Queen Anne furniture that is so popular in the 1960's was far below that of William and Mary furniture. Nevertheless, prices of William and Mary furniture had been cut in half since the 1929 peak, and the index stood at 150 percent in 1932.

In the Herbert Lawton sale held at the American-Anderson Galleries on April 2 and 3, 1937, a small New England walnut cabinet on stand, made about 1690–1710 and not a beautiful piece, brought $2,600, a very high price for the times.

This piece was, however, an exception to the trend in the late 1930's. At the William Randolph Hearst sale of November 1938, a six-leg walnut flat-top highboy brought the small sum of $300.

In 1939, a walnut and pine slant-top desk with ball feet which may have been added at a later date brought $50.

Prices between 1932 and 1939 had now been halved, and William and Mary furniture seemed to drop from fashion. The index now stood at 75 percent.

War and the Postwar Era

This was, however, not the bottom of the market for William and Mary furni-ture. A part of the Lockwood collection was sold in the Mrs. Luke Vincent Lockwood sale of November 7, 1942. This sale included a burl walnut and maple six-leg New England highboy, *c.*1700–1710. It brought exactly $220 despite its illustrious background, and even though it was illustrated in Lockwood's *Colonial Furniture in America.*

American William & Mary highboy of burl walnut and maple.   Parke-Bernet,
1942, $220.   (*Photo: Taylor & Dull*)

On May 2 of the same year, another highboy was sold by the same gallery—Parke-Bernet. This was also a New England model, *c*.1770, and with specifications similar to the Lockwood highboy but with some restorations. It brought $100.

By 1942, the first full year of the entry of the United States into the war, the price index of William and Mary furniture had declined to 50 percent—where it was at the beginning of the 1920's.

The war inflated prices, and by 1945, the last year of World War II, the price index had doubled and stood at 100 percent—the same as the 1926 level. At the sale of the belongings of Mrs. J. Amory Haskell in April 1944, a walnut six-leg highboy *c*.1700 brought $675. Still in December 1945 a walnut and burl ash six-leg highboy of New England origin, made between 1700 and 1705, brought only $325.

The 1950's and 1960's

By 1950 prices had risen to a limited degree and the index stood at 150 percent. At the sale of the belongings of Mrs. Henry Ford, October 17 to 19, 1951, at the Parke-Bernet Galleries, a small gate-leg turned maple table, forty inches wide, brought $675.

Three years later the significant Luke Vincent Lockwood sale was held on May 13 to 15, 1954. At this sale a six-leg turned maple flat-top highboy from New England, made in the early eighteenth century, brought $750. And at the Maurice Rubin sale held in October of the same year, an inlaid walnut lowboy made in New England *c*. 1700 brought $600.

By 1955 the index had struggled upward to a level of 200 percent compared with 150 percent in 1945. On March 26, 1955, the Parke-Bernet Galleries sold a walnut chest-of-drawers with ball feet, made in New England, illustrated in Lockwood's book and once owned by Lockwood, for $400—not a princely sum for a piece with such a background. In the same sale another William and Mary piece did better, however. An inlaid walnut and mulberry wood highboy, five feet three inches high, brought $900.

For the next five years the index pushed upward at more or less of a snail's pace. In 1960 it stood at 250 percent. In February of that year, a carved and painted armchair with a caned seat was sold by Parke-Bernet for $250. The carving was of extremely fine quality and the chair was made about 1700. On October 20 the same gallery sold a New England side chair of carved cherrywood with Spanish feet for $250. In the same sale a carved maple side chair brought $150. Earlier in the year a painted walnut side chair brought only $80.

In January 1964 an item was sold that indicated that all interest in American William and Mary furniture was not dead. A painted and decorated pine corner court cupboard of New England origin, 55 inches high and 39½ inches wide, a simple, country piece, brought the amazing sum of $6,750. Still, the index can be considered to have risen to only 300 percent, up 50 points in five years. At a retail establishment in Greenwich, Connecticut, a flat-top six-leg highboy was offered in mid-1965 for about $1,000. A very early six-leg highboy was offered privately to me for $500, although an appraiser valued it at $2,200. It was inlaid and in reasonably good condition, but it required some minor restoration.

In New York in late 1966 a good William and Mary lowboy was bringing $2,500 to $3,000, a price level well under comparable pieces of the later Queen Anne era. A very fine highboy was offered for sale by a leading dealer in American furniture. It was unusual in that it was made of solid curly maple. (Such a William and Mary piece is usually of walnut or veneered pine or gum.) This piece was also unusual in that it was once in the excellent and well-known Garvan Collection. Its price was $5,000 in late 1966.

A third item which was about to appear on the New York market in late 1966 was a burl ash veneered desk with ball feet, one of the finest examples of a William and Mary desk. Its probable retail price was from $5,000 to $6,000.

All of these quotations are on the "better-to-best" grade of William and Mary furniture. The lesser items seemed scarcer at this time and prices were slightly higher, although there was certainly not a bull market in William and Mary antiques.

Prices are not the only important factor marketwise about William and Mary furniture. An equally important factor is that it is generally not featured and illustrated in auction sales. Another significant factor is that there is not much of it on the market, and there has not been much on the market since the early 1930's. The pieces that are offered are frequently of nondescript variety, many of them over-restored, particularly the long trumpet-turned legs under the carcass. The furniture is not in vogue at the present time, although there are signs that there may be some return to favor.

American William and Mary Prices

Date	1926 Equals 100%
1926	100%
1929	300
1932	150
1939	75
1942	50
1945	100
1950	150
1955	200
1960	250
1965	300

AMERICAN HEPPLEWHITE AND SHERATON DINING ROOM OF THE FEDERAL PERIOD.
A Baltimore Hepplewhite table is shown with inlaid chairs of Sheraton design.
Courtesy of Ginsberg & Levy, Inc., New York.

CHAPTER TWENTY-THREE

American Hepplewhite and Sheraton
Hepplewhite—1785–1800
Sheraton—1795–1815

EPPLEWHITE AND SHERATON FURNITURE is the last group of furniture to be produced in the eighteenth century, that era of excellence in design and construction. Since American styles followed English styles (from which they originated) by a decade or two, both of these styles of furniture ran into the nineteenth century and are thus not solely eighteenth-century types. American craftsmen carefully copied the English designs well into the first quarter of the nineteenth century.

Hepplewhite and Sheraton furniture has never experienced the crazes or the vogues that many other types of furniture have, such as the present French vogue or the earlier Duncan Phyfe craze. Although Duncan Phyfe furniture, at least the early Duncan Phyfe, can be classified as Sheraton, the later furniture is what is known as American Empire. We have considered Duncan Phyfe to be a separate classification of furniture.

While Hepplewhite and Sheraton furniture are very close to each other style-wise, they are still usually distinguishable, although there are some cross breeds that create a problem of classification. These, fortunately, are not so numerous as to make classification impossible.

American Hepplewhite Furniture in the 1920's

As in other types of American furniture, we start tracing prices with the 1920's. In this era the vogue of collecting antiques developed in force, with the result that prices began to rise significantly.

In 1920 American Hepplewhite furniture was some of the lowest priced of the entire gamut of antiques. On November 5 and 6, 1920, the Anderson Galleries sold a rare sideboard with carved front and sides. It had tapering inlaid legs, and was made in about 1800. It brought exactly $105.

On November 13, the same gallery sold an inlaid card table of cherry, maple and ebony with square legs and a sunburst medallion. It was made in about 1790, and it brought $35. In the same sale a cherry chest-of-drawers brought $70. Still another piece was offered in the same sale—a secretary-desk of cherry wood and maple with oval brasses and escutcheons. It was made around 1790, and it brought $150.

343

On November 16 and 17, 1923, the Jacob Margulis sale was held in New York. Here prices of American Hepplewhite furniture showed a little more strength. A mahogany swell-front bureau with French feet, an average piece, brought $180. One of the pieces of furniture that are so popular today, a tambour desk, brought $230. It was inlaid, had original brass, and was made in about 1790.

The classification of a piece of Hepplewhite furniture as being American or English is sometimes difficult. Not only is it hard even if the piece is examined in detail, but it is vastly harder to do from a photo. Often the leading auction houses did not so classify pieces of furniture. In these cases, the piece was not used in this survey. Here, in the case of the Margulis collection, it is hard to tell from the photo if the swell-front bureau described above is American or English. There is no designation, but the sale was of "Early American" furniture, and it is presumed that this was one of the early American pieces.

By 1925 some fairly respectable prices were achieved by American Hepplewhite pieces. On March 29 the Anderson Galleries sold a fair inlaid mahogany sideboard with a serpentine front for $1,000. On January 21, the American Art Association Galleries sold a beautiful inlaid mahogany and curly maple writing desk, 46 inches high and 40 inches wide, for $380.

On January 23, 1926, a mahogany sideboard with a shaped front and square ends, made by Daniel Edgecomb of Connecticut, brought $1,800, a much higher price than the preceding one and a vastly higher price than the one that sold for $105 in 1920. Of course, this sideboard sold in 1926 was by a known maker and this attribution gave it a higher price. In the July 1927 issue of *Antiques* magazine, H. O. Valentine of Richmond, Virginia, advertised an early inlaid mahogany sideboard six feet long for $2,250.

In January 1926 a mahogany sofa, six feet five inches long, was sold by the American Art Association Galleries for $475. On November 5 the same auction house sold a settee with a back in the form of three chairs for $1,450. In the same sale, twelve dining chairs were sold for $2,280.

Between early 1925 and late 1926, prices rose measurably and substantially. With the price index at 100 percent in 1920, by mid-1925 it had tripled and stood at 300 percent. By the end of 1926 it had doubled again and stood at 600 percent.

But by 1926 it had run its course, and it still stood at 600 percent in the peak year of 1929. At the Rubin sale of February 1 and 2, 1929, held at the Anderson Galleries, a serpentine mahogany inlaid sideboard, *c.*1785, brought $1,700, and at the famous Reifsnyder sale held at the American Galleries on April 24 to 27, 1929, an inlaid mahogany card table of serpentine shape, made in Maryland *c.*1790 and illustrated in various books, a fine antique, brought $900. In the same sale, an inlaid slant-top mahogany desk with original oval brasses, made in Philadelphia *c.*1795, brought $450. It was an average piece.

The Debacle of the 1930's

On January 2, 3 and 4, 1930, the Philip Flayderman sale was held at the American-Anderson Galleries, and it will do no harm to repeat that this was one of the greatest sales of American antiques ever held in the United States. One piece of furniture achieved a price so far out of line with other Hepplewhite antiques as to be unique. It was an important inlaid tambour secretary, *c.*1790, with John Seymour's label. It brought $30,000; but even with the Seymour label and with Seymour's excellence of design and workmanship, such a price is hard to justify except that at this sale a number of wealthy people were competing for a fine antique.

In the same sale a curly maple swell-front chest-of-drawers, *c.*1790, brought $500; an inlaid mahogany sideboard with a serpentine front, *c.*1790, brought $1,700 and six shield-back carved mahogany side chairs, *c.* 1790 and attributed to McIntire, brought $1,800—$300 a chair.

At the Garvan sale held at the American-Anderson Galleries on January 8 to 10, 1931, an East Hartford, Connecticut, shaped-front inlaid mahogany sideboard, *c.*1785–1795, brought $1,300; an inlaid mahogany circular drop-leaf card table, made in Virginia or Maryland, brought $300, and an inlaid cherry and maple bow-front chest made in Rhode Island brought $225. The prices of these Hepplewhite pieces were not significantly high in this distinguished sale.

In the notable Clifford Carlisle Kaufman sale held on October 30 to 31 of the same year at the American-Anderson Galleries, a fine serpentine inlaid mahogany sideboard brought $2,000. But an inlaid cherry and curly maple swell-front chest with bracket feet brought only $140, while a fine mahogany Pembroke table 40 inches deep brought $350 and a Pembroke table of Philadelphia origin brought only $200.

Inlaid mahogany Hepplewhite tambour-secretary of the Federal period with the original John Seymour label.   American-Anderson, 1930, $30,000.

In the Benjamin Flayderman sale of October 5 and 6, 1932, prices were certainly no better. A finely inlaid mahogany serpentine-front sideboard brought the low price of $450, and a mahogany and satinwood card table brought $90.

There were still some high prices in 1932, however, the year of the Depression bottom. On April 8 the American Galleries sold three splendidly carved mahogany shield-back side chairs for the high price of $3,900—over $1,000 apiece.

The Sack sale of January 9, 1932, saw the generally highest prices of the year for Hepplewhite furniture. Two of the Hepplewhite pieces had been sold to Mr. Sack in the Flayderman sale held exactly two years earlier. We thus have some indications of the effect of the Depression on American Hepplewhite prices:

Comparative Prices of Hepplewhite Pieces
Sold in January 1930 at the Flayderman Sale
and Again in January 1932 at the Sack Sale

Item	1930 Price	1932 Price
Inlaid cherrywood and mahogany sideboard with American eagle decoration, c. 1790, 39¼ inches by 5 feet 11 inches	$1,900	$ 700
Inlaid mahogany sideboard with label of Frothingham, c.1780–1790	5,500	1,500

The cherrywood sideboard had declined in price to 37 percent of the 1930 price. The Frothingham sideboard was down to 27 percent of its 1930 price.

From a set of three American Hepplewhite shield-back side chairs.   American Art Association, 1932, $3,900 the set.

As in the case of many other price comparisons, it must be pointed out that the 1930 prices were still boom prices to a great extent. The press was talking about a temporary economic setback in early 1930, and collectors were still hoarding their cash for fine specimens of furniture like the Flayderman pieces. But by 1932 there was no doubt in anyone's mind that there was a major depression or that stock prices had collapsed. An air of gloom was over the country. It is thus felt to be correct procedure to disregard some of the extremely high prices of furniture in the late 1920's and in early 1930 at the famous Flayderman sale in determining price trends.

Several other Hepplewhite pieces were sold in the Sack sale. Six New England shield-back chairs (one armchair and five side chairs) brought $1,200. An inlaid mahogany and satinwood chest-of-drawers brought $400. A Seymour inlaid tambour secretary brought only $700. It will be remembered that a Seymour tambour secretary had brought $30,000 in the Flayderman sale.

An inlaid mahogany and satinwood swell-front chest brought $950, but an inlaid mahogany break-front secretary brought the relatively high price of $3,600.

Prices by 1932 were down to 300 percent. They were cut at least in half as compared with 1929.

There was no improvement in Hepplewhite prices as the country pulled out of the Depression in the late 1930's. On November 3 and 4, 1933, the American-Anderson Galleries held the Dr. and Mrs. Morris Murray sale. An inlaid mahogany card table, 35 inches long, brought $75, and at the April 1937 sale of the Herbert Lawton collection, a Rhode Island carved mahogany side chair brought $240. On April 1, 1939, an inlaid mahogany sideboard made in Baltimore or Philadelphia brought only $300.

Prices in 1939 were still at the 300 percent level.

The War and Postwar Years

By 1940, with the European phase of World War II underway, prices of American Hepplewhite furniture showed no improvement. Mrs. Frederick S. Fish's collection was sold at the Parke-Bernet Galleries on October 3 to 5, 1940. One of the now highly desirable tambour secretaries of inlaid mahogany brought $110. It was of New England origin, c.1800. A pair of late eighteenth century carved mahogany shield-back side chairs brought $380.

In the next year, the Wallace Nutting collection was sold at the Parke-Bernet Galleries. A rare mahogany side chair attributed to Goddard brought only $180, while an inlaid mahogany butler's sideboard of convex and concave design, illustrated in Nutting's book, brought $575.

By 1942 prices weakened somewhat. The collection of Mrs. Luke Vincent Lockwood sold at Parke-Bernet on November 2, 1942, saw a carved mahogany shield-back side chair bring $50, an inlaid mahogany and birdseye maple chest with high bracket feet bring $160 and an inlaid mahogany and satinwood swell-front chest bring $510.

In January 1942 four carved mahogany shield-back side chairs were sold at the Parke-Bernet Galleries for $480. The distinguishing feature of these chairs is that they had belonged to Benjamin Rush, one of America's great patriots and one of the distinguished founders of the line. Today these chairs would probably bring ten times this figure.

On May 7 an inlaid mahogany bow-front sideboard of New York origin from the van Courtlandt family, a well-known and illustrated piece, brought $675.

Early in the year an inlaid mahogany card table with a hinged top brought $100, and late in the year an inlaid mahogany and satinwood tambour secretary brought $140. The onset of the war had cut prices in half, and the price index now stood at 150 percent, with the base of 100 percent being 1920.

By 1944 prices had improved, and at the Mrs. J. Amory Haskell sale at the Parke-Bernet Galleries on April 26 to 29, 1944, a pair of carved mahogany shield-back side chairs that had been exhibited at the Metropolitan Museum of Art brought $1,250—$625 each. Three more shield backs brought $540 for the lot, and a New Jersey mahogany serpentine sideboard brought $1,100.

Prices in The 1950's

Nevertheless, by 1950 there was no further improvement in prices. A mahogany serpentine-front settee, seven feet six inches long, brought $1,000 at the April 29,

American Hepplewhite card table.   Parke-Bernet, 1954, $185.   (*Photo: Taylor & Dull*)

1950, sale at Parke-Bernet. On January 12 the same gallery sold an inlaid mahogany serpentine-front sideboard, with some repairs and restorations, for $900. But many items sold for a few hundred dollars, and a sewing table sold on February 11 for $50.

Two important sales were held in 1954. The Luke Vincent Lockwood sale of May 13, 1954, held at the Parke-Bernet Galleries, saw some Hepplewhite pieces offered. An inlaid branch satinwood and mahogany bow-front chest made in the late eighteenth century brought $600.

Prices in 1955 still stood at the 400 percent mark, where they had been in 1945 and 1950. By 1960 prices had risen, but still the galleries were not featuring Hepplewhite furniture. Very little of that offered was considered important enough to illustrate, although many of the sales contained Hepplewhite pieces. A survey of the antique magazines also showed few offerings of American Hepplewhite furniture.

Prices in the 1960's

On March 3, 1960, the Parke-Bernet Galleries sold a New York carved mahogany shield-back armchair for $850.

American Hepplewhite bow-front chest.   Parke-Bernet, 1954, $600. (*Photo: Taylor & Dull*)

Other prices of Hepplewhite furniture were also higher in 1960. A Connecticut inlaid cherrywood sideboard made in about 1800 brought $650 on January 15 in New York. The next day a Pembroke table with some imperfections brought $400. In February a swell-front chest brought $375, and in March an inlaid cherrywood chest brought $375. Prices were moving up, but they were not of a height which would attract anyone's enthusiastic attention. The general price level was about 50 percent over that of five years before, and the index now stood at 500 percent.

By 1964 and 1965 nothing of a startling nature had happened to prices of Hepplewhite furniture, and, again, few items were illustrated. The emphasis was on other types of furniture. It was clear, however, that there was some demand for American Hepplewhite furniture. In October 1965 the Parke-Bernet Galleries sold an inlaid mahogany *demi-lune* card table with two swinging legs for $400. Another one, but with small imperfections, went in the same sale for $350. On the previous day another went for $450. A Madison Avenue dealer offered a fine pair of arm-chairs with shield backs, showing the influence of Robert Adam, for $3,600. On the other hand, my wife and I at the same time bought a fairly good *demi-lune* table with one moving leg and a few imperfections for $135 from a less exclusive New York dealer. This was no discovery. The dealer knew exactly what he was selling.

By 1965 no huge increase in the prices of American Hepplewhite furniture had taken place. The index stood at 600 percent—about the same place it had stood in the middle and late 1920's.

At the famous Stout sale held at the Parke-Bernet Galleries January 22, 1966, several Hepplewhite items were sold, but none in the super-fine category. They

Inlaid Connecticut Hepplewhite sideboard.   Parke-Bernet, 1960, $650.   (*Photo: Taylor & Dull*)

illustrate what ordinary Hepplewhite furniture was bringing. A mahogany Pembroke table made in New York, c.1795, with an oval hinged top brought $775. An inlaid mahogany swell-front chest-of-drawers with bracket feet, made in Massachusetts in the late eighteenth century, brought $500. A mahogany eight-leg dropleaf dining table with a rather plain top but with fluted square tapering legs, 56 inches long and 54 inches wide, brought $1,500.

An inlaid mahogany swell-front sideboard made in Maryland in the late eighteenth century, five feet seven inches long, brought $1,650. It was finely inlaid but was repaired.

A carved mahogany and brocade armchair made in the late eighteenth century, with a stretcher, a slightly arched back and tapering legs, brought $1,400, and a nineteenth-century carved arch-back armchair with square, tapered, stretchered legs brought $1,800.

The October 1966 sale held at the Parke-Bernet Galleries in New York saw some very good Hepplewhite pieces sold, and at some rather high prices. A late eighteenth-century inlaid mahogany Pembroke table brought $450. An inlaid mahogany serpentine-front sideboard from the early nineteenth century, with small imperfections, brought $1,400. A Salem, Massachusetts, shield-back mahogany armchair with square legs and a stretcher brought $450. A Salem inlaid mahogany and satinwood sofa, attributed to William Hook, c.1800, brought the relatively high price of $3,600. An inlaid mahogany tambour secretary, c.1800, by John Seymour, brought $4,000, but a carved mahogany tester bedstead attributed to John Goddard of Newport brought the very high figure of $5,250.

Prices in one year had strengthened for Hepplewhite furniture of American origin.

American Hepplewhite Prices

Date	1925 Equals 100%	1920 Equals 100%
1920	33%	100%
1925	100	300
1926	200	600
1929	200	600
1932	100	300
1939	100	300
1942	50	150
1945	133	400
1950	133	400
1955	133	400
1960	167	500
1965	200	600

American Sheraton Furniture

American Sheraton furniture occupies a unique position in the price history of antiques. It is some of the best made and most beautifully designed furniture ever produced. It is of a size and general contour admirably suited to today's smaller houses and apartments. Yet, in the entire history of prices of antiques, American Sheraton furniture can never be considered to have been in great demand or to have achieved consistently high prices. There have been top-notch designers and makers of American Sheraton furniture, but even pieces by their hand have not brought high prices. There are few Sheraton pieces to compare with the John Seymour Hepplewhite tambour secretary that brought $30,000 in the 1930 Flayderman sale. Sheraton and Hepplewhite furniture are closely related in design and construction, and it might be expected that they would move together price-wise. Yet there are divergences, the most notable being that Sheraton prices have never seemed to "get off the ground."

Prices in the 1920's

Like a good many other pieces of furniture sold in the early years of the 1920's, American Sheraton attracted little attention and brought low prices—little above the level of "secondhand" furniture. An example of these prices was a mahogany side chair of rectangular design made in the late eighteenth century that brought $20 when it was sold in the Anderson Galleries on November 5, 1920. Few Sheraton pieces were illustrated in sales catalogues, and few of these illustrated pieces brought prices that were worth recording.

If the 1920 price index is considered as 100 percent, prices five years later had doubled. In February 1925 the American Art Association Galleries sold a small urn-back settee for $275, an excellent piece of furniture. In the same sale, a carved tulipwood secretary-bookcase, seven feet four inches high, brought $600. On March 7 the same gallery sold an inlaid mahogany secretary, four feet four inches high, with original brass, for $125. On October 9 the Anderson Galleries sold a mahogany secretary-cabinet five feet six inches high, for $300. On October 14 the same gallery sold six side chairs for $325; in the same sale a three-part mahogany dining table, twelve feet six inches long, brought $200. Certainly, such prices cannot be considered of much significance in the antique market.

The years 1925 and 1926 saw a rapid increase in prices of many types of antiques, and some prices rose tremendously in late 1925 and early 1926. But this situation did not obtain in American Sheraton furniture. In 1926 prices were about the same as they were in 1925, and 1925 did not represent a huge increase as against 1920, at least as compared with other antiques.

On January 9, 1926, the American Art Association Galleries sold an armchair for $65 and a matching side chair for the same price. Three days later they sold an inlaid mahogany and satinwood card table with straight tapered legs for $90.

By 1929 prices had gone up rapidly and were now at the 600 percent level. In April the Anderson Galleries sold a pair of inlaid card tables with hinged folding tops for $450 the pair, very much above the price of the card table that brought $90 in 1926. The following month the American Art Association Galleries sold another card table of similar design for $300. The same gallery sold a late eighteenth-century inlaid tambour secretary, made in New England in about 1795, for $1,500. This is one of the items so popular today.

In the Reifsnyder sale of April 24 to 27, 1929, a pair of carved mahogany side chairs brought $275 each, a very high price in comparison with prices five years earlier. A pair of carved mahogany armchairs of Philadelphia origin, illustrated in Nutting's book, brought $900 each.

The Depression

By the time of the Flayderman sale of January 2, 3 and 4, 1930, American Sheraton prices had not been reduced greatly, although the country was going downhill economically. In fact, an inlaid mahogany small settee from New England, c.1790–1800, with a long and illustrious history, brought a high price—$6,000. In the same sale, an inlaid mahogany and branch satinwood card table, made in New England c.1800, brought $280, and an inlaid mahogany tambour secretary brought $475.

In the Garvan sale of January 8 to 10, 1931, held at the American-Anderson Galleries, a mahogany and maple inlaid chest, originally made either in Pennsylvania or Maryland, brought $200, a small sum for the piece and for the quality of the sale in general. In the Benjamin Flayderman sale of October 5 and 6, 1932, a rare Sheraton mahogany card table, c.1800–1810, with the national emblem, brought $320.

At the Sack sale earlier in 1932, several excellent Sheraton pieces were sold. A pair of inlaid satinwood and mahogany card tables brought $600. A small New England mahogany sofa brought $1,550. A Samuel McIntire carved and upholstered mahogany sofa brought only $650. A bow-front chest with the label Samuel

American Sheraton tambour secretary. American, 1925, $125.

Curly-maple swell front chest of drawers. Flayderman Sale, 1930, $500.

One of a set of four Sheraton side chairs. Parke-Bernet, 1939, $180 the set.

American Sheraton satinwood inlaid card table. Anderson, 1920, $80.

American Hepplewhite card table. American Anderson, 1933, $75.

American Sheraton secretary-bookcase. Parke-Bernet, 1939, $300.

S. Noyes, East Sudbury, Massachusetts, brought only $225. An inlaid mahogany serpentine-front sideboard brought $1,700.

On April 8, 1932, the American Art Association Galleries sold a mahogany two-part dining table by Ephraim Haines, seven feet five inches long, for $1,050.

The Depression cut prices approximately in half. They *appeared* to remain high only because of the excellence of the pieces offered after 1929 and in earlier years. In 1932 the index stood at 300 percent.

The Plateau of the 1930's

In 1936 a fine piece of American Sheraton furniture was sold at the Marsden J. Perry sale, held at American-Anderson Galleries on April 3 and 4. A rare mahogany side table, 45 inches long, made in Baltimore *c*.1795, brought $875.

The next year, four excellent pieces of Sheraton furniture were sold at the Herbert Lawton sale at the American-Anderson Galleries on April 2 and 3, 1937. All were McIntire pieces. A mahogany sofa brought $875 and a dressing table $900. A card table brought $500, and a very fine mahogany sofa brought $3,100. All attained high prices for American Sheraton furniture considering the times.

In the following year prices appeared to collapse, partly in response to the Depression of 1938. A pair of semicircular card tables by John Hewitt, New York, were offered at the Erskine Hewitt sale at the Parke-Bernet Galleries on October

One of a pair of American Federal semicircular card tables by John Hewitt, showing Sheraton influence. Parke-Bernet, 1938, $200. (*Photo: Taylor & Dull*)

American Sheraton inlaid mahogany and satinwood card table.   Parke-Bernet,
1939, $45.   (*Photo: Taylor & Dull*)

From a set of twelve carved mahogany dining chairs, American Sheraton, circa
1790.   Parke-Bernet, 1964, $6,600 the set.   (*Photo: Taylor & Dull*)

18 to 22, 1938. These tables had been exhibited at the Metropolitan Museum of Art, at the Colony Club and at the Museum of the City of New York. They brought $200 for the pair. In the same sale, a New Jersey inlaid mahogany card table, c.1800–1810, brought $80, and a New York inlaid mahogany writing bureau brought $75.

The William Randolph Hearst sale was held a month later. An inlaid mahogany bureau with the label of Michael Allison, New York, brought $175.

On February 4, 1939, the Parke-Bernet Galleries sold an inlaid curly maple card table with a serpentine-hinged top and reeded legs. It brought $60. On October 6 the same gallery sold an inlaid mahogany and satinwood card table, 35½ inches long when opened, for $45. Prices were now down to the 100 percent level—the low point of the early 1920's.

The War and Postwar Period

At the Wallace Nutting sale held at the Parke-Bernet Galleries on October 4, 1941, an inlaid mahogany and satinwood swell-front chest illustrated in Nutting's book brought the somewhat better price of $400.

In 1945, at the war's end, prices were distinctly better. A mahogany sofa with straight fluted legs brought $500 on January 27 at the Parke-Bernet Galleries. On the same day, a serpentine-back sofa attributed to McIntire brought $900. On December 8, a mahogany butler's sideboard, c.1810, once owned by General Israel Putnam and from the collection of William Whiting Nolan, brought $1,900. Prices

From a set of six chairs, including two arm chairs, of the Federal period, New York, circa 1795, made from a design by Sheraton. Sold in the early 1950's, $2,750 the set. *Courtesy of Ginsberg & Levy, Inc., New York.*

of American Sheraton furniture had now returned to about the 1932 depression level.

By 1950, however, featured offerings of American Sheraton furniture had all but disappeared in American auctions. In January 1950 a late Sheraton inlaid mahogany writing cabinet with tambour cupboards, c.1820, brought $275. The next month a carved mahogany drop-leaf breakfast table brought $125. Many items offered were unillustrated. The vast majority of these American Sheraton items brought under $100, and a number of them brought under $50. American Sheraton furniture was in the doldrums. The index was back to 100 percent, the wartime low of 1942.

The Sheraton Price Recovery

At this point a general upward price movement set in—not of boom proportions by any means, but a steady upward push. On October 9, 1954, the Parke-Bernet Galleries held the Maurice Rubin sale. A small carved mahogany bow-front sideboard with a secretary desk by McIntire brought $550, certainly a small price for any piece by McIntire. Four inlaid carved mahogany side chairs of Salem, Massachusetts origin, with reeded legs, but of plain design, brought $300.

On January 22, 1955, a carved and gilded wood and gesso mirror made in Salem, Massachusetts, c.1800, with *églomisé* decoration, brought $800. A new England inlaid mahogany and branch satinwood secretary-bookcase brought $370.

From a set of nine American Sheraton chairs, and a sofa, inlaid with satinwood (one chair is now in the Sleepy Hollow Collection). Sold in the 1950's for under $10,000 the set. *Courtesy of Ginsberg & Levy, Inc., New York.*

Drop-leaf breakfast table, American Sheraton, circa 1810. Parke-Bernet, 1964, $675.

Mahogany work table, Massachusetts, circa 1815. Parke-Bernet, 1966, $1,000.

One of a set of four Salem Sheraton side chairs. Parke-Bernet, 1954, $300 the set.

Mahogany Pembroke table, New York, circa 1810. Purchased by the author, 1964, $150.

Most of the rest of the items sold during the year were unillustrated and brought upward of $100, most of them under $200; but some still brought less than $100. Prices had about doubled since 1950.

The important thing about sales and prices of American Sheraton furniture in the 1950's is that almost no items offered were considered important enough by the auction house to illustrate in the catalogues, although there were many offerings. For the most part they brought low prices.

By 1960 American Sheraton furniture returned to the attention of the auction houses, and more pieces were illustrated in response to greater demand and somewhat higher prices. On January 16, 1960, a carved mahogany three-pedestal dining table with a center section of a later date (such substitution tends to hurt the price severely) brought $850 at the Parke-Bernet Galleries. In February an inlaid mahogany satinwood sofa table brought $310 despite imperfections. Later in the year, a mahogany card table inlaid with the American eagle brought $250. Some of the unillustrated items were bringing over $200 and even over $300. The price index had gone up 100 points to 300 percent and was again at the 1932 low!

In 1964 (June 18), the Parke-Bernet Galleries sold four carved mahogany side chairs with a latticework splat and fluted and stretchered square tapered legs for $1,400—over $300 a chair. On the same day twelve carved mahogany dining chairs (two arm and ten side) were offered for sale. The backs were square, there was a stepped crest rail, the splats were pierced, and the carving was of drapery swags and Prince of Wales feathers. The set had belonged to General Winfield Scott. It brought $6,600—over $500 a chair.

In the same sale, a carved mahogany drop-leaf breakfast table with six legs, c.1810, brought $675. In October 1965 an inlaid mahogany sideboard brought $2,100. Prices had risen 150 percent since 1955 and now stood at 450 percent.

Although the Stout sale held at the Parke-Bernet Galleries on January 22, 1966, was noted for its extremely fine American antiques, very few fine American Sheraton pieces were offered. An early nineteenth-century mahogany card table with one swinging leg and a hinged serpentine top, 29½ inches high and 35½ inches long, brought $225. The next lot was a mahogany high-back open armchair, c.1820. It brought $700.

American Sheraton settee.   Flayderman Sale, 1930, $6,000.

A carved mahogany tester bed made in Salem, Massachusetts, c.1795, a bed of slender, graceful design, brought $2,000. A mahogany three-pedestal extension dining table made in the late eighteenth century (extending to ten feet four inches) brought $1,100.

Finally, a good mahogany lady's work table of the eighteenth century, 30 inches high and 24½ inches wide, brought $2,100.

On October 22, 1966, some fine pieces of American Sheraton furniture were offered at the Parke-Bernet Galleries, and prices were by no means low. A set of six carved mahogany side chairs with balloon-shaped seats, made in Philadelphia c. 1795 and attributed to John Connelly, brought $3,000—$500 a chair. A similar pair of side chairs that differed in that they had square seats, square legs and stretchers, brought $2,200—$1,100 a chair. A Boston inlaid mahogany sideboard, c.1795, brought $1,250. All of these pieces had originally been sold by Ginsberg and Levy, which provided a stamp of authenticity and excellence.

One might make out a case for American Sheraton furniture rising at least 50 percent in one season, based on these prices.

At about this time (the middle 1960's), a distinction in price had begun to be made. In general, prices of Sheraton furniture, English or American, have never increased greatly or reached very high levels. But in the middle 1960's the distinction between American Sheraton and English Sheraton became more pronounced. The items sought after in the American auction houses and in American dealers' shops were American Sheraton pieces rather than English Sheraton, and American pieces were tending to rise more rapidly than English. As the already short supply of American pieces grows more scarce in relation to the much larger general supply of English Sheraton furniture, it can be expected that American Sheraton prices will rise much more rapidly than they have in the past, particularly in view of the general excellence and small size of American Sheraton furniture.

American Sheraton Prices

Date	1925 Equals 100%	1920 Equals 100%
1920	50%	100%
1925	100	200
1926	100	200
1929	300	600
1932	150	300
1939	50	100
1942	50	100
1945	150	300
1950	50	100
1955	100	200
1960	150	300
1965	225	450

DUNCAN PHYFE ROOM, circa 1800.   *Courtesy of the Museum of the City of New York.*

CHAPTER TWENTY-FOUR

Duncan Phyfe
1790–1847

THE FURNITURE OF DUNCAN PHYFE is essentially Sheraton and for that reason might be classified as a Sheraton substyle. In his later years, Phyfe became more and more influenced by the French Empire style, and his furniture may be considered to fall into the category known as "American Empire," the American adaptation of French Empire. Nevertheless Duncan Phyfe furniture is so distinctive as to form a separate category.

In Ridgefield, Connecticut, there was a sofa for sale in the summer of 1965 that had all of the elements of Phyfe, but was it a later Phyfe copy? We felt it was a later piece. Had it been of the period we would have paid up to $1,200. If it had been of the period but not Phyfe, we would have paid perhaps half that figure, and if it was done later in the style of Phyfe we would have paid $200, at most.

Also in the summer of 1965, a light-colored Pembroke table with casters was sold at one of the lesser auction houses in New York. The style looked like Phyfe to me, but I was not quite sure that the piece was of the period and I was much less certain who the maker was. I let it go by. It brought only $100. When I learned that the buyer was the largest dealer in American furniture in the city, I started to do research and I quickly came to the conclusion that the piece was almost certainly by Duncan Phyfe. A fair asking price for that piece would be about $1,200. This was one that got away.

While there is now a limited demand for the pieces of Duncan Phyfe, a few dealers are buying up this furniture very quietly and putting it away. These dealers are adding Duncan Phyfe to their stock with the feeling that it will shortly come back in active demand. It almost certainly will.

There are other reasons for including a chapter on the furniture of Duncan Phyfe. In the 1920's there was a "Phyfe craze," and his furniture was not only in tremendous demand, but it was considered that Phyfe was as fine a cabinetmaker as America ever produced. Authorities made this statement over and over again in newspapers and magazines. Even if the design is not in the greatest demand today, the overall quality cannot be denied, and tastes can change in a very short period of time so as to create another Phyfe boom.

Of course, Duncan Phyfe, like all the other famous furnituremakers, had to come in for his share of criticism as well as exultant praise. In *The Saturday Evening*

Post of March 29, 1930, Wallace Nutting, dean of authorities on American furniture, says of Phyfe, "Poor man, he began well, imitating for the most part good late Sheraton or early Empire and lapsing with the decline of taste to supply the clumsy crudities of the 1830's and '40's."

Duncan Phyfe was born in Scotland in 1768 and came to America in 1784. In 1790 he set up shop in New York City, and in 1795 he opened a shop in what later became Fulton Street. Here he remained until his shop closed in 1847.

At first Phyfe manufactured in the English Sheraton style, the furniture most in vogue at about the turn of the century. But to this furniture he added French elements—elements of the period following the Louis XVI style. This was *Directoire*, then Consulate and finally Empire. But whereas the *Directoire*, Consulate and Empire furniture tends to become heavier and heavier in appearance, the furniture of Duncan Phyfe is light and graceful, particularly in his early period. The French furniture made after the Louis XVI Period was larger in size. But Phyfe did not follow this trend to large size and he thus avoided one of the poor elements of later French furniture.

The proportion of his pieces was superior to much of the French of the period. While it is recognized that in the late 1960's French Empire furniture is growing in popularity, it is still heavy and of cumbersome proportions. For the most part, the proportions of the furniture of Duncan Phyfe are excellent.

Finally, the later French styles were heavily ornamented with all kinds of forms. There were animals, sphinxes, Egyptian heads, symbols of freedom, and so forth. Duncan Phyfe did not err on the side of overornamentation. He used a few simple motifs and usually carried them out by carving.

Characteristics of Duncan Phyfe Furniture

1. Relatively small size. The size was more like Sheraton than like the French of the period.
2. Use of small members. Arms and legs were of slender diameters, thus adding to the feeling of grace.
3. Excellent proportion. With the exception of a few bases for tables and some finials on the underside of tables, the proportion of the furniture of Duncan Phyfe is very good.
4. Highest grade construction. Phyfe used ample materials to stand the strains to which the furniture would be put, with some resulting feeling of heaviness. The workmanship is the best.
5. Extremely subtle lines to give a clean-cut appearance. His use of classic curves was masterful.
6. Predominant use of Cuban mahogany, a wood of excellent quality and appearance.
7. Carving as the chief means of ornamentation. Important design elements included:

      Acanthus leaf
      Water leaf
      Oak leaf

Acorn
Ribband
Thunderbolt
Egg and dart
Wheat ear
Prince of Wales feathers

8. Placement of carved ornaments on the top rails of sofas and chairs. This placement was extremely characteristic of Phyfe.

9. Flat surfaces for top rails on chairs and sofas for general good design and to provide a medium for the carving.

10. Low relief carving of extreme precision. By looking at the care with which the flat surfaces of sofa and chair backs are prepared, and noting the type and quality of design, a long step is taken in identifying a particular piece as having been done by Phyfe as compared with someone working in the style of Phyfe.

11. Backward curve to the top of sofas and seats on which the carving is placed.

12. Precision fluting of front and side seat rails of chairs and sofas. This was not always done, but it is characteristic of many of his pieces. The precision of this work and the excellent widths and depths of the fluting are also means of identifying the work of this maker. This pattern was also used on table legs.

13. Sharply incised carving on chair, sofa and table legs.

14. Great use of the lyre, not only as a design element in carving, but also as a support for tables.

15. Use of the Regency table pedestal.

16. Use of finely proportioned and well-made brass mounts.

17. Use of multiple curves on small tables, particularly on the leaves of Pembroke tables.

18. Concentration on furniture other than case furniture. Phyfe was a specialist in tables, chairs and sofas. He also made sideboards and even pianos. But he was not known for making cabinets, commodes, tallboys or other storage furniture.

19. Great use of casters on tables of all kinds.

20. Very slender legs on tables, particularly the small tables. The extremely graceful leg is one means of identifying a Phyfe piece. These legs were almost invariably reeded and gently tapered.

The Duncan Phyfe Boom of the 1920's

In the November 1922 issue of *Antiques* (one of the first issues), Duncan Phyfe furniture was the main topic of the entire publication. And by the June 1923 issue, it was clear that a Duncan Phyfe boom was in the making. The inside of the front cover is a Phyfe advertisement, and throughout the various issues of the magazine around this time there appears to be a disproportionate number of ads for Phyfe pieces. When one considers that all of the Phyfe furniture came from one relatively small shop, it is hard to understand how there could be enough furniture on the market for a boom to take place!

But by 1929 Phyfe had become so popular that *Antiques* contained an article entitled "The Essence of Duncan Phyfe." Even after the stock market collapse and Depression of the early 1930's, the August 1935 issue of *Antiques* comments that Duncan Phyfe items are always high in price.

The rise in the price of Duncan Phyfe during the decade of the 1920's and particularly during the last half of the decade was not equaled by any other group of American furniture. It is obvious that furniture prices did not move in the same manner as the stock market averages did; but, as far as the boom of the 1920's is concerned, Duncan Phyfe furniture did its best to parallel the rise of the stock market to its peak in late 1929!

In 1925, a mahogany three-part dining table by Duncan Phyfe brought $600 at the American Art Association Galleries, and a three-part extension dining table brought $675. In the following year a dining table brought $925 and another $1,500. This is the pattern of most antique furniture in the years 1925 through 1929. The one year, 1926, shows an extremely sharp increase in prices. In that year, two settees went for $325 and $900.

Now let us see what happened to the price of Duncan Phyfe sofas by the boom year of 1929. At the Reifsnyder sale at the American Art Association Galleries on April 24 to 27, 1929, a sofa brought $4,100. This high price was no exception for Duncan Phyfe furniture. At the sale of the belongings of Mrs. H. H. Benkard at the Anderson Galleries April 13, 1929, one sofa brought $3,100 and another $4,750. A three-part dining table brought $2,300, and a secretary-bookcase brought $1,900.

If we start the price index on Duncan Phyfe at 100 percent in 1925, we find that by the next year it had doubled, and by 1929 it stood at 800 percent.

By January 1930, several months after the stock market crash, the Philip Flayderman sale of top-grade antiques was held at the American-Anderson Galleries. At this sale an important set of nine carved mahogany shield-back chairs was offered. They had fluted and stretchered legs and were made by Phyfe at about the end of the eighteenth century. They brought the high price of $1,000 each.

Duncan Phyfe lyre sofa table. Anderson, 1926, $550.

"Martha Washington" sewing table by Duncan Phyfe, New York, circa 1810. Parke-Bernet, 1939, $275.

At the important Garvan sale in January 1931, a Pembroke table forty inches long brought $175, certainly not a huge price. However, at the Kaufman sale in October of the same year, a two-part dining table made in 1805 and having a carved pedestal brought $2,600, certainly something above a depression price. This, too, was an important sale of fine American furniture.

In January 1932 the Israel Sack sale was held in New York, and the furniture offered was generally of superb quality. A Phyfe lyre-back mahogany sewing table brought $750, a pair of mahogany card tables brought $1,700 and a carved mahogany and upholstered sofa brought $2,050—low prices as compared with 1929, but certainly not give-away prices.

The Benjamin Flayderman sale later in the same year saw some lower prices. A carved mahogany lyre-pedestal card table brought $230, an important Phyfe sofa of Sheraton style brought $650 and a breakfast table brought $260.

At the Louis Guerineau Myers sale in April 1932, a settee was sold for $1,100 and another for $975. A work table was sold for $900, another for $1,100, a breakfast table for $1,900 and three card tables for $800, $350 and $360.

Beautifully carved sofa table, New York, circa 1810. In the Phyfe style and attributed to Michael Allison. Sold in the early 1940's for $800. *Courtesy of Ginsburg & Levy, Inc., New York.*

With prices of Phyfe furniture at 100 percent in 1925, 200 percent in 1926 and about 800 percent in 1929, prices were now about 500 percent. This was a big drop, but not a disastrous one, and certainly not a drop which was comparable with many other goods of various kinds at the time.

But as the depression receded into the past there was no recovery of Duncan Phyfe prices. By 1939 the index stood at 250 percent. Prices were half of what they were in the Depression low of 1932. The highly important sales that were held in the Depression undoubtedly helped to hold up the prices of Phyfe furniture.

By 1942 the index which had stood at 250 percent in 1939 had fallen to 200 percent. At the Charles McCann sale held at the Parke-Bernet Galleries November 17 to 21, 1942, a carved mahogany drop-leaf pedestal table 47½ inches long brought $425.

The war had an upward-pulling effect on the prices of American furniture in general; by 1945, the last year of the war, Duncan Phyfe prices had risen to 300 percent—up 50 percent since 1942. One reason for the general rise in antiques during the war was the drastic cutback in the production of new furniture: The demand spilled over into antiques. But while this explanation has some merit, most of the demand spilled over into plain second-hand furniture.

In December 1945 two settees brought $1,500 and $950. A carved mahogany drop-leaf pedestal breakfast table brought $1,900, and a good Martha Washington sewing table brought $650. Earlier in the same year, an important set of seven carved mahogany dining chairs with curule legs and caned seats brought $600 for the lot.

By 1950 prices had dropped materially from the end of the war figure of 300 percent and were at the 100 percent level. They remained at 100 percent for the next five years.

At the Maurice Rubin sale held at the Parke-Bernet Galleries October 9, 1954, there was hardly any improvement in prices. A pair of side chairs brought $200,

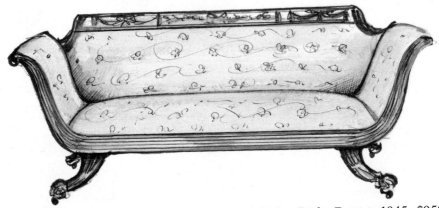

Carved mahogany sofa by Duncan Phyfe, circa 1805.   Parke-Bernet, 1945, $950.

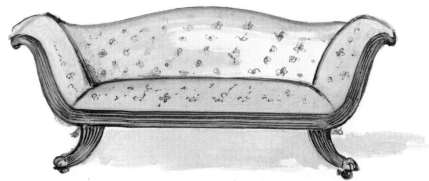

Carved mahogany lyre sofa by Duncan Phyfe, New York, circa 1810. Parke-Bernet, 1945, $1,500.

"Martha Washington" sewing table by Duncan Phyfe, New York, circa 1800. Parke-Bernet, 1945, $650.

One of six Phyfe side chairs. Parke-Bernet, 1960, $840 the set (and a set of four to match, $520).

Phyfe mahogany settee, circa 1810.   Parke-Bernet, 1954, $385.

another pair brought $200, a similar pattern sofa brought $385 and a three-pedestal dining table brought $550.

In *Antiques* magazine during 1954, a pair of Phyfe side chairs was advertised for $300, and in 1955 a Phyfe card table was advertised for $140, certainly no high prices.

By 1960 the price index had doubled from the extremely low 100 percent of 1955. In October 1960 a carved mahogany sofa with reeded legs and a scrolled crest rail decorated with wheat sheaves, swans and bow knots brought $1,600. On the other hand, the Parke-Bernet Galleries on March 3, 1960, sold six carved mahogany side chairs made in 1815 for $840 and four more to match for $520. Another side chair was sold two days later for $120.

Work table by Duncan Phyfe.   Sold in the mid-1950's for about $1,500.   *Courtesy of Ginsburg & Levy, Inc., New York.*

Carved mahogany dressing table by Duncan Phyfe, New York, circa 1820. Parke-Bernet, 1966, $4,000.

One of a pair of Phyfe side chairs. Parke-Bernet, 1954, $200.

Carved mahogany sofa by Duncan Phyfe, circa 1820. Parke-Bernet, 1966, $4,000.

But something else was happening to Duncan Phyfe furniture in this period from the early 1920's up to the present time. It was virtually going off the market. Each year less was offered, and of the Phyfe furniture that was offered, less and less was illustrated in the auction catalogues and less and less was considered important.

On February 20, 1965, the Parke-Bernet Galleries sold a Phyfe Napoleon table made about 1815. It had four supports and was nine feet three inches long. It had been on loan to the Smithsonian Institution in Washington and had been used by Presidents Kennedy and Johnson. It brought $2,000.

The index in 1965 stood at 250 percent, a figure comparable to the middle 1920's (when dollars had a higher purchasing power than they did in 1965). The 250 percent figure compares with 800 percent in the peak year, 1929.

We have not heard the end of Duncan Phyfe furniture, however. This is probably the biggest "sleeper" in antiques in America. A fine piece will bring a good price; and American dealers, while not featuring Duncan Phyfe, do not ask small prices. A good sofa will be priced at $2,000 or $2,500 even though it will not sell for a long time. The minor dealers will ask perhaps $350 for a good card table or Pembroke table.

There is absolutely no question that if prosperity continues, Phyfe will stage a sizable comeback in price. It is of excellent quality and fine design, and on its intrinsic merits it must gain a lasting place in the hierarchy of antiques.

On January 22, 1966, the most significant sale of furniture since the 1920's, as far as Duncan Phyfe goes, took place at the Parke-Bernet Galleries. The sale was of the estate of the late Mr. and Mrs. Andrew Varick Stout. In this sale Duncan Phyfe pieces went at prices that were astronomical as compared with earlier sales, and these prices presaged a possible new Phyfe boom.

Drop-leaf breakfast table by Duncan Phyfe, New York, circa 1800.   Parke-Bernet, 1945, $1,900.

Duncan Phyfe carved mahogany lyre-back armchair, circa 1815.   Parke-Bernet, 1966, $2,000.   (*Photo: Taylor & Dull*)

One of a pair of carved and inlaid mahogany card tables by Duncan Phyfe, New York, circa 1820.   Parke-Bernet, 1966, $1,900 each.   (*Photo: Taylor & Dull*)

Pair of lyre-back armchairs by Duncan Phyfe.   Sold in the early 1960's for about $8,000.   *Courtesy of Ginsburg & Levy, Inc., New York.*

Duncan Phyfe carved mahogany window seat (exhibited at the Girl Scout Loan Exhibition).   Parke-Bernet, 1966, $7,500.   (*Photo: Taylor & Dull*)

One item was a carved mahogany window seat 42 inches long. The end supports had splats in the form of lyres. It had animal legs and paw feet. Aside from the fact that there are very few Phyfe window seats in existence, this was not a particularly unique and wonderful piece of furniture. Yet it brought $7,500.

A carved mahogany dressing table with ogival legs (one repaired), with leaves carved on the upper part, and paw feet, 58 inches high and 34½ inches long, brought $4,000. A typical Phyfe carved and inlaid mahogany card table, 36 inches long, with some repairs, brought $1,900. It was a late piece, made in about 1820 as was the preceding piece. A matching table with some repairs and imperfections brought a similar price.

In the same sale a mahogany drop-leaf table 50 inches long brought $800, a carved mahogany library table brought $1,000, and ten early Federal carved mahogany side chairs brought a total of $2,000.

A carved mahogany sofa with a paneled crest rail carved in relief and with finely reeded apron, legs and arms brought $4,000. Finally, an armchair was offered with a leaf-carved lyre-shaped splat. The arms were finely reeded and of reverse curve design running from the top of the crest rail to the seat rails. The legs were animal in form with paw feet. One important feature about this chair is that it was displayed in the famous Girl Scouts Loan Exhibition of 1929. It realized $2,000, the price of a good French, Chippendale or Queen Anne armchair.

If this one sale were representative of the prices for the entire year, the Duncan Phyfe index would be back at the 1929 peak of 800 percent. But the sale was noted for its record prices for all kinds of fine furniture. Still, a level of 500 percent had almost certainly been reached, representing a doubling in one year.

Duncan Phyfe Prices

Date	1925 Equals 100%
1925	100%
1926	200
1929	800
1932	500
1939	250
1942	200
1945	300
1950	100
1955	100
1960	200
1965	250
1966	500

PENNSYLVANIA GERMAN ROOM, showing furniture and decorations of the eighteenth and nineteenth centuries.   *Courtesy of The Metropolitan Museum of Art.*

American Country Furniture
1790–1890

ANTIQUE STORES THROUGHOUT THE United States sell more country furniture made in America than any other type furniture, with the possible
exception of Victorian. In any event, much of the Victorian furniture
which is sold is of a primitive country type, so that the two categories overlap to
a great extent. Together, they amount to the great bulk of what the American
antique shops sell today.

In the category of American country furniture is a great deal that is genuine
antique and that should technically be included in the chapters on Chippendale,
Queen Anne, etc. The reason this furniture is not so included is that it is of a
lesser quality than that included in those chapters. It is not fine, city-made antique
furniture. The country versions of the city pieces are extremely far removed in
quality from the city prototypes. In fact, the country American versions of city
furniture are very much like the French provincial versions of Louis XV furniture.
French provincial is not in the same quality category with Paris antiques and is
strictly rustic.

Hardly a week goes by that does not see American country versions of city
styles sold through the New York auctions. If we take the week this chapter was
written, both the Parke-Bernet Galleries and the Plaza Art Galleries offered such
pieces in their regular sales. A good city piece would probably bring three times as
much as a good country piece of the same type and age. That is the approximate
differential between city and country furniture.

In the 1920's country furniture became the rage in the most sophisticated city
homes, and whole rooms were filled with what was called "Early American." Now
the fad has passed, and the price of such furniture bears a more realistic relationship to the sophisticated pieces.

But there are a few dim signs of the return of the fad. One of the leading
department stores in New York has just opened a "Country American" salesroom
in one part of the store's antique department. In this section pots and pans are
hung from the walls and ceiling, the country pieces are jammed in or scattered
about, and the whole place gives the impression of an old-time country barn sale.

The most wanted antiques are of the eighteenth century—that is, earlier than the
year 1800. Antiques up to 1830 are still respectable, and they include the highly

popular French Empire style and the English Regency style. While a number of American country pieces come within these "magic cutoff dates," a great deal of the furniture was made at a later time. The difficult part of classifying such furniture is that it was made in about the same way for a very long period. The piece may have first appeared in Revolutionary times but continued to be made in the same way until, say, 1850. One cannot definitely establish age in many of these pieces so as to distinguish those made in 1790 from those made in 1805, or those made in 1825 from those made in 1850. The difference in these dates is of vital importance in valuing antiques, but the date often cannot easily be established.

Pennsylvania German furniture and decorations of the eighteenth and nineteenth centuries. *The Metropolitan Museum of Art.*

CHAPTER TWENTY-FIVE

Thus, in this chapter we may be talking about what are technically antiques, or simply discussing old furniture which is not antique.

American country furniture is somewhat unique from a market point of view. In most countries of the world there is a sharp cleavage between the sophisticated city pieces and the country or provincial pieces, the former bringing by far the higher prices. In fact, the provincial pieces are generally in the low-priced category.

In American country furniture, there is a premium-priced category—the furniture of the seventeenth century (Pilgrim Century). This premium is present even though the furniture may be just as lacking in sophistication as the later country furniture. It must be remembered, of course, that early in American history a great deal was by nature crude because the country was new and undeveloped and had little civilized history.

In the October 1966 New York City Armory Show, one dealer from New Hampshire offered several pieces of seventeenth-century furniture. The first was a Brewster chair dated about 1670, one of perhaps a dozen in the United States. The price was $6,000 for this single chair. He also offered two Carver armchairs, dated 1650 and 1660. These were priced at $2,800 and $4,500. A pair of Carver side chairs was priced at $2,000, while a hutch table made c.1720–1730, a very crude piece of furniture, was priced at $775.

This is not exactly furniture of the Age of Elegance, and it does not fit in with sumptuous surroundings. It is bought for the most part by specialist collectors. It has risen in price in recent years like most antiques, only perhaps faster, and it is possible that in the past year prices have as much as doubled.

SEVENTEENTH CENTURY AMERICAN FURNITURE. Left to right: The chair-table is New England, circa 1675; the chest, attributed to Thomas Dennis, Ipswich, Massachusetts, 1675; the cradle dates about 1625–1675, and the Carver armchair, 1650–1700. *The Metropolitan Museum of Art*, Gift of Mrs. Russell Sage, 1909.

What we are concentrating on in this chapter is not the furniture of the Pilgrim Century, but the closely related furniture that appeared in later years. Although basically of the same type, this later furniture is vastly less valuable.

Typical American Country Pieces

CHAIRS

Hitchcock Chairs. These are painted black or a very dark brown and ornamented with stenciling, often of fruits and flowers. The legs are straight and stretchered. Solid seats of wood are used as well as rush and cane seats. The back slats are wide. The chairs are small and of cheap construction and materials— usually maple. But they are very decorative.

Empire Chairs. These are based directly on the French Empire chair of a slightly earlier period and closely resemble the earlier chair. A few years ago we bought a pair of excellent curly maple Empire chairs for $50, and at auction we bought five with caning in excellent condition for $19 apiece. Hitchcock chairs and Empire chairs account for more sales than probably all other types of nineteenth century chairs on the market. Both types are small, and if they are not in good condition they can usually be repaired with a minimum of expense.

Shaker Chairs. Both side chairs and rockers were turned out by the Pennsylvania Shakers in the first sixty years of the nineteenth century. These pieces are extremely rudimentary. The legs and the upright posts are not turned because the Shakers believed in simplicity, although they were apparently not against comfort, since the chairs are fairly comfortable. The seats are of rush or splint, and the chairs resemble the slat-backs to be described now.

Slat-back Chairs. The most prominent feature of these chairs is the back which is high and contains a number of parallel slats. Both side chairs and armchairs were made. Such chairs can sometimes be bought for $50 or less.

Banister-back Chairs. These are an earlier and more elegant variety of the slat-back chair.

Boston Rockers. The production of these rocking chairs was started in the first decade of the nineteenth century and continued into the 1860's. The Boston rocker was made all through the United States, not just in Boston, but it has a rustic New England appearance. Boston rockers can often be purchased for $50.

Windsor Chairs. This is an extremely popular chair in America. In the era of the 1920's a number of these sold for several hundred dollars each, and the Windsor chair at this time gathered a kind of aura. It is still attractive, but not the most important collector's item. In 1917 famed dealer Wallace Nutting published *American Windsors* which possibly started the glorification of the Windsor chair. This book details how the best variety of this chair should be constructed, classifies the chairs into bow-backs, fan-backs, writing arms, comb-backs, etc., and then assorts them as to area of origin. The Windsor is a rather good-looking lightweight rustic chair with a farm-type charm.

TABLES

Table-Chairs. This is an intriguing piece of furniture that is a table when the top is in position, but when the top is lifted on one side it becomes a chair.

Trestle Tables. This is a simple form of refectory table like an Italian Renaissance or Jacobean table, but much more primitive. The top consists of one or two boards resting on blocks which in turn rest on trestles. These trestles are held in position and kept from collapsing by flat stretchers which connect the two main stretchers.

Sawbuck Tables. These are very similar to trestle tables, but they are more like the sawhorse that was and is used on American farms for sawing logs.

Harvest Tables. These all-purpose tables are six or seven feet long and have a drop leaf on each side over straight, undecorated legs. They were used for dining on the farm as well as for any other purpose to which a large table could be put.

Tavern Tables. The top of such tables is oval or rectangular. They are more refined than the trestle, sawbuck or harvest table. They are smaller than the long trestle or sawbuck table, and they got their name from the fact that they were used in taverns to serve guests.

Table Stands. This is a little table of square or curved design. Under the top are one or two drawers. The tables were used to hold candles or lamps, or they were used as sewing or bedside tables.

Joint Stools. This is a very early type of seat or table. It was sometimes used to sit on and sometimes it was used as a base for other things. Sometimes, under the top, there is a drawer. Like most stools of all countries and of most eras, these pieces are fairly rare and in some demand.

Storage Furniture

Blanket Chests. This was a universally popular piece of furniture from the middle of the eighteenth century to almost the middle of the following century. It is also known as a pine chest or dower chest, and the Renaissance chests have been described earlier as being directly related to these American chests-of-all-purpose.

Seamen's Chests. While the blanket chest is a rudimentary piece of furniture, the seaman's chest is more rudimentary. It, too, is a pine chest, but even more like a box than the blanket chest. Its purpose originally was to carry the seaman's belongings when he went to sea.

Shaker Chests. While the blanket chest is extremely common and the seaman's chest is no rarity, the Shaker chest is very rare. There is a low Shaker chest that contains drawers and a high Shaker chest with a series of long drawers and one or two rows of two drawers at the top. The piece resembles the bureau or commode that has existed from Renaissance Italian times in almost identical form.

Apothecary Chests. These were made for apothecaries to keep their wares. They contain a series of drawers with china pulls.

Open-top Dressers. This is an item that is in some demand at the present time, both because it is very useful for storage purposes and because it often has some artistic merit. It consists of a series of shelves which are open or which have guard rails in front of them, and these shelves are placed on top of a cupboard which may have two parallel drawers at the top and cabinet doors below the drawers. This piece of furniture was used for the storage and display of china, glassware and kitchenware.

Corner Cupboards.   This piece of furniture is even more popular at the present time than the open-top dresser to which it is related. It is the country version of a very popular city piece.

Kitchen Cupboards.   This is a shorter piece of furniture than the above two cupboards. It is about five feet high and three feet wide. The top is flat but has a plain wooden gallery that runs around the back and the sides. Below this top are two drawers, and below these drawers are two doors enclosing a cupboard. The cupboard is fitted with shelves. The feet are simply continuations of the wood on the sides of the cupboard. Kitchen cupboards were made throughout most of the nineteenth century.

Water Benches.   These are very primitive pieces of furniture common to most of the nineteenth century. They were placed outside the kitchen door and contained a pitcher of water for washing the hands and face.

Dry Sinks.   This is the forerunner of our modern kitchen sink, and the modern sink resembles it very closely in shape. Essentially, the dry sink is a low cupboard about the height of a modern sink. It has a sunken washing compartment which is sometimes lined with zinc or copper so the water does not damage the wood. Behind the washing compartment may be a low backboard which rises above the top of that compartment. Sometimes it rises very high and has a hood. Beneath the sink part are two doors enclosing storage space. The dry sink often appears on the market—in shops and in auctions. We purchased a fairly good one in 1964 for the low price of $50.

DESKS

Desk Boxes.   These are merely boxes with a top that slopes downward toward the writer. They have no legs and are less than a foot high in most cases; they have to be placed on another piece of furniture to be used. The top, which is the writing surface, is hinged so that writing materials can be kept in the box.

Schoolmasters' Desks.   If one put four plain rectangular or square legs on the desk box and installed a drawer, he would have the schoolmaster's desk.

Traveling Desks.   This is a portable but elaborate desk box. It has a drawer at the side, unlike the desk box, and it has a writing surface which is slanted beneath the top, not integral with the top. The writing surface can be opened in order to reveal storage space and sometimes compartments. There is also a carrying handle made of brass.

Desks-on-frames.   This is a more elaborate and larger schoolmaster's desk.

SOFAS

Windsor Settees.   These are attractive settees based, as the name indicates, on the Windsor chair. In effect, they are simply stretched-out Windsor chairs.

Settles.   These are little more than flat benches with flat backs that rise to a height of perhaps five feet. The sides of the settle are wide and sometimes wing-shaped. The top of the back may be in the form of a hood, designed so that the piece would keep away the breezes that blew through early American windows that did not fit very closely.

Painted Settees. These have eight legs, some of which may be turned or shaped. Some painted settees resemble the Hitchcock chair and even have decorations like that chair.

Painted Cradle Settees. These were produced in the era of the painted settee. They were, however, set on rockers, and the solid seat was divided—one part for the cradle and the other part for the sitter. The sitter could rock the baby and, at the same time, rock herself. These pieces were often painted.

Country Sofas. These are essentially modified daybeds, cut down and upholstered. Sometimes a back was added or else arm rails.

Wagon Seats. These are simply movable seats that were placed on wagons. When they were not on the wagons, they were used in the home. They are like double slat-back armchairs or double Windsor chairs with spindles. Sometimes they were painted and were supplied with splint or rush seats. In the last few years another type of wagon seat has become extremely popular—the later wagon seat with low flaring sides and back and longitudinal springs.

In addition all manner of beds were made in the "Primitive American" Period.

There is also a whole series of country versions of Hepplewhite, Sheraton, Empire and even earlier styles of furniture. These pieces superficially resemble the well-made and beautiful city pieces, but are crude because they were made by country craftsmen for use in country homes or farm houses. They are now coming onto the market in the major auctions more than ever, and are beginning to command some respectable prices—although not of the level of the fine pieces of the era.

Painted softwood corner-cabinet, Pennsylvania German, circa 1760. Anderson, 1922, $575.

Banister-back chair, Connecticut, circa 1725. Anderson, 1922, $85.

Pair of hickory windsor chairs, American, circa 1780. Anderson, 1922, $70 the pair.

Important sawbuck or "X" table, Pennsylvania, circa 1675. Anderson, 1922, $325.

Prices of Country American Furniture

Perhaps the furniture of the Pilgrim Century (seventeenth century) should not be classified as Country American at all. For that reason, the dates given for the furniture considered in this chapter are the 1700's to 1890. Ralph and Terry Kovel in 1965 published a highly informative book on such furniture: *American Country Furniture, 1780–1875* (New York: Crown Publishers). The title is particularly significant. While country furniture was most certainly made in the eighteenth century, and even earlier than that, these dates encompass what is generally sold in the market as Country American.

Price-wise, American furniture of the more primitive variety shows a unique pattern. The pieces of the seventeenth century and some of the early eighteenth century are sold at premium prices. (The Brewster chair, for instance, brought $6,000.) The market for this unique furniture, even though of crude design and finish, is a specialist market. It is composed for the most part of collectors who buy because of the unique nature of the piece and who have at least as much knowledge of what they are buying as the dealer who sells it. The buyer is akin to the stamp collector, the coin collector and the individual who will pay $25,000 for an antique automobile.

At the other end of the Country American scale are the simpler pieces of country furniture. While the unique pieces have perhaps doubled in price in one year, these run-of-the-mill pieces, many of the late nineteenth century, have risen little and can be bought for little. In fact, as far as furniture for utility goes, they are some of the best buys on the entire antique market. The cash outlay to purchase them is small. They do the job as furniture, and it is difficult to see how they can go down in value, even in a depression.

Early eighteenth-century walnut tavern table with vase and ring turnings.   Anderson, 1920, $45.

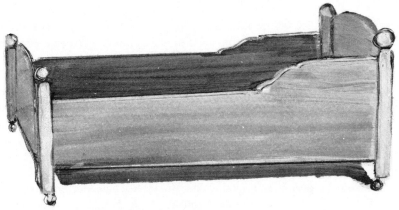

Painted softwood trundle bed, Pennsylvania German, circa 1750.   Anderson, 1922, $50.

Hooded pine settle, early American, circa 1720.   Anderson, 1922, $275.

Painted bridal chest, Pennsylvania German, dated 1832.   Anderson, 1922, $190.

Slat-back chair. Plaza, 1964, $15.

Black and gold lacquered fancy chair, American, circa 1830. Purchased by the author, 1959, $15.

Oak and pine paneled chest, New England, circa 1680–1700. Anderson, 1928, $1,250.

Pine wash stand, nineteenth century.
Plaza, 1964, $27.50.

Pine chest of drawers, American, nineteenth century.   Savoy Auction, 1964,
$30; mirror with pine frame, $15.

Country pine dry sink, American,
nineteenth century. Savoy Auction,
1964, $50.

Walnut chest of drawers, marble top,
American, nineteenth century. Purchased by the author, 1958, $40.

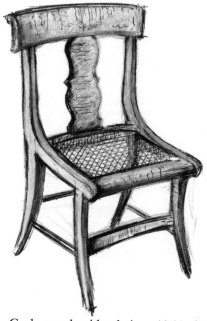

Pine side chair, circa 1830. Plaza, 1964, $20.

Curly maple side chair. 1964, $50 a pair.

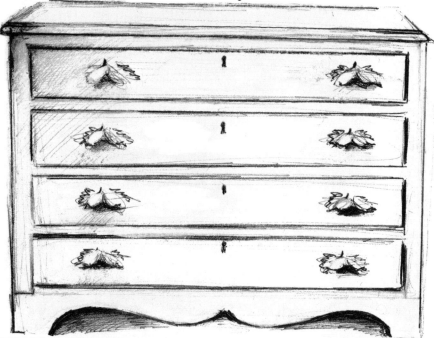

Country four-drawer commode. Savoy Auction, 1964, $40.

Pine slant-front desk on frame. Plaza, 1966, $30.

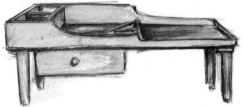

Pine cobler's bench, nineteenth century. Plaza, 1966, $30.

Pine occasional table, nineteenth century. Plaza, 1966, $25.

Maple and pine commode, late nineteenth century. Plaza, 1966, $20.

On October 27, 1966, the Plaza Art Galleries in New York offered a large group of this simple, highly unsophisticated furniture for sale. These are some of the prices realized at this sale:

Stained pine miniature china cabinet, nineteenth century	$40.00
Walnut hanging corner shelf	12.50
Small pine lift-top box (desk box)	18.00
Set of four Hitchcock maple side chairs—rush seats	30.00
Pine and oak wagon seat—later type (with springs)	60.00
Small pine occasional table, early nineteenth century	12.50
Pine cobbler's bench, nineteenth century	30.00
Turned pine single-drawer occasional table, nineteenth century	20.00
Pine bench and pine woolwinder floor lamp (converted piece)	15.00
Small pine desk on frame	30.00
Stained pine two-drawer occasional table, nineteenth century	25.00
Cherry rectangular drop-leaf table, nineteenth century	17.50
Two assorted pine chairs, nineteenth century	20.00
Pine two-drawer serving table, nineteenth century	20.00
Pine caned-seat side chair, small occasional table and a hanging shelf	40.00
Maple and pine chest of three drawers, nineteenth century	20.00

For these 23 separate pieces of furniture, $410.50 was paid—about $18.00 apiece. For a very modest total outlay, a very substantial group of furniture could be purchased at just one sale, and it is difficult to see how the investment could be lost if the buyer some time moved away to another city and decided to auction off these things again.

In 1960 we purchased a number of similar items, including pieces converted to coffee tables, lamps and end tables. We bought them at retail for perhaps 25 per-

Pine and oak wagon seat, later model. Plaza, 1966, $60.

Turned pine occasional table, nineteenth century. Plaza, 1966, $20.

Cherry rectangular drop-leaf table, nineteenth century.   Plaza, 1966, $17.50.

Two pine chairs, late nineteenth century.   Plaza, 1966, $20 the lot.

Pine serving table, nineteenth century.   Plaza, 1966, $20.

cent under these prices. At retail, prices of such low-end items have probably increased 50 percent in five years, but the number of dollars we are talking about is minimal.

Between this low-end group of American furniture of the simpler variety and the collectors' items of the seventeenth and early eighteenth century, there is a great group of American Country furniture—furniture that is not so simple as to be suitable only to the country home or the recreation room, yet not so expensive that only wealthy collectors can afford to buy it. It is this furniture that forms so large a percentage of the stocks of most American antique and semiantique dealers.

In the fall of 1966 price samples were taken of a group of this in-between furniture. These are the prices of some representative pieces:

Windsor high-back chair	$165
Ladder-back armchair, c.1730	165
Blanket chest, one bottom drawer—refinished	145
Settle—refinished	295
Maple corner cupboard (Connecticut) refinished	550
Boston rocker	85
Small country ladder-back chair	25
Pair of simple country chairs	60
Country drop-leaf table	200
Country bureau	60
Six tiger maple side chairs, c.1840	200
Hitchcock chair	35
Dry sink, no liner	115
Pine shelf cupboard (Pennsylvania), four doors	150
Veneered tiger maple and maple chest-of-drawers, made before 1800	165
Tavern table (Pennsylvania), three feet by six feet	148
Cherry drop-leaf table	75
Slaughter bench converted to coffee table	30

Prices in the past five years have better than doubled for this intermediate group of Country American furniture, and there were no signs of price weakening. Demand in the fall of 1966 was high.

To summarize price movements for Country American furniture, the unique and earlier items rose perhaps 100 percent in the 1966–1967 season alone. The low-end very simple pieces rose perhaps 50 percent in the past five years. This is by no means furniture of the Age of Elegance and cannot be expected to benefit in price or demand by this movement. Nor can most dealers afford to handle a great deal of it. The number of dollars to be made on each piece sold is not great.

The intermediate group has a certain amount of elegance and many of the pieces have been refinished to look like genuine antiques. Such items might even be placed in elegant homes to good effect. This group has better than doubled in price in the past five years.

*A comparison of furniture styles
and selected average prices in today's
antique market*

ENGLISH
JACOBEAN, $800

ENGLISH WILLIAM
& MARY, $750

ENGLISH QUEEN
ANNE, $1,500

ENGLISH
CHIPPENDALE,
$1,000

AMERICAN
JACOBEAN, $2,000

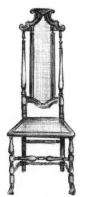

AMERICAN
WILLIAM & MARY,
$275

AMERICAN
QUEEN ANNE,
$15,000

AMERICAN
CHIPPENDALE,
$3,000

LOUIS XIV, $800

RÉGENCE, $900

LOUIS XV, $2,500

LOUIS XVI, $2,000

ADAM, $1,500

ENGLISH
HEPPLEWHITE,
$750

ENGLISH
SHERATON, $250

REGENCY, $350

VICTORIAN, $100

AMERICAN
HEPPLEWHITE,
1,000

AMERICAN
SHERATON, $500

DUNCAN PHYFE,
$2,500

COUNTRY
AMERICAN, $150

VICTORIAN
(BELTER), $300

FRENCH
PROVINCIAL, $500

DIRECTOIRE, $900

FRENCH EMPIRE,
$500

RENAISSANCE
ITALIAN, $350

PAINTED ITALIAN,
$750

Comparative Prices of Good Quality Armchairs* in the Late 1960's

1. Louis XIV	$1,000	16. Hepplewhite	1,000
2. *Régence*	1,250	17. Sheraton	600
3. Louis XV	2,500	18. Regency	500
4. Transition	1,500	19. Victorian—English	100
5. Louis XVI	2,000	20. Victorian—American	200
6. *Directoire*	800	21. American William and Mary	1,000
7. Empire	500	22. American Queen Anne	3,000
8. French Provincial	300	23. American Chippendale	2,000
9. Renaissance	400	24. American Hepplewhite	1,250
10. Painted Italian	1,250	25. American Sheraton	600
11. Jacobean	800	26. Duncan Phyfe	1,000
12. William and Mary	800	27. American Country	150
13. Queen Anne	1,250	28. Fine American Seventeenth	
14. Chippendale	1,500	Century (Carver)	3,000
15. Adam	1,250		

Comparative Prices of Good Quality Commodes in the Late 1960's

1. Louis XIV	$ 5,000	16. Hepplewhite	1,000
2. *Régence*	5,000	17. Sheraton	600
3. Louis XV	20,000	18. Regency	1,500
4. Transition	10,000	19. Victorian—English	150
5. Louis XVI	12,000	20. Victorian—American	300
6. *Directoire*	3,000	21. American Wm. and Mary	800
7. Empire	3,000	22. American Queen Anne	3,000
8. French Provincial	1,250	23. American Chippendale	3,000
9. Renaissance	1,000	24. American Hepplewhite	1,750
10. Painted Italian	15,000	25. American Sheraton	750
11. Jacobean	750	26. Duncan Phyfe	2,500
12. William and Mary	750	27. American Country	250
13. Queen Anne	2,000	28. Fine American	
14. Chippendale	2,000	Seventeenth Century	3,000
15. Adam	3,000		

*These are average, prices for good chairs. The comparative pictures of chairs are of specific chairs most of which have been sold for specific prices.

FRENCH ANTIQUES

Louis XIV	1648–1715
Régence	1715–1723
Louis XV	1723–1774
Louis XVI	1774–1794
Directoire	1795–1799
Consulate	1799–1804
Empire	1804–1815
French Provincial	1715–1850

ITALIAN ANTIQUES

Renaissance	1400–1700
Painted Italian	1680–1820

ENGLISH ANTIQUES		AMERICAN ANTIQUES
Jacobean	1603–1689	—
William and Mary	1689–1702	1700–1725
Queen Anne	1702–1714	1725–1750
Chippendale	1749–1779	1755–1790
Georgian	1714–1820	—
Adam	1760–1793	—
Hepplewhite	1780–1795	1785–1800
Sheraton	1795–1810	1795–1815
Regency	1795–1830	1810–1840 (Empire)
Duncan Phyfe	—	1790–1847
Victorian	1830–1900	1830–1900
American Country	—	1700's–1890

Antique Periods Peculiar to America

The term "Colonial Furniture" describes furniture made at and before the time of the American Revolution of 1776 and includes William and Mary, Queen Anne, Chippendale and Early Georgian as well as the scarce American Jacobean furniture.

The term "Federal Period Furniture" describes furniture made from the establishment of the Federal Government in 1789 on to 1830 or even as late as 1840, and includes Hepplewhite and Sheraton as well as American Empire and Late Empire (1830–1840) and the limited production of American Directoire (1805–1815).

CHAPTER TWENTY-SIX

The Antique Price Index

A T ANTIQUE AUCTIONS AND antique fairs there seems to be one topic of mutual and perpetual interest—prices. There is hardly an auction or a fair at which the level of prices is not discussed. In any event, a summary is made in the minds of those making the comments which (1) includes most of the items at the auction or the fair, and (2) depends on what the antique market was prior to the sale to provide a base for determining whether prices were higher or lower.

At this point in this study, we have attempted to establish an average price index of the antique market and to work out this average by years from 1925 to the present. Some of our reviews of prices have started with the 1860's to show what has happened to, say, Louis XVI furniture over a period of many years. In the case of Louis XVI furniture, prices back this far were readily available and could be traced up to the present time. For other types of furniture, prices were not available very far back.

We have started this overall price index at the year 1925 for several reasons. The first is that prices of most important types of antiques are available back to that year. Second, many of the more significant of these items were illustrated in the auction catalogues back to the year 1925. Without illustrations, we cannot be certain what we are talking about.

The third reason for starting the index in the year 1925 is that forty years are included in the index, not too long a span for an investment. A person is not vitally concerned if he could have bought a BVRB *bureau plat* in 1897 for $200 and it is now worth $50,000. He is more concerned if he could have bought it in 1925 for $2,500 and can now sell it for $50,000, and he is very much more concerned if he could have bought it in 1960 and made a profit on it by selling it now (or by just realizing that the value did go up materially).

Philadelphia carved mahogany Chippendale highboy.   Sold to George Horace Lorimer, editor of *The Saturday Evening Post* in the 1920's for about $1,500 (with a lowboy to match, the two pieces were about $3,000–$3,500). It was repurchased at Lorimer's death by Ginsburg & Levy and resold in the 1930's. It was then sold in the 1940's at auction for about $8,000. In the summer of 1966, Mr. Ginsburg valued it at between $20,000–$30,000. It sold at Parke-Bernet on October 22, 1966 for $22,000.   (*Photo: Courtesy of Ginsburg & Levy, Inc., New York*)

The fourth reason for starting the index in 1925 is that things began to happen at about that time. The year 1926 in antique furniture bears the same relation to 1925 that the year 1929 bears to 1928 in the stock market. The 1920's saw an antique boom the like of which we may never see again; a boom that was as important in the antique field as the 1929 boom was in the securities field. And it is possible that there were as many investors in antiques in this period as there were in securities.

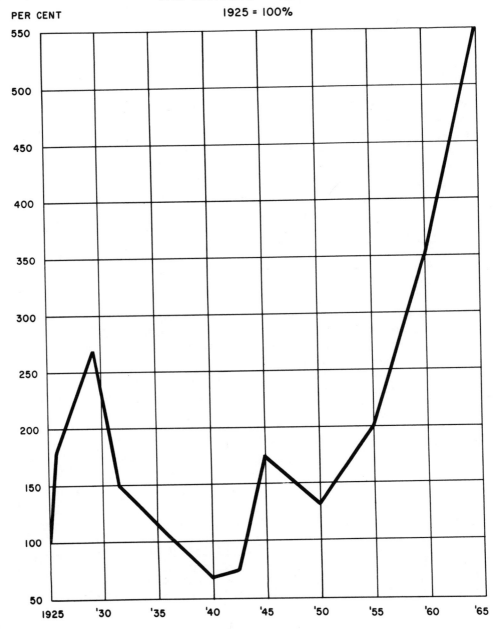

THE ANTIQUE PRICE INDEX

1925 = 100%

The forty-year span of the price index for antiques from 1925 to 1965 includes some notable occurrences which affected the antique market. In the first place, there was the 1920's boom in antiques which was not entirely based on prosperity. The present prosperity far exceeds that of the 1920's and is much broader based. Yet at the present time there is nothing like the antique craze of the 1920's.

The forty-year span includes the prosperity and the stock market boom of the late 1920's, so we can see what happened to antique prices under this set of conditions.

The next thing that can be observed is what happened to antique prices in the crash and in the recession and depression of the early 1930's. It is possible that some forecasts can be made of the future of antique prices in times of business depression based on this history.

The next phenomenon observed was the effect of the recovery of the late 1930's on antique prices. Then came the effect of the outbreak of the war in Europe in 1939 and the full entry of the United States into the war at the beginning of 1942. The progress of the war and the end of the war in 1945 had a definite effect on antique prices.

The five-year period from the war's end to 1950 was a time of economic readjustment as well as a preparation for the long period of postwar prosperity which continued through the late 1960's. The only interruptions of any significance were a few periods of moderate stock market decline and a slowing down of business, which in no way compared with the Great Depression. Yet antique prices did not closely parallel economic conditions.

In the middle 1960's the country, and much of the entire world, was in an economic boom with accelerating inflation. What was the effect of these phenomena, and of the psychology of boom and inflation, on antique prices?

Types of Antiques Included in the Price Index

In France the main antiques sold are French. Some Italian furniture is sold, a small amount of English, relatively small amounts of German, Austrian and other Continental antiques—and practically no American. Thus, a price index confined to French antiques and possibly including some Italian items plus some other European types would measure the Paris antique market. English furniture would not have to be included. There would be no question of including American furniture since it is almost unknown in the Paris market.

An English antique price index, on the other hand, would include English furniture which could largely be disregarded in the Paris market; but it would also have to include French, since this is sold in significant amounts (and at high prices) in England. The English price index could ignore American antiques as few American items are sold there. Italian antiques might be included.

In America, American antiques would obviously have to be included since they are sold here in large volume. So are English antiques and French antiques. A few Italian antiques are sold, and the rest of the continental European antiques could be ignored. The last appear not infrequently, but they are scattered as to country of origin—one piece from Sweden, one from Holland, a set of chairs from Austria, a German table, etc.

Thus, in summary, *a price index for antiques must be made for the market in which it is to be used*. The index we have developed is for the *American market*.

It includes American, English and French furniture of various types. But we have also prepared subsidiary indexes for English furniture and for French furniture as well. A combination English-French index might be used to measure the English market a little better than the combined American-English-French index. The French index which we have developed is not strictly applicable to the French market, although to some extent it uses Paris auction prices. It is based primarily on French pieces sold in London and in New York, and these prices are not entirely comparable to Paris prices of French furniture. At the present time and in the immediate past, the Paris market has offered more eighteenth-century and early nineteenth-century French furniture of generally better quality and at lower prices than has London or New York.

The index has been developed to measure antique prices in America over the years. But the English-French index, which measures the English market, does not vary too greatly from the American-English-French index, so that this three-part index does provide some measure of the London market. Our English furniture price recordings, however, are not confined to sales in England. They are based to a great extent on prices realized in New York for English furniture, so there is some bias. There is by no means a perfect market in antique furniture; and, when prices of English furniture rise in New York, English sellers do not immediately stop selling in London and ship their furniture to the New York auctions.

In some types of antique furniture, there were so few sales in early years (even as late as the year 1925 when our index starts) that these could not be included in our final index because they would exert a disproportionate influence on the final index number. When such types of furniture did become important, they were included in a second index which we have developed using the year 1950 as the base equal to 100 percent.

French Furniture Prices

1925 Equals 100%

Date	Louis XV	Louis XVI	Louis XV & Louis XVI	Régence	All French
1925	100%	100%	100%	100%	100%
1926	100	100	100	100	100
1929	100	100	100	200	133
1932	67	87	77	100	127
1939	34	43	38	25	34
1942	83	43	63	200	108
1945	166	93	129	100	120
1950	166	93	129	200	153
1955	166	93	129	300	186
1960	500	186	343	400	362
1965	700	533	616	500	578

FRENCH FURNITURE PRICE INDEX
1925 = 100%

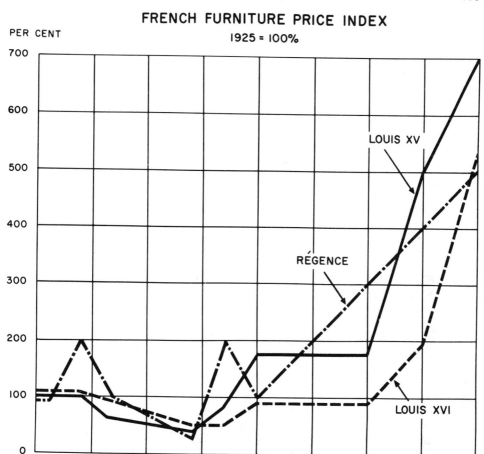

With 1925 equal to 100 percent, French furniture stood at 578 percent in 1965. A separate index consisting of only Louis XV and Louis XVI furniture was prepared, since these two types of furniture are responsible for most of the sales of French furniture on the international market. Not only are relatively fewer pieces of *Régence* furniture offered for sale, but the price level of *Régence* is lower than that of the furniture of the Louis'.

If, then, we eliminate *Régence* furniture, the index consisting of Louis XV and Louis XVI rose to the higher figure of 616 percent. Louis XV furniture rose further and faster than Louis XVI.

Still, the 1925 base of 100 percent does not indicate the magnitude of the rise of Louis XV and Louis XVI furniture or the price rise relationship between these two. If we take the year in which French furniture was in the doldrums—1939— and make that year equal to 100 percent in the case of both Louis XV and Louis XVI furniture, then Louis XVI rose to 1,240 percent in 1965 but Louis XV soared to 2,060 percent.

However, if we use 1939 as a base and determine the rise to the year 1960, Louis XVI rose to 430 percent but Louis XV rose to 1,500 percent. The last five years has been a period of catching up for Louis XVI furniture as Louis XV became scarcer and its prices skyrocketed.

LOUIS XIV PRICE INDEX

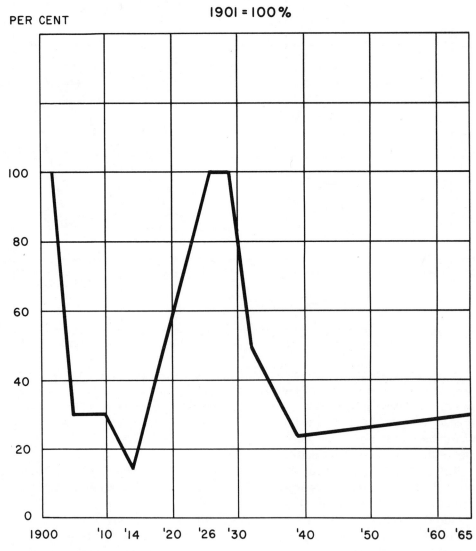

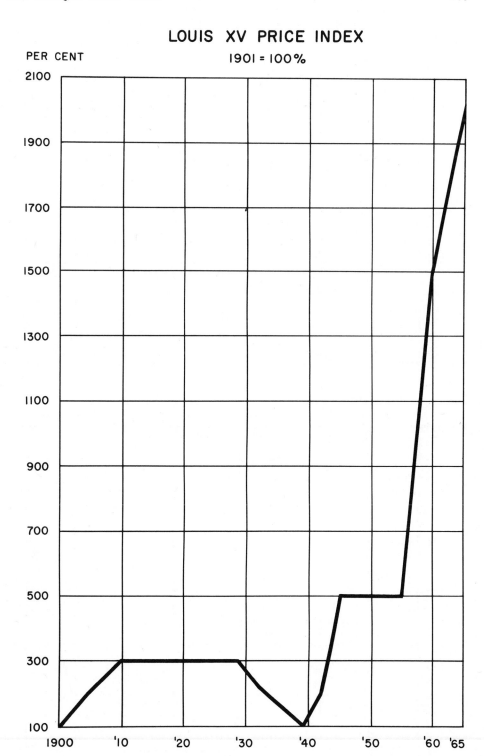

LOUIS XV PRICE INDEX
1901 = 100%

TRANSITION LOUIS XV - LOUIS XVI PRICE INDEX

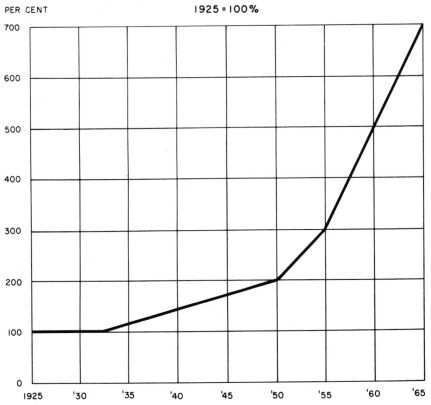

LOUIS XVI PRICE INDEX

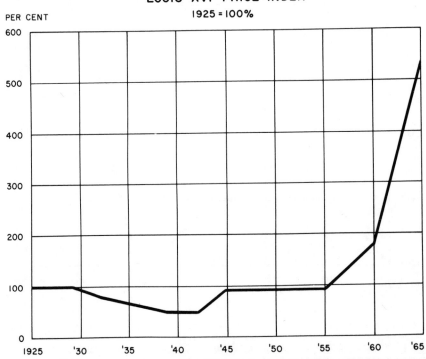

RÉGENCE PRICE INDEX
1905 = 100%

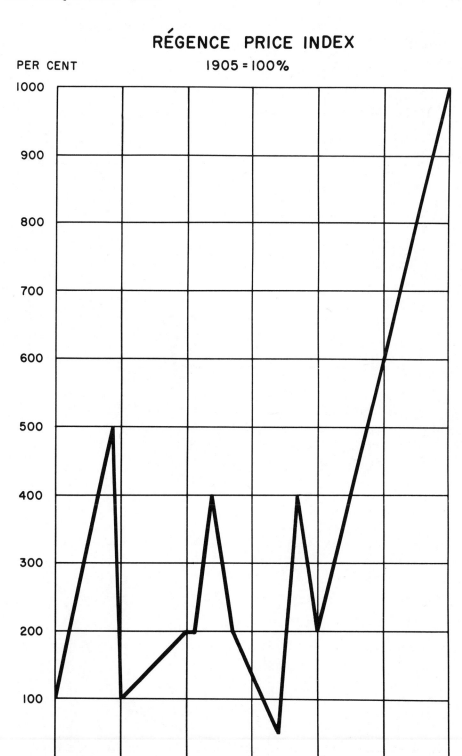

FRENCH PROVINCIAL PRICE INDEX

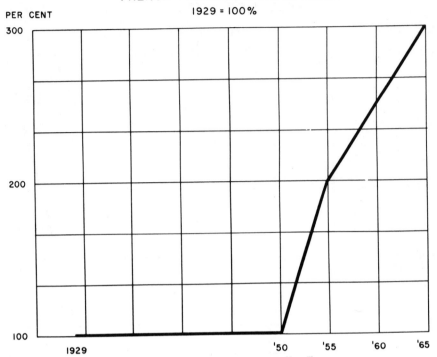

FRENCH FURNITURE COMBINED PRICE INDEX

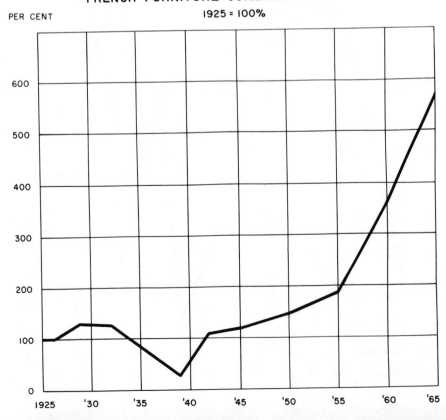

FRENCH EMPIRE PRICE INDEX
1950 = 100%

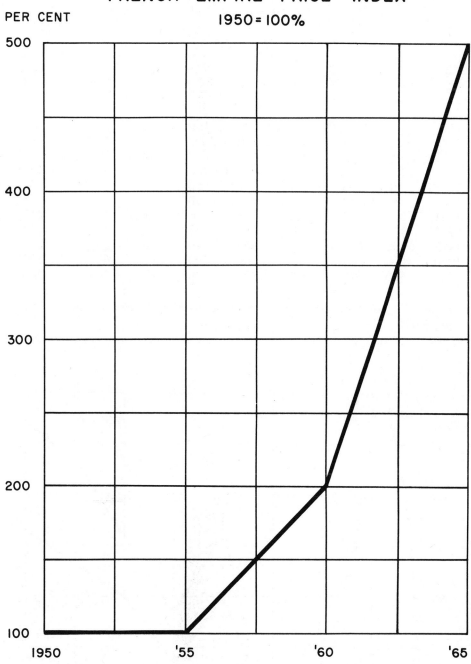

English Furniture Prices

1925 Equals 100%

Date	Chippen-dale	Hepple-white	Shera-ton	Queen Anne	William & Mary	Jacobean	Adam	All English
1925	100%	100%	100%	100%	100%	100%	100%	100%
1926	150	150	100	500	100	200	150	193
1929	150	200	150	1,000	100	300	200	286
1932	100	133	100	400	100	150	150	161
1939	30	67	100	20	50	60	75	57
1942	50	100	100	40	50	40	100	76
1945	300	133	150	500	70	200	150	215
1950	100	67	150	250	50	100	150	124
1955	300	133	168	500	40	100	200	206
1960	400	267	225	700	100	300	600	370
1965	500	400	300	800	120	350	1,200	524

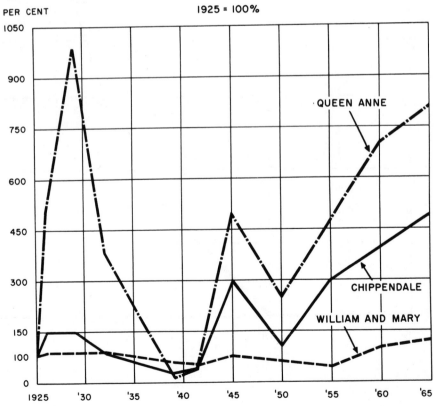

EARLIER EIGHTEENTH CENTURY ENGLISH FURNITURE PRICE INDEX

PER CENT   1925 = 100%

LATER ENGLISH FURNITURE PRICE INDEX

PER CENT   1925 = 100%

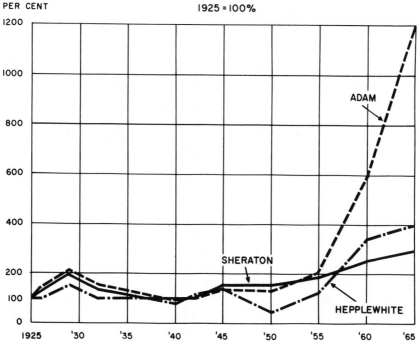

With the year 1925 equal to 100 percent, English furniture rose to 524 percent by 1965; but if we take the low year for antique furniture in general—1939—the index rose to about twice this figure. At the same time that there was a boom in business and in the stock market in the late 1920's, there was a boom in Queen Anne furniture, particularly in England, and Queen Anne furniture established price records each year in comparison to all other types of furniture in 1928, 1929 and 1930. In 1929 the index for Queen Anne stood at 1,000 percent, and this gigantic rise tends to distort the overall English price index simply because of the magnitude of the figure 1,000 while all other prices were in the low hundreds. Queen Anne, although the highest priced category of antique furniture, is only one of the seven categories of English antique furniture sold. While the highest priced category cannot be omitted from the index, it should be pointed out that if it were excluded, the index in 1929 would have been about 100 points lower than the 286 percent it achieved.

Adam furniture is generally the group with the greatest rise since 1925, although Queen Anne is certainly in a class with Adam in degree of rise as well as general price level.

The difficulty of using any one year as a base is indicated in the case of Jacobean furniture. Jacobean shows a relatively high rise from 1925 to 1965—350 percent. Yet dealers know that its rise has not been spectacular. If we compare the present price level of Jacobean furniture with the boom year 1929 when the price level was 300 percent, it can be seen with little need for any computation that there has been almost no rise to 1965.

ENGLISH QUEEN ANNE PRICE INDEX
1901 = 100%

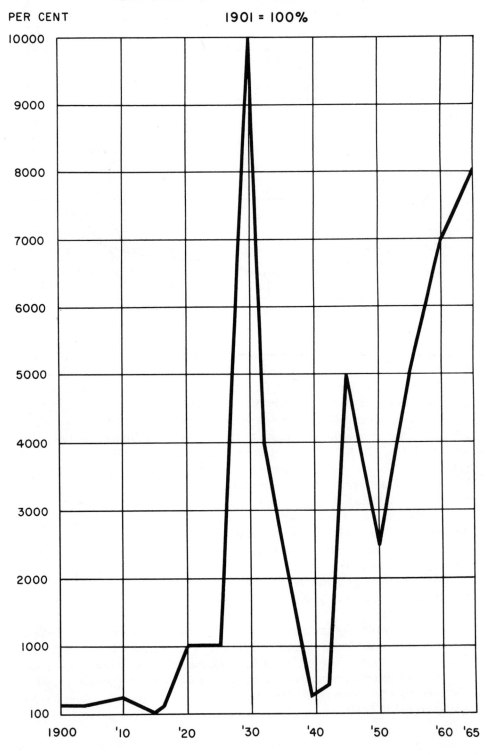

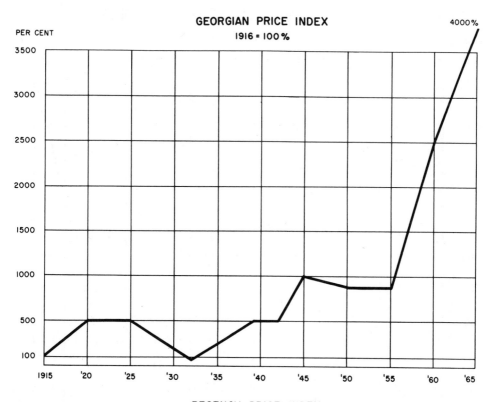

GEORGIAN PRICE INDEX
1916 = 100%

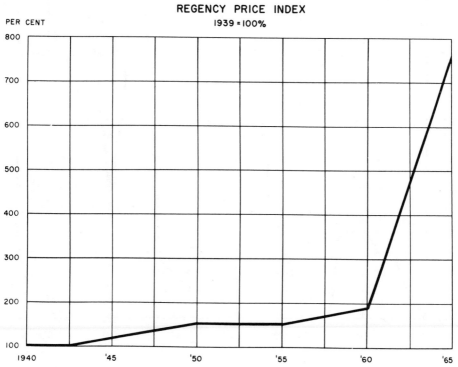

REGENCY PRICE INDEX
1939 = 100%

ENGLISH CHIPPENDALE PRICE INDEX
1901 = 100%

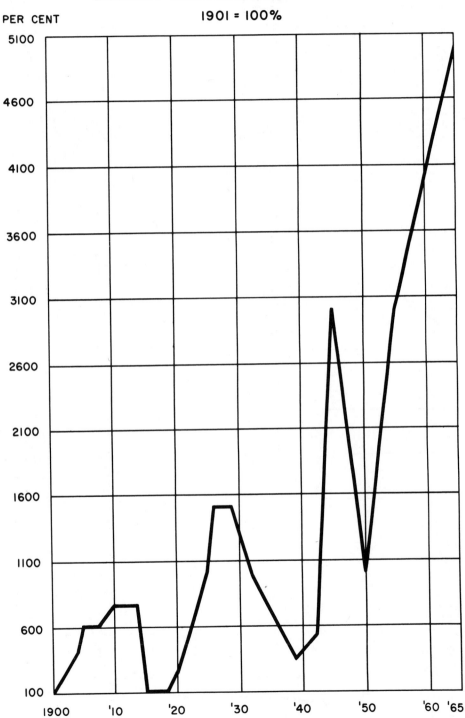

PER CENT

JACOBEAN PRICE INDEX
1901 = 100%

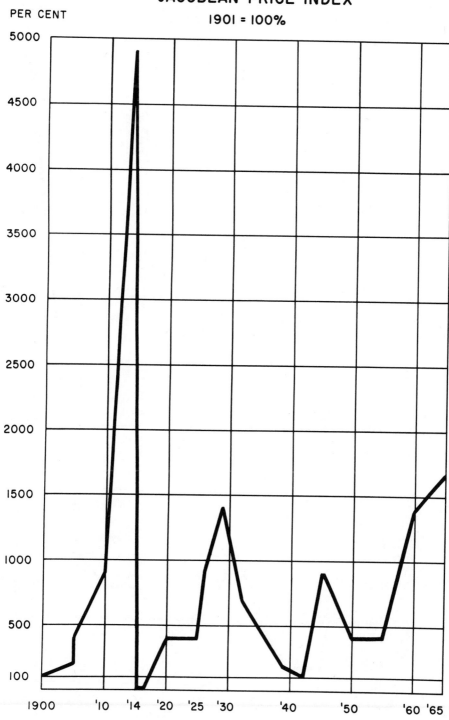

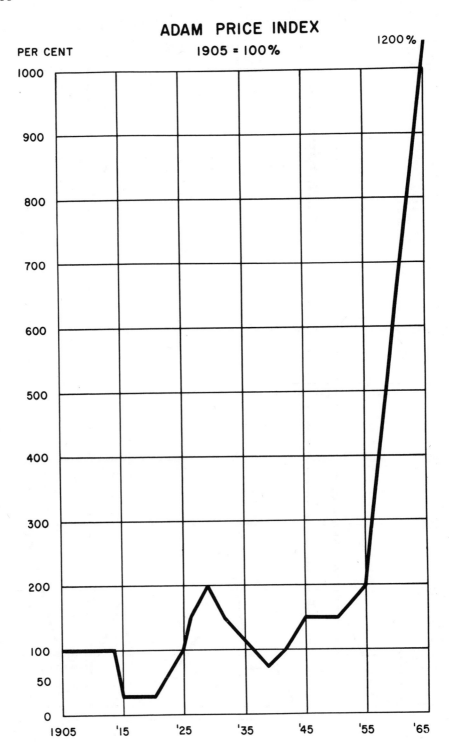

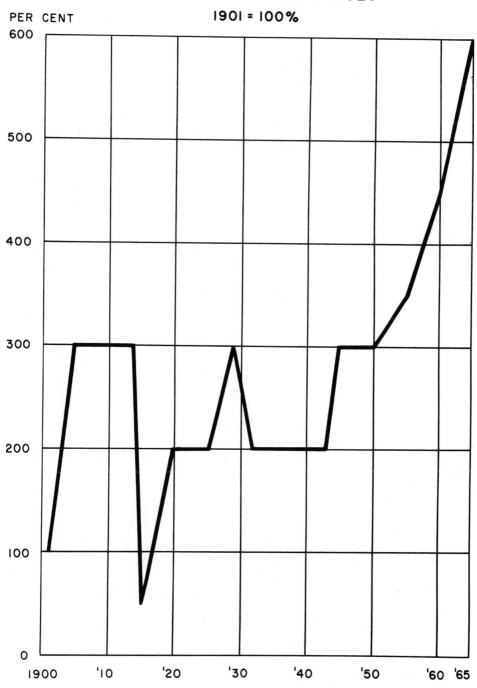

ENGLISH SHERATON PRICES

1901 = 100%

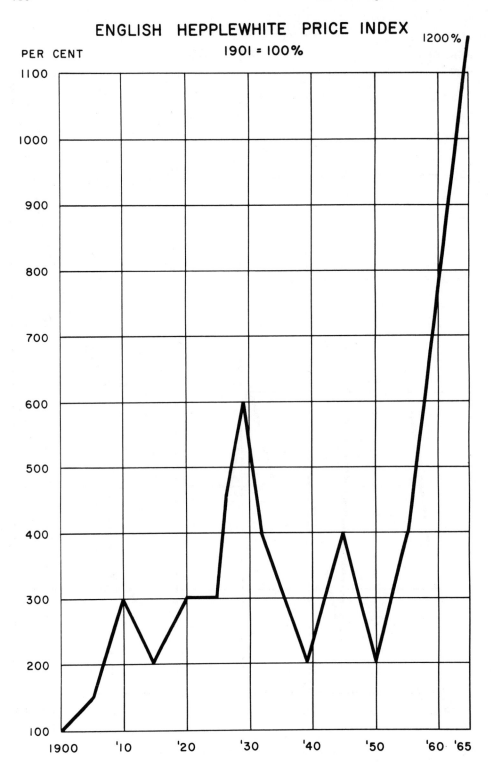

ENGLISH HEPPLEWHITE PRICE INDEX
1901 = 100%

PER CENT

1200%

WILLIAM AND MARY PRICE INDEX

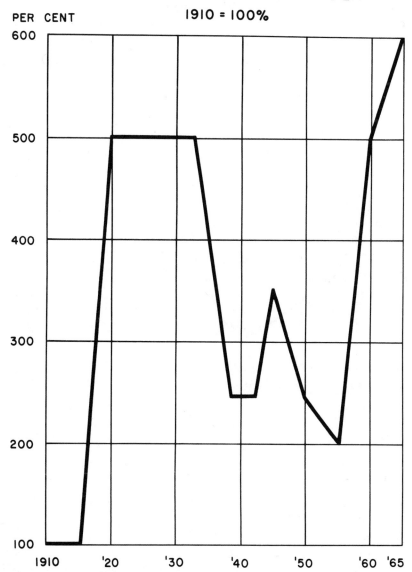

Another difficulty in combining types of furniture to form an overall index is illustrated by Sheraton furniture—and Jacobean as well. Sheraton is not a high-priced type of furniture. Yet it is given equal weight in the English furniture price index. Dollar-wise, however, Sheraton forms a very large group of what is offered on the market both in England and in the United States, and in England much Jacobean furniture is sold, so that not much of a wrong impression is given by including these items in the index as being of importance equal to the higher priced types. Statistically, this simple averaging of Queen Anne, Sheraton, Adam, etc., amounts to giving exactly equal weight to every type of furniture.

ENGLISH FURNITURE COMBINED PRICE INDEX

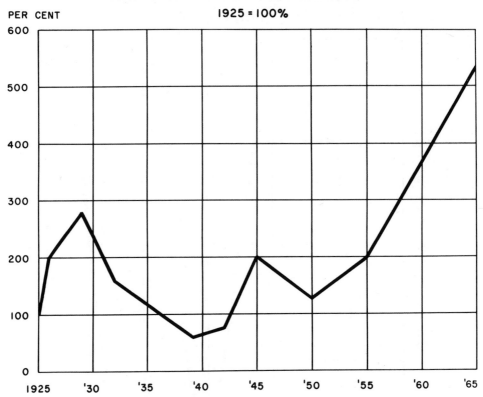

PER CENT   1925 = 100%

American Furniture Prices

1925 Equals 100%

Date	Chippen-dale	Hepple-white	Sheraton	Queen Anne	William & Mary	All American
1925	100%	100%	100%	100%	100%	100%
1926	200	200	100	250	200	190
1929	300	200	300	250	600	330
1932	140	100	150	100	300	148
1939	100	100	50	50	150	90
1942	40	50	50	50	100	58
1945	100	133	150	100	200	137
1950	100	133	50	150	300	147
1955	200	133	100	300	400	226
1960	400	167	150	400	500	323
1965	600	200	225	1,200	600	565

EIGHTEENTH CENTURY AMERICAN FURNITURE PRICE INDEX
1925 = 100%

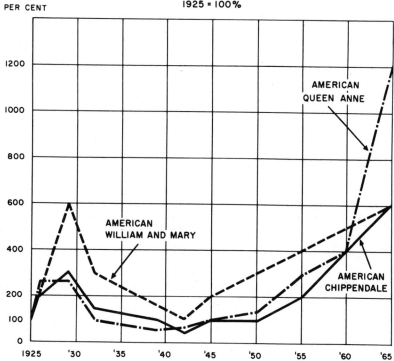

PER CENT

AMERICAN
QUEEN ANNE

AMERICAN
WILLIAM AND MARY

AMERICAN
CHIPPENDALE

LATER AMERICAN FURNITURE PRICE INDEX
1925 = 100%

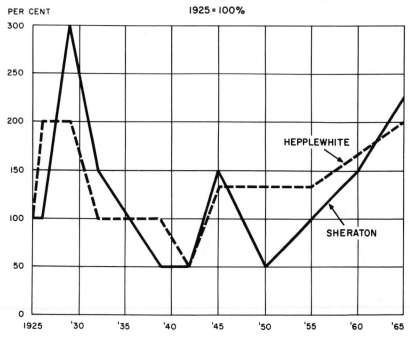

PER CENT

HEPPLEWHITE

SHERATON

AMERICAN WILLIAM AND MARY PRICE INDEX
1926 = 100%

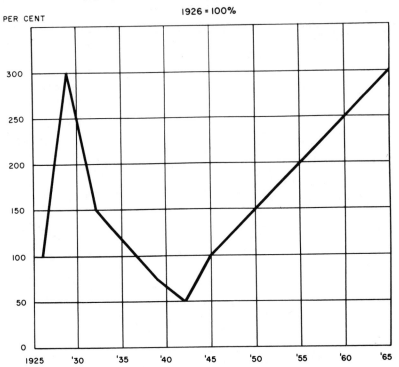

AMERICAN HEPPLEWHITE PRICE INDEX
1920 = 100%

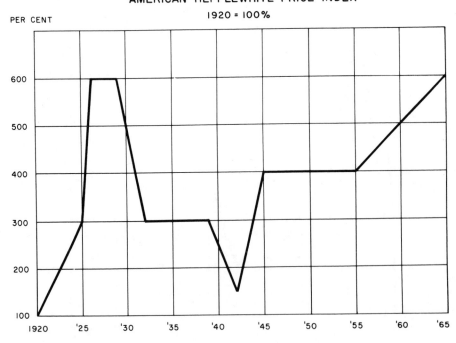

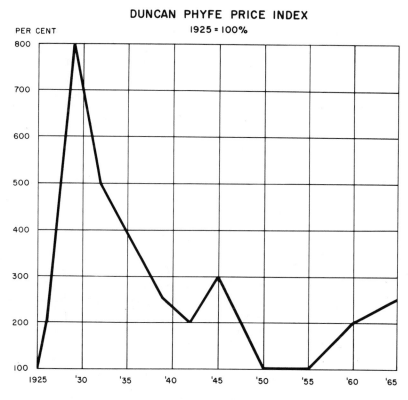

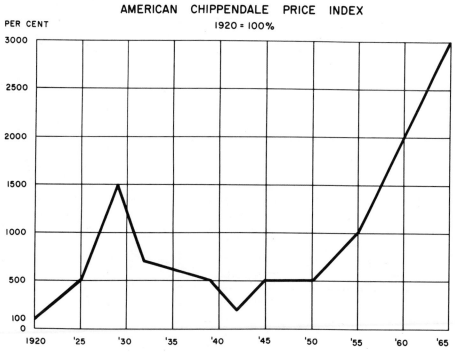

AMERICAN SHERATON PRICE INDEX
1920 = 100%

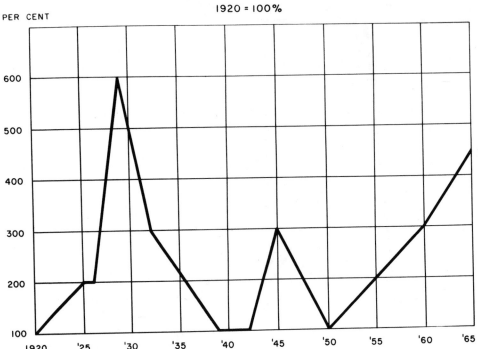

AMERICAN QUEEN ANNE PRICES
1920 = 100%

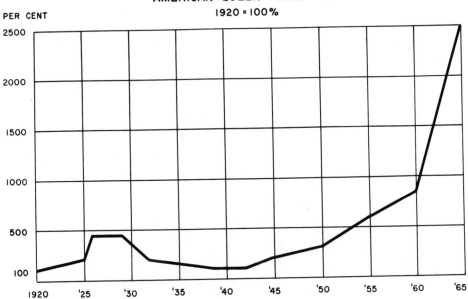

Between 1925 and 1965 the prices of American furniture rose about five times—from 100 percent to 565 percent. Queen Anne furniture rose the most, and this high figure was no doubt helped by the enormous increase in popularity of the low-boy and the highboy. The high figure of 1,200 percent for the one category of Queen Anne furniture in 1965 tends to distort the average of all American furniture and make it a little higher than it would be without this large number bias. Hepplewhite and Sheraton furniture, on the other hand, rose relatively little, and the prices of Sheraton furniture are the lowest of all types of American furniture included in this index. Yet the sales volume of Sheraton furniture is so large as to help offset the low price bias of Sheraton in the index.

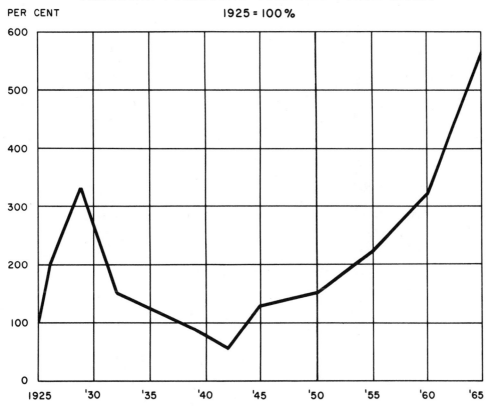

AMERICAN FURNITURE COMBINED PRICE INDEX

PER CENT   1925 = 100%

Italian Furniture Prices
1925 Equals 100%

Date	Painted Italian	Renaissance	All Italian
1925	100%	100%	100%
1926	200	200	200
1929	400	300	350
1932	200	30	115
1939	200	5	102
1942	200	30	115
1945	300	40	170
1950	300	50	175
1955	600	60	330
1960	900	75	487
1965	2,400	85	1,242

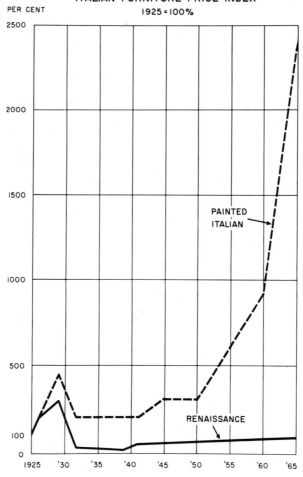

ITALIAN FURNITURE PRICE INDEX

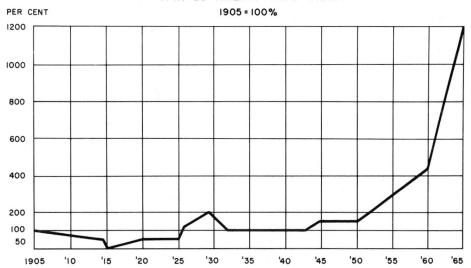

PAINTED ITALIAN PRICE INDEX
1905 = 100%

PER CENT

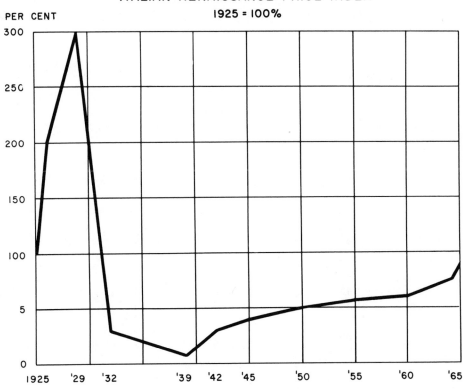

ITALIAN RENAISSANCE PRICE INDEX
1925 = 100%

PER CENT

There is no more striking example of divergent price movements than in Italian antique furniture. The real vogue for Renaissance furniture existed before the base year of the index (1925). By 1925 other types of furniture were certainly of as much importance from a prestige and price point of view as Renaissance. By the early 1930's Renaissance furniture had collapsed in price. At the same time it went out of vogue and has never returned. It is one of the few types of furniture that have not been sufficiently buoyed by the present rising antique market to exceed the peaks of the 1920's.

The common denominator of Renaissance Italian furniture and painted Italian furniture is that they both came from Italy. Stylistically, however—and price-wise as well—they might as well come from opposite ends of the globe; to combine the two into an index labeled "Italian Furniture" is stretching the meaning of the term "average." Furthermore, neither Renaissance nor painted Italian furniture is sold in very large volume in England, America or France.

While the 1965 price level of painted Italian furniture was 2,400 percent, and the price level of Renaissance was 85 percent, a good quality painted Venetian commode could be worth from $25,000 to $35,000 and more, while a fine quality Renaissance *credenza* could be purchased for less than 10 percent of this figure. Thus there is bias in both degree of the price rise and level of price.

All of these things militate against creating an average of these two types of furniture and labeling the resulting figure "Italian Furniture." If, however, each of these two types is included in a final index consisting of many types of furniture (thereby diluting the importance of each), the objections largely disappear. Neither Renaissance nor eighteenth-century painted Italian furniture can be ignored. Both are elements of the antique market.

The Antique Price Index
(14 Types of French, English and American Furniture)*

1925 Equals 100%

Date	Combined Index
1925	100%
1926	179
1929	270
1932	148
1939	66
1942	68
1945	175
1950	133
1955	202
1960	349
1965	552

*Italian not included in this index

This antique price index is the final result of combining all of the fourteen types of furniture (excluding Italian) recorded in the earlier tables. In forty years the index rose to five-and-a-half times. In 1939, however, antique furniture prices hit their low point. If we consider 1939 to be the base equal to 100 percent, then the 1965 index number becomes 840 percent. Prices in 1965 were eight times what they were in 1939.

Index of French Louis XV and XVI
and all English Furniture
(Simple Average of Two Groups)

1925 Equals 100%

Date	*Combined Index*
1925	100%
1926	146
1929	193
1932	119
1939	47
1942	69
1945	172
1950	126
1955	167
1960	356
1965	570

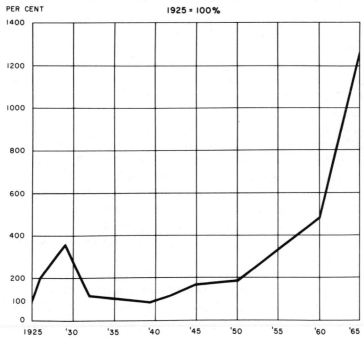

ITALIAN FURNITURE COMBINED PRICE INDEX

PER CENT   1925 = 100%

It can be argued, particularly by those in England and France, that the only antique furniture with a truly worldwide market and sold in the leading art and antique centers is French and English. (A Frenchman may argue with some persuasion that only French furniture occupies the position of being internationally traded antiques).

If we consider that French and English furniture is sold in roughly comparable volume, it is a simple thing to average the two groups with equal weight given to each. The new index can be used as a check on the combined price index just presented. There is also a good deal of logic to the argument that the new index is applicable to the New York market. Certainly the leading American auction houses sell much more antique French and English furniture than American.

We have left *Régence* out of the French Index since its volume is so small in relation to the furniture of the Louis'.

With 1925 as the base, the French-English Index rose to 570 percent in 1965. The overall index was 552 percent.

French Furniture Prices

1950 Equals 100%

Date	Louis XV	Louis XVI	Régence	Transition	Directoire	Empire	Provincial	All French
1950	100%	100%	100%	100%	100%	100%	100%	100%
1955	100	100	150	150	167	100	200	138
1960	300	200	200	250	200	200	250	230
1965	400	573	250	350	233	500	300	372

The use of 1950 as a base has several advantages. In the first place, the year 1925 is more in the nature of ancient history and is of less importance from an investment point of view than a much more recent year. In the second place, the picture of the differential of rise in price as among the various types of furniture is much different using the later 1950 base year. And in the third place, other types of furniture can be added to create a more complete picture of the antique market. In the earlier years figures were not available on certain types of furniture. They were not featured by the antique market because they were not offered in great volume, or their price was too low to merit much buyer interest.

Thus, in addition to Louis XV, Louis XVI and *Régence* furniture, we can now use Transition Louis XV-Louis XVI, *Directoire*, Empire and Provincial. The combined French furniture index rose from 100 percent in 1950 to 372 percent in 1965. Louis XVI becomes the leader in price rise because Louis XV had already realized its increase. Now also, Empire furniture is recognized as an important riser, just behind Louis XVI. The lowest rise was registered by *Directoire*. This style furniture was generally low in volume on the market and can with some force of logic be characterized as a simplified or economy version of Louis XVI. Louis

XIV furniture can be omitted from the index since it is not offered in very large volumes, and the kind offered for sale is not the very scarce and elegant variety, but is the cruder lower-priced kind. It is not generally illustrated in sales catalogues.

English Furniture Prices
1950 Equals 100%

Date	Chippendale	Hepplewhite	Sheraton	Queen Anne	William & Mary	Jacobean	Regency	Adam	All English
1950	100%	100%	100%	100%	100%	100%	100%	100%	100%
1955	300	200	117	200	80	100	100	133	154
1960	400	400	150	280	200	300	125	400	283
1965	500	600	200	320	240	350	500	800	439

Between 1950 and 1965 prices of American furniture rose to a little over four 100 percent to 439 percent. The less expensive Sheraton furniture rose the least. Adam was the standout that outran the others and the market in general. Regency furniture was not particularly featured in earlier years, just as French Empire was not. In the last decade, however, there has been something of a Regency vogue, and the name Regency has become attached to sundry items for the purpose of creating prestige (for instance, the Regency Hotel, Regency Room, Regency Model, etc.). Regency furniture rose from 100 percent in 1950 to 500 percent in 1965.

American Furniture Prices
1950 Equals 100%

Date	Chippendale	Hepplewhite	Sheraton	Queen Anne	Duncan Phyfe	William & Mary	All American
1950	100%	100%	100%	100%	100%	100%	100%
1955	200	100	200	200	100	133	156
1960	400	125	300	267	200	167	243
1965	600	150	450	800	250	200	408

Between 1950 and 1965 prices of American furniture rose to a little over four times. The index of American furniture in 1965 stood at 408 percent. Queen Anne was the type which rose the most, followed by Chippendale; and while Sheraton showed a substantial rise, the average price of a piece of Sheraton furniture was so low in 1950 that a substantial rise in percentage meant a relatively small increase in number of dollars. In 1965 it was distinctly below Hepplewhite in price.

Duncan Phyfe furniture has been added to the index. Since it is only one of six styles included in the index of American furniture, it does not distort the index a great deal. While Duncan Phyfe furniture is becoming important, it does not compare in volume of sales with any of the other categories of American furniture. Between 1965 and early 1966 its price rose greatly.

Italian Furniture Prices
1950 Equals 100%

Date	Renaissance	Painted Italian	All Italian
1950	100%	100%	100%
1955	120	200	160
1960	150	300	225
1965	170	800	485

A great deal of the price rise in painted Italian furniture was realized since 1950—the price level rose from 100 percent to 800 percent. During the same period, Renaissance furniture rose from 100 percent to 170 percent. It must again be stressed that the two types of furniture are diverse, and painted Italian is more like the furniture of the Louis' than it is like Renaissance furniture. On the other hand, Renaissance furniture is more like English Jacobean than it is like painted Italian. Moreover, the 170 percent price level achieved by Renaissance furniture in 1965 represents perhaps less than 10 per cent of the actual price of painted Italian. Renaissance furniture is extremely low-priced antique furniture.

The Antique Price Index
(23 Types of French, English, Italian and American Furniture)
1950 Equals 100%

Date	Combined Index
1950	100%
1955	150
1960	250
1965	415

This is the most comprehensive index which has been prepared. It includes all 23 types of antique furniture used to make up the 1950 base year French, English, American and Italian price indices. Each of the 23 has equal weight. While in actuality they do not have equal weight because they are sold in different volumes, the fact that there are 23 types of furniture and not some small number assures that bias is kept to a minimum.

In the combined index with the 1950 base equal to 100 percent, prices rose to 415 percent in 1965.

In order to prepare the overall antique market price index using a 1925 base, only fourteen types of antiques were used. Prices as early as 1925 were not readily available for some types of antiques. If for these fourteen types of antiques used in the overall index we use 1950 as a base instead of 1925, we get the following index:

The Antique Price Index, Based on Only
14 Types of Furniture

Date	Combined Index
1950	100%
1955	152
1960	263
1965	415

There is not enough difference in the two indices to bother about, and the accuracy of the original index, which goes back to 1925, is fairly clearly demonstrated.

1965 Antique Furniture Prices Using 1960 Base Year as 100%

FRENCH FURNITURE   *Price in 1965*

Louis XV	133%
Louis XVI	287
Régence	125
Transition	140
Directoire	117
Empire	250
Provincial	120
ALL FRENCH	167%

ENGLISH FURNITURE

Chippendale	125%
Hepplewhite	150
Sheraton	133
Queen Anne	114
William and Mary	120
Jacobean	117
Regency	400
Adam	200
ALL ENGLISH	170%

ITALIAN FURNITURE

Renaissance	113%
Painted Italian	267
ALL ITALIAN	190%

AMERICAN FURNITURE

Chippendale	150%
Hepplewhite	120
Sheraton	150
Queen Anne	300
Duncan Phyfe	125
William and Mary	120
ALL AMERICAN	161%
COMBINED INDEX	172%

The final subdivision of the antique price index uses 1960 as a base in order to see what happened to antique prices in the past five years. A noteworthy fact is that the furniture of all *countries* represented moved up by a comparable percentage. In America, Queen Anne furniture was the greatest performer, in Italy painted Italian, in England Regency, and in France Louis XVI and Empire.

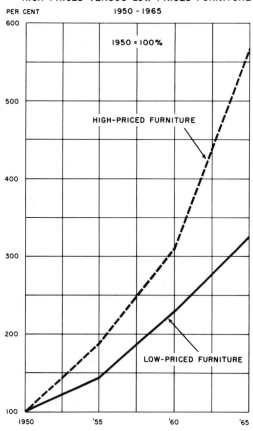

HIGH-PRICED VERSUS LOW-PRICED FURNITURE
1950 - 1965

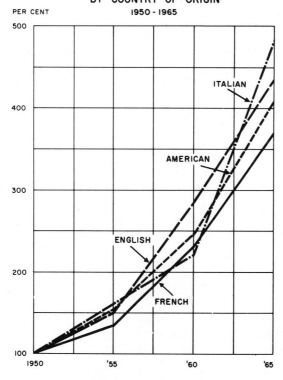

COMPARISON OF FURNITURE PRICE RISE
BY COUNTRY OF ORIGIN
PER CENT   1950 - 1965

High-Priced Furniture Index*

1950 Equals 100%

1950	100%
1955	186
1960	307
1965	570

Low-Priced Furniture Index**

1950	100%
1955	145
1960	230
1965	328

In the painting market, higher priced art tends to rise faster and higher than lower priced art. Until an extremely high price is reached per painting, the "big names" in a particular school of art outdistance the lesser names price-wise. The same tendency can be observed in the antique furniture market. "High-priced" means both the schools or types of furniture in vogue and the finer pieces. The

*Index includes Louis XV and Louis XVI; English Chippendale and English Queen Anne; American Chippendale and American Queen Anne, plus painted Italian.
**Index includes *Directoire*, Empire and French Provincial; English Hepplewhite, English Sheraton and English Jacobean; American Hepplewhite and American Sheraton, plus Italian Renaissance.

division of types of furniture into "expensive" and "cheap" is, of course, somewhat arbitrary, but it is a basically correct procedure. Between 1950 and 1965 the less expensive types of furniture rose to 328 percent in price, while the more expensive types rose to 570 percent.

Antique Prices Versus the Stock Market

A large number of mathematical correlations were made in order to try to determine what economic facts (1) measured and (2) caused rises and falls in the prices of antiques. Antique prices were compared with the price level in general, with gross national product, with national income, with personal income, with disposable personal income, with personal consumption expenditures, with personal savings and with many other series.

The outcome of all of these comparisons was that no single series seems to measure or explain the rise and fall of antique prices, but the series which has the closest correlation with antique prices is the stock market.

The series on the stock market which was finally chosen was the Standard and Poor's Monthly Average of Weekly Indexes—five hundred stocks. It is felt that this series is more representative of stock movements in general than the old standby, the Dow-Jones Industrial Average, which includes only thirty stocks (although thirty of the largest corporations, to be sure). In actuality, the Standard and Poor's 500-Stock Index and the Dow-Jones Industrial Average do not vary greatly one from the other.

If we start both averages at the year 1925, we find a fairly close correlation between antique prices and stock prices up until about 1950. From 1925 to 1929 antique prices rose faster than stock prices. They fell less than stock prices in the Depression low of 1932; but, whereas stock prices then began a fairly steady rise which continued up until the war, antique prices fell. Antiques were not "the thing" in this period. They were out of style and not considered to be a particularly good investment as compared with other things.

By 1942 the drop in antique prices, which began in the 1930's, had been arrested. But stock prices were slumping, and the two indices almost met in that year. In other words, they bore almost the same relationship that they did in 1925, when they were both arbitrarily made 100 percent for comparison purposes.

For the rest of the war period, antiques rose in price faster than stocks, but in 1945 the trends of the two series were reversed. For the next five years the stock market rallied while antique prices slumped. In 1945 the antique price index had been above the stock price index. By 1950 these positions had been reversed and stocks were ahead.

Now both series began to climb. Since five-year intervals have been used from 1950 on, the slumps in the stock market in 1954, 1958 and 1962 are not apparent. After each reverse, stock prices recovered and continued their long upward march. Antique prices paralleled this long upward movement, but stock prices ran ahead through the year 1965. Then, in 1966, the stock market dropped while the antique market did not show any significant diminution of its rate of increase. The result was that by the fall of 1966 the two indices were at almost the same point. The antique price index now stood at 673 percent and the stock index at 690 percent. Both indices had risen to almost seven times in the 41-year period. But in 1965 the antique index stood at 552 percent of the base year, 1925, and the stock price index stood at 823 percent. Up to this point, stocks had been better performers than antiques, and it must not be forgotten that stocks usually pay dividends each year while antiques do not.

Yet a different picture is painted if one uses 1950 as a base of 100 percent for both antique and stock prices. By the fall of 1966 the antique price index stood at 506 percent of the 1950 level, while stock prices stood at 418 percent. In other words, if a person had a choice of investing in antiques or stocks in 1950, he might have done better in antiques. Had he sold out in 1965, he would have done a little better in stocks (498 percent as against 415 percent).

Suppose, finally, that a person invested in 1960. By 1965 his antiques would have increased in value 68 percent while his stocks increased 64 percent—an almost identical increase; but, had he held both stocks and antiques until 1966 and then sold in the fall of that year, his antiques would have almost doubled in value, while his stocks would have shown an increase of only 38 percent. The comparison between stocks and antiques as investments thus depends upon when a person invests, or technically, what year is chosen as the base period.

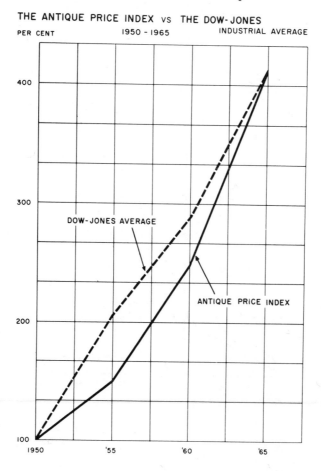

THE ANTIQUE PRICE INDEX vs THE DOW-JONES

PER CENT   1950 - 1965   INDUSTRIAL AVERAGE

Antique Price Index vs. Standard & Poor's 500 Stocks—1925 to 1968

1925 Equals 100%

Year	Antique Prices	Stock Prices
1925	100%	100%
1926	179	113
1929	270	233
1932	148	62
1939	66	108
1942	68	78
1945	175	136
1950	133	165
1955	202	363
1960	349	501
1965	552	823
1968 (Spring)	785	801

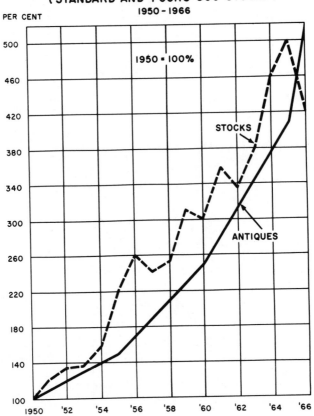

ANTIQUE PRICES VERSUS STOCK MARKET PRICES
(STANDARD AND POOR'S 500 STOCKS)
1950-1966

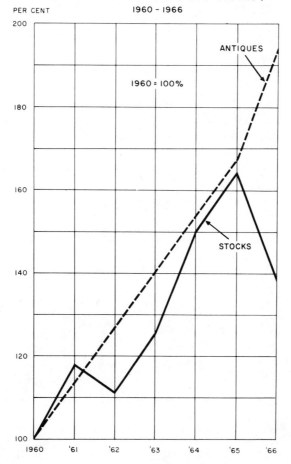

ANTIQUE PRICES VERSUS STOCK MARKET PRICES
(STANDARD AND POOR'S 500 STOCKS)

PER CENT 1960 - 1966

Antique Price Index vs. Standard & Poor's 500 Stocks—1950 to 1968

1950 Equals 100%

Year	Antique Prices	Stock Prices
1950	100%	100%
1955	150	220
1960	250	304
1965	415	498
1968 (Spring)	562	486

Antique Price Index vs. Standard & Poor's 500 Stocks—1960 to 1968

1960 Equals 100%

Year	Antique Prices	Stock Prices
1960	100%	100%
1965	168	164
1968 (Spring)	225	160

Hall of the Van Rensselaer Manor House, Albany, New York, built circa 1765–1769. *The Metropolitan Museum of Art.*

CHAPTER TWENTY-SEVEN

Channels From Seller To Buyer

U NQUESTIONABLY, THE MOST publicized of all channels through which antiques pass from seller to buyer are the major auction houses. The Georges Lurcy sale of art held at the Parke-Bernet Galleries in November 1957 made the public in general, not just the art-and-antique-buying public, realize that there was a boom in art objects. The whole event had the air of an opening night stage performance. Many prospective buyers and spectators were dressed in formal clothes, and such notables were present as the Henry Fords II, the Chester Dales, the Billy Roses, Mrs. Eleanor Roosevelt and James J. Rorimer, Director of the Metropolitan Museum of Art.

The sale of the Erickson painting collection in the fall of 1963 had quite a different aspect. Everyone felt that a record of at least some kind was going to be broken—either total volume of cash realized or highest price ever received at auction for a painting. The galleries were bright with illumination for television, the floors were covered with heavy cables for television cameras and sound equipment, and there was a proliferation of technical personnel with earphones, trailing wires and cables. There was testing and retesting of equipment, and there were rehearsals by the auctioneers and "dry runs" of the auction, so that the cameras and sound equipment could "get it just right." This Erickson sale was like a Presidential inauguration in elaborateness of preparation and downright significance for everyone concerned.

The Parke-Bernet Galleries in New York are becoming ever more of a social gathering place—not just at the major sales, but at the weekly ones and even at the weekly previews. There is hardly a time when one drops in at these galleries during the week that he does not find at least one Rolls-Royce with chauffeur parked at the curb—or double-parked. The doorman is a person of considerable dignity and distinguished appearance, and one can well imagine that he has his own limousine and chauffeur.

In 1965 Parke-Bernet was further glorified through redecoration. The lobby now resembles Marie-Antoinette's parlour. The walls are finished in an elaborate figured red fabric. There are crystal chandeliers, and the carpets are of a particularly deep and luxurious pile. Usually on display in the lobby are some items which will appear in a future sale. The only fault that can be found with this gallery is that its attraction has become so great that the elevators are sometimes overcrowded. Thus one cannot gaze with sufficient tranquility on the elegant people in the same elevator who, one feels certain, must at least be dukes and duchesses, but one can rub shoulders with them.

Auction Sales

Comprehensive figures on all sales of antiques and other objects of art are not available. Figures for the major auction houses are available, however, and have been used in this study as some measure of the antique market in general. Parke-Bernet, Sotheby's and Christie's are the largest auction houses in the United States and in England, and in volume of sales they overshadow all other auction houses in the world.

The sales pattern of these three major houses is one of the most unusual of any sales pattern in any industry. At the same time, the pattern of all three is alike. From the middle 1950's, the sales of each house rose steadily. In 1956 (the 1955–1956 season) the sales of the Parke-Bernet Galleries were $5,567,538. For the 1964–1965 season they were $13,737,808. They had increased two-and-a-half times in this period.

In 1955 Sotheby's sales were £1,698,825 ($4,756,710), and in 1965 they were £12,112,165 ($33,914,062). In this period they had increased seven times.

In sales rise Christie's was somewhat of a lagger, but nonetheless exhibited an almost identical pattern of growth. In 1958 their sales were £1,687,373 ($4,724,644), while in 1965 they were £8,500,000 ($23,800,000). They had increased in this shorter period five times.

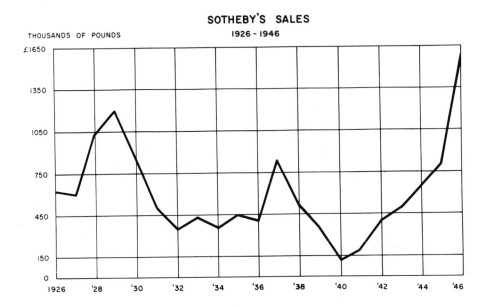

SOTHEBY'S SALES
1926 - 1946

PARKE-BERNET GALLERIES SALES (INCLUDING PREDECESSOR)
1929 – 1946

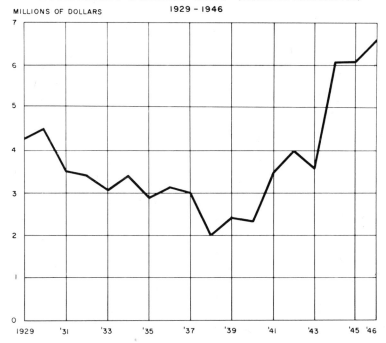

SOTHEBY'S SALES
1946 - 1965

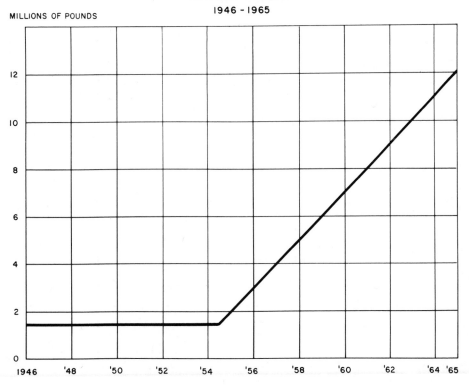

PARKE-BERNET GALLERIES SALES
1948 - 1965

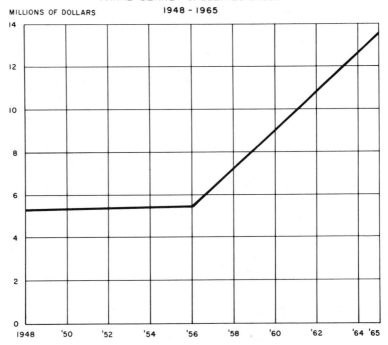

MILLIONS OF DOLLARS

PARKE-BERNET GALLERIES SALES
1946 - 1950

MILLIONS OF DOLLARS

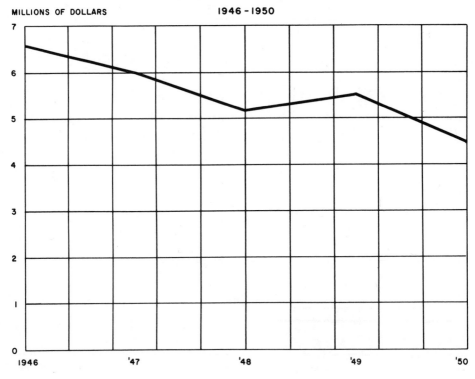

In 1965 the two English auction houses had a combined total of $57,714,062 in sales, and all three galleries totaled $71,451,870, of which the Parke-Bernet total amounted to a little over 19 percent. In 1964 Sotheby's acquired the Parke-Bernet Galleries, a move which made Sotheby's far and away the largest auction house in the world.

Auction Sales, 1966 Season

Sotheby's (London)		$36,446,816
Parke-Bernet (New York)		23,519,067
	Total Sotheby's	$59,965,883
Christie's		20,276,580
	TOTAL—THREE AUCTIONS	$80,242,463

Although Christie's sales slipped in 1966 as against the previous year, Sotheby's London sales were up 6 percent. The total sales of the two London auctions— Sotheby's and Christie's—were almost the same in 1966 as in 1965. The major

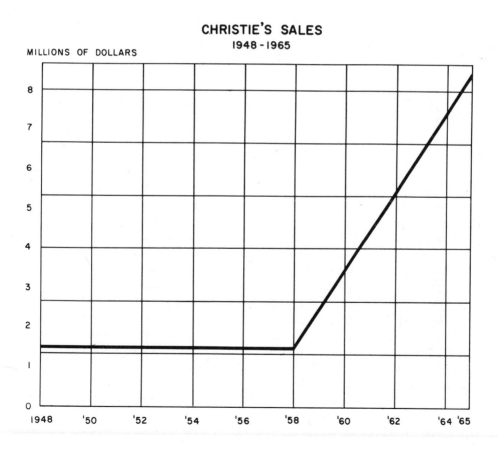

CHRISTIE'S SALES
1948 - 1965

TOTAL SALES OF THREE AUCTION HOUSES 1946-1950

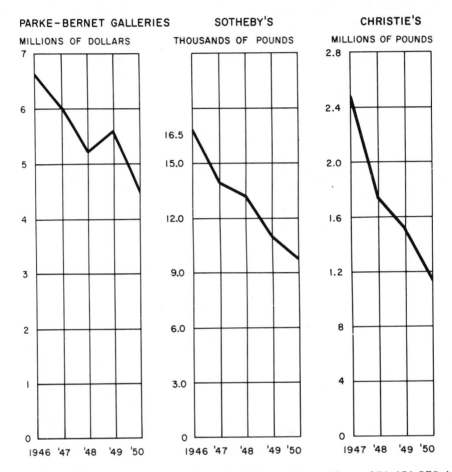

PARKE-BERNET GALLERIES   SOTHEBY'S   CHRISTIE'S

MILLIONS OF DOLLARS   THOUSANDS OF POUNDS   MILLIONS OF POUNDS

factor in the total increase in sales of the three auctions (from $71,451,870 in 1965 to $80,242,463 in 1966) was the incredible increase in the sales of Parke-Bernet from $13,737,803 to $23,519,067—over 70 percent. In one year Parke-Bernet's total share of the combined sales of the three auctions rose from 19 percent to almost 30 percent. In part, of course, the explanation lies in the merchandise Sotheby's allotted for auction in London and for auction in New York. Since Sotheby's and Parke-Bernet are under the same management, that management obviously has a great deal to say about where particular goods will be auctioned.

The three leading galleries exhibited growth patterns in sales that are remarkably similar. The growth started at approximately the same time for all three galleries (1957 for Parke-Bernet, 1956 for Sotheby's and after 1958 for Christie's).

This similarity of pattern holds true in a most unique way for the period immediately *preceding* this era of growth. The charts on total sales for each of these three leading auction houses show the picture most effectively. At the end of the war, or shortly thereafter, there was a plateau in sales volume for all three galleries.

The flat line uses just two points rather than a point each year to show this trend (or rather the lack of trend). While sales for each gallery for the years between the war's end and the beginning of the mid-1950's rise in sales certainly do vary from a straight line, they vary remarkably little. For this reason the line is flat.

Now, if we go back to the first year after the war (1946) and compare sales trends of all three auction houses to 1950, we find a pattern of *decline*. This pattern is not shown in the charts covering the longer period because it is quickly erased for all three galleries after the year 1950, but it exists nevertheless. In 1946 the sales of the Parke-Bernet Galleries were $6,684,043; in 1950 they were $4,537,142. In 1946 Sotheby's sales were £1,556,698 ($6,273,493); they were £968,104 ($2,710,691) in 1950. Christie's sales in 1947 were £2,487,046 ($10,022,795) and in 1950 they were £1,125,718 ($3,152,010). The Parke-Bernet Galleries lost 32 percent of its sales volume; Sotheby's lost 38 percent and Christie's (in a shorter period) lost 55 percent.

The sales decline in this immediate postwar period can best be explained not so much by a decline in popularity of art and antiques, as by competition from new sources for the art and antique buyer's dollar (or pound sterling). During the war profits and wages were high, and with war shortages, demand went in the direction of art and antiquities simply because these were some of the relatively few items available for purchase. At the war's end, goods such as automobiles, electric refrigerators and other appliances, plus major items like houses had first call on funds. When the drastic shortages were made up, people once again became art and antique conscious.

One of the most important facts that must be emphasized in the case of auctions compared to other types of businesses is that demand cannot be satisfied by producing more. If more automobiles are desired by the buying public, more can fairly easily be turned out. If more milk can be sold, more milk cows are raised; and after a short delay, more milk finds its way to consumers.

But antiques are in a different category. To a great extent, an auction house must wait until estates come to it. True, a "ball of fire" like Sotheby's Peter Wilson can get out and rustle up art and antiques for sale; but if no major estates are available because the owners are still alive and would like to keep their belongings, Mr. Wilson cannot always get them.

The art and antique auction houses exhibit a unique sales pattern in still a different period, and this pattern can best be illustrated by charts on sales from the 1920's up to the war's end (at which point the previously mentioned charts start). Until the late 1930's there was no Parke-Bernet Galleries. However, this firm considers the American-Anderson Galleries to be its predecessor, and records of that gallery are used here. (American-Anderson was organized in 1929 by merger of two predecessor companies, the American Art Association and the Anderson Galleries. By early 1938 the Parke-Bernet Galleries were in business, organized by a group of employees who left the American-Anderson Galleries en masse. In 1938 the American-Anderson Galleries literally died.)

For the 1928–1929 season, the American-Anderson Galleries had sales of $4,330,238. The next season (1929–1930) saw the stock market crash of October

1929 and the rapid decline in business thereafter. Nevertheless, the American-Anderson Galleries actually showed an increase in business in that season as against the prior one. Sales were $4,603,253, of which furniture and allied items amounted to $2,792,486. From this point on, however, there was a steady drop. By 1932 antique furniture sales were down to $2,079,773, and to $2,021,567 in the 1934 season. In 1937 they were $1,913,338, but by 1939 they had been drastically reduced to $969,641. Without this furniture drop, *total* sales for this gallery in technically its last year of existence would have shown no decline.

The Depression was very slow in coming to the art and antique business, and the total drop into the Depression was far less than in many other types of business. It is also noteworthy that whereas art and antiques would appear to be remote from necessities and would quickly be curtailed in the spending programs of individuals, the figures do not support this thesis.

Another unique sales pattern of art and antique galleries is the decreasing proportion of sales volume accounted for by antique furniture. In 1952 the Parke-Bernet Galleries reported antique furniture sales separately but not antique furniture alone—rather antique furniture in conjunction with other items of a somewhat allied nature, like rugs. Antiques in 1952 were $3,803,760 out of total sales of $5,727,759. These are the subsequent figures:

Parke-Bernet Galleries
Total Sales and Sales of Antique Furniture (1956–1966)

Year	Antique Sales	Total Sales	Antique % of Total
1956	$3,518,541	$ 5,567,541	64%
1959	4,500,000	10,208,879	44
1960	Over 4,000,000	9,240,982	43
1961	Over 4,000,000	8,430,306	47
1963	3,160,184	11,848,966	27
1964	3,500,000	10,820,242	32
1965	3,811,537	13,737,808	27
1966	4,253,395	23,519,367	18

It is abundantly clear that antique furniture is forming a smaller proportion of total sales. This is true because of the relative stability of antique furniture sales volume and because of the increasing importance of paintings.

Sotheby's sales do not show quite the same pattern of rise prior to the crash of 1929 and fall into the Depression. In 1925 Sotheby's sales were £500,864 ($2,414,164). In 1929 they were £1,223,889—more than double. By 1930 they had dropped to £845,207 ($3,431,540)—about 30 percent in one year. And by 1932 they were down to £356,000 ($1,246,000)—a drop of over 70 percent from 1929.

From the Depression low to the start of World War II, however, the sales patterns of the Parke-Bernet Galleries and Sotheby's were the same—and unique as an industry as compared with other industries taken as a whole.

If a trend line were drawn for both galleries, one gallery in England and the other in the United States, between the years 1934 and the war's start, the patterns would be identical. The degree of slope would be almost identical, too. In this period sales of art and antiquities were down rather than up like industry in general, and the drop in both cases was substantial—over 50 percent. Sotheby's made some recovery to 1937, but there was a steady drop thereafter. This drop was not caused by the war, since the war did not start until 1939. There was no recovery to 1937 for the Parke-Bernet Galleries' predecessor. For the year 1938 the picture is confused for this gallery. Both American-Anderson and Parket-Bernet were operating—with two houses in two locations to secure both stocks of merchandise and customers. The American-Anderson Galleries had $2,020,974 in sales that year, and the Parke-Bernet Galleries had $1,251,917 for the period from January 7, 1938, to the season's end. It has been pointed out in the detailed study of prices that prices, too, showed a sharp decline in the period of the early 1930's to the late 1930's. Unquestionably, antiques and works of art in this period were "not the thing to buy," and the business cycle of art and antique houses at this time was remarkably different from business in general.

Sotheby's sales sank to a low point of £136,195 ($548,866) in 1940, not only because of a lack of interest in antiques, but as a direct result of continual bombings of London. Still, the Parke-Bernet Galleries also did not show any strength in sales in 1940. Their sales that year were approximately at an all-time low for the overall period covered by the chart—$2,329,330.

From this low in 1940 both galleries had a sharp upsurge in sales. Parke-Bernet reached $6,684,043 in 1946 and Sotheby's reached £1,556,698. The sales of Parke-Bernet almost tripled, while those of Sotheby's increased over twelve times. During the war the Parke-Bernet Galleries became the chief auction house in the world. The European auction houses as a group were seriously affected by hostilities if not completely closed down, and much business gravitated to America. (Some sea shipments of antiques from Europe even reached our shores during hostilities.)

The British and American auction houses provide some measure of the art and antique market in general. In the case of England, the Statistical Office of Her Majesty's Customs and Excise compiles figures on exports and imports of antiques and works of art. These have been tabulated by David Coombs for *Connoisseur* magazine. The Coombs figures have been brought up-to-date through the addition of another year.

Antiques exports from England in 1938, the year before the war, were £465,338. In 1947, two years after the close of the war, they had better than tripled and stood at £1,635,239. In the same period, antique imports dropped from £526,484 to £112,660. In this period, the pattern was about the same for works of art, so that the market total (art and antiques) shows the same pattern.

In the six-year period from 1952 to 1958, total art and antique exports from England did not quite double: They rose from £5,217,855 to £9,172,079. In the next six-year period (from 1958 to 1964) they tripled. The 1964 figure was £26,785,000—$75,000,000. From 1952 to 1958 antique exports alone rose only slightly—from £3,003,186 to £3,652,837. By 1963 they had doubled and stood at £7,435,138. From 1952 to 1958 England's imports of antiques rose from £430,255 to £1,029,321—more than double. By 1963 they had quadrupled. From 1952 to 1958 imports of art and antiques to England rose from £694,927 to £8,052,972 and then tripled by 1964 when they stood at £23,000,000.

If we break down the imports of antiques into England by country which sent them, we find that by far the greatest value of shipments came from the United States. Of a total of £2,643,327 of antiques imported into England in 1961, by far the major source was the United States which supplied £1,025,382 in value— $2,870,000. Of the £5,877,316 of English antique exports in the same year (1961), the largest portion by far went to the United States—£2,887,513 ($8,083,000). This was about 50 percent of the total antique exports from England. Over one million pounds sterling (£1,039,521) was imported into England and then reexported.

While the United States supplied most of the antiques shipped into England from abroad, France was the next largest contributor by far. And, whereas the United States took most of England's exports, Italy came next in importance as a recipient of English antique exports.

The Rest of the Auction Houses

Writers in this country and England are chiefly concerned with what goes on at the large auction galleries, particularly who was there and who bought what for what fantastic sum of money. It is true, of course, that Sotheby's and Christie's are far and away the largest auction houses in England as are the Parke-Bernet Galleries in the United States. No auction houses in either country approach these in volume of sales, and the competition from other auction houses is minimal. Serious competition may well arise in the future, but it is not here now or even on the way.

The very best estates gravitate to these "big three," while the other houses get the lesser estates and very often the rejected estates and turned-down merchandise from the big houses.

In sheer volume, then, the three main auction houses are the leaders, and this is the first distinguishing characteristic of these houses compared to the rest of the auction houses. The second characteristic is closely allied—they get the best estates and the best merchandise.

Next, their proportion of antiques and works of art to total volume of objects sold is much higher than in the case of the rest of the auction houses. In a typical furniture sale at the Parke-Bernet Galleries, for instance, *most* of the items offered for sale are genuine antiques. If to these genuine antiques are added fine reproductions, we can account for approximately 90 percent of the merchandise offered. There is a tendency in Parke-Bernet auctions to feature fine reproductions more and more and to illustrate them more and more in the sales catalogues, probably in the hope that as antiques become rarer, the buying public can be induced to settle for reproductions.

Whereas the Parke-Bernet Galleries cling to the antique line, Sotheby's and Christie's have a tendency to take almost anything that is offered for sale. In addition, the condition of antiques and other art objects offered by the Parke-Bernet Galleries tends to be far better than the condition of the items offered by Sotheby's and Christie's. The Parke-Bernet officials will suggest that the owner have the item put in good condition before it is auctioned.

With the items in good condition, the display galleries at Parke-Bernet look like the grand salon of a château or an English town house, and sometimes even of a palace. There is a serious attempt made, and successfully, to do an excellent decorating job of the offerings of antiques and art objects for every sale. There is never any "piling in" as there often is in London .And in London the condition of the antiques can be anything from perfect to falling apart.

The lesser American auction houses are more like the English auctions in accepting most of what is offered in the "as is" condition in which offered. The furniture to be sold is placed around tastefully *if* there is not much to be sold. The more there is, the more the display halls look like furniture stores. And if there is a very great volume, as in the case of "back-gallery sales" (the really low-grade offerings), the display halls look like warehouse storage rooms.

Presumably one sends his wares to the Parke-Bernet Galleries because all of the splendor secures a better grade of customer who will pay more. The Parke-Bernet Galleries do get higher prices for high grade merchandise (as do Sotheby's and Christie's) because they consistently attract buyers who are willing to pay higher prices. The lesser auctions do not habitually attract this type customer and thus do not get as good prices. In the field of paintings, once in a while a masterpiece or near-masterpiece sneaks by in one of the smaller auction houses. On the other hand, the major art galleries and antique dealers, but not always, have their scouts out looking at the weekly offerings of the smaller auctions as well as the offerings of the major ones. In London, a partner in one of the major art and antique houses will usually personally visit every auction house on display days.

Leslie Hyam, late president of the Parke-Bernet Galleries, believed that about 75 percent of the Parke-Bernet sales went to private buyers for their homes and the remaining 25 percent to dealers. Only 10 percent of Parke-Bernet's total sales, he felt, turned up in the shops of dealers. It is believed that these percentages are low. Near Christmas in 1964, six Adam chairs were sold at the Parke-Bernet Galleries for $300—$50 a chair. They turned up in a dealer's booth at the East Side Settlement House show and were priced at $2,400—$400 a chair! Of course, they had been reupholstered. Another set of chairs of Queen Anne design appeared in the same show. These had been purchased at the Parke-Bernet Galleries (with perfect upholstery) for $2,400. They were offered for $4,800. Many similar items previously sold at auction have been observed in the shops of antique dealers.

In London it is standard procedure for major dealers to buy at auction and reoffer the items at substantially higher prices. The items may even have been illustrated in the auction house sales catalogues so that they can be traced to find out their auction prices. Very often the dealer price is several times the auction price. In London, dealer purchases at auction are far greater than at the Parke-Bernet Galleries in New York.

While top-grade merchandise certainly brings the highest prices when sold at the leading auction houses both in America and in England, the second-rung merchandise seems to do just as well price-wise in the lesser auction houses. While the Parke-Bernet Galleries may not be a "dealer" auction, some of the smaller auction houses are definitely dealer auctions, and certainly so as compared with Parke-Bernet. This simply means that at these smaller auctions the dealers form a larger percentage of the customers at each sale, and that a larger percentage of sales is made to dealers.

In March 1966 an American serpentine-front commode sold at one of the lesser auctions for $3,500. This was not a top-grade piece of furniture and probably would not have sold for more at the Parke-Bernet Galleries. On the other hand, there is probably a greater opportunity to make real buys at the smaller auctions. In 1964 an American bow-front Sheraton commode in perfect condition sold at the Plaza Art Galleries for just $50. At a sale in 1965 a large, superb English Sheraton sideboard brought exactly $160. It is difficult to visualize a piece of furniture of this quality selling for such a low sum at any major auction today. At the same gallery in late 1966, a drop-leaf Sheraton table in perfect condition brought $100. It was bought by America's leading dealer in American furniture. It was a Duncan Phyfe piece that had sneaked by.

Volume and Type Merchandise in Smaller Auctions

In London it is accepted procedure for all major art dealers to visit all the auction galleries every week. This is a necessary form of competition to get paintings in today's very tight painting market. The list of auctions visited includes not only Sotheby's and Christie's, but Philips Son and Neale, Newcombs, Bonhams and some other galleries.

Here are some of the relative total volumes of sales of these galleries for 1964:

Sotheby's	£ 13,251,455
Christie's	£ 4,300,000
Philips Son and Neale	£ 2,026,754
Newcombs	262,000
Bonhams (est. from 6-months fig.)	920,000
SMALL GALLERIES TOTAL	£ 3,208,000
	($8,982,000)

The total of just the three smaller houses compares with a volume in the same year for the Parke-Bernet Galleries of $10,820,242.

It is difficult for a person who has never visited London to realize the magnitude of the art and antique business in that city. There are at least fifty dealers selling paintings of first quality, and at least one hundred dealers selling fine antique furniture just in London's downtown section.

The bulk of the Parke-Bernet merchandise is antiques or quality reproductions. An important distinguishing characteristic of the other New York auctions is that the majority of furniture sold is so-called secondhand merchandise—merchandise which is not antique. It may be anything from Victorian and nineteenth-century Country American furniture to a living room suite covered in $150-a-yard material and made in 1964. In strictly secondhand merchandise, the very best buys are secured in the larger of the secondary auction houses.

The larger secondary auctions probably do not have over 60 percent of their total dollar *sales volume* in secondhand things. The remaining 40 percent falls into the antique category. As we go down the line in quality of the secondary auction houses, the percentage of secondhand merchandise to total volume increases. Thus, if a buyer is concentrating on antiques, he might well confine his regular visits to the Plaza Art Auction Galleries, the Savoy Art and Auction Galleries, the Coleman Auction Galleries and perhaps the Fischer Auction Gallery and the Astor Birnbaum Galleries. Of course, a great find may turn up occasionally at some of the other galleries.

While the Parke-Bernet Galleries claim many customers who are buying for their homes, the smallest auction houses in New York can confidently claim the same thing—but in a different way. These smallest galleries are often "Saturday" galleries catering to families furnishing their homes with secondhand items. The in-between-in-quality galleries (in-between Parke-Bernet and "Saturday" houses) are the chief hunting grounds for the dealer group, and they come from New York, from the suburbs of New York and from all over the United States. One Dallas dealer sends an enormous truck to pick up his auction purchases at the various houses. When it leaves New York it is filled to the tailgate with antiques and secondhand furniture.

Probably 50 percent of the sales of these in-between auction houses are to dealers. Another 10 percent of sales are to collectors who are on a par with dealers in furniture knowledge, and the remaining 40 percent goes to ultimate customers for home furnishing and decoration. Possibly because of its strategic location, the Savoy Art and Auction Galleries have a larger proportion of ultimate customer business than do the other comparable auction houses.

Sources of Auction Merchandise

While it is true that all auction houses must wait for some goods to be offered to them, only a certain percentage of offerings are on a strictly fortuitous basis. Such residual estate business—merchandise in an estate after the demise of the owner—probably amounts to 25 percent of most auction house sales. Private individuals and collectors are a source of perhaps 35 percent more, making about 60 percent coming from individuals or their estates. This 60 percent might also be classified as resulting from "deaths and moving." Dealer merchandise probably accounts for the balance. And ten percent of this dealer merchandise can be classified as "tired" or "stale" items which the dealer has not moved in some time and which he is tired of looking at. The rest of the dealer merchandise is good items which the dealer wants to sell or which the auction house induces him to put up at auction.

All of the Parke-Bernet merchandise and all of Sotheby's and Christie's merchandise is consigned and is not owned by the auction house. This is not true for some of the other auction houses, and many of them at one time or another have purchased outright either particular items or complete estates and sold them by the auction procedure. Some auction houses buy abroad, particularly in England; and while many of the items offered are certainly technically antiques, they are often the dregs of this category. But the word "antique" has a magic for buyers which is often far out of proportion to the intrinsic value of the "antique" offered for sale.

The trouble with the house buying merchandise and then auctioning it is that too many buyers think the item will be sold for the highest bid, no matter how low the final bid may be. This situation, unfortunately, does not obtain, and an auction house that has paid $100 for a French table is not going to let it go for a high bid of $10. Collectors and professional buyers are well aware of this "owned merchandise" type auction and are not inclined to be too enthusiastic about their offerings. What the uninformed public thinks it is getting is another matter—and a problematical one.

To a certain extent, buying from some galleries is like buying from dealers. If there is any kind of reasonable markup, the auctioneer lets the item go—for instance, if he can get $500 for a table for which he paid $400. At these auction houses, however, the chase and the thrill of auction buying are absent, except for the buyer living in a fool's paradise!

But "owned merchandise" is not the only protected merchandise sold at auction. The items supplied to the auction by dealers are not going to be "given away" by these dealers. They frequently place reserves on them or are present to protect them through bidding themselves. At a recent auction in New York, one dealer bid in as many times as he sold, and took the items home with him.

Sometimes the auctioneer himself bids against the bidder in order to raise the price of an item. He often views the consignor as being his client—particularly a dealer consignor. He thus, on his own, may force up a price for the benefit of the consignor, or even bid on the item rather than see it go for too little.

Sometimes private individuals place reserves on items. The bidding appears to go along normally, except the last bid is the auctioneer's if the reserve price is not reached.

Often, too, auctioneers help to get things started. The auctioneer may ask, "Will anyone bid $50?" He will then say, "I have $50." Then he says, "Now I have $60." There may well be a pause while he appears to be waiting for a further bid. Then he will suddenly reverse himself in a burst of frankness and say, "All right, will anyone start this item at $25?" My wife always urges me to get into the bidding early so the auctioneer will not play his game of bidding the item up by himself to too high a figure. As soon as he sees my bid, he can relax as he then knows he has someone willing to pay something, at least.

The Scale of Auction Charges

The Parke-Bernet Galleries issued its new rate schedule in March 1966:

RATES OF COMMISSION

For all property consigned to us for sale after May 1, 1966, standard rates of commission will be as follows:

FURNITURE AND WORKS OF ART: 20% on lots fetching $500 or less; 18% on lots fetching over $500 and up to $3,000; 15% on lots fetching more than $3,000. The same commissions apply to decorative paintings included in furniture sales.

JEWELRY: 15% on lots fetching $5,000 or less; 12½% on lots fetching more than $5,000.

BOOKS AND MANUSCRIPTS, and all other literary property: 20%.

PRINTS: 20% on lots fetching $500 or less; 18% on lots fetching over $500 and up to $3,000; 15% on lots fetching more than $3,000.

Rates for paintings, sculpture and drawings remain as set May 1, 1965: 15% on lots fetching $5,000 or less; 12½% for lots over $5,000. Commissions are applied on the value of individual items and not on the value of groups of items.

These rates include all expenses of sale after the property is received at the Galleries, with the following exceptions: insurance; and color plates and special advertising where these are considered advisable.

The chief British auction houses have generally charged 10 percent of sales as commission, and it is understood they cut this percentage in order to get a particularly attractive piece of business. Continental galleries may charge between 16 percent and 21 percent.

Charges by the smaller New York City auctions vary. One auction house charges private individuals 23 percent of sales and dealers 20 percent. It is believed that most galleries charge a straight 20 percent of sales. The gallery that charges the dealer 20 percent may charge him only 10 percent of the highest bid if the item is not sold and has to be returned to the dealer. Or it may charge him a flat $25 for each item that remains unsold, without regard to price reached. One auction house claims that it is as much trouble to handle items which are unsold as those which are sold, and it tries to collect the same commission on nonsales as on sales, the base figure for the charge being the highest bona fide bid from the customers at the auction.

The "Ring"

As mentioned previously, many, if not most, auctions in the middle range (that is, below Parke-Bernet but above the "Saturday" auctions) have a dealer ring in operation. It also operates on occasion at Parke-Bernet. This is a group which numbers up to about sixteen members who buy together so as to at least eliminate competition among themselves. One member of the ring does the bidding. Directly after the item is bought and the auction is over, these dealers hold their own little auction among themselves (the "knockout"). The highest bidder gets the item, and the difference between the final high bid of the dealer ring and the buying price of the item at the real auction is divided among the members of the ring.

For instance, if the ring spokesman bought a chair for $100 at the auction and then at the "knockout" one member of the ring was willing to pay $150 for the chair, the difference—$50—would be divided among the other members of the ring. Theoretically, a member of the ring might earn a living simply by being a member of the ring and never buying or selling any merchandise!

From the point of view of the buying public, the ring is not as important as it might seem—nor is it as detrimental. The dealer who paid the high price of $150 for the chair must resell it, and he must be within the dealer market price of say $300. The ultimate customer or collector bidding against the ring at the auction can afford to pay a higher price and one nearer the market value of $300. He would normally have to pay such a price at a dealer's establishment, and he does not have to resell at a profit.

Furthermore, the ring bids on only a relatively small proportion of items. Possibly 30 percent of *all* dealer purchases at the auctions in between the Parke-Bernet Galleries and the "Saturday" auctions are ring purchases, possibly less.

The professional buyer or collector can often profit from the ring. This is done by utilizing the expert knowledge of a large group of dealers who belong to the ring. If one sits with or near the ring and picks up conversation and watches bids, he can check his own judgment on the authenticity and quality of items being offered for sale and can use this knowledge to outbid the ring. The author has done this on more than one occasion. Of course he had to visit many auctions to determine who the ring members were.

Not all items sold at the New York auction houses go to New Yorkers. Perhaps 8 percent of all the sales of the lesser of New York auctions goes to suburban buyers and another 12 percent goes to other out-of-town buyers, principally dealers.

Authenticity of Descriptions

There appears to be an honest attempt made by auction houses to label antique furniture correctly. Attempts at upgrading are generally ridiculed by dealer buyers and collectors so that such upgrading is not tried again. Of course, legitimate mistakes along an optimistic line are made. Then, too, in a few cases unpardonable mistakes are made; for instance, a thoroughly experienced auctioneer twice announced from the rostrum that a table was eighteenth-century French, not eighteenth-century English as the catalogue stated. He was presumably honestly correcting a mislabeling in his catalogue. The piece was inspected after the sale and found to be not even remotely eighteenth-century French. It was shown to a partner of the auction house who readily agreed that the piece was not eighteenth-century French, but no attempt at restitution was made. (Frequently, catalogues will read Chippendale "style" when the auctioneer is doubtful of a piece's authenticity.)

On the other hand, in the spring of 1966 the Plaza Art Galleries offered a *marquise* for sale labeled "in the style of Louis XV." An inspection showed that the piece was genuine Louis XV of the period. The author bid to $290. The piece was purchased by the ring for the next bid—$300. Shortly thereafter it appeared in the shop of a member of the ring—for $1,250!

The volume of auction business is difficult to determine. One leading auction official stated publicly to *The New York Times* that all auction business amounted to less than one percent of all art and antique business. It is believed this percentage is low when one considers that their are far more auctions than Sotheby's, Christie's and the Parke-Bernet Galleries, and far more than the celebrated auction houses in Vienna, Paris, Cologne, Zurich and elsewhere. Every major city in the United States, as far as can be determined, has at least one auction house, and to the auctions conducted by these houses must be added auctions set up for the specific purpose of liquidating just one estate or the contents of just one home. If to total United States sales of genuine antiques one adds Victorian and Country American furniture, glassware, china and various kinds of semiantiques and knickknacks, auction business in total may amount to not over one percent of all "antique" business in this country. Thus, total business calculated in this way to cover the entire gamut of items might amount to $1,000,000,000 per year.

Antique Shows

Antique shows are proliferating throughout the United States. Many smaller cities and towns are inaugurating periodic antique shows set up for a few days or a week, in which various dealers have booths to sell their wares. The Rye, New York, antique show held at the Playland Amusement Park in late 1965 (another one was held in a Rye church in March 1966) was a mammoth affair. So was the one in Ridgefield, Connecticut, at which a person could spend almost an entire day trying to see all the items offered for sale.

In the United States there are at least 2,000 antique shows held per year. This number has increased from about 1,800 three years ago. But more important than number of shows held is the size of each show. The 1966 antique show in the New York Coliseum had ten more dealer exhibits in 1966 than it had in 1965. The Wilmington, Delaware, show was started just two years ago. In those two years it grew into one of the biggest shows in the country. There are now dealers who sell only through these antique shows, and some of these dealers sell in over fifty shows per year. One such show-selling dealer comes from Potomac, Maryland. He does not even have a shop in his home town; he sees potential customers only by appointment when he is in town. Show sales probably amount to over 10 percent of the total volume of antiques, near-antiques and bric-a-brac sold in this country.

The Dealer Structure

The largest volume of antiques by far is sold by dealers rather than auction houses. The number of these art and antique dealers amounts to the amazing total of 20,000. This is the number of names which will probably be included in Boleslaw Mastai's forthcoming issue of the *Classified Directory of American Art and Antique Dealers*. This number is an increase of 15 percent from the number in the last issue of the Directory which appeared in 1961. Mastai, who has been preparing issues of this directory for the past 25 years, indicates some of the difficulties in tabulating art and antique dealers by primary line of business. Among the problematical classifications are the following which actually exist:

> Groceries and Antiques
> Infants' Wear and Antiques
> Antiques Old and Modern
> Antiques Made to Order

There is some radical overlapping of lines of business in the antique field. A very large wholesaler of delicatessen products purchased a leading art magazine and became its publisher, thereafter devoting the major portion of his time to artistic matters.

Using two Mastai Directories, a tabulation has been made of antique dealers located in various cities in the United States at the close of World War II, and again in the last year of publication of the Mastai Directory—1961. The growth cities of Los Angeles and Houston were selected, plus the more or less stable cities of Washington, D.C., Boston, and Philadelphia. (New York was tabulated separately.) These were the number of dealers in each city by years:

Number of Antique Dealers By Selected Major Cities—1945 and 1961

City	1945	1961
Los Angeles	71	128
Houston	24	56
Washington, D.C.	52	62
Boston	67	124
Philadelphia	86	120

Substantial growth was realized in every city but Washington, D.C., which has shown a consistent general decline in retail sales in the central city as the result of mass migration to the suburbs since the war's end. Even such stable cities as Boston and Philadelphia have shown growth. Between 1950 and 1961, Washington, D.C., Boston and Philadelphia had actual declines in number of antique dealers, while Los Angeles and Houston continued to show a growth pattern.

The number of antique dealers in Manhattan (New York City) has been tabulated for a number of years between 1950 and 1966. These are the total numbers, realizing, of course, that there may be errors resulting from several listings by the same dealer:

Manhattan Antique Dealers—1950–1966

Year	Number of Antique Dealers
1950	544
1955	534
1960	539
1963	562
1964	592
1965	639
1966	632

In total numbers of antique dealers, there was not an outstanding record of growth to 1960. In fact, there appears to have been a slight decline. Thereafter, there was definite growth, although the rate of growth was nothing like the growth in the volume of antiques sold. It is possible that in the period of three years—from 1965 to 1968—antique volume in the United States showed an increase of 100 percent.

This is a tabulation based on Kelly's *Post Office London Directory* in which he lists antique dealers in London:

London Antique Dealers—1938–1963

Year	Number of Dealers
1938	490
1947	458
1948	433
1950	568
1960	804
1963	770

Between the prewar period and 1948, there was a static condition in number of antique outlets in London, and this situation corresponds with the flat trend line of antiques sales in this period. But by 1950, growth had started. Ten years later the number of antique dealers was over 40 percent greater than it was in 1950; however, by 1963 the number had dropped back to 770.

Business Done by Dealers

In the late spring of 1966 I mailed a questionnaire to 385 antique dealers throughout the United States. Its purpose was to (1) to see what was happening to sales and prices of antiques at the dealer level, (2) to find out something about the customers and (3) to find out the sources of dealers' antiques.

The questionnaire was a particularly searching one, and it was expected that returns would be low. Matters were gone into that dealers in general are not inclined to discuss. There were 74 useful returns—about 20 percent. A number of questionnaires were returned with the explanation that the dealer did not handle antique furniture, but sold glassware or china or something else besides furniture. A few were returned with the comment that this was none of the author's business. A number of blank questionnaires were returned in the self-addressed envelope as a kind of silent protest.

The 74 returns did represent, it is felt, a fairly good sample of large and small dealers from all over the country. What is very important, from the point of view of adequacy of the sample, is that there was a good deal of agreement on most questions among the dealers replying.

The questionnaire asked, "About how many pieces of antique furniture do you sell per year?" The average number of pieces of furniture handled was 344. The average dealer in antique furniture is not large, and certainly not large in the sense of an automobile or electric appliance dealer. Two dealers stated that they sold about 2,000 pieces a year and one 1,000. The rest did not approach the 1,000 figure. One dealer sold only 15 antiques a year, and this number probably represents a generally common volume for smaller dealers who handle andirons, sleigh seats, antique decoys and Victorian glassware along with various kinds of furniture. Most dealers stated that they handled a few hundred pieces.

One interesting fact about dealer sales volume is that while the dealers in the large cities tended to have the greatest volume of sales, this situation was by no means universal, and some of the very largest dealers were located in very small cities or towns. One of the largest dealers in antiques in the country is located in a town about fifteen miles from Louisville, Kentucky, but he is of sufficient importance for me to have paid a cab fare of $10 to visit him and look over his stock. Large volume dealers in smaller communities is a unique feature of the antique business and will be explained more fully later.

The average dealer is long established—unlike the operators of boat sales agencies or trailer dealers or lawn equipment dealers. The average antique dealer has been in business 26 years. One dealership was stablished 121 years ago and one 105 years ago. Only thirteen dealers in this survey have been in business for less than 10 years. Just one dealer was in business for a year or less. Three were in business for 3 years. It should be pointed out, however, that *Antiques* magazine's list of dealers was relied on heavily for the names selected to receive the questionnaires, and listing in a magazine is not necessarily the first thing a newly established dealer thinks about. The longer he has been in business, the more time and opportunity he has to seek a listing.

The next question dealt with sales volume, and this was a highly important element of the questionnaire. The dealers stated that their sales volume had increased an average of 31 percent in the past year. Since the returns came in April and May 1966, we are comparing the antique season of 1966 with that of 1965. The antique season starts in September and ends about the following June. (In most of the rest of this book, however, the calendar year was used for price comparisons.) One dealer stated that his sales had fallen by 30 percent for local reasons. Practically no one stated that his sales had not increased in the past year. Four dealers reported that their sales had doubled in the year, and one dealer stated that his sales had increased by 125 percent.

The next question was all-important—the percentage of price increase for the year. The average figure was 22 percent. The important thing about this average is that it is *not* a composite of extremes, say 125 percent, 3 percent and 58 percent. Most of the dealers were in general agreement as to the magnitude of the rise. Only four dealers reported rises as high as 50 percent.

Buyers of Antiques

The next question in the questionnaire was aimed at finding out who bought antique furniture and whether new people were coming into the antique market: "Have your old customers been buying more pieces of furniture in the past year?"

Forty-two of the dealers who answered this question stated that their old customers were stepping up their antique purchases. Twenty dealers stated that their old customers were not increasing their purchases. Two stated that "to a certain degree" their old customers were increasing their purchases. One dealer stated that his old customers were "continuing their purchases." One answered "possibly," and one made the important comment "unless they are full."

This latter comment is important because it has to do with a unique characteristic of the antique market. When the older, well-established families of the country were interviewed, it was found that a great number of them were interested in the value of antiques not as *buyers,* but as potential *sellers.* They are apparently "full up" and have been for years. They may even be thinking of moving into smaller quarters and disposing of some of their antiques to get them out of the way. Antiques are thus not like the second car or the third car or the boat, which can be added as one gets more affluent. There is no place to put additional furniture, and the process of "refining one's collection" by getting rid of the poorer antiques and adding better ones is not a very common procedure for most antique owners. This "full up" comment indicates some limits to the ever-expanding antique sales.

The next question was, "What percentage of your sales are to new customers (that is, new to your shop)?" The average percentage of sales to new customers turned out to be 40—almost half of the total sales. An antique dealer is thus not exactly like the electric company or the dairy where there is great customer stability and new customers are added slowly—as new people move to town.

The next question was aimed at finding out the new antique buyers who were just coming into the market for the first time. It asked, "About what percentage of your sales are to people who have never bought antique furniture before?" The average percentage turned out to be 15. One dealer reported sales to new antique buyers as being 60 percent of his total volume. Two dealers reported 50 percent. But five dealers stated that they had no customers who had never bought antique furniture before.

It has sometimes been stated that young people are becoming antique conscious and are buying antiques instead of department store or furniture store merchandise to furnish their first homes. The next question asked the percentage of sales to people under 30 years of age. The percentage turned out to be 13, not an enormous figure. Three dealers reported no sales to people under 30. One dealer reported one percent of his sales to this group. Three dealers reported 2 percent and ten dealers reported 5 percent. Only one dealer reported over 25 percent of his sales to the under-30 group, and he reported 60 percent.

Sales to the next older group were, however, a different matter. We asked the percentage of sales to the 30-to-40-year-old group. The average turned out to be 31 percent. This is, of course, a relatively young group considering the overall level of incomes of this group and the general "expensiveness" of all of their purchases. Thirteen dealers out of a total of 65 who answered this question reported a majority (at least 50 percent) of their sales to this particular age group. Only two dealers reported less than 10 percent of their sales to this group, while two dealers reported 75 percent of their sales, and another stated that 70 percent of his sales came from this group of buyers.

The next question was along the same line: "Are sales to people under 40 years of age increasing? Rapidly?" Thirty-nine of the dealers who answered this question stated that sales to this group were simply increasing. Four stated that they were not increasing and one could make no comparison. The overwhelming number of dealers indicated a rise in sales to this younger group of antique purchasers.

The next group of questions had to do with the kind of antique furniture that people were buying from the dealers. It asked, "What is the most popular antique furniture *you sell* (French, English, eighteenth-century American, Country American, Victorian, etc.)?"

Forty-four dealers stated American, 26 English, 14 French and 3 Italian. Some dealers answered with more than one type, so that the total of all of the above-mentioned types adds up to more than the total number of questionnaires.

This is a somewhat "loaded" question. It has to be. Most dealers in the United States sell American furniture, and it does not make any difference whether French furniture is the elite furniture of the world or not. They do not sell it and they do not usually have access to it. It is available in quantity only in the largest cities. The dealers sell the furniture they can buy and this is, for the most part, American and English.

The second bias in this question is that it was sent to a great extent to dealers listed in *Antiques* magazine, and this magazine is chiefly concerned with American antiques, particularly the finer antiques of the eighteenth century. Dealers handling this category of antiques can be expected to seek listing in this magazine more than in others. Little Italian furniture was mentioned in the returns because little is available for dealers to purchase. Nevertheless, if there were consistent calls from customers for Louis XV furniture, this preference could be expected to be reflected in the replies of the dealers, and it is known that in many large cities and in many antique-conscious cities, American is the preferred antique furniture, not French or Italian.

The next question was designed to bring out preference still further: "Is any type of antique furniture that you handle growing especially fast in popularity?"

The largest number of dealers (eleven) stated "Queen Anne." A cross-check of the dealers to see whether they handle American or English or both types of antiques indicates that this means *American* Queen Anne for the most part, but it also includes English Queen Anne to a lesser extent. In total number of replies, English furniture in general was mentioned by eleven dealers, but eight dealers mentioned Chippendale, and here the cross-check indicates that most of them mean *American* Chippendale. Nine dealers simply mentioned eighteenth-century American furniture. Two more dealers just said American furniture and another one mentioned early American.

There seems to be some interest in the earlier furniture. Oak and walnut were mentioned by one dealer, seventeenth-century oak by four, and American Country furniture by one. It will be remembered that American Country furniture was the rage in the middle 1920's.

American Empire furniture was mentioned by one dealer as growing in popularity, and one dealer listed American Sheraton.

Three dealers mentioned French, two mentioned Spanish and one mentioned Italian. Two dealers simply stated "no"—no furniture that they handled was growing especially fast in popularity. Three answered "all," which may amount to the same thing.

The remaining answers are extremely important from the point of view of customer preference. They were not especially elicited by the questionnaire. Rather, they represent the extra individual thoughts of the dealers who answered the questionnaires.

One dealer stated that good small American pieces were growing especially fast in popularity. This is the general market tendency, to place emphasis on fine furniture of apartment or modern house size.

One reply stated that formal furniture was growing rapidly in popularity. This shows the influence of the "Age of Elegance" and indicates a turn away from rustic, crude pieces.

The next answer amounts to about the same thing—"pieces of refinement." The final reply of especial note is "unusual pieces." The run-of-the-mill pieces are apparently not in the greatest demand. Instead, people want the unique piece.

The next question is the reverse of this question. It asked, "Is any type of antique furniture going out of fashion?"

Most dealers (eighteen) stated that no antique furniture was going out of fashion, a reply to be expected from the largest group of dealers.

The next largest group of dealers (fifteen) answered that Victorian furniture was going out of fashion. This reply probably indicates that as antique buyers become more knowledgeable, more sophisticated and more wealthy, they pass from Victorian to the types of furniture considered finer, more elegant and more in the mode. Perhaps the "lower level" shops, those handling secondhand furniture and knickknacks of various kinds, would find less demand for secondhand things and more for Victorian, but the questionnaire went to antique dealers and not to the lower level merchandise shops.

The next largest group of dealers (six) stated that American Empire furniture was going out in preference. This is in a sense on a level just above Victorian, and it certainly occupies this level price-wise. It is also closely related to Victorian in style and in size. Both American Empire and Victorian furniture tend to be large and less refined as compared with eighteenth-century types.

Two dealers stated that crude pine and rustic furniture was going out in preference, and this reply is entirely in keeping with other replies to this question as well as with the replies to the preceding question. One dealer stated that early American furniture was going out, by which he may have meant seventeenth century—as is to be expected. One dealer mentioned Regency, and he probably means that, as tastes develop, eighteenth-century furniture is preferred as against early nineteenth-century furniture—including American Empire and Victorian. One dealer felt that William and Mary furniture was not preferred, so that at both ends of the eighteenth century we see preference dropping off.

One dealer stated that Spanish furniture was going out. Most Spanish furniture sold in this country is of the large, dark, rustic type.

The last two replies to this question were unsolicited. One dealer stated that large pieces were going out, and one dealer stated that "junk" was going out. Both answers are entirely indicative of the trend to the refined furniture at the Age of Elegance.

The final question elicited the most interesting information from a marketing point of view. It asked, "Are your customers located mainly in your city? If not, please explain."

On the surface, there is every reason to believe that an antique shop in Danville, Kentucky, let us say, would sell mainly to the people living in Danville and nearby areas—as would the paint store or the auto dealer. But the antique business is almost entirely unique from a marketing point of view. Only seven dealers indicated that their customers were chiefly local. Twelve indicated that they came from a wide area. Many of them stated they served a radius of up to 100 miles. No fewer than 34 dealers stated that they sold all over, which could mean that they sold to customers from major cities and towns located at some distance, or even to more or less the entire United States. In fact, many dealers stated that they did sell all over the United States. Interviews with dealers located in various parts of the country substantiate the fact that the market of an antique shop located almost anywhere can be nationwide, depending on the quality of the merchandise handled, the advertising policy of the dealer and the length of time he has been in business and built his customer clientele. There are few, if any, other retail stores located in small towns that can sell to the wide area that antique shops can. Furthermore, the overwhelming majority of antique dealers have only one shop. Just two dealers reported having three shops, and four reported having two. (It is known, however, that several dealers actually have several shops by "backing" other shops).

Two dealers stated that they sold by advertising and did a walk-in business. These dealers apparently sell from nonstore locations on the basis of advertising. One dealer stated that he specialized in exhibits. It is known that several dealers have no shops at all, but operate from their homes and sell principally though the antique shows.

One dealer stated that he sold only to museums. To supplement this reply, he indicated that over the years he had emphasized sales to museums and he described pieces of furniture that he had sold, pieces of top quality and of American origin.

Many dealers stated that a major percentage of their sales were to local customers, while a large percentage were to customers located at a great distance from the shop. They covered both the local and the distant market.

Sources of Antiques

We now go back to an earlier set of questions included in the questionnaire. These were designed to find out the sources of antiques. Although it was feared dealers might not be willing to reveal this confidential information, the entire set of questions dealing with sources of the dealer's antiques elicited full and extremely valuable answers.

The questionnaire asked the dealers to break down purchases by origins to percentages. Blanks were left to fill in the usual sources of antique furniture.

The dealers reported that they bought, on the average, one-third of their stock of antiques directly from abroad. A survey of telephone directories in various cities, as well as other advertising, indicates that many dealers believe it to be a great virtue to advertise that they import. Many dealers proudly proclaim that they handle only imports, as if imported furniture were like imported champagne. It should be stressed, however, that imported furniture must be higher in price in the United States than it was abroad in order to cover transportation, insurance and the markup of the dealer abroad who sold the furniture to the American dealer, as well as the markup of the American dealer. French, English and Italian furniture in general can be purchased in the United States by dealers and resold by them at a lower price than imported furniture.

Fourteen dealers reported that they imported no furniture, while three reported that they imported 100 percent of their stock. Six more reported that 90 percent or more of their stock was imported. While the dealers reporting high percentages of imports to total purchases are in general big dealers, there are many big dealers who import few or no antiques. Importing is a matter of business policy rather than a natural development which takes place as a dealer grows in size. Of course, the smallest dealers have less means to import directly.

While, overall, one-third of the antiques in the stock of the dealers would appear to come directly from abroad, 17 percent come from purchases from other dealers. This is a characteristic of antique furniture dealing that is somewhat unique, but in this industry it is quite common. At the various regional and local antique shows, such "swapping" often goes on just prior to the opening, and a dealer will openly state that he just bought a piece of furniture at the show that he is offering for sale, even though the potential customer's reaction may be to forget about buying it since it has involved two dealer markups. On the other hand, dealer discounts of 20 percent are common at such shows, and the buying dealer may have bought the piece at 20 percent off and will offer it at the original dealer's retail price.

In replying to the questionnaire, one dealer stated that his entire stock comes from purchases from other dealers. On the other hand, there are many wholesaling dealers, dealers whose principal business is to sell to other dealers. Along Third Avenue in New York City as well as in the University Place area, there are many dealers who place a sign in the window "To the Trade Only." Some of these dealers mean what they say and will ask a private buyer to leave the shop. Others will sell to anyone who has the cash—dealer or private individual.

Twelve dealers reported that they bought nothing from other dealers, while eighteen more bought less than 10 percent of their stock from other dealers. The entire question might well have been ignored by dealers as it is believed a somewhat bad impression might be created for a dealer who simply pays another dealer his markup and then adds his own markup to the piece of furniture. There is even more inter-dealer selling than the questionnaire brings out, and piece after piece has been traced from one dealer to another in New York City. It is also significant that the average of 17 percent of all stock coming from other dealers is not a modal figure, but rather a composite of highs and lows, some dealers stating that they buy a great percentage of their wares from others while some stated they buy little or nothing from others.

The third source of the stock of dealers was estate sales upon the death of the owner, and this source accounts for 15 percent of the stock of the dealers answering the questionnaire. One might have supposed that this percentage would be much larger. An explanation of the small percentage is that this is a common source of business for auction houses, which depend heavily on estates for their merchandise. It is natural for executors and administrators to sell estates at auction.

Nine dealers stated that estates accounted for 50 percent or more of their sales, but 32 dealers stated that estates accounted for little of their stock—less than 5 percent. This 5 percent is probably a fairly accurate answer. Dealers like to give the impression that they are offering merchandise that comes from an estate; and as they describe the estate, one has the impression that it is just a little finer than the J. Pierpont Morgan estate. They also like to give the impression that they are offering the piece at an extremely low price because they were able to buy it very low since the owner was dead and everything had to be sold. Finally, they like to give the impression that they just got the particular piece directly from the estate and other potential customers have had no chance to see it and snap it up.

Surprisingly enough, people calling the dealer by phone or dropping in to see him about things they have for sale account for only 10 percent of antiques bought by dealers. Of course, a large dealer located in a small town or a suburb and selling to customers all over can be expected to have few walk-ins or call-ins. On the other hand, some of the big city dealers are so elegant in appearance and so formal looking that they might well frighten off potential sellers of good antiques. It is significant that no dealer stated that a large percentage of his stock came from this source, but most stated that some did.

The next source of the stock of antiques was from people moving away from the area or into a new house, possibly a smaller one. Ads appear all the time in local newspapers of people who are transferred in their jobs and who are selling an antique or a few antiques. This source accounted for 8 percent of the stock of the dealers who answered the questionnaire. No dealer reported that a substantial part of his inventory came from this source.

The same percentage of stock (8 percent) came from wholesalers, volume dealers who specialize in selling to the trade. The line between buying from other dealers and buying from wholesalers is a fine one and to a certain extent an artificial one. In New York, a retail dealer regularly sells to a very large dealer located uptown; but this uptown dealer is primarily a wholesaler with one of the largest stocks of antiques in the country, so that a dealer buying from him would have to report purchases from wholesalers. Yet the wholesaler would report purchases from other dealers. As a matter of fact, probably most dealers do some wholesaling and they usually have a wholesale as well as a retail price, or at least expect to take less from another dealer. One dealer reported buying 80 percent of his stock from wholesalers, another reported 70 percent, and another 50 percent; but, in general, the dealers reported low percentages of stock secured from this source.

Local auctions were reported as supplying 4 percent of the stock of the dealers, and the big-city auctions as supplying another 4 percent, so that all auctions supplied 8 percent of the merchandise. In New York City, at least, it is expected that auctions supply a much larger percentage of the stock of most of the medium size and smaller dealers; and at most of the auctions held in New York, the same old faces of the dealers appear time after time. The dealers form a kind of fraternity. They usually sit together and they often bid together. One dealer reported that all of his stock came from the city auctions, but no fewer than 48 dealers reported that they purchased nothing from city auctions, and 37 reported that they purchased nothing from local auctions.

The answers to these two questions are not entirely homogenous. For a dealer in East Haddam, Connecticut, a local auction means one in nearby towns, while a big-city auction may mean one in Hartford, Connecticut, as well as New York City. But for the New York City dealer, a local auction means one in Elmsford, New York, and a city auction means one in his own city. To him, a New York City auction is a local auction.

The dealers reported that 2 percent of their stock came from individuals who consigned the merchandise to them for sale. This percentage seems lower than it should be. One dealer located in Westport, Connecticut, is stocked 100 percent by individual consignments, and many dealers have one or a few pieces on consignment, but sometimes many pieces. One dealer reported 35 percent of his merchandise as being consignment merchandise, but the rest all reported very low percentages. Forty-six dealers reported no consigned merchandise at all.

A still lower percentage was reported for merchandise consigned from other dealers—one percent. The highest percentage reported by any one dealer was 30. No fewer than 57 dealers reported that they had no merchandise consigned from other dealers. In New York, the largest and probably the most elegant dealer in antiques had in stock items consigned by other dealers; and, although to this question the dealers emphatically answered "never," there does not seem much stigma attached to taking on consigned antiques, especially elegant ones, from a dealer who, for the most part, does not have elegant customers and who would like to reach such customers via the elegant shop.

This is the breakdown of sources of dealer merchandise:

Source of Dealers' Antiques

Direct imports from abroad	33%
Purchases from other dealers	17
Estates sales upon death of owner	15
People calling or bringing in antiques	10
People moving to another location	8
Wholesalers	8
Local auctions	4
Big-city auctions	4
Consignments from individuals	2
Consignments from dealers	1

If the percentages of antiques secured by the dealers from their various sources are totaled, it will be found that the sum is 102 percent, not 100 percent. This error is caused by questionnaires of several dealers who reported percentages which add up to over 100 percent. One dealer's total percentage amounts to 175 percent, and one put down 65 percent for each of three categories. The error on individual questionnaires is so small, when included along with all the other questionnaires, that it can be disregarded.

There are a few other sources of antiques. One dealer reported that he was selling antiques that he had collected over the years. In other words, he is a collector-turned-dealer. In Washington, D.C., a large dealer complained bitterly about these collectors-turned-dealers who are apparently more numerous than the questionnaire might indicate. The large dealer stated that these new dealers sold well below the market and thus damaged the market; but, as soon as their collections ran out, they had to buy at high replacement costs and had to price along with the established dealers.

Two dealers reported that they secured 20 percent of their stock from appraisers who called in, or from owners who had appraisals made and then wanted to sell once they found out how vaulable their antiques were.

Two dealers reported that they bought collections when they were disposed of as well as museum collections when they came up for sale. Strange as it may seem, museums, including the Metropolitan Museum of Art, have been wonderful sources of antiques as well as other art objects.

One dealer reported "private buying" in addition to his other sources, by which he probably meant the seeking out of antiques. In the early 1900's this was great sport, particularly after the automobile was developed into a reliable vehicle which enabled the buyer to comb the countryside and visit farmhouses in order to persuade the owners to part with antiques. This type of buying is not much practiced lately, as far as can be determined.

One dealer stated that 5 percent of his stock came from pickers and runners, while another stated that 55 percent came from this source. In a sense, pickers and runners are at the bottom of the antique barrel. They generally handle the low end, or cheaper, antiques. They buy these for quick resale to dealers, generally the smaller, less illustrious ones. Or they merely locate items which dealers then buy directly (the pickers and runners thus do not have to employ any capital which, with them, is often a scarce commodity). Or they take the item from the seller on consignment.

Sometimes runners find treasures. Dr. William Suida, late Curator of the Kress Collection, reported the instance of a runner who had a painting for sale in Vienna. After the runner's daily efforts of trying to sell it for the equivalent of a few hundred dollars, he would check it in the cloakroom of a hotel or restaurant for the night and pick it up again the next day when his selling efforts would begin again. The runner eventually showed the painting to Dr. Suida, who immediately identified it as a Piero Della Francesca, one of the rarest and most valuable artists in the world in the Old Master category. The painting now reposes in the Frick Collection in New York and is worth well over $1,000,000!

Important Philadelphia Chippendale Furniture: High chest of drawers, circa 1765;
tripod table, 1760–65; side chair, 1770–80.

CHAPTER TWENTY-EIGHT

The Value of an Antique

T HE VALUE OF AN ANTIQUE IS NOT an absolute thing, unalterable and time-enduring. As of today, it has a certain value, but that value changes with time. It is not a static thing determinable by static standards. There are, however, certain determinants of value for any antique. They can be applied at any time, in the year 1901 or in the year 2000, but their application would of necessity produce a far different dollars-and-cents figure in 1901 than in 1967 or in 2000.

What Is in Style

No matter how excellent any particular piece of furniture is—its wood, its excellent proportions, its detailed craftsmanship or its durability—it will have value and consequently a high price only if it is in style; only if it is in vogue. In the 1960's Louis XV and Louis XVI are the fashionable thing, and probably the former more than the latter. This was not always so, but it is at this time and probably will be for the next few years at least.

On the other hand, in the early part of the century Renaissance Italian was in vogue; and even as late as the mid-1930's a simple three-legged Renaissance Italian chair brought $23,500.

At the present time Louis XV stands at the top of the value pyramid for a complex of reasons. Probably the main one is the "Return to the Age of Elegance." Louis XV stands out and commands attention. It is beautiful and anything but unobtrusive. It screams, "I cost money," and is thus a good outlet for the funds that were made so rapidly in the 1960's.

There are certainly many elements creating a vogue, such as the religious, political and economic situation and the pendulum of taste. These were taken up earlier in great detail. One final one should be summarized and this one, to some extent, begs the question. If a vogue or fashion can simply get started, if it can "get off the ground," forces are generated which tend to strengthen the vogue. There is nothing quite so persuasive as to what is in vogue as a rising price curve. It works like a snowball. The more it rolls on, the more important it gets.

A friend of mine had a catalogue of a forthcoming London auction. In it he had selected several items to bid on, and alongside these items were the bids he had given to the New York office of the London auction house. He placed these bids— two of them in six figures—without having seen the items offered for sale. "But," he pointed out to me, "two of my friends are going to bid on items in this sale, and I can bid just as well as they can." Such an attitude cannot help but strengthen vogue or fashion, and it is significant that all of this man's bids were for the items most in vogue in 1964, and every item French!

Particular Items That Are in Style

In the 1960's the furniture that consistently brings the highest prices are commodes of the Louis XV and Louis XVI Period. Chairs are of less importance *compared with commodes* even though of comparable excellence and even though stamped by the same maker.

Prior to World War II, the exact opposite situation obtained. A set of chairs brought a great deal of money, and commodes were decidedly a secondary item.

For their size, probably the most valuable of all pieces of furniture are the very small occasional tables of eighteenth-century French design, and no end of labor was expended on the marquetry and parquetry of some of the finer ones.

Importance of the Maker

The vast majority of furniture that appears on the antique market was made by makers who are unknown, even the fine French furniture. But if the maker can be identified by style and workmanship, the value is immediately increased. If there is a label of the maker affixed to the antique or if the piece is stamped with the name of the maker, the value is increased even more.

To a certain extent, the value of the piece of furniture depends on the excellence of the maker. The better furnituremaker, *ipso facto*, in general makes better furniture. In American furniture the names Goddard, Townsend, Savery and Gostelowe, if they can be definitely attached to a piece of furniture, at least double the value of the piece. This list can be extended, of course, to include other American greats such as Duncan Phyfe and Seymour.

The initials B.V.R.B. on a Louis XV piece place it at the top of the value list if the quality is comparable to the name. The same magic applies to the names Riesener, David Roentgen and perhaps two dozen other top makers of the era of the Louis'. If, in addition, the bronzes can be assigned to Caffiéri or Gouthière with some degree of certainty, the value goes up significantly.

At one time the name Chippendale could be insisted on in the buying of antiques. In other words, items from Chippendale's own shop could be purchased. Now they are extremely rare; if a piece can be shown conclusively to have come from his own shop, the price is probably tripled, or raised even more. The Harewood Desk made by Chippendale holds the world auction record for a piece of English furniture.

Size

From these decidedly intangible value determinants we go to very practical ones. In general, the larger pieces are not so much in demand as the smaller ones because they require more space in the smaller houses and apartments of today. Those who have larger living quarters do not find so much buyer competition for these larger pieces.

One notable exception to this rule of size is large bookcases, particularly Chippendale and Georgian ones. These are enormous pieces, but they almost invariably bring high prices. The explanation is not hard to find. Built-in bookcases, when considered an item of furniture, are large indeed, even when they are made today. They are meant to hold a number of books, and generally the more space for book shelves in a home the better. Frequently the entire side of a room is devoted to these built-in bookcases. The Georgian or Chippendale bookcase is simply a substitute for these built-in ones; and if it is large, so much the better. It will hold more books.

Another exception to the rule of size is the large English kneehole desk, even though such an item does take up a good deal of space. Here we run into the element of rarity which is discussed later.

The rule of size is most obvious in the case of the slant-top desk, American or English, of the eighteenth century. None of these desks can be considered a large piece of furniture, and few are as large as a medium-sized Louis XV commode. But the larger desks invariably bring less money than the small ones of comparable quality, and the shrewd buyer is always quick to point out that the writing top is so high that the ordinary chair will not allow him to write comfortably.

Conformance to Certain Characteristics Considered Good

Cabriole legs are a characteristic of Louis XV furniture. A dealer in France is said to make this test in selecting chairs he purchases: He places a yardstick against the leg of the chair he is considering. He holds the end of the yardstick. The other end he places on the floor as though he were measuring the height of the chair from the floor. In reality, he is determining whether the legs slant inward or outward or go straight down.

The angle of slope of the legs would indeed seem to be an artificial determinant value, but the fact of the matter is that the slope of the legs does affect value.

One of the simplest types of foot on American furniture (or English) is the bracket foot. It is not curved and does little more than serve the purpose of connecting the piece of furniture—highboy, tallboy, desk, etc.—with the floor. The ogee foot is a curved foot, more difficult to make and probably better looking. As a matter of fact, it is double curved like a compressed cabriole leg. These feet impart a greater value to furniture than do bracket feet.

In every type of furniture there are certain characteristics of the design and construction that are considered good, and the presence of these characteristics makes the piece more valuable. Some of them may seem incomprehensible, but they are important price-wise. For instance, in a Louis XV *bombé* commode two drawers are better than three, and it is best if the two fit closely together so that only the wood of the two drawers can be seen when they are closed, and no part of the body of the commode is apparent.

Elaborateness

It is a somewhat strange fact that, in general, the more elaborate the piece the higher the price it brings. This fact has held true with a few exceptions throughout the history of antiques. In the 1930's the United States, as well as many European countries, went through a depression. During this time there was a turning away from elegance and an emphasis on "design following function." The simpler designs were preferred in everything, including apartments, houses and automobiles.

Yet even in this austerity period, the rule held true that the more elaborate the greater value. The Louis XV commode with marquetry, parquetry and ormolu mountings was worth more than a plainer one.

In the slant-top desk the value depends directly on the elaborateness of the piece. The more fanciness the item has, the more it is worth. If it has a finely finished interior under the slant top, it is of greater value. If the tops of the letter compartments are arched, the value is greater than if they were simply squared off. If there are shells carved on the inside, so much the better, and the more shells the greater the value. If, on the outside, there is a shell or a sunburst, the value is higher, and two are better than one—three are better still. The best of all is the indented front called the block front. There is no category of American desk more valuable than the block fronts. They are now almost unobtainable.

In Chippendale chairs, those with simple splats and straight feet bring the least. The more carving on the splats the better, and the more intricate the splats the better. The ball-and-claw foot is better than the straight foot; and if the seat rails are carved or if the knees of the legs are carved, the value is increased materially. While it may be aesthetically debatable as to whether elaborateness is synonymous with beauty, the fact is that in the market the more elaborate the piece and the more finely it is carved, the higher its value.

What Is Considered Beauty

Some years ago my wife took a fancy to a piece of furniture owned by a friend of ours in Washington. It was an American chest-on-frame, a somewhat unusual piece of furniture, but not a great rarity. It had four long drawers, the deepest being at the bottom. The higher drawers were progressively more shallow. Above the highest of these four long drawers were two small parallel drawers. The whole piece stood a little over five feet high, small for this article of furniture, and it stood on cabriole legs that ended in nicely carved Spanish feet. The apron was scalloped and the top was flat. The piece was obviously from Pennsylvania and probably from Philadelphia. The owner, a member of a prominent Philadelphia family, told us that as far as she knew, the chest had been made in the middle eighteenth century for her family.

Finally, my wife summoned enough courage to ask her if she would sell the piece. I was rather surprised at her response. She said, "You mean that monstrosity downstairs near the door? Surely you don't want that!"

The upshot of this inquiry was that we purchased the chest-on-frame for a figure that to us was reasonable but to her was a heaven-sent gift.

Everyone was pleased with the transaction. But her reaction started me wondering about just how fine the piece really was from an aesthetic standpoint. We had not been specialist collectors of American antiques, and I began to wonder exactly how good a purchase we had made for our home, since we buy only to use and not to sell.

To a certain extent we were versed in American antiques in the characteristics generally accepted as establishing beauty as well as worth. This chest-on-frame measured up pretty well. But when I tried to put myself in the seller's position when she called the chest a "monstrosity," I began to appreciate her viewpoint. The whole piece was large in relation to the size of the legs. In other words, it had the appearance of a big dog with short legs. To a certain extent it looked as though if the drawers were filled, the legs might first bow out and then collapse.

To some degree all American and English highboys on cabriole legs have this characteristic, yet the finer examples are among the most prized of any antiques.

We have come to love our Philadelphia chest and have turned more to American antiques. Absolute beauty is another matter. Our eye has become sharpened to what is *considered* beautiful and also fashionable and valuable; and this process, if one is willing to admit it, takes place in connection with an appreciation of all artistic things. Nothing was ridiculed more than Impressionist paintings when they first went on display in France, but hardly anyone makes fun of a Renoir today.

Perhaps there is such a thing as abstract beauty, the kind I felt I was witnessing when I looked at a shapely sailboat. And I know little or nothing about sailboats. But usually I unconsciously try to conform in my judgment of what is beautiful in antique furniture to the standards of beauty which exist today in this field.

A most valuable service is performed by Albert Sack in *Fine Points of Furniture: Early American* (New York: Crown Publishers, Inc., 1950). In this book he illustrates American pieces of the eighteenth century and rates them into three categories of "Good," "Better" and "Best." This is one of the easiest ways of determining what is considered beautiful in this type of antique furniture. The more one studies furniture, the more he learns what is considered good quality and beautiful.

This same process must be performed in every field of fine furniture. While beauty may be to a certain extent absolute, it is to a greater extent learned—one must learn what the best critical opinion in the field of antiques considers beautiful.

Comfort

The original purpose of furniture was, of course, use. Commodes were intended to hold clothes and other items; desks were for writing and storing business and other papers and correspondence, and chairs were to sit on. Long ago, however, this primary purpose was modified as the furniture took on decorative qualities and became symbolic of elegance and wealth as well as objects of investment. Although the perennial slant-top desk is in constant demand today, its use characteristics are decidedly secondary to other characteristics that make it a desirable possession.

Nevertheless, antique furniture is still used, and it is interesting to note that the antique chairs in the very greatest demand, namely Louis XV and Louis XVI, are sold in Paris primarily on a comfort basis; that is, the most comfortable chairs tend to bring the highest prices.

There is little question that this furniture when it was originally constructed was furniture par excellence from every point of view—materials, design, workmanship, quality of carving and upholstery. And not the least important element was comfort. Good Louis XV chairs look comfortable and were originally designed for comfort. In Paris today, the emphasis of the buyer is not simply on comfort so that he may sit more pleasantly; comfort is a kind of test of authenticity. Eighteenth-century chairs were not only reproduced all through history since they were made, but they were faked as well. Since one of the main objectives of the chairmakers of the eighteenth century was comfort, a test of whether a particular chair was in effect made by one of these master ébénistes is, "How comfortable is it?"

Provenance

The Davanzati Palace in Florence is a beautiful structure, although it does have the lack of comforts characteristic of the Renaissance furniture of the same period. However, in the area of Renaissance furniture, a background of having come from the Davanzati Palace increases value enormously. The famous Volpi sale of furniture from the Davanzati Palace was conducted in 1916, and this sale will never be forgotten in the antique world. The examples sold were excellent, for the most part, and the prices realized were very high, particularly for the year. When a piece originally from this Palace appears on the market today, this background alone increases its value perhaps 50 percent over what it would be had it not been in the Davanzati.

Obviously, Versailles Palace contained the very finest French eighteenth-century furniture. When an item appears on the market that was once in Versailles, the piece not only creates a kind of bond with royalty, but it establishes the excellence of the particular piece. Such pieces with this provenance command huge prices.

Probably the most celebrated sale of American furniture was the Reifsnyder sale. The collection was so celebrated and the pieces so fine that prices ranging up to $44,000 for one piece of furniture were realized. Here again, the Reifsnyder provenance increases values greatly.

From time to time, antiques come onto the market that were originally owned by J. Pierpont Morgan and William Randolph Hearst. The collection of each of these tycoons contained many good items, but at the same time, however, they were so large, especially the Hearst Collection, that the fact that a piece belonged at one time to this collection does not necessarily make it distinguished.

Former ownership is significant to most collectors. In America, no authority was more celebrated than Wallace Nutting, whose *Furniture Treasury* has long been a bible of early American antiques. Some few antiques appear on the market which were once in Mr. Nutting's own collection. The fact that this expert and collector thought enough of the piece to add it to his collection supplies a kind of certificate of authenticity as well as excellence which adds value to any antique.

Historical or Aristocratic Connections

Recently, a table was offered for sale which had been used by the late John F. Kennedy when he was President. Mr. Kennedy was not a true connoisseur of excellence in furniture, nor was he in the class of Wallace Nutting as a specialist on American furniture. But he was President of the United States and his name is particularly prominent. The fact that he owned the table increased its value, and the Parke-Bernet Galleries noted this fact in the description of the table. It had been in the White House, and the person who bought it at the auction can point to it and say, "This table you are eating at was once in the White House and was used by President Kennedy."

In the 1920's historical connections were vastly more important in increasing antique values than they are now; and, if it could be stated authoritatively that a set of Chippendale chairs was owned by George Washington, those chairs might be worth three times what they would be worth without such a historical connection. In the 1920's there was great emphasis on patriotism and on the early struggling days of the new United States, an emphasis that resulted in the purchase of the crude, early simple types of cottage furniture, chiefly pine and maple. This same resurgence of Americanism placed somewhat artificial values on pens used by the signers of the Declaration of Independence, Benjamin Franklin's chair, etc.

One such item to bring a good price at the time it was sold was Mme. Du Barry's bed. The same bed without the connection with Mme. Du Barry would have brought far less than it did. The price was close to $1,000, and beds have never been in great demand as antiques.

Original Condition

Perhaps the most important single element in determining the value of an antique is original condition; or, rather, what is *left* of the original condition. The vast majority of antiques on the world market are over 150 years old, the best and highest priced ones dating back to the eighteenth century and earlier. Thus there must, of necessity, be some wear.

Original condition can vary all the way from a deep scratch on the top of a table to only one piece of original wood left in an entire chair.

We have divided the changes or defects of any antique into four categories. The least serious changes or alterations are those contained in Category One. These changes leave the piece in the condition nearest to what it was when it originally came from the cabinetmaker's shop. Alternatively, Category One antiques are nearest to original condition and are the best. Categories Two, Three and Four get progressively worse.

Within Category One, the change or defect of the least importance is the first one listed. The second one listed is more serious and more damaging to authenticity and, so on. The same classifications of changes or defects are made under Categories Two, Three and Four. We have thus tried to classify alterations within each category from those that damage authenticity the least down to those that practically destroy any semblance of authenticity. Value fairly well follows the degree of authenticity.

While Category One alterations diminish the value of the antique the least, the more of these changes there are the lower the value. It is conceivable that enough Category One changes could lower the value of any antique to Category Two (or even lower).

This categorization is only a guide, but without a knowledge of how alterations change quality and value, antiques cannot be intelligently valued or purchased.

CATEGORY ONE ALTERATIONS

1. Surface stains and fly specks.
2. Surface dents and cuts.
3. New drawer runners (these are the strips of wood under each drawer on which the drawer slides).
4. New seat blocks under the cushion where the seat rails join each other.
5. Replacement of brass—on American and English furniture. This substitution is vastly more serious on French furniture, particularly on eighteenth century French furniture.
6. Filling in of holes left over when new glass and ceramic knobs and pulls were put on in Victorian times and when these Victorian holes were filled in and the original type brass put on in modern times. This filling in was done on both American and English eighteenth-century pieces to "bring them up to date" in the nineteenth century.
7. Small additions of wood where original wood chipped off or rotted away.
8. Warping, if not too serious, which can often be overcome by heating and pressing.

CATEGORY TWO ALTERATIONS

1. Separators installed inside each drawer where none was originally placed, provided the wood of the drawer is not cut out in too large amounts.
2. New inner seat frame on chairs where reupholstering and constant use have worn out the original.
3. Removal or replacement of drawer separators which are attached to the carcass between the drawers.
4. New bottom of the entire piece (a part which is not seen).

5. New back (which is against the wall and not supposed to be seen in the case of most furniture, but not such pieces as Louis XV *bombé* commodes, which were often finished on the backs so they could stand in the middle of the room).

6. New small drawers located under the top in slant-top desks.

CATEGORY THREE ALTERATIONS

1. Cutting off of feet, replacement of feet or splicing original cut-off feet back on. The last procedure is not as rare as it might seem. The piece was often lowered in height by removing the feet, yet these feet were not thrown out. They were often put back on later to restore as much of the original condition of the piece as possible.

2. New paint—or the amount of new paint—on such pieces as Venetian commodes where paint is essential to the beauty of the piece.

3. Placement of a bonnet top or broken arch top on an originally flat-top piece—English or American antiques. To restore the piece, a new flat top must be made.

4. New flat top where the old one wore out or rotted out.

5. Replacement of important parts of the frame of a table.

6. Removal of the insides (like knife box interiors) which was often performed to "update" the piece.

7. Loss or replacement of tambour slides (the wood, but not the canvas; canvas is expected to wear out).

8. New chair stretchers.

9. New crest rail.

10. New chair arms or arm supports. This substitution is sometimes made to convert a side chair to an arm chair with resultant damage to the rest of the piece through cutting in order to fit on the arms and supports.

11. New replacement stretchers on tables—often of a more elaborate variety to upgrade the piece.

12. New veneer. The more of this that is replaced the worse for the value of the piece; and if veneer is of the essence, as in Louis XV commodes, value can be completely destroyed. New inlay, marquetry and parquetry also damage value most seriously.

13. Missing door or a new door.

14. Absence of bed rails, especially large ones, which were intended to be seen.

15. Embellishment of interiors of desks, mainly by carving sunbursts on American pieces.

CATEGORY FOUR ALTERATIONS

1. Replacement of drawers or drawer fronts—the large front drawers.

2. Additional carving, inlay, veneer, marquetry or parquetry.

3. Reshaping the splat.

4. Piercing and recarving the splat.

5. New splat.

6. New wooden seat.

7. Re-turning, rereeding or recarving bed posts to make them more slender and more artistic.

8. Loss or replacement of bonnet top or broken arch—on American highboys.

9. Different shape imparted to drop leaves on tables and aprons of chairs or tall furniture.

10. Changing the size or shape of a bureau or highboy.

11. Changing the shape of a sideboard—from straight to curved or serpentine.

12. Creation of a bow front or a block front from a straight front—desk or highboy.

13. Loss of headboard—on a bed.

14. Different top on the bottom. Here what is left of two pieces is stuck together. This process is called mismarriage, an obviously derogatory term.

Rarity

Perhaps it is very late in the listing of value determinants of antiques to place rarity, but most of the other characteristics have to do with *what* is sold—the nature of the item offered. "How many are on the market" is immensely important from a value point of view. Prior to the sale at auction in London of the famous Roentgen commode for over $176,000 in 1964, I used to talk at length to a friend of mine, a museum curator, about the antique market. In one conversation I stated that I was furnishing my living room exclusively with pieces by David Roentgen. Although this may not seem much of a joke when it appears in print, it did occasion a laugh at the time. David Roentgen furniture is almost nonexistent. To begin with, it is excellent furniture, but on top of this excellence it is of extreme rarity.

The rarity, in order to add to value, must be *rarity of an excellent item*, and an excellent item *long recognized by the market as a valuable item*, one that is wanted by collectors as well as other members of the buying public. Only then does rarity add to the value.

High Public Price

In the first place, a price history, if well established, is in itself a price determinant. If this were not so it would not be possible to estimate prices at auction with any certainty at all, and many of the major auction galleries make advance price estimates on each major item offered for sale. (These estimates will be given to prospective buyers on application.) The estimates are surprisingly close when one considers that everything offered for sale in the category of art and antiques is, to a considerable extent, unique. Each item has its own individual characteristics which are, for the most part, unlike the characteristics of any other offering. My own estimate on the 24 items offered in the Erickson sales was less than 10 percent off in the total dollar amount realized from the sale, including the famous Rembrandt "Aristotle" that brought the unprecedented price of $2,300,000.

A price history tends to pull a particular item up to or down to the level of items of a like kind which have been sold in the past.

Public prices and price histories are more important than simply serving as a guide line for future prices. A high public price is an attribute of prestige. When the Roentgen commode sold for $176,000, the most important question was, "Who bought it? Who had the kind of money to put $176,000 into one commode?" The high price itself immediately adds to the luster of the buyer and to his prestige as a collector. It also adds to his reputation as an extremely wealthy man, and such an attribution is extremely important to many. It is just possible that if the Roentgen commode had been sold privately, it would not have brought near this newsworthy, published price.

THE ADAM ROOM from Croome Court, Warwickshire, a superb example of authenticity. Featuring Gobelius tapestry (after designs by Boucher) from a set of six tapestry chairs and two settees of carved and gilded wood documented as the work of the firm of Ince and Mahew, 1769. *The Metropolitan Museum of Art*, gift of Samuel H. Kress.

CHAPTER TWENTY-NINE

Authentic or Fake?

O NE OF THE BIGGEST CONTRIBUTIONS that can be made by this book is the creation of apprehension on the part of prospective antique buyers— the raising of a perpetual doubt whenever a so-called antique is viewed. The purpose of this chapter is not to indict the dealer organization of the country, or any particular dealer, nor is it to indict the auctions for mislabeling or failing to conduct their examinations of items offered in their sales thoroughly enough. Dealers and auction houses alike are fooled by antiques, and a survey of the high points of faking should make this point clear.

A 1954 issue of a prominent picture magazine contained a highly interesting story entitled "How to Make a Fast Antique." The article explained that Florence, Italy, surpassed all other cities of the world in the faking of antiques, and it wrote up one Sergio Tacchi who, the article said, turned out two hundred such fakes a year. The article went on to describe how he made these antiques, and ended up by saying that he sold only to dealers. He was strictly a wholesaler!

Let us go back sixteen years earlier to December 1938. The magazine *Arts and Decoration* contained an intriguing article entitled "Antiques Made to Order." The article divides the fakers into two types, the commercial faker and the expert or master faker, the first being much further down the artistic line than the second.

Let us cite another example in the same year, 1938. The January issue of *Asia* contains a good description of some of the fine work that comes in above the expert faker category. Margaret Mackay states:

> In musty workrooms . . . the craftsmen of modern Peiping are bending over their crude tools making new objects old. . . . The best of the fakes are almost perfect. Their creation is a fine art in itself. . . . A certain master cabinet maker who fashions matchless "Chien Lung" chests, cabinets and screens of inlaid lacquer requires 18 arduous months to make a single splendid fake. When at last he is finished, he not infrequently sells his product to some western Connoisseur who has not been mistaken for years —at a price befitting a beautiful object from the Palace of Chien Lung!

The astounding statement was made in the *Literary Digest* of May 15, 1937, that the U.S. Treasury Department estimates that in the 28 years since the passage of the Morgan Act of 1906 giving preferential tariff treatment to antique imports, it lost $500,000,000 in taxes through the importation of spurious antiques that went through duty free as real antiques. The article estimates that between 75 percent and 85 percent of the imports which are supposed to be antiques could not possibly be anything but fakes.

In 1930 the problem was severe enough for Senator Wagner to introduce a bill dealing with fakes. It was directed specifically against the sale of spurious antiques.

The era of the 1920's was probably the heyday of faking. The U.S. Appraisers' Stores, an agency of the United States Government, made an estimate in the December 29, 1928, issue of *The Saturday Evening Post* that 90 percent of the imports from England of what purport to be antiques are genuine. The estimate for French antiques was that 50 percent are genuine and 50 percent fakes, but that 90 percent of Italian "antiques" are fakes.

F. J. Kracke, the United States Appraiser at New York, stated in *The Saturday Evening Post* of January 9, 1926, "The proportion of counterfeits in the mass of supposed antiquities is so large . . . that I am continually amazed at the picture it presents of American gullibility. Two-thirds of all merchandise imported into America comes into this port and filters through our appraising machinery, which is essentially a human machine. The proportion of the antiquities coming to the U.S. imported through New York is even larger than two-thirds." Mr. Kracke concluded that over two-thirds of all supposed antiquities coming into New York are fakes.

The faking of the 1920's had an immense impact on the buying public. The April 11, 1925, *Literary Digest* said, "Mr. ———— believes that the decline in the French and Italian styles may have been due in part to a general disillusion over the amount of fraud . . . practiced by certain unscrupulous dealers."

The Saturday Evening Post of May 30, 1925, contained an astounding story entitled "Faking by an Old Antique Dealer." The article was not signed for obvious reasons. It starts out, "I have dealt in antique furniture for thirty years; I have bought it, sold it and faked it, and I haven't the faintest doubt but what I can fool the shrewdest collector alive. Only one master craftsman can detect another's forgeries. . . . All the earmarks by which the collector tests his finds of antique furniture for authenticity may be counterfeited."

All of these citations are by way of a prelude to the fact that I have never heard an antique dealer, a furniture dealer or any functionary of an auction house in recent years characterize even one piece of furniture as a fake. There must have been literally tens of thousands, possibly hundreds of thousands, of fakes made from the 1920's to the present time, but where are these pieces today? Did they disintegrate over the years? Did they just disappear? Or did they become discovered by collectors or dealers or both, who then threw them out or chopped them up for firewood?

The most logical answer is that *they are still in existence.* When estates come onto the market by private sale to a dealer or by public sale through auction, whatever the estate contains is sold. If the Parke-Bernet Galleries do not take an estate, some other auction most certainly will. And one can go on down the line until he finds an auction house or dealer that will take the most humble collection, even overstuffed borax made in the 1930's. In some of these estates, there must certainly be a part of this vast production of fakes.

There are many pieces of furniture in the "antique category" sold by dealers and auction houses that are described simply as "Queen Anne" or "Chippendale" rather than as "Queen Anne—eighteenth century," or "Chippendale—eighteenth century" or "antique Queen Anne" or "antique Chippendale." Such an absence of an age designation often means "This is not of the period," or "We do not believe this is of the period," or "Make up your own mind about this piece—we don't know for sure."

Yet such pieces are never described by the sales personnel, even informally, as fakes. They are "later reproductions" or "made a few decades later" or "not quite of the period."

To some extent, the entire antique industry is to be blamed for this attitude toward fakes. It is an attitude of overlooking their existence. Fakes do exist, except now they are forty years older than they were in the Twenties when many of them were made. They are "aged" forty-plus years. One authority suggests that fakes will have fallen apart in this period of time or deteriorated so much that they will now be obvious fakes. But use gives the impression of age, and patina develops with time. It is logical to believe that the longer a well-made fake is in existence, the greater will be its appearance of authenticity.

Writings in the antique field have too often avoided the subject of fakes because of a fear that talk of fakes will cause the buying public to lose faith in antiques in general. This may be so, just as talk a few years ago of poisoned cranberries caused the public to "lay off cranberry sauce." But is it not better for the industry to warn the public so that collectors and even museums will not buy worthless things? Such purchases can well result in worse discrediting of the industry.

The job of authentication is not an easy one, as will be made clear later. A New York dealer in French antiques stated that he guaranteed the item to be antique "to the best of his knowledge"; if the buyer could prove it was not an antique he could get his money back. This was not a process of throwing the burden of proof onto the buyer. It was probably a sincere desire to make good but to avoid the necessity of making an absolute representation of authenticity. The dealer explained that for one customer this guarantee was not enough. He wanted the piece he proposed to purchase authenticated by *several* experts *before* he purchased it. Accordingly, the gallery got in four experts. Their findings were highly significant. Two of the experts found the piece to be absolutely genuine. The other two found it to be not of the period!

If one lesson can be learned from this chapter, it is that there are a number of fakes on the market which are "growing more antique every year" and that even the best galleries and auction houses can extremely easily make a mistake and label an item "antique" which is not. Of course, the reply might be "What's the difference? If it fools the experts, it's just as good as an antique."

The answer is that if and when a $50,000 double block-front "Goddard highboy" is proven to be not of the period and thus not by Goddard, its value on the market is $1,000 or less, not $50,000. It is in the same category as a Rembrandt which is proven to be by a later artist. One pays a Rembrandt price for a Rembrandt, and a copy price for a copy. The buyer expects to be able to get out of Goddard or Rembrandt the high price of an original should he ever have to dispose of it. The market recognizes the genuine as being worth a great deal and the spurious as worth almost nothing.

Earlier Faking

One of the most interesting documents in the entire field of antiques is the "Daily Consular and Trade Report" for November 24, 1909, issued by the United States Department of Commerce and Labor. It states, "Consul Maxwell Blake, in writing . . . of the frauds which are still perpetrated on the inexperienced collector of old silver and china and period furniture by dealers throughout the United Kingdom and continental Europe, says:

> The United States is reputed by the well informed to harbor more "artistic atrocities" that were purchased as genuine than any other country in the world, and we may even see a greater influx of pseudo works of art to American shores unless these frauds are detected by government experts or rejected by the public taste. The purpose of this article is to state facts, not opinions, and it is not addressed to the experienced collector. A real service, however, may possibly be conferred by warning the inexperienced— those who, perhaps, go abroad for the first time and find the curiosity shops places of interest, and many of whom, doubtless, can little afford to be so heavily penalized for their credulity by antique dealers.
>
> Difficulties thicken as the subject of old English furniture is approached. Large stakes are here frequently played for and the cunning of the dealer amounts to sheer genius.
>
> It is no exaggeration to say that such episodes are a daily occurrence in the antique trade, except that, generally speaking, the ignorant purchaser seldom gets in exchange for his investment even so much as a good modern copy. Many so-called antique shops actually carry on business without having one genuine piece of antique furniture in their establishments. Fine pieces of period furniture bring higher prices in London than in New York, and the inexperienced American collector has little chance of outwitting the alert dealers and connoisseurs of England when it comes to securing something for nothing.
>
> To successfully collect nowadays requires expert knowledge and technical training, since it may be generally stated that nothing but the veriest trash is to be found in 90% of the antique shops of Great Britain and the Continent!

Each time we move back a few years, the prevalence of faking seems to be greater! Here are some quotations from the February 1906 *Good Housekeeping*:

> About ninety percent of the things sold nowadays as antiques are bogus. That is, they are not what they pretend to be, or just what is claimed for them.
>
> In ways that are dark and tricks that are vain, and lucrative, the heathen Chinee was never so peculiar as the dealer in antiques. Almost every one of them has in his back room or basement anywhere from half a dozen to a score of workmen busy manufacturing antique furniture.

Antiques magazine in 1946 thought enough of this article to reproduce long sections of it in order to warn the public about fakes.

While the desire to keep the entire antique industry from falling under suspicion or even into complete discredit is certainly one very strong reason for the lack of publicity given to fakes in the antique press over the years, there are other reasons for this void of information—information which would be of inestimable help to collectors and museums. Dealers and auction houses do not know when they see a clever fake and so cannot warn the public. A survey of the literature on the subject of antiques forces one to arrive at a rather startling conclusion: The level of scholarship in the field of antiques is not as good as it was in the past. We are so used to seeing "frontiers pushed forward" in such fields as aviation, nucleonics, chemistry, medicine and surgery, it is difficult to realize that in some fields knowledge and expertise have gone backwards. How many furniture experts today have the knowledge of Wallace Nutting? The field itself does not push forward. Here there are never new and more advanced earth satellites. There is the same old furniture, and on this subject knowledge has not been accumulated as fast as it might have been.

While laboratory techniques can help in determining the age of the wood and the composition of the glue, who takes the trouble or goes to the expense to take the furniture apart, examine it microscopically and make the necessary chemical tests? These things are not done.

The furniture designer after whom an entire style of Victorian furniture was named, Charles L. Eastlake, tells of certain practices in the Soho district of London—manufacturing medieval furniture which was sold in Wardour Street. He says in *Hints on Household Taste*, published in 1869, "As a rule, the 'Glastonbury' chairs and 'antique' bookcases which are sold in that venerable thoroughfare will prove on examination to be nothing but gross libels on the style of art which they are supposed to represent."

The 1870's appear to be an era of intense activity on the part of forgers. One particular group was located at Cologne, Germany, and specialized in Gothic cupboards. A little later in the nineteenth century, factories for the production of fake furniture were to be found in Paris, Nuremburg, Cologne, Constance, Venice and Brussels.

The greatest piece of furniture ever made in France was probably the *Bureau du Roi*, started by Oeben and finished by Riesener as well as several other *ébénistes*. Otto Kurz in his interesting book, *Fakes* (London: Faber and Faber, 1948), points out that the Wallace Collection in London contains such a fake commode by, presumably, Reisener. He states, "It bears the spurious and misspelt signature RIESNER, is of German workmanship and dates from 1800. This commode was for a considerable time regarded as an authentic work by Riesener." (The collection also contains a copy of the *Bureau du Roi*.)

The faking of French furniture around the turn of the nineteenth century appears to have been very widespread. When Mme. Vigeé-Lebrun, the famous French artist, visited Moscow in 1800, she observed furniture in the palace of Prince Bezborodko which was brought from the workshop of the famous Paris upholsterer Daguerre in the first years of the Revolution. In her *Memoirs* she said, "When I went to see him he showed me rooms full of furniture, bought in Paris from the workshops of the famous upholsterer Daguerre. Most of this furniture had been imitated by his serfs, and it was impossible to distinguish between copy and original."

One does not know what became of this spurious furniture, but if it was impossible to distinguish it from the originals in the year 1800, how would it conceivably be possible to distinguish it today?

How To Market Fakes

Verified stories of selling fakes are more than hard to secure. The seller of fakes is unlikely to tell the story of how he swindled a buyer out of his money. The buyer of a fake is even more unlikely to tell a story that will make him the laughingstock of his friends. There are stories by people who sold reproductions as such and found out later that they were resold as genuine antiques. A few experts have been honest and sincere enough to tell how they were almost taken in (or were taken in) by a fake. Finally, there are some court cases involving fakes with printed transcripts of the testimony. Some of these stories are so fantastic that they would form a major sequence in a whodunit picture—or in a comedy.

The "Daily Consular and Trade Report" of November 24, 1909 contained an interesting account by Consul Maxwell Blake:

> An instance of recent occurrence may be cited: What purported to be some exceptionally rare Chippendale chairs were sold by a well-known dealer to a certain nobleman who unhesitatingly accepted the dealer's word that they were genuine. Some time after this, however, the services of an expert were employed to further examine them, when it was revealed that a swindle had been perpetrated, the chairs being nothing more than fine modern copies. The customer informed the dealer of this discovery, demanding on penalty of exposure, that the full purchase price be immediately refunded. Much to the purchaser's surprise the dealer refused to make restitution under circumstances which involved both his reputation and his honor. But to put it differently, if the customer would simply state his dissatisfaction with his purchase, then he (the dealer), knowing the chairs to be genuine, would thank him for the privilege of being allowed to recover them, but, it must be distinctly understood, only upon the terms and conditions of an ordinary sale. The dealer thereupon offered about $1,000

over and above the sum for which the chairs had previously been purchased. To this, of course, the nobleman demurred, protesting that he desired no profit from an unfortunate venture; but in the end, in order to secure the recovery of his money, he was prevailed upon to acquiesce in this extraordinary proposal.

The chairs having been duly returned, no great time elapsed before another customer took their purchase under consideration. A sale had now, however, become much simplified, for not only could the source of the purchase be pointed to with pride, but actually the check was exhibited, showing beyond all doubt that the chairs had been purchased from Lord _____, the well-known collector, at a price indicative of their apparent worth. Thus the dealer, shadowing his own dishonesty by this clever ruse, contrived to snatch even a further profit out of this second and more unscrupulous transaction.

Now if the "Chippendale" chairs of Lord _____ were put on the market today with the bill of sale from Lord _____ to the dealer who hoaxed him, and the date of the bill was 1909, this would be the best possible kind of authentication of the chairs! Then, too, 55-plus years would have been added to the age of the chairs to provide wear and mellowing.

At least one faker had the gall to boast of his hoaxes in the press, without, of course, revealing his name. The story was carried in *The Saturday Evening Post* of May 30, 1925:

> The Washington style sofa is a rare antique, always in demand. I had some useless parts of an old fireside chair. I combined the front and back legs and the stretchers of the chair with the lower portions of the square legs of an old drop-leaf table, virtually the same in shape and color, and had the bulk of a Washington sofa. The rest of the chair, which was covered with upholstery, made the filling of the sofa. Very little remained to fill in, and this I supplied with odds and ends. The wood was newer and did not match up precisely, but the very absence of uniformity was the best proof to the average collector that the sofa was genuine.
>
> I really had no intention of selling it as an authentic Washington sofa. A collector of prominence came in and began to study the sofa through the corners of his eyes. He flirted with the sofa every time my back was turned, eventually made up his mind that it was genuine. But did I appreciate that it was genuine? He doubted it, and offered me a price far below what a true Washington sofa was worth. Because it was faked, I let him have it at that price. I've wondered since if I did know my business. Despite its fabrication the sofa is a rare specimen in the original state.

This story indicates several things. In the first place, the dealer offered something that most certainly could have been mistaken for an antique without any explanation that it was a fake. He was perpetrating a fraud because the sofa was made with the intention of fooling someone into believing it was an antique. Otherwise, the dealer would have explained that it was a "put together piece."

But the story also indicates a good deal about many collectors. They are out to beat the dealer if they can. If the dealer has a real antique but thinks it is a reproduction, the buyer will rarely go to the trouble to explain the dealer's error of judgment to him. On the other hand, the dealer is never exactly a naive boy; and because he is a dealer, he certainly has a good deal of expert knowledge of what is genuine and what is false.

This is not the only story that this faker had to tell:

> Another collector once asked me to be on the lookout for a good old piecrust-top table, always hard to find and costly. He had seen several, he said, but the price always was too high. I found him the piecrust-top table and at a reasonable price. I used a genuine claw-and-ball-foot table that had a plain round dish top. I scalloped the edges, cut in the molding, and made it a grade finer than the average piecrust edge. I matched the finish of the top with the balance of the finish, of course. It was well done and my customer got the table in the original condition; he did not have to take my word for it.

This procedure of upgrading antiques is quite common, and I have seen many examples of such fakes. One of the more recent ones was the carving of the front of a highboy. This later carving was of good quality but obviously not original; it made the piece almost valueless as an antique.

Still two more stories by our faker:

> Once I had a genuine antique Hepplewhite card table with serpentine front. The front rail had a square plain veneered panel. I removed this and replaced it with an inlaid American eagle. In the lower right-hand corner I inlaid the date, 1785, in very small figures, faint in color. It would take two looks to see it.
>
> I sold it to a well-known Connecticut collector for a stiff price. Six months later he dropped in to tell me that he had discovered the date, 1785, faintly inlaid in the table, and that he regarded the piece as the gem of his collection.
>
> Some years ago I made a four-post bedstead for a woman customer. The bed-posts were turned down thinner from other very high posters which I used to import from South America. The drapery work was beautifully done, and as the wood was old and hard mahogany it took an excellent finish. My customer's husband died recently, and she sold everything. The sharpest collector in town bought only one item. That was my high-post bedstead, for which he paid the widow one thousand dollars— a lot more than she paid me.

The faker thus performed a fine and charitable service. He made a profit on his investment and the widow collector made a profit and secured cash in her time of need!

One of the most interesting legal cases (in the field of antiques certainly) is the Adolph Schrager case. During World War I Schrager was in the rubber business.

That business prospered and he turned to buying antiques for his home, Kent Lodge, Westgate-On-Sea, England. The antiques were bought from Basil Dighton, Ltd., of London, dealers in antiques. Schrager had spent £84,887 on antiques by the time the case was heard in 1923—about $388,000.

Some time after buying the furniture, Schrager found himself in need of cash and asked a dealer in antiques to come to his home to look at an antique table Schrager was thinking of selling. The dealer would not buy the table as an antique.

Schrager then sent for a specialist in antiques, Herbert Cesinsky. (Cesinsky was certainly one of the most publicized experts in the era of the 1920's.) Basil Dighton had claimed Schrager's furniture came from Royston Hall. Cesinksy testified that there was no Royston Hall.

The old Chippendale lamp stands were not quite as represented. Cesinsky testified: "The legs were obviously new, and the stem had probably been made from a child's four-post bed. The price of £450 was ridiculous. As secondhand furniture they would be worth £8/10s." Schrager had bought some old oak paneling which had come in part from a dairy. The rest had come from a carpenter's shop. It had cost the dealer £300 or less.

Of an "eighteenth century blue lac cabinet" Cesinsky said: "It was not Queen Anne, but was recently made up in a factory. The 'lacquer' was merely French polish and the brass work of a well-known Birmingham make." This item cost Schrager £850.

Next came a Queen Anne red lacquer writing bureau. This was a somewhat novel piece. The body was Dutch, and onto this body was affixed an Oriental chess board. It cost Mr. Schrager £800.

The next item the expert considered was a "Charles II walnut table with marble top." This, Cesinsky concluded, had no period at all. It was worth about £10 and was sold to Schrager for £375.

Next came two particularly fine and expensive items, a pair of Chippendale side tables. Schrager paid £1,100 for this pair. Cesinsky stated that they had modern carvings and were worth £7 apiece.

The court suit was for the price paid for the antique furniture by Schrager to Basil Dighton, Ltd.—£84,887. But Basil Dighton, Ltd., countersued for £25,000, the balance due for furniture sold to Schrager, delivered to him but not paid for by him.

Strangely enough, the plaintiff, Schrager, did *not* win this case. The point on which the decision apparently turned was that in the recently made pieces, *at least some part was old*. Therefore ,there was no misrepresentation about the "antique" nature of the furniture!

H. Avray Tipping, an authority of some note on antiques, said,

> The case has demonstrated to the full probity of Messrs. Dighton, but at the same time I think it will add to what has for some time been the growing conviction that the genial art of faking in its higher and more artistic heights has reached such a state of perfection that even the experts

may be deceived. We have seen some of them come to opposite conclusions though each claimed to know the genuine article by sight, smell or touch. One gets the impression that they are not so clever as they think they are and that the 'faker' can at times deceive them. . . . The mere amateur who wants to buy old stuff cannot go into the open market and not be taken in.

The dean of American antique authorities (as well as the dean of authorities on antique American furniture) was Wallace Nutting. There is probably no collector of American antiques who does not own his book, *Furniture Treasury* (The Macmillan Company, 1963). Nutting was a great collector in his own right, and J. Pierpont Morgan bought the Nutting Collection of early American furniture and presented it to the Wadsworth Atheneum in Hartford, Connecticut.

Nutting wrote in *The Saturday Evening Post* of March 22, 1930:

> The writer once possessed a wonderful Windsor chair. He copied it for one who posed as a friend. The copy was avowedly new and looked new. It turned up at an auction some time after and brought $500. The original price had been nineteen dollars—not hundreds. A dealer offered the auction purchaser $1,000 for the chair. The owner had become suspicious and asked me if I made it. After a careful examination of certain birthmarks I answered that I did make it. The dealer offering $1,000 was so informed. He replied, "I believe it's old and so does my client. Here is your $1,000." His client died. It was sold for forty dollars to a dealer; he went out of business, selling it again for a small price at auction. No man on earth but the maker could have identified this chair as new. The faker had washed off the finish, and then, no doubt, subjected it, in some purlieu, to the summer's rain and sun, rain and sun. In six months this treatment would give it every appearance of antiquity.

The fantastic part of this story is that when the purchasing dealer was informed by an expert cabinetmaker that he had made the piece, he refused to believe it; or else, having fooled his client into believing it was genuine, was determined to carry through with the hoax.

The figure of $44,000 for the famous highboy that was sold in 1929 was remembered for many, many years. The comment on this piece by Wallace Nutting himself in the March 29, 1930, *Saturday Evening Post* is worth quoting exactly: "People were startled out of their boots last spring by the fact that a highboy fetched $44,000. They would have been far more startled had they known that the styles of the carving on the two parts of the highboy had nothing to do with each other."

The "fake in reverse" is something of a rare animal. Nutting in the same article quoted above says, "One of the finest Connecticut-built chests I ever saw bore a silver label bearing a legend that the piece was brought from England by the owner's ancestors about 1600. He believed it."

Here one had a piece of furniture worth more because it was American, yet he stated, and was convinced, that it was English!

Good Housekeeping of February 1906 tells the story of one woman antique collector:

> She had bought from a well-established dealer a claw-foot sofa. It was sent to her while she was away from home. On her return she examined the piece while it was in the freight house and found that the original claw feet had been sawed off and imitation ones put in their place. The old feet were, of course, put on a new sofa which was thereby classed as a genuine antique.

Since on many sofas and wing-back chairs little of the wood shows but the feet, the process of faking by this method is highly economical.

A story which gives the background of faking and the environmental factors out of which faking arose is told by Wallace Nutting in *The Saturday Evening Post* of March 29, 1930. Not much faking is involved on the part of the dealer, but the factors creating temptation in any era of rapidly rising antique prices are made clear:

> For the best table ever found in the country, the dealer paid two dollars. After long delay, he sold it for $125. It was then sold for $600. The buyer, after keeping it awhile, and not feeling the importance of it, returned it at such a figure, by way of exchange, that I bought it for $400, and was delighted to see it turn up again in the market. The next morning the dealer called me; explained he knew I never sold anything from my collection, but that, as this piece was still in the shop, he thought I might gratify a collector by allowing him to have it at an advance of $100. Grudgingly, I let it go, to be told later that the real advance secretly obtained by the dealer was a good deal more!
>
> The collector who took the piece away from me shortly sold his whole collection to a department store. The table was sold for $3,000. The buyer was told by a friend that the top was not original. The last dealer had fitted the two pieces of the top by taking off just a shaving. The table was, therefore, returned to the department store. I bought the table then for $1,600. It passed in my collection, presented by Mr. J. P. Morgan, to the Hartford Atheneum. Its latest valuation there for insurance purposes was $15,000, but since it is the only large table, with feet intact, carrying carving on the frame, there is little doubt that some buyers, intent on the best and rarest, would, given the opportunity, pay more than that sum.

In 1956 my wife-to-be and I were trying to buy furniture and paintings with which to set up housekeeping. I was in Baltimore negotiating for a few items when the dealer suggested I visit the home of a woman who had some priceless things— provided he could arrange to get me in. He got me in. But the "plants" were not very clever. There was far too much furniture for anyone's home. The paintings were not only hung on the wall, they were standing around on the floor, on tops of bureaus and *armoires*, in the closets—everywhere. In fact, while my dealer and

I were looking the things over, another prospective customer came in with another dealer for the same purpose.

Where are the fakes today? And have not a good many more been added in Europe as well in the United States in the three-and-a-half decades since the 1920's?

It must be remembered that not one stick of eighteenth-century furniture has been made since that century. If there is disappearance through wearing out or just throwing out, is it reasonable to assume that the fakes wore out or were thrown out faster than the genuine pieces? If so, is not the percentage of fakes in the total supply of antiques just as high as it was in the 1920's when the problem was so acute? Yet, and I repeat, I have never heard one prospective buyer or one dealer or one auction official say that there was the smallest possibility that a particular piece of furniture might be a fake!

Tell-tale Signs of an Antique—and How To Create Them

Ideally, an antique buyer should be armed with at least a decade of intensive study of antiques. Wallace Nutting says, "Speaking broadly, one may say that twenty years of careful study is not enough to render a buyer fairly certain of his ground." ("Antique Humbugs," *The Saturday Evening Post*, March 22, 1930).

A buyer should ask the dealer or auction house selling what purports to be an antique to take the antique apart. Once it is in pieces, with the upholstery off, the prospective buyer ideally should get out calipers, straightedge, high-powered magnifying glass, scrapers, a low-power microscope and a few more complicated devices for determining age of wood and age of paint. Then, after perhaps a day of study, he can arrive at a decision as to the true age of the piece, what members have been replaced, what the general condition is, and how fine the construction is.

No prospective buyer that I have known, or heard of, does these things or ever has done so. The dealer or auction house will not permit such a procedure, even though the prospective buyer might have the knowledge, the equipment and the time to conduct such an examination.

In the auction house, however, it is quite common practice to permit dealers to tear apart the upholstery (most usually the muslin under the seat) and examine the frame. If the piece is authentic, this ripping apart can only enhance the value; and, if it proves not to be authentic, then the piece was not worth much and would not have brought any more had it remained intact and unproved—so goes the theory under which the destruction takes place, at any rate!

GENERAL IMPRESSION

Usually, the first thing a connoisseur notes when he considers a piece offered for sale is the general impression. Here is where knowledge is important, for a fake or copy will usually give itself away by some flaw in the style, the carving or some detail. One of the greatest dealers in the country says that if his first glance does not give him the feeling that the piece is "right," he passes on to something else without making any detailed examination.

Probably the explanation of the importance of this first impression is that we want to read into antiques what we would like them to be. We would like to believe that we have located something genuine and fine, that we have made a discovery of an excellent piece that perhaps we can buy under the market.

The next step after the overall impression is a detailed examination; and in order to make a meaningful examination, it is absolutely necessary to know the structural and surface characteristic of period furniture.

The overall style of a piece of furniture is indicative of two things: The first is the excellence of design (or the absence of it) and the second is the authenticity of the piece.

For over a year in an antique store in Larchmont, New York, there was a pair of what appeared to be Louis XV chairs that had been waiting for a customer. Both chairs were stamped with the maker's name. But the chairs found no buyer. The trouble was that they were all out of proportion. They were too small and the legs too short for almost any purpose; and the backs were too low in relation to the rest of the chair. How any self-respecting eighteenth-century French *ébéniste* could have turned out such chairs is beyond comprehension. Finally, the gilt appeared to be of the nineteenth century, and without any further examination I would have to discard them as being much later than the eighteenth century.

PATINA

This is an indefinable quality which is extremely illusive to the untrained eye; and yet without the correct patina, or what appears to be the correct patina, no knowledgeable collector, connoisseur, dealer or other professional buyer would touch a piece of furniture. The patina is the look of antiquity of the exposed surface wood. It is the first sign of age that one sees when he starts to make a close-to examination—after he has seen the piece from a distance and formed his first impression of it and noted whether the overall style appears to be authentic.

When one looks at the genuine patina of age on, for example, the top of a table, he seems to be looking below the surface and he can see a good many of the signs of age. Very often patina is extremely reliable as a means of determining age just because of its color. Mahogany of certain types lightens (fades) with age and may even approach a light yellow or cream color which appears to be covered with discolored varnish.

Patina can be faked in any number of ways or it can be removed by extensive refinishing. Many antique dealers are refinishing to the extent that very little of the original wood surface remains. In fact, such pieces often look new. Why such refinishing is done one can only guess—perhaps the original wood surface was very much damaged, or perhaps buyers in the price category of these pieces want a "new look"; or perhaps the original piece looked so nonauthentic, particularly the patina, that the dealer thought it best to avoid any discussion of the original nature of the patina by removing it entirely.

OLD VARNISH

Old varnish is one sign of age. Old varnish is discolored, often deeply, and the older the piece of furniture, the more deeply is the original varnish discolored.

Varnish can be faked with brown stain, and the more one wants to hide, the more stain he puts into the old varnish. In fact one can buy varnishes which are described as "old oak varnish," "light mahogany varnish" and "deep mahogany varnish." These contain wood stains. We have bought such varnish to give the pine stairs in our eighteenth-century Connecticut house the appearance of age.

SURFACE DAMAGES

No surface can have come through 150 or 200 years without showing some damage. A minor form of damage is an ink stain which can easily be faked and easily removed. But an old ink stain on an old desk often goes a certain distance in proving the piece.

Grease marks are also common. They do not particularly damage the value of a piece of furniture, but they go deeper than ink stains. They also give an appearance of age.

Many American country pieces have burned rings where overhot pots and pans were placed on the surface. This is probably one of the reasons for refininshing pieces completely.

Although they certainly do nothing to improve the piece of furniture, deep gouges help to indicate authenticity, particularly if the gouge appears to have been made many decades ago and shows signs of having been polished again and again so that the original cleavage is well rounded. In time the gouge itself takes on the patina of age. Of course, a deep gouge looks better on a country cabinet than on a Louis XV *bombé* commode!

Two other types of surface damages are important: artificial wormholes and "banging."

The subject of wormholes has been one of bitter debate. The debaters align themselves into one school that says certain methods are used to produce wormholes and those who say it is impossible to use such methods. The first of these methods is firing a shotgun at the piece. This method has been described as absolutely impossible by "expert" after "expert." Yet *Life* magazine published a photograph of one faker with the gun in his hand, ready to make wormholes in the fakes—fakes which he produced in great volume. The trouble is that the pellets must be picked out or they give away this form of faking to even the novice. The other objection is that the holes do not curve after entry, and real worms or beetles usually do not, if ever, bore in a straight line.

In Dijon, France, a number of years ago a farmer was hauled into court and charged with raising worms for the purpose of selling them to antique fakers. There is a school of critics who say it is impossible to produce in captivity either worms or beetles which will eat furniture as it should be eaten in order to give a look of authentic age. They are probably wrong. Too much evidence has been produced to uphold the raising of worms and beetles for the purpose of performing this valuable function!

It is often pointed out by learned students of faked antiques that one can never see the channel of the worm—only the little hole of entry or exit. Thus an open channel means that the piece of furniture was made out of wood that was cut or planed to reveal the wormholes, and so the piece must be made of old and reworked wood.

We have a piece of eighteenth century antique furniture that has a few channels on the surface. It is genuine. The explanation is that the worms bored under the paint, and when the paint wore off, the channels were revealed. This often happens to painted Italian furniture—with a gesso undercoat. Sanding will also reveal channels which are close to the surface. An expert will look for the point of entry of the worms; and in Italian furniture the feet, on authentic pieces, will show the holes of entry on the bottom and will also be slightly rotted or worn.

The drill is another method of faking wormholes, but here the critics point out that such faking can easily be detected since the drill goes in straight. The fakers answered with a flexible drill that bends as it cuts. The job of the worms is thus well simulated, but a magnifying glass in the hands of an expert will tell the difference. This type of faking will fool only the inexpert buyer.

"Banging" is also a form of surface damage. A framemaker in New York keeps a chain which she slams on the wood to make new frames look old. She in no way attempts to fool anyone. It just looks better to have a worn-looking frame on an old picture. She also paints in a discolored paint to make the frame go with the picture. But banging with one implement or another is also used to age fakes. Over a period of years all furniture gets banged around. It does not hang on the wall away from wear as a painting does. It is moved; it is banged into other furniture; it is kicked. Some means must be devised by fakers to simulate this aging.

Another thing can be done in the category of banging. Chairs are often moved by holding the top rail of the back and dragging them on their back legs, which tends to round off the outside of the back feet. This rounding process can be performed artificially. The top rail must also have some finish rubbed off by the many hands that have pulled the chair around for centuries. One "chair manufacturer" in Venice proudly pointed to his technique of simulating this wearing process by thinning the finish on the chair top rail.

Old Boards

In the 1920's early American farm and country furniture was the rage. After the close of World War II, such primitive American furniture again came back in fashion. The number of spurious pieces of this furniture increased, too, in response to greater demand and higher prices. One characteristic of a number of these fake pieces is many knots. To a number of buyers, knots mean authentic rusticity. But anyone buying a piece of wood, even to repair the roof of a garage, avoids wood with knots, particularly the kind of large knot which falls out after the piece is nailed securely in place. But these "early American pieces" are often filled with the type knots that would fall out as the piece dried with age. Woodworkers of the eighteenth century were vastly more concerned about the quality of the wood they used than are the mass furniture producers of today; and even more concerned than the cabinetmakers of today who are, for the most part, furniture repairers and not cabinetmakers. The early makers would never have used such knotty wood. Thus, even from across the room, one can arrive at the tentative conclusion that such pieces are not authentic.

The old makers also used wide boards. The fewer the boards the better the piece, as a general rule. Some of the later fakes have narrow boards.

The stock of all lumber yards consists of particular grades, particular widths and particular thicknesses. This is the way the wood comes to the yards from the mills, and anyone who has bought even one piece of wood from one yard is at once made aware of this standardization. The early cabinetmakers used what wood they could get. It was hand cut. The result is what one calls random widths, and in buying an old house the real estate agent will proudly point to the "random-width floors." Thicknesses, too, were not standardized as they are today, so that if all the pieces of a table, let us say, are made of wood exactly the same width and thickness, the presumption is that it is not early and not of the eighteenth century.

The surface of a piece had to be flat, but it could be flat only within the limits of hand planes. Even though the piece was finally finished with a sander, the plane marks are still visible. The finest of all surfaces had to be achieved on panels to be painted by the great artists. On our wall is a painting by the great Dutch artist Miereveld. In a certain light, every plane mark is visible on this panel.

If one places a rule on the surface of a piece of antique furniture and moves it around so that it does not run the long way with the plane marks, he will see the undulations left by the plane. If he shines a light on the rule he can easily see the places where it does not touch the surface. There are no plane marks on modern wood. One learns the feel of a hand-planed surface very quickly.

The ends of boards and the backs and bottoms of pieces of furniture are not highly finished. They do not have to display the degree of finish that the front and sides do. On these pieces, saw kerf marks can be seen. The circular saw leaves circular cuts, and this circular saw was not used in the eighteenth century. It was not widely used till 1840 in the United States. The early saw was the pit or frame saw which cut straight, and this was the saw used on antique furniture.

Legs and other members made on a lathe were turned at low speed in the eighteenth century. The power was often hand power or horse power or, in some cases, water power. But it was low power and it turned the lathe slowly. The cutting tool used at this low speed leaves certain knicks and other characteristic marks of low-speed turning that can be easily identified with the use of a high-power magnifying glass.

The very best wood used was taken from the center of logs, and the annular rings or grain of pieces cut from this place in the log are very clear and characteristic. In modern times the wood comes from any place on the log, so long as the wood holds out for the saw to do its job. The use of center wood is a test of age.

Warpage takes place in wood over a period of time. In general, the greater the length of time the greater the warpage. The warpage does not occur to any appreciable degree the long way (in the length) but it takes place laterally—in the width. There is little warpage the way the grain runs, but much across the grain. Thus a table top will shrink in one direction much more than in the other. In examining a tilt-top table which started its life round, one looks immediately to see whether it is "out of round." A rule will indicate that the diameter of the top is less across the grain than the long way (with the grain). This difference in diameter is sometimes ⅜ to ⅝ of an inch. This proves the table top to be old. But how old? An 1830 table should show such warpage just like a 1790 table. At least where there is this much warpage, however, the presumption is that the table is not a fake.

The day this chapter was written, the Parke-Bernet Galleries were offering a tilt-top table of American make which had an authentic top which met this test. The gallery pointed out, however, that the top did not go with the bottom. The two parts were mismates. Thus, if the top were proven, the bottom might still remain unproven and perhaps be of later manufacture.

This same shrinkage or warpage differential is responsible for the pulling away of the top boards of some tables from the bottom. The results look disastrous, but such an appearance sometimes helps to prove the piece.

In Windsor chairs the front legs come up through the solid seat. With time, the legs do not shrink as much as the seat gets thinner. The grain of the seat is parallel to the sitter, but the grain of the legs is vertical. Thus, the passage of time tends to leave the leg ends projecting above the flat seat, and cleaning and polishing do not wear off the wood against the grain as much as the wood with the grain. Polishing and shrinkage thus both tend to leave the legs projecting.

This shrinkage differential also appears in turned legs, and a caliper will show that one thickness of the leg is not the same as the thickness taken at right angles to the original measurement.

Aging wood and staining are also important considerations. Aging is a subject for an entire book in itself. The wood can be left out in the sun, wind and rain for months. Or it can be steamed in a kind of Turkish bath which does the job faster. Or the wood can be buried for a time. Several authorities on faking have suggested burying the wood in a manure pile to give the wood just the right patina. Ammonia applied to the wood over a period of time accomplishes something of the same thing.

In the past some bizarre methods of aging have been used. New wood was placed in smokehouses for a period of days. Or a solution of strong lye and mud was placed on the new wood. Or very strong tea or coffee was used to stain it. Or there were infusions of oak or butternut bark.

An expert looks at unvarnished areas—the color of the back of a piece, the color of the interior of the carcass and the color of the inside, back and bottom of the drawers. If a piece of wood is left in the light it tends, in most cases, to darken. The back of a piece of furniture thus tends to become very dark. At the same time, it should be noted that this part against the wall and the bottom of the drawers tend to have very prominent hand plane marks as they were not finished with the same care as the parts to be seen.

The inside of the carcass should be a lighter brown as it is subjected to less air and light. The backs of the drawers should be still lighter. And the backs of the little drawers of a slant-top desk, under the top, should be the very lightest.

An important thing about color is uniformity of the color of the back, uniformity of the interior of the carcass, and uniformity of the drawer backs. In the first place, the color should be right for the age of the piece, and one can check what the color should be by studying authentic pieces. One is thus constantly taking a "refresher course."

If the color is not uniform, it may have been tampered with and may represent the best a faker can do. Or it may mean that some of the pieces are not original. It is almost impossible to get the same color in any two pieces of a pile of old wood. But where the piece grew old together, it grew the same shade of brown together; and the less exposed to the light it was, the lighter the color.

Staining is a process that makes the wood look old. One of the easiest ways to tell new wood is to see the color. Since most wood tends to darken with age, the back or the interior of one of the drawers or a shelf should be checked. If it is the color of new wood, the presumption is that this part is a replacement. But staining takes care of this.

Areas of Surface Wear

One of the most polished parts of any antique is the table top. The surface itself wears, but one of the most obvious areas of wear is the edge. Originally the edge was fairly sharp since it was cut with a saw and then smoothed with other tools. But over the decades polishing rounded the edge. In the same way, the edge of dished-top and piecrust tables show wear and a rounding off. Here again, 125 years of wear is a considerable amount, and such wear is not readily distinguishable from 150 or 200 years of wear.

Certain chairs are made with finials at the ends of the side posts of the back. These often rise above the crest rail. They characteristically show a good deal of wear on the back. The explanation is not that the chairs were stored against the wall, but that the sitter became fatigued from sitting straight up in such chairs and leaned the chair back against the wall so as to be in a more comfortable position.

The back of the back feet also show wear which took place when the chair was pulled backward and away from the table, but there is also wear on the front of the front feet where the crest rail was held while the chair was pulled forward.

Front stretchers close to the floor were used to rest the feet. Wear showed up very quickly on these stretchers. In fact, it is not unusual to have these replaced simply because they wore out or became unsightly.

Some types of tables show great surface wear. This is true of tavern tables of early American times (1780–1830) and their English equivalents. These were used in taverns, as the name implies, to serve guests. The surface wear became great over a period of 150 years or more. The members of the frame holding the top are placed so that the grain runs perpendicular to the top (from the floor to the top). On the top of the table the grain runs the other way—horizontally. Horizontal wear is greater than vertical wear, as indicated earlier. The wear thus tends to reveal the ends of the legs which come through the table top since they wear less than the table top.

The runners under the drawers must show wear if they are in an antique piece of furniture because years of use must be on the runners. Conversely, if the runners are not worn, one can be fairly certain that the piece is not antique. As a matter of fact, it is so common for these runners to be worn out completely that it hardly hurts the value of an antique if it has replaced runners. In any event, the runners that remain on antique bureaus must be worn. This situation posed a real problem for one faker. How could he simulate years of wear? The conclusion was so simple as to be almost overlooked. How? Hire a man to open and close drawers all day long. In one day the normal opening and closing of decades was made to take place, and the antique showed the normal type of wear that would take place.

Odor of Old Wood

It is absurd to think that a person can read any book, no matter how authoritative and how detailed it may be, and go into a shop, smell a piece of furniture and be able to declare "This is an antique" or "This is not an antique." Nevertheless, if a person has been around a good deal of antique furniture, he notes the smell of certain types of antiques.

There is, of course, the opposite reason for smelling the piece of furniture—to determine whether it is a "new job." The smell of varnish indicates at least that the piece has had some varnish put on it recently. A varnish smell would of course alert us when a seller states that he just got the piece from an old house that had been vacant for ten years!

The smell test might also yield an odor of newly cut wood. Of course, the newly cut wood might only indicate that repairs had been made. On the other hand, it might mean that extensive replacements had been made and that the smeller should investigate further.

To develop an ability to determine the odor of old wood, one has to smell old wood and remember what it smells like, and this means smelling an authentic antique in a reputable dealer's establishment or in a museum.

Hard Paint

Many ancient pieces of furniture are painted. This painted furniture was made in the eighteenth century in Venice as well as in other parts of Italy. It was also made in the same general style in southern France, and was made in Paris, England and even in the United States.

One characteristic of old paint is that it is extremely hard and brittle. There is no such thing as an entirely original painted item of furniture—unless it has lost pieces from wear and chipping over the years and these have *not* been replaced. In such an event, the piece often looks so poor that it is difficult to understand how anyone is able to endure it around the house. Cutting with a knife on an inconspicuous part will reveal the age of the paint. On some pieces all the paint will come off and will have the appearance of being soft. This is *new* paint, not old. Very often there are seven or eight layers of overpaint. The later ones are the soft ones; the earlier ones have been hardened. (In the United States, milk was used as a base on early painted furniture, and this paint is just as hard as European paint.)

Antique Joints and Fastenings

The wooden dowel was extensively used in antique furniture and is characteristic of such furniture. The dowel is a wooden peg that fits into a hole in a piece of wood. It can be glued into that hole so that, theoretically, it need never be removed. Then the other end can be fitted into another piece of wood; and if the fit is tight and perhaps if glue is used the dowel holds the two pieces together indefinitely. The top rail can be held to the side rail of a chair by means of a dowel. Screws or nails can be seen from the outside, but a dowel cannot. In certain places a dowel is thus better to use than a screw, nail or other fastening device.

The presence of doweling is some indication of age. It was used in ancient times and in the eighteenth and nineteenth centuries. In fact, it is still sometimes used. But the old dowel is a characteristic dowel. It was made of hickory, oak or ash. It was not turned on a lathe in ancient times and is not perfectly round. It is oblong at times and sometimes almost a square. The old dowel has an old appearance like the surface of old furniture.

It was driven into place and held because the hole was smaller than the dowel. Glue may have been used, but not often in antiquity.

One chief characteristic of antique construction is the mortice-and-tenon joint. If a side rail and a top rail of a chair are to be joined together, the two pieces can simply be nailed or screwed together. Or a dowel can be used to run from one piece to the other. Or a slot can be cut in one piece (a mortice), and the other piece can be cut away so that there is a protruding piece (a tenon) which exactly fits into the slot (mortice). This joint is held together by a wooden pin that goes through the mortice pieces and catches the tenon in place. These pegs are visible in old furniture; they are "out of round" and have an appearance of age.

A dealer in antiques in Rye, New York, sold me a Hepplewhite chair. He explained that he had rebuilt the chair, and he assured me that his inspection of the chair when it was apart indicated that it had mortice-and-tenon joints.

The inside of the mortice should show the wear that should take place over the years when various strains were put on the joint. But new joints can be burned with acid of various kinds and rinsed out. Then the ends can be covered with glue and dust can be sprayed on the glue so that the glue holds it in place. The immediate impression is one of great age.

Still another interior inspection can yield important results in the determination of age. Chair legs must be drilled in order to receive the stretchers. Prior to the middle of the nineteenth century, the so-called pod drill was used. The bottom of the hole which was drilled with this tool was rounded. The later gimlet-point drill left a flat bottom with the walls of the hole perpendicular to the bottom.

In antique furniture the rungs of the chairs were thoroughly seasoned, while the legs were either unseasoned or seasoned very little. When the seasoned rung was put in place it did not shrink. It had already been shrunk. The leg, on the other hand, began to shrink around the rung, with the result that the joint became tighter and tighter. In old furniture, in consequence, chair rungs have a tendency to remain firmly in place.

After one makes a quick survey of how the piece looks from a stylistic point of view, he then looks more closely at it to see the patina. If the piece passes these two quick looks, he opens one of the drawers (if it is a piece that has drawers) and looks at the dovetailing. This is the eighteenth-century and early nineteenth-century way of joining interior wood together at right angles, particularly drawer joints. It is also used, particularly on American pieces, on exterior surfaces such as sides and tops of eighteenth-century slant-top desks.

A wedge-shaped edge was cut on one of the members to be joined. The other member had a piece cut out of it of the same shape. These members were fitted together (like a puzzle) and often nailed in place.

If a brief examination by opening one drawer shows recent machinemade dovetails and relatively new wood, we do not usually bother to check further, although, conceivably, the particular drawers we looked at were replacements. A good faker can, of course, make an ancient-looking dovetail. But the fact of the matter is that most fakers do not make dovetails that look authentic.

Before the middle of the eighteenth century, the dovetails were very large and very few per drawer, particularly in America. Frequently there were only one or at the most two. As time went on, the dovetails became smaller and at the same time more numerous. In the 1830's and later these dovetails began to be made by machine.

Dovetailing, however, is not the only early method of joining drawer sides and fronts. A much simpler method was also used in the early eighteenth century: overlapping one piece and then nailing it in place.

Early Moldings

Early moldings were a difficult and time-consuming ornament to produce. There were no machines to make moldings in the early years, and they had to be produced by hand planes. Of necessity, they were simple in design. These moldings were held in place by small nails, not by glue. Nothing of very complicated design was produced even by a shop with thirty or so planes.

Old Hardware

Eighteenth-century pieces of furniture used square or rectangular nails forged by hand. This type of nail was used as early as Roman times, and its use continued until the 1790's when the machinemade nail came in. This latter nail was of the same angular shape as the handmade nail, and it is still made in volume today.

It has the characteristic of holding firmly to the wood in which it is imbedded.

The hand-forged nail was made in quantities as is to be expected. The tops are frequently crudely made: The rectangle is off center and the edges crooked.

The common nail of the twentieth century is the wire nail. This is just a section of cut wire with a small head. The hand-forged nail was made until the 1790's, and the machinemade square nail of the same shape was made for the next hundred years, after which the round wire nail took over while the square one continued to be made in limited quantities. But even after 1790 hand-forged nails were still used. The cabinetmakers had supplies of them and they were a good product. A square nail can be hammered over on the end much more easily than a round nail, and for this reason the square nail has uses to which the round nail cannot be put as easily. If the nail is used in a wagon, for instance, the square variety shakes loose much more infrequently than the round one. Hand-forged nails, however, of necessity varied in length since they were a hand product. Where the ends of the square nails are bent over in a piece of furniture one sees a difference in length of the bent-over part in one nail as compared with another. This is one method of proving the use of handmade nails.

Of course, old nails can be pulled out of discarded pieces of furniture and kept for the purpose of "authenticating" new pieces. Rust in itself means little. Sulfuric or other acid can "age" a new nail of any kind in a few minutes.

The wood screw, sometimes called the screw nail, goes back centuries. It was used in the sixteenth century. The screws of antique furniture are handmade. A thread on a screw is a most difficult thing to make by hand—if the finished product is to screw into the wood and not get stuck halfway down .The threads are very uneven, as can be seen without any magnifying glass. These hand-forged screws were used in America beginning in the early part of the eighteenth century and for the next ninety years.

By its nature, the handmade screw was not the best possible item to do the job. In addition, it was complicated to make and was expensive. Once the uniform machinemade screw came in, the handmade item suddenly went out of use. Because they were expensive to buy, the cabinetmakers had only small stocks of them to be used up. This transition came about at the beginning of the nineteenth century. The new machinemade screw was, however, not quite like our modern machinemade screw. It had a blunt end like the old handmade product. The modern screw has a sharp end and can often be "started" without the use of a gimlet. The old handmade and early machinemade screws could not. The head of the old type was small and often imperfectly made, and the slot was not only shallow but often off center.

The machinemade blunt screw was made from about 1810 to 1845 after which the modern screw, sometimes called a gimlet, took over. If one wants to "antique" a new piece of furniture, he can remove the new gimlet screws and replace them with old handmade screws retrieved from old pieces of furniture, farm implements, etc. An examination of the hole into which the screw fits will show two sets of threads, however.

In early American times (up until the late eighteenth century), the village smithy made the hardware for furniture in his shop, including hinges, exterior pulls and other items.

Before the middle of the seventeenth century, the old type hinge called the strap hinge was used in America. One piece was fitted over the other (like a strap on a piece of harness was fitted over a piece of metal and then riveted in place). In the case of hinges, no rivets were required as nails were used to go through the holes and fasten the hinge to the piece of furniture. These nails were bent over to hold the hinge in place.

Toward the end of the eighteenth century, a considerable amount of ironware and brassware was imported into the United States from England, much of it turned out by machine even at this early date. In the early years of the nineteenth century, mass-produced butt hinges of this early type were made. Then the modern hinge came in. The modern hinge did not consist of two layers of metal folded together, one over the other.

One of the earliest types of hinges used in America is the interlocked cotter pin hinge. It is nothing more than two wire cotter pins hooking into each other to form a hinge. The ends are driven into the wood, but they generally do not stay too long. In America this type of hinge was used between the middle of the seventeenth century and the first quarter of the nineteenth century. This hinge was also common on Italian Renaissance furniture. All hinges on these pieces of furniture look old, and they are so primitive that real age is almost possible to determine. It can be stated with absolute finality, however, that they last a very short time when used constantly. They pull out of the wood very readily, or they sag so much that the doors will not close. The hinges have to be constantly adjusted or replaced.

Some of the most popular items on the modern hardware market are the strap hinge, the H-hinge, the HL-hinge and the butterfly hinge. These are extremely ornamental for kitchen cabinets and bars. They are closely patterned after the originals. The butterfly hinge was made before 1760. The H and HL types were made in the last half of the eighteenth century and up until about 1840. From 1730 on, the present-day style rectangular hinge was used.

An important examination which can be made in connection with hardware consists of removing the original brass (where there is original brass). The wood under the brass was not exposed to the elements and should be of a much lighter color than that of the rest of the surface which was exposed. The fakers, being for the most part a lazy lot, often finish the entire wood in one color and then apply the brasses.

The earliest brass pulls were hand made and some had crude stamped designs. Original hardware on any piece of antique furniture is a rarity today, even though old brass may have been put on an antique to make it at least antique all over. This old brass, whether original with the piece or not, has a very characteristic light color. It is pale yellow compared with ordinary brass alloys such as those used on much later brass beds. This lighter color is caused by incorporating much zinc and tin in the alloy as compared with copper.

The earliest brasses used a kind of cotter pin to hold them in place. The brasses were cast and punched with a design and the edges were filed. Later in the eighteenth century brass sheet was nicely cut and the edges scrolled.

Early bail handles were hand threaded, and these threads were much shallower and rounder than on the later machinemade items. The threads were also much more irregular. One of the things that I have been trying to get around to for years is to make a trip to Philadelphia to get a bail handle for a Philadelphia chest-on-frame of the eighteenth century that is missing a handle. A firm in the Philadelphia area makes authentic reproductions of this early brass. Of course, this brass, being made by hand, can be treated in various ways so that it looks like old brass.

Stamps and Labels

If an eighteenth-century French piece of furniture has any maker's stamp on it, no matter how minor, the value of the piece goes up materially. If the stamp is a Riesener or a Roentgen, the value goes to great heights. A few of these stamps are still in existence, however, and there is no reason why they cannot be used again on faked pieces of furniture. André Mailfert devoted his life to the production of fake antique furniture, but he never learned that the eighteenth-century French ébénistes used just one plate for stamping their names to their pieces of furniture. He used a separate stamp for each letter.

On the other hand, if the faker does not have an original stamp left over from the eighteenth century, he can secure the imprint of the stamp by using dental wax on an authentic piece of furniture. The metal casting of a stamp from this wax impression is very easy. The stamp is then heated and the metal placed on the furniture in the right place. The burned impression is then scrubbed with a wire brush, and the scrubbed place can be cleaned with ammonia to eliminate the recently burned smell.

A label is usually an excellent way to prove the authenticity of a piece of furniture, and genuine labels have proven pieces of the most prominent American makers. But a label is not hard to fake. One buys some old books dating back to the eighteenth century and tears out the unprinted pages. He thus has paper dating back to the required time. The photoengraver makes a cut of an authentic label, or even a copy of an authentic label. Then the printer mixes ink until he gets the characteristic brown of age, and hand presses on the old paper. The "label" is now treated with chemicals or is exposed to the sun for a few months, and it is as authentic as one could wish.

Classification of Fakes

Fakes range all the way from mild suggestions that the piece of furniture is much finer than it really is to the elaborate manufacture of items—manufacture which may consume months. This is a classification of fakes from the simplest to the most complex:

1. *Simple Misrepresentation.* The most common form of fake is to represent the furniture as being something that it is not. Louis-Philippe furniture, which was manufactured in France during the era of Queen Victoria, is sometimes represented as being Louis XV furniture, produced about one hundred years earlier. A Louis-Philippe love seat might sell for $500 and a Louis XV love seat for $5,000. We have an example of the former. It was valued several years ago by a leading firm of auctioneers as "Louis XV"—at $2,500. This was an honest mistake. With dishonesty present, it would not be hard to pass off the sofa as genuine Louis XV.

Venetian furniture was produced in the eighteenth as well as in the nineteenth century. Very often a nineteenth-century piece is passed off as an eighteenth-century one, again sometimes unknowingly. But the difference in value between an eighteenth-century Venetian piece and a nineteenth-century one is vast. At the turn of the twentieth century, a large production operation was in existence in Venice to turn out furniture in the old style. They now have 60-plus years more age on them!

This type of fake is really a misnomer. The piece itself may be all right. It is what is said about it, how it is represented, that makes it a fake. This type of hoax (rather than fake) is very prevalent.

2. *Restored Piece.* When a piece of furniture becomes aged it often becomes infirm, and it is standard practice to restore it. If the restoration is made for the purpose of putting it back into condition and not for the purpose of deceiving anyone, there is no faking involved. But if it is restored to deceive, or if the dealer knows of the extensive restoration and fails to so notify the prospective purchaser, then there is a misrepresentation, and the piece of furniture is a form of fake.

Take Venetian furniture, for example. Much of it has had the paint worn off over the past two hundred years. This is to be expected. It is also to be expected that it is restored. Otherwise it will look too "moth eaten" for anyone's home. But if the restoration is, say, at least 50 percent of the original paint, if the paint is made to blend in with the original, if the dealer knows of this restoration and fails to so notify the prospective customer, then there is a misrepresentation and the piece can be labeled as partially fake.

3. *"Pieced-in Piece."* We have in our home an Italian Renaissance *cassone*. It is small and beautifully carved. The only trouble is that the sides are replaced. The dealer did not so inform us depsite the fact that he had been dealing in Italian furniture for fifty years and knew Italian pieces well. We felt we knew them too, and we paid him the price of a "semi-fake." Perhaps the repair was for the purpose of making the piece useful. Perhaps it was for the purpose of faking. Such a piece can be a fake depending on the intent of the dealer or the remaker.

4. *Reconstruction.* This is a major replacement. We know of a Venetian desk that is absolutely genuine, and most of the paint is original. It is a very rare type of slant-top desk of the early eighteenth century with angular corners and covered with *chinoiserie*. The only trouble is that the slant-top part with the pigeon holes is a much later replacement. Originally there was probably a cabinet on the top. This was evidently replaced by

the later slant top. The piece has very little value as an antique. It is not really a slant top at all. As it was originally it would be worth perhaps $25,000. Now it is worth less than $1,000. The dealer represented the slant top as being an original eighteenth-century Venetian slant top—which it is not.

5. *Mismarriage.* A dealer in Connecticut has a Queen Anne lowboy with a replacement top. In fact, it was originally a highboy, but the top part was removed and a flat top put on. Maybe the flat top is old. But the piece has next to zero value as an antique.

Wallace Nutting implied that the great highboy sold in 1929 was a mismarriage. Had this been common knowledge at the auction when it was sold, it is hard to believe that a price in five figures would have been achieved; and this piece brought in the middle five-figure range.

What was the motive in marrying these two parts—a top that was not made to go with the bottom? Maybe the original top or bottom was lost and, after much searching, this was the best that could be done to salvage the part that was left. On the other hand, no mention in the catalogue was made of the mismarriage. Maybe it was forgotten. Or maybe it was "conveniently" forgotten, in which case the piece was a fake.

6. *Transformation.* Since French furniture of the eighteenth century is generally the most expensive furniture on the market today, it should be gone over most thoroughly in order to determine its authenticity and the degree of originality. Where the market is high, there is much room for "improvement."

One of the types of nonoriginality for which to examine the French piece of furniture is the "transformation." A chair is sometimes cut in two through the middle—from top to bottom. The front and back seat rails and the back rails are extended, and what started out as a chair ends up as a sofa, a piece of furniture very much bigger and more valuable. Essentially, the things that prove an American piece of furniture also prove a French piece, and one should look for the same kind of piecings and new wood.

Another transformation is the conversion of a large chair into a smaller and more useful one. In the case of Louis XVI chairs, the designs are continuous, and it is easy to reduce the scale of straight line elements of construction. Louis XV pieces are curved and the designs are noncontinuous and thus not easily made to flow evenly after the operation has been performed. To remake a large curved piece of furniture with noncontinuous curves in the structural elements and continuous designs requires artistry of a high order, and these fakes must bring a high price to cover labor involved in turning them out.

A cane-back chair is not usually as valuable as an upholstered-back chair. A third type of transformation is to turn the former into the latter, of course concealing the cane holes.

7. *Upgraded Piece.* This is almost always an outright form of faking. The tilt-top tables of the eighteenth century are very nice things to have, but the dished-top tables and piecrust tables of the same era are vastly to be preferred and vastly more valuable. It is quite a job to cut in the top and

shape the rim, and it requires a real craftsman to do this. But the results are worth the time in increased value. Sometimes the pedestal is plain. Carving will make it far more attractive and far more valuable.

The front of a highboy or chest-on-frame is usually plain. If it were carved it would be very much more attractive and more valuable. Shells are particularly wanted, and we saw in a large shop in Connecticut some beautiful shells carved on the front of a chest-on-chest that obviously did not have shells originally. As an antique, such an item has almost no value.

Some upgrading is most difficult to detect. The most valuable Chippendale chair is the highly decorated one, and some of the most valuable decoration is the piercing of the back splat. The chair with an unpierced splat is the least valuable. So we start out with piercing with a saw. But the value depends on something *which is not there*, rather than on something which is added. The *holes* give the piece value. Therefore, one must look carefully at the edges of the piercing to see if he can possibly detect later tooling. One must be more than an amateur to perform this feat of authentication.

8. *Old Wood Piece.*   The most common type of out-and-out fake that is produced today is the piece made of old wood. One of the first things an expert or connoisseur looks at in order to determine the authenticity of an antique is the age of the wood. It is relatively easy to get old wood and proceed to make furniture out of it. It then passes the "old wood" test of an inexperienced buyer.

Italy is full of makers of furniture using old wood. Strangely enough, the vast majority of the "old wood" cabinetmakers do not attempt to fool buyers. The Naples cabinetmakers who have shops in their sales places do not try to hide what they are doing. They offer a genuine antique table for $250, but point out that the prospective buyer can secure as good a table made out of old wood for $50.

These copies made of "old wood" are highly respectable. Some of the best department stores and importers in New York sell them; and they sell them for what they are—reproductions made out of old wood. The price is that of a good reproduction and not of an authentic period piece. No one is fooled.

It is, of course, obvious that pieces have been made of old wood that have been used by unscrupulous persons to fool the public into believing that they are buying antiques. It is also reasonable to believe that the shop owners know that they are making pieces that will shortly be sold as antiques. Perhaps they are accessories before the fact in that they are assisting in the perpetration of fraud. If they are, this status does not seem to particularly worry them.

9. *Antiquized New Piece.*   This is probably the most fake of all the types of fakes. It is a thoroughgoing job from beginning to end and is made for no other purpose than to fool the buyer. Over the years, the perpetrators of this type of fraud have been extremely able, and the products of their art have sometimes rivaled the originals made in the eighteenth century.

To this end, every method described in this chapter has been used— the making of artificial wormholes, or the keeping of "trained worms" in

infected wood who will attack the new "antique" when given the opportunity; and the banging, inking, staining, varnishing, vaporizing, burying,
rubbing, gashing, burning, darkening, bleaching, and using of old labels
and every other trick in the book, plus a few others which we shall probably never know.

Extent of Fakes on the Market

The job of determining what is a fake and what is a genuine antique can usually be bypassed. One determines whether the item is *almost certainly* an antique,
provided that is what he is out to buy. Whatever other category the piece may fall
into, aside from genuine antique, he need not determine. It is sufficient that a piece
under consideration is 99 percent antique. One can almost never be 100 percent
certain, so 99 percent certainly will have to be enough. Now all the other pieces of
furniture besides the 99 percent antique can be lumped together—(1) genuine
reproductions made recently, (2) old reproductions including Centennial pieces,
(3) pieces made just a little later than the period wanted but made with no attempt
to fool anyone, (4) true pieces misrepresented as to era or place of origin, (5)
overrestored pieces and (6) fakes.

A few pessimistic quotes will be used to close this chapter. They are pessimistic
in that they may not be quite true, but they serve to warn anyone who is so foolish
as to think fakes in large quantity are not on today's antique market.

Sepp Schuller in his book *Forgers, Dealers, Experts* (New York: G. P. Putnam's
Sons, 1960, originally published in German by Franz Ehrenwirth Verlag, Munich,
Germany, 1959) says:

> In 1957 a huge fraudulent organization, dealing in "antique" wood-
> carvings and furniture, was unmasked in France. The chairman of the
> Paris art dealers' syndicate announced that information obtained by him-
> self and the police proved that over 90 per cent of all "antique" furniture
> sold in the last fifty years had been forged. A ring of swindlers was dis-
> covered, belonging to a concern with many ramifications, which supplied
> almost the whole world with spurious works of art. The biggest markets
> were stated to be America, Holland, Belgium and southern and western
> Germany.

The second quote is from an anonymous dealer and faker who told his story
in the June 1, 1929 issue of *The Saturday Evening Post* under the title of "Art
and Artful Art." He says:

> In the days when the all-desired Louis Quatorze and Louis Quinze things
> were made, France was, after all, a comparatively small country. The
> masses were very poor, the middle class little better off, and wealth con-
> centrated into the hands of a limited number of nobles. It happens that the
> qualities which specially distinguish the furniture of these times were elabo-
> rateness and expensiveness. Consequently, there were not a great many
> people in France who could afford such luxuries, and the export business

was then still limited. Again, in the rack and ruin of one hundred and fifty to two hundred and fifty years, much of the stuff then made must have perished. Ten per cent would probably be a very high estimate for the survivals. If we now deduct the old pieces which have been taken over by French and other European museums, placed permanently in the palaces and reliquaries of the French government, held by old families in their many châteaux and city houses or sold to collectors and social pretenders before the Americans came on the scene, we must conclude that not a great deal of genuine fine stuff can have been on the market at any time within fifty years or so.

There are several unmistakable indications that the rapid rise in antique prices in the 1960's is at last spawning a new crop of fakers and fake-passers. In the fall of 1966 an antique dealer in the Old Bond Street section of London offered us an eighteenth-century butler's tray. She was quick to point out that it was a genuine antique and stated: "London is flooded with copies of these. I could have bought ten."

In response to a questionnaire sent out by the author in 1966 to secure information from antique dealers, Mr. Seiburn White of Seiburn White Antiques, of Murray, Kentucky, volunteered an entire essay which was so valuable that permission was secured to print it in its entirety:

> In this affluent society there are many new-rich. These people hunger for the elegancies they have never known. The fleece is thick and rich, and there are those who are amply prepared and equipped to take it. Witness that there is a quantity of so-called antique furniture in the United States today sufficient to fill every house and cottage in the British Isles thrice over—and it is still coming in by the ship-load. Much of this furniture has merit as well-constructed hand-crafted reproductions, but it should not be considered in the same breath with antique furniture. It is regrettable that this fake furniture is appearing in the advertisements in our trade publications. Such was hardly the case even ten years ago, and certainly twenty years past.
>
> More than thirty years ago both Wallace Nutting and Edgar G. Miller stated in their books that more than 90 percent of the English furniture being imported at that time was faked. Then and now this faked antique furniture had or has no enduring value.
>
> Any book dealing with the investment value of antique furniture should not overlook the flood of fakes being fostered off on a gullible naive new-rich U.S. public.

A corner of the Duncan Phyfe room. *Courtesy of the Museum of the City of New York.*

CHAPTER THIRTY

Are Discoveries Possible

I T IS PROBABLY THE DREAM OF EVERY antique collector to walk into a secondhand furniture store and there, in the corner, find a dressing table for $50 which turns out to be the one used by Marie Antoinette at Versailles Palace. Or perhaps in a barn in Virginia he can pick up for a song what turns out to be George Washington's desk which .was originally in Mount Vernon. And any collector of American antiques would probably like to find a block-front desk, in someone's attic, that the owner insists on selling for $250.

Discoveries in antique furniture are all but impossible, and if not quite "all but impossible," then rare indeed. When we are talking about discoveries we are not talking about picking up at auction a genuine Sheraton commode, of the period and completely restored, for $50. This we did in 1964. It was just a wonderful buy, but it was quite clear exactly what the item was—to the people attending the auction and to the auctioneer. There just happened to be no one at the auction that day who wanted the piece, and we were lucky.

When we talk about discoveries in the field of antique furniture we have to talk about great works in this field.

In the late 1960's the most treasured works of art in antique furniture are the pieces of Louis XV and Louis XVI. These often sell in the high five figures and a few go into six figures, like the $176,000 David Roentgen commode.

Within this French school we are concerned with the works of the greatest *ébénistes and menuisiers*, the pieces that are of definite authorship, preferably signed. Thus the scope of discoveries is relatively limited.

If we had to list the great French furnituremakers of the eighteenth century in order of importance, the most important being at the head of the list, then the list might be the following. Of course, such a list is to a considerable extent arbitrary:

Bernard van Riesen Burgh II
Jean-Henri Riesener
Jean-François Oeben
David Roentgen
Jacques Dubois
Guillaume Beneman
Roger Vandercruse—(Lacroix)

Adam Weisweiler
Jean-François Leleu
Georges Jacob
Jean-Baptiste Sené
Louis Delanois

The first of the group are the *ébénistes* (cabinetmakers) and the last three are *menuisiers* (primarily chairmakers).

In May 1965 the Lubin Galleries in New York held a sale of the contents of a Waltham, Massachusetts, house. At this sale a mellow brown *bombé* commode with a marble top was offered for sale. It had two drawers and fine bronze fittings. A New York City dealer thought the piece looked very good and was determined to use a buying technique which he thought would secure the piece as well as a few others for him. Alongside the piece in his auction catalogue he put "$30,000," and he placed similar high figures alongside other pieces in which he was interested. He then made a point of showing his "proposed top bids" to another dealer who, he felt, would spread the word around among other dealers—which he did. This technique was designed to scare off the other dealers and make them give up before they even started to bid.

Then, in order to back up this technique, he used another novel technique at the sale itself. At around $600 to $700 most of the bidders dropped out, some because they felt the piece was worth no more, others because they did not have any more money. From $700 our particular dealer jumped to $1,000. The next bid was $1,100, whereup our dealer jumped to $2,000. The next bid was $2,100, and our dealer countered with $3,000. At this point all other bidders were frightened off, and our dealer secured the piece for $3,000.

Three thousand dollars is no trifling sum of money, except that the commode was made and stamped by Oeben! The true value was well into five figures.

At the same sale our dealer bid on an inlaid table, the inlay being mother-of-pearl and the table being of beautiful design and workmanship. He got the table for $850. It turned out to be a Bernard van Riesen Burgh (BVRB) signed piece!

He resold both commode and table to a large collector the same day, which was lucky for our dealer in view of the fact that he did not have sufficient funds in the bank to cover his purchases at the auction. The commode and table are now in a museum.

In December 1963 a lady who resided on East 39th Street in New York came into the store of a dealer and inquired about a French *armoire* which the dealer had for sale. In the course of the conversation with her, it became known to the dealer that this lady had a *Régence* commode and a fall-front desk which she said were eighteenth-century French and which she would consider selling. He went to her home and examined the desk. It appeared to be a fine piece. It had a fall front and drawers below the front. It was inlaid with squares and had fine ormolu ornamentation. The top was original and of gray marble.

The price agreed upon was $250. As soon as the dealer got back to his shop with the piece he called another dealer, a larger one but still not a leading dealer in any sense of the word. This dealer, without examining the desk, offered $1,500 for it on the phone. Just then, however, a large collector came into the shop, caught the drift of the conversation and offered $1,800, which was accepted.

The desk was signed "Beneman."

Two months later this same dealer went to visit the apartment of a lady on Central Park South who said she had a table for sale. It turned out to be an *escritoire*, a lady's writing desk. However, the hinges had come off the lid, the finish was bad, and the bronze needed regilding. The lady said she wanted $1,000, but our dealer was not quite ready to buy. He therefore put a deposit of $50 on the piece and took the evening to think it over. He thought correctly, for the next day he came by the lady's apartment, paid the $950 balance and took the *escritoire* with him.

As soon as he got back to his shop, he called a collector who was an old customer of his and offered him the desk. The dealer stated to the customer that the desk had cost him $2,000, instead of the $1,000 that it had really cost. But it was obvious to both dealer and collector that the piece was a gem. The dealer then proposed to sell the collector the desk for the amount of cash he said he had in it— $2,000—but, in addition, he wanted a small sketch by Renoir that the collector had in his office. The collector agreed and the sale was consummated.

However, before the desk was actually delivered, a large uptown dealer saw it and offered $4,300 for it. Still another uptown dealer raised the offer to $6,000.

Why such offers? The *escritoire* was a signed Riesener.

There are many stories about finds, but it is difficult to verify them. In the case of these pieces, however, it was possible actually to examine the checks paid for the items, and better still to talk with the seller. When the auction house sells an item, it is next to impossible to find out where it came from; and even if it is possible to locate the former owner, it is most difficult to question him about where the piece came from originally.

In the case of the Beneman desk and the Riesener *escritoire*, the former owner gave the background on each piece. Each was bought in Paris in the early 1930's in the Rue Faubourg St. Honoré. They were bought for a sum of money in excess of the price the final buyer paid in the middle 1960's. When the lady who owned them gave up her home in Paris and moved to New York, she had to store the pieces where they gradually "ate themselves up" in storage charges. Rather than have the storage fees go on, the lady chose to sell, and did very little shopping around among dealers before she disposed of them.

All of the items used in these tales now reside in museums.

Let us turn to a collecting story by my wife and myself. In the summer of 1964 we dropped into a shop in lower New York. We very quickly spotted a set of some of the most unusual antiques we had ever seen. Antique knife boxes are usually of the slant-top type, and these boxes are often found in pairs. The rare type is the urn-shaped knife box where the top raises up to reveal holes in the interior to hold knives, forks and sometimes spoons. Once in a while an urn-shaped knife box of the eighteenth century appears on the market, and sometimes a pair. The best dealers in English and American furniture sometimes have such pairs. But these were very extraordinary in that there was a third and smaller box to go along with the pair. This was for spoons. The boxes were of medium height—24 inches for the large pair and 23 inches for the smaller matching box. They were of dark wood with inlaid bands running lengthwise in lighter wood. They also had inlaid rosettes of light wood along the top rim under the lid.

After a close examination we made up our minds that the set was definitely of the eighteenth century. Just as we were about to talk price, we noticed a label inside one of the covers: "Art Treasures Exhibition of 1928, No. 129." This label, of course, could have been an attempt at faking, and there might have been no Art Treasures Exhibition of 1928. We asked the dealer about the label, but it was apparently new to him—or so he made us believe. At the price asked, however, no one would have hesitated to buy, even though the knife boxes were reproductions— $150 for the pair. On further thought, the dealer said he would take an additional $20 for the small knife box, or $170 in all. We made out our check in a hurry and took the boxes away with us.

Then started a period of research. We looked in *The New York Times Index* for the "Art Treasures Exhibition of 1928." We studied the *Readers' Guide to Periodical Literature* and the *Industrial Arts Index*, but no "Art Treasures Exhibition of 1928." A careful review of *Antiques* magazine also revealed no such exhibition.

We were about to give up when we thought of the Metropolitan Museum of Art's Card Index. Sure enough, an Art Treasures Exhibition of 1928 was held under the auspices of the British Antique Dealers' Association in London in 1928; and the Library had a catalogue of the exhibition, an exhibition which included the finest pieces offered by the leading British dealers.

Item No. 129 was "Three Adam knife boxes, circa 1775" placed on exhibit by M. Harris who, at the time, was one of the two leading London dealers. The value of this set of knife boxes? At least $2,000!

We did very well on the purchase of these knife boxes. On the other hand, the dealer, James LePere did very well too, as we found out over a year later. He and his wife, Jean, called on us and we showed him the knife boxes displayed in our dining room. He then told us the rest of the story. "Now I'll tell you where I bought those knife boxes that you are so proud of," he said. "The garbage man came by and offered them to us a day or two before you came in. We bought them for $40!"

CHAPTER THIRTY-ONE

A Look to the Future

I N THE LATE 1960's THERE were strong elements of boom in the antique market. There was not a full-scale boom, but one had started. By a boom, we mean the kind that took place in the late 1920's. The most interesting thing about the immense demand for antiques in the 1920's is that it had such a broad base. It was by no means confined to the rich, but took in a very large group in the upper middle class.

There was another interesting element present. Homeowners and housewives often became "occasional" dealers. While they could hardly be classed even as part-time dealers, they did buy *and sell* antiques for a profit. This owner-dealer development has not taken place in the current rise in the antique market, and it may not take place.

The Supply of Antiques

The analysis of future prices of antiques is like the analysis of future prices of any other item. We look at the prospect for supply and we look at probable demand, and the interaction of the two results in a price forecast. Objects of art are no exception to economic laws.

As a general thesis, the supply of antiques is definitely fixed. There is a certain number of antiques in existence and more legitimate ones cannot be made, so that if demand increases with the supply fixed, the price should reasonably be expected to rise. We can follow through with this logic and show that in a given number of years all the antiques of this fixed supply will be exhausted and there will be no more antique market, or that there will be an infinitely high price for the few antiques that do come onto the market.

This was the thinking in the 1920's, and it was widely forecast that shortly there would be no more antiques for sale. This was not how things worked out, however. In the 1930's the demand for antiques fell off, although not so rapidly as the demand for stocks and bonds. And there were plenty of antiques still on the market to satisfy the diminished demand. Prices dropped and had great difficulty in recovering.

While it is true that the supply of antiques is absolutely limited, the supply *on the market at any given time* is the supply factor that counts in determining price. The most important single element in determining the supply on the market is the estates offered for sale, sometimes privately but for the most part at auction. It is difficult to forecast deaths and the distribution of the antique estates of those deceased. In some years there are many estate distributions and in some years very few. If there are many, there is a tendency for antique prices to be lower than in those years when few estates are put on the market.

There will undoubtedly be more selling of antiques in order to realize a profit with the rise in the market. In paintings, some collectors sell individual items or whole collections in order to realize profits and also to rotate collections. The owners' tastes change and selling refines their collections. This type of selling is not practiced much in the field of antiques, although it is by no means uncommon.

There is some actual disappearance of the supply into museums. The very best items will go into museums as they have done in the past. This disappearance never will be as great, however, as it is in paintings. Paintings do not take up much space in museums and antiques do. And most museums are perennially short of space. Then, too, there is a greater demand on the part of the museum's public to see paintings than to see pieces of furniture. The public has been educated to Old Masters far more than to antiques.

But to go back to the gloomy forecast of the 1920's that shortly antiques would be off the market: To a degree this forecast has already been fulfilled. There are probably no estates left that contain antique furniture of the quality of the Flayderman Collection and the Reifsynder Collection. If there are no such estates left, there will be no such estates to come onto the market. As for the specific antiques from these two great estates, they are now dispersed over a very wide area, and many of the items are in museums. One or two items from these original great collections will appear from time to time, but no such aggregation.

Certainly excellent individual items can and will appear. In private hands is a Derby chair of the set that is in the Metropolitan Museum of Art, and perhaps more than one. There is no more celebrated American chair than this. There was on the market a Chippendale tassel-back chair of the set in the Van Rensselaer Room of the Metropolitan Museum. But these are individual items, not sets and not collections.

The tax laws are set up to promote contributions to museums, churches and educational institutions. A fair present valuation is allowed as a deduction against income before the tax is determined. If a person with an income of $100,000 donates an antique worth $30,000, he can deduct this $30,000 from his income before determining his tax. (This 30 percent is the maximum he can deduct, so that even if the fair present value of the donation is $40,000, he can only deduct 30 percent of his income.) This law is extremely effective in securing donations for educational and charitable institutions, and it also preserves for posterity those cultural objects which should be made available to the public for all time.

A few remarkable collections are still in private hands and may one day be placed on the market or in public institutions. The Getty Collection of furniture, particularly the furniture of the Louis', is superb, as is the Costantino Collection. So is the Untermeyer Collection of English furniture, and the Charles B. Wrightsman Collection of French furniture.

The Demand for Antiques

The most important single element in the demand for antiques is economic prosperity. As prosperity continues, free spendable income increases (that part of income which is not required for the necessities of living). It increases disproportionately to income. The essentials of living—food, clothing, lodging and medical care—represent an ever smaller *proportion* of income as that income increases, and there is more money left over for cars, trips, vacations, the theater, eating out, etc. In this category of nonnecessities are antiques. They come quite far down the line, and for most people a Cadillac comes ahead of them. But after the Cadillac and other similar items like a fine home have been purchased, antiques become more and more attractive.

A concomitant of economic prosperity is a rising stock market and capital gains from selling securities as well as from selling other things that have appreciated in value, such as real estate and privately owned companies that were started by their owners with relatively little investment. This selling out of businesses or stocks in businesses has been responsible for some very high bids on art objects.

The factor of greatest importance in the demand for antiques, aside from the wherewithal to buy which comes with prosperity, is the Age of Elegance. This is just about upon us, and advertisements indicate clearly that unless we have a background of antiques in our homes and/or a collection of paintings, we have not "arrived."

The Age of Elegance is not simply an age of antiques. It is an age of overall elegance. It is expressed in top quality automobiles; it is expressed in the ownership of large and expensive houses, with a good deal of land; it is expressed in yachts. The age of the large house and the age of yachts is back after a long absence since the 1920's. The proper furniture to go in the finest houses and to go along with yachts is antique furniture. It is not only well designed, well made and beautiful, but it represents the outlay of a great deal of money, and this is a most important consideration to those who wish to partake of the Age of Elegance.

Quite aside from the factors of free spendable income and the return to the Age of Elegance, antiques are a prime investment. In the stock market, unfortunately, many stocks run counter to the rising trend, and as the overall market hits new all-time highs, some stocks are hitting new lows for the year. Then, periodically, the whole stock market collapses. The situation in the antique market is far different. Antiques rarely go down in price today. While tastes change, and over a long period of time certain types of antiques go out of fashion—and will go out of fashion in the future—tastes do not change enough in the short run to affect the market; and tastes are now changing *to* antiques.

It is entirely possible to demonstrate this overall rising market by buying slowly and wisely, holding the antiques a relatively short period of time, such as a year or two, and then selling. I did this with a group of antiques to prove out the theory.

It proved out with a holding period of one year in the case of my purchases and sales. I better than doubled my investment.

Most people can afford only "low-end" antiques—the pieces other than prime. But these are the antiques which have risen the most in the past year or two. The noncollector has been coming into the market more and more to make his home a place of elegance. And he enters the market, at least at first, with modest investments. This new demand which was not expressed earlier has had a disproportionate effect on the so-called cheap antiques, and these have risen greatly in value in recent years.

There is another investment element in antiques which must not be overlooked. This is "the inflation hedge." It is certainly a key element in the thinking of the more sophisticated and wealthy investors, and it is becoming more and more important to the average person with money to invest. In certain countries of Europe where inflation takes place so fast as to be obvious to everyone, there is a mad scramble for inflation hedges. This fear has driven up the price of painted Italian furniture about 1,000 percent in six years. That means that an item costing $50 six years ago now costs $500. This is about the price pattern of the lower grade painted Italian commodes.

Although some economists state that a rising price level is not necessarily a bad thing, it is much better to have one's funds in something like antiques which are rising more rapidly than the price level rather than in cash which diminishes in value with the rising price level.

It should be reemphasized that the price of antiques is extremely dependent on a continuation of the economic boom that we have at the present time. A slight decline in business activity such as we experienced in 1958 will not necessarily pull down the antique market. A long one most certainly will. The stock break of 1962 did not have much effect on antique prices. Another year of such a decline and the market for antiques would have very severely felt the decline. In 1962 business activity did not decline. An economic decline like that of 1958 *plus* a stock market decline like that of 1952, if they occurred together, would have forced the antique market almost to a standstill.

We must, however, divide the antique market into two parts; and we have already indicated this dichotomy exists and will exist so long as we are in the rebirth of the Age of Elegance. The expensive pieces, the antiques of museum quality or near museum quality, will rise in a gradual and orderly manner. They are bought by very knowledgeable buyers (those who know both quality and values). These buyers want the best; they will wait for the best, and they will pay high market prices for the quality they are buying.

The other division of antiques is those for the home, to be considered articles of furniture or objects of art which may be used occasionally if they are not used too vigorously. These are the antiques at the lower end of the price scale. In the immediate past they have been the ones which have risen by the greater percentage. The Linsky commode which sold within the past few years at $176,000 would not very easily bring $352,000 if sold today. But an eighteenth-century American slant-top desk which sold for $400 two years ago may very likely bring $800 today. A doubling of prices at the lower end of the antiques price scale is much easier than a doubling in the higher prices where many more dollars are involved. New buyers of antiques come in at the low end and thus increase demand for this type of antique.

If, in the next two years, the price of the cheaper antiques increases 50 percent, a corresponding increase in the more expensive antiques might be 25 percent. The price *increase* in the cheaper antiques might reasonably be expected to be twice that of the more expensive ones.

Forecast by Types of Antiques

Antiques that are highest priced and highest in fashion in the middle 1960's are French pieces of the period of Louis XV and Louis XVI. Louis XV is the more popular style and the higher priced. Many pairs of Louis XV chairs sell in the five-figure range.

There is no indication whatever that there will be any weakening of demand or prices for the furniture of the Louis' in the absence of a severe stock market break and/or a serious economic decline. Prices will continue to rise and will probably rise faster than the stock market rises.

It is expected that there will be an increase in the demand for Louis XVI furniture *in relation to Louis XV*. In Paris, prices of Louis XVI chairs are low in comparison with Louis XV, and the larger sets of side chairs, although certainly much higher in price than five years ago, cannot help but increase even more. The oval-back chairs in sets of ten or twelve were not popular a few years ago. These will gain enormously in price and popularity. There is no intrinsic reason for the price of such chairs to be under the square backs; and in other types of furniture, the larger the set the greater the price of each piece. This will certainly be the situation in regard to Louis XVI chairs in the future.

The important point in the relationship between Louis XV and Louis XVI is that there is no intrinsic difference in beauty of construction. The Louis XVI *ébénistes* were every bit as good as the Louis XV group. The larger, more flowing and highly ornamented Louis XV pieces tend to be a little too flamboyant looking. The Louis XVI items are slightly more restrained and consequently easier to live with. These facts will all be in favor of the equalization of prices between the two types of furniture.

Painted Italian furniture, of which Venetian is in the greatest demand, has been spotty in its market price. In Italy the demand is huge and price is on a par with the furniture of the Louis'. In America there is much less of such furniture. It is not so well known in America and is consequently in much less demand. Then, too, almost every week New York is combed by Italian dealers buying for shipment back to Italy. This procedure tends to keep such furniture off the market and make it unkown here. There is also little shipment of the very best Italian painted furniture from Italy to the United States. It can be sold too easily in Italy. When shipping is added to the price along with the dealer markup in America, the price here becomes too high for the furniture to find a ready market.

The next important category is eighteenth-century American furniture. In the late 1960's a good piece of American furniture brings a huge price, no matter how humble the shop of the dealer selling it. A very large roadside furniture emporium in Connecticut was offering a Philadelphia lowboy, maker unknown, but a good piece, for $5,500. A fine small French piece would hardly bring more. The future price pattern of fine American furniture will probably be much the same as the pattern of fine French furniture. The market for American furniture will for the most part, of course, be in the United States.

Behind fine American furniture in popularity will come fine English furniture. The American market is interested in American furniture rather than English, and this demand in this country has a limited supply to meet it. For that reason American prices tend to be disproportionately higher than for comparable English pieces.

The very finest English pieces like the Chippendale Harewood House desk will bring high prices that will not be surpassed by the prices of American furniture, but grade for grade English will be behind American furniture. If we move downward from masterpieces like the Harewood House desk to fine English furniture that is not of strictly museum quality, we get to particularly fine gilt Adam and Hepplewhite furniture, especially chairs made in the Louis XVI style.

The finest furniture of the Golden Age of the Eighteenth Century must include Sheraton. The furniture of this designer is in no way inferior to the furniture of any other Englishman or American. Yet it is the least expensive at the present time of all of the great furniture of the eighteenth century. A modest set of English eighteenth-century Sheraton chairs can be bought for $100 a chair, and the best can often be bought for under $500 a chair. American Sheraton chairs can be bought for under $500 a chair. Comparable quality American Chippendale chairs would cost at least $2,000 each—four times as much. Sheraton furniture is available and at reasonable prices.

One category of furniture that is certain to rise in the future—and substantially— is Duncan Phyfe. This price rise forecast is made for several reasons. In the first place, the furniture is of excellent design and construction. It is not over-plentiful in the market. It is uniquely American and there is the fact that dealers are salting this furniture away, buying when they can. They buy Phyfe furniture not only for immediate resale, but to put away for a future price rise. This they can do because the furniture does not represent too great a cash investment to hold for a period of years.

The future of Victorian furniture is problematical. It has been problematical ever since Victorian furniture first appeared. This is not an unqualifiedly bad type of furniture. On the other hand, it has not managed to get very many plaudits over the years. From time to time a forecast is made that "now Victorian is going to be in demand." But to date nothing like a large demand has arisen, nothing like a demand which would raise prices of Victorian furniture above the prices of any secondhand furniture of some quality. One of the leading home magazines indicated that the rapidly increasing prices of ancient houses (sixteenth through eighteenth centuries) mean that the prices of Victorian houses were rising simply because the earlier ones were no longer available at reasonable prices. There may be a trend to Victorian houses, but there is not a strong trend to Victorian furniture.

If we point to *percentages* we can show that Victorian is going up as rapidly as any of the leading antique categories, Louis XV included. But it has gone from $25 an item last year to say $40 this year. The rise is certainly real but the sums are trifling, and the furniture is still not considered to be of much importance as antiques.

There are indications that the situation may not always be so. The large galleries are now not only taking the better Victorian furniture, but they are trying to promote it through illustations in the sales catalogues. The higher priced furniture in the next few years, like J. H. Belter furniture, should increase in price, perhaps in the neighborhood of 25 percent, while the cheapest items may well go from $40 to $80—still no great price and certainly not prices to place Victoriana in the category of important antiques.

The Shift of Interest to Later Styles

In the late 1960's the choicest and most wanted furniture is the French furniture of Louis XV and Louis XVI. American Chippendale and Queen Anne furniture is equally high priced. In English furniture, the most wanted periods are Chippendale, Queen Anne and Adam.

In Italy the furniture in greatest demand is the early eighteenth-century painted furniture and Italian Louis XV and Louis XVI painted furniture.

In summary, the most wanted furniture in the world today, and the highest priced, is that which was made from the second decade of the eighteenth century up to, but not including, the last decade of that century.

As the middle 1960's were approached, this furniture became scarcer and higher priced. In English furniture, Hepplewhite, the next later period furniture, came more into demand, and then the still later Sheraton. Yet Sheraton has by no means come into its own in the market. Of course, after Sheraton has run its course pricewise, one type furniture to be in demand would logically be Victorian, since the rule of art and antique buyers is to move forward in interest to more recent types.

In French furniture Louis XV rose from the middle 1950's to the early 1960's when its rise was greatest. In the early 1960's the market interest centered on the next later style—Louis XVI. Louis XV had already achieved price heights that created some buyer resistance so that interest to a great extent was transferred to Louis XVI.

The middle 1960's saw an increasing interest in *Directoire* furniture as well as the antiques of the short-lived Consulate. The greatest interest centered on Empire furniture because there was enough of this on the market while *Directoire* and

Consulate was relatively scarce. Good Empire furniture, particularly fine pieces with human or animal forms in brass, often brings prices comparable to similar items of the period of the Louis'.

In early April 1966, toward the end of the 1966 season, the Parke-Bernet Galleries held a most unusual sale. It was unusual in that French furniture, very nearly exclusively of the middle nineteenth century, was offered for sale. Over five hundred items of this general era were offered, and the furniture was for the most part made from the beginning of the reign of Louis Philippe (1830) to the founding of the Third French Republic (1870). The period of course parallels the English Victorian era. The furniture was ornate, highly carved, colored, large and often based on the eighteenth-century French styles, but less subtle.

There was a good deal of criticism of this sale, all the way from Ph.D's from Heidelberg to small art and antique dealers. Many called the items junk and pointed out sadly that in the "old days" Parke-Bernet would never have offered such things for sale. But the sale may very well turn out to be a milestone in style preference, and it is simply a step in the movement of interest from the early to the later periods. In the middle 1960's glassware, pottery, jewelry and art objects of the *Art Nouveau* era of the early 1900's were all extremely popular and going up in price, and these *Art Nouveau* items are not very dissimilar to the nineteenth-century French furniture.

In American furniture the interest has moved from Queen Anne and Chippendale to Hepplewhite, and a Hepplewhite piece of furniture is often as high in price as a Chippendale item. By the middle 1960's it was all but impossible to locate a set of American Chippendale chairs of the period anywhere in the United States, particularly a large set of the beautiful, elaborately carved city variety. It is also next to impossible to locate an important set of English Chippendale chairs in the United States.

At the present time interest is moving to Sheraton, and in five years it is expected that American Sheraton furniture will be not only high in price, but hard to find. In the mid-1960's good New England Sheraton pieces with a combination of dark and light woods were not hard to find. These are some of the finest pieces of furniture produced anywhere.

In the late 1960's there is also a tremendous amount of interest in English Regency furniture, and although its price level is not high as antiques go, it is rising fast and will continue to rise in the future.

The Shift of Interest in Earlier Styles

It is only logical that as the furniture of the middle 1700's becomes scarce and high priced, the interest of buyers should move not only to later styles but to earlier as well. It has moved backward, but to a much smaller degree than it has moved forward. Good William and Mary pieces of furniture (both English and American) have been in somewhat greater demand, but the nature of the style is such as to secure a good deal of resistance from present-day buyers. It is often large, generally of darker wood, a little less delicately designed and proportioned than Queen Anne and Chippendale, and sometimes over-ornamented with large turnings, particularly on high case furniture such as highboys. Still, the relationship of this furniture to Queen Anne and Chippendale is clear, and William and Mary does mix well in a room with this later furniture.

Some interest has been shown in the still earlier and much different Jacobean style with its very dark woods, rectangular shapes, crude finish and large size. It is apparently felt that whereas one would not choose to fill a present-day home with such furniture, still a few such pieces go very well with antiques of later style and with modern furniture.

The furniture of the Italian Renaissance has received some interest in the market throughout the world, and along with Italian Renaissance furniture goes the closely related Spanish Renaissance style. In fact, so great is buyer interest in having just a few pieces of Spanish furniture that there is a brisk import business in the United States in newly made Spanish furniture of Renaissance style.

In France the furniture which corresponds to Jacobean and Renaissance is Louis XIII, and this furniture has been receiving even more interest in France than Jacobean and Renaissance furniture has received in England and the United States. Still, in the late 1960's this furniture from all countries has not received the interest or experienced the price rise that the later eighteenth-century and early nineteenth-century furniture has. In the near future, earlier furniture will certainly rise in price.

Quality

There is little question that the antiques at the lower end of the price scale have risen the most *in the past two or three years*. Antiques at this level are rising the fastest now. As the Age of Elegance becomes more and more recognized, the low-end demand builds the fastest as people realize that "antiques are the things to have."

From a purely investment point of view, it might seem that these lower priced antiques are the best ones to buy. They are going up the fastest and they tie up the smallest amount of cash.

As long as antiques are growing in popularity and new low-end buyers are coming into the market, cheap antiques will rise greatly. The higher priced antiques are bought more by owners of the finer homes and wealthy connoisseurs who have been buying at about the same pace over the past several years. It is true that some of the postwar millionaires have come into the antique market to drive it up just as they have come into the painting market. But even these additions do not drive up the higher quality antiques as fast as the lower level antiques have been rising.

Very often a "good" antique can be distinguished from a "poor" one simply by the number of wormholes. If there are enough wormholes it must be "genuine," and if there are none it must be a reproduction and thus worth nothing as an antique. Sometimes the piece is so lacking in artistic merit that the only merit it has is the clearcut evidence of age which makes it a genuine antique. This authenticity alone often gives value to an antique.

If and when tastes change, these are the antiques that will first go down in value and will go down the most. They also respond the fastest to declines in economic conditions and to drops in the stock market. The finer the piece, the less it is affected by poor times, and it was seen that some of the very highest prices for antiques were secured in 1930 and in 1931 at the two sales of really fine antiques.

The fine antique of top quality always has a market and at a good price. The commode by Roussel which was sold in Washington to a local dealer for $11,000 was immediately resold by him for $12,000. He bought near the market and he resold at a reasonable markup. On the other hand, a short time ago a collector of conglomerate antiques proposed to sell some of his lesser things. To this end he called in several dealers. The prices they offered were in some cases under what he had paid. Unfortunately, he had bought several items of poor quality, which did not rise sufficiently in value. However, the better items sold at a profit.

Despite the fact that the cheaper antiques are often rising the fastest, the usual private individual rarely "trades" in antiques. He does not buy and sell like a stock trader. He cannot do this. Moving, storage and restoration expenses are too great, and it is too much trouble to try to deal in antiques as an individual. Antiques are too cumbersome and break too easily. Then, too, the dealer who sells for $1,000 frequently buys not for $800 or even $500, but for $200 or even $100. The Duncan Phyfe table that recently brought $100 at auction will almost certainly be sold by the acquiring dealer for a sum in excess of $1,000. The dealer can more easily buy a Goddard block-front kneehole desk for $10,000 and immediately place it with a customer for $11,000, than buy a $50 piece and resell it for $250. It can easily be demonstrated that it is much more profitable to buy expensive items and resell them quickly at a small markup than it is to buy cheap items to resell at big markups. Cheap items may have to be held a much longer time. The fact of the matter is that buyers are always looking for the fine items while the cheap items have to be held in stock.

Thus, from a purely investment point of view, it is better to (1) buy high-priced items of the finest quality and (2) hold them for a number of years, or better still, (3) forget about resale and enjoy them with the knowledge that if a financial crisis should strike the family, these items can be sold at a price which bears a reasonable relationship to the original buying price.

As in the purchase of paintings and other works of art, and probably in the purchase of everything else, the question must always be asked, "Is the *quality* there?"

Index